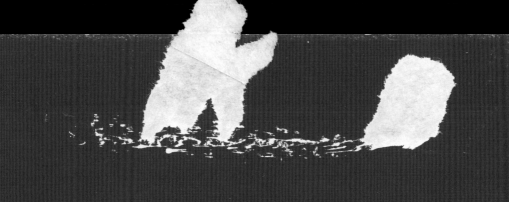

Managing Food Safety

Published by Chadwick House Group Limited
on behalf of

 Chartered
Institute of
Environmental
Health

Chadwick Court
15 Hatfields
London SE1 8DJ
UK
Tel: +44 (0)20 7827 5800
Fax: +44 (0)20 7803 0643
Email: customersupport@chgl.com
Website: www.cieh.org

ISBN 1 902423 72 0

Contributing Editor
Claire Nash BA (Hons) FRSH MRIPH MIoD
Associate member CIEH
VisàVis Publications

Design Director
Sarah Dobinson
Axiom Partners

Authors   **Dagmar Maria Dorothea Engel** Dipl. -Biologin FRSH
                   Associate member REHIS, member Deutsches Trainertreffen (TT-Netzwerk)

                   Donald MacDonald BA (Hons) MREHIS

Illustrator   **Mark Hackett** BA (Hons)

Additional material Justine Johnstone BA (Hons) MA
                        Ifan Payne

Editorial team Julia Bruce MSc
                   Nicola Bull MA MSc MPhil
                   Robyn West
                   Member SFEP

Contents

Contents

Introduction

Managing Food Safety is a new book for a new century and takes a fresh and pragmatic approach to the vast subject of managing the safe production and sale of food.

As food safety is often one of many demands on busy managers striving to produce excellent food on time, to budget and for profit, the book keeps the everyday operational practicalities of food businesses firmly in mind.

Designed for managers and would-be managers with responsibility for some or all aspects of food safety in any sector of the food industry, the book provides both practicable management guidance and clear information about the science and legislation behind accepted good practice.

The book is an essential study aid towards advanced-level food safety examinations and also provides a valuable, compact source of reference for disparate aspects of the subject.

Threats to consumer health from unsafe food are ever present worldwide, despite many new methods for producing safer food with a longer shelf life. Over the last three decades of the twentieth century food scientists, producers,

legislators and law enforcers developed new ways of tackling these old problems — mainly through food hazard analysis and food safety risk management.

These 'new' approaches have tended to be bolted on to old-established ways of considering the subject.

Now *Managing Food Safety* integrates the approaches. At the heart of the book is the management of hazards and risks, without enslavement to any particular system of food safety management.

The legislative framework of the book is that of the European Union, with detailed information provided about food safety legislation in the UK. Even so, the *principles* enshrined in these laws are valid for countries around the world.

Examples are included throughout the book of food safety problems encountered around the world and ways of dealing with them. While the threat to consumer health is global, the challenge to find the right solution is local.

For ease of reading the book uses the phrase 'your business', even though many managers are not proprietors and some food operations are non-profit making.

The book assumes that you have at least a basic-level knowledge of food safety and are familiar with the organisation and processes of a food business. Even so, the book explains all the topics step by step, gradually building confidence in the management of food safety issues. Not all the topics may seem immediately relevant to your workplace or your current job responsibilities, but it is still important to get a firm grasp of all the issues discussed.

The book consists of four parts, a Reference section and a number of feature pages. Each part of the book asks and answers a simple question — what is food safety, why do we need to manage food safety, what do we need to manage and how should we manage food safety? After a general introduction to the topics covered in that part, the book is divided into sections, chapters and subchapters.

At the start of each section is a list of the **KEY POINTS** underlying effective food safety management and the **KEY WORDS** which are crucial for the understanding and management of food safety matters. The **KEY WORDS** are also *highlighted* in the text. Explanations of many of the **KEY WORDS** are expanded in the Glossary,

which also includes many other words and phrases that are useful in the context of food and food safety.

By the end of the book you should be able to discuss all the **KEY POINTS**, giving, wherever possible, examples from your own workplace. You should also be able to explain all the **KEY WORDS** in your own words.

If you are preparing for an advanced-level food safety examination, refer to the **KEY POINTS** and **KEY WORDS** during your revision. You should find the sidebars — the brief notes in blue in the margins — useful for this purpose too.

As the role of a manager includes setting a good example to others, supervision and and at least some responsibility for training, the book includes two types of summary — **MAKING IT EASIER FOR OTHERS** throughout the book and in Parts 3 and 4, **MANAGEMENT MATTERS**. Use them to inspire you to find the best possible ways to help your staff to produce, serve or sell safe food.

The Reference section is an indispensable compendium for anyone managing the safety of food, so keep it close to hand even when you are familiar with the contents of all the chapters.

1 What is food safety?

1 What is food safety?

STAYING ALIVE
Safe enough to eat
In good hands

2 Why do we need to manage food safety?

Managing Food Safety

3 What do we need to manage?

4 How should we manage food safety?

People have been known to survive without food for three weeks or longer, but it is rare for humans to live without water for more than ten days. Food and water are indeed the stuff of life and it is evident that we cannot live without them.

They are, however, more than just a means of sustaining life. In societies where starvation is not an immediate threat, eating and drinking frequently feature in family, social and leisure activities, often creating pleasure and a general sense of well-being in addition to providing nourishment. What's more, food and drink have a central part in many religious customs.

In the 'developed world' we generally assume that the food we buy is safe to eat, whether we are consuming it at home or eating out. The statistics for cases of food-borne illness in the UK alone indicate that this assumption is not always valid. *Managing Food Safety* looks at ways in which you can help to predict and prevent the problems that lead to illness from food.

First, however, we need to check what we mean by *food safety* and indeed what exactly we mean by *food*. This we do in the first chapter of Part 1, where we introduce the key concepts of *hazard* and *risk* that are then developed throughout the book. In the second chapter we look briefly at the responsibility for food safety, a theme which is picked up in Part 2 and expanded in Part 4.

The important points and the key words to remember in this section are listed on page 3. As you read through the book, you will find that the definitions of some key words are expanded. All key words are included in the Glossary, together with many other words and phrases that are frequently used in the discussion of food safety.

STAYING ALIVE

🔑 KEY POINTS

KEY WORDS

food
substances that can be ingested (eaten or drunk) to maintain human life and growth, items of no nutritional value used for human consumption, ingredients used in food preparation, and chewing gum and similar substances.

food hygiene
all the processes involved in keeping food safe to eat.

food safety
the protection of human health by preventing edible substances, which are defined by law, from becoming hazardous and by minimising the risks from those hazards. Also used to indicate the *absence* of harm to people from food.

hazard
a source of danger: any thing, condition or circumstance that could cause harm to the consumer.

person in charge
the person given the authority by the employer to take charge of food premises at any given time.

risk
a measure, or scale, of the likelihood (or probability) that a hazard will occur.

unfit
food which is not fit (suitable/safe), as defined by law, for people to eat.

SAFE ENOUGH TO EAT

We grow up, quite literally, with food. It is so obvious that food is something we eat, that adults rarely need to define it. Indeed, few books dealing with food safety bother to do so. However, it is important to explain exactly what we mean, not only because legislation does so, but also because this book deals only with the *safety* of food and cannot cover every aspect of the topic of food or of human safety.

FOOD DEFINED

Food is usually defined as a substance that is taken into the body to maintain life and growth. It is fair to assume from this simple definition that the word covers anything we ingest (eat or drink) for nourishment — in other words, to maintain life. As we know, however, nourishment is not always the reason for eating or drinking and many people drink alcohol for pleasure, even though it is not defined as a nutrient, or chew gum, even though it provides little, if any, nutritional value.

Legislation is usually specific about the substances that are included and excluded under the heading of food. The criteria may vary slightly from country to country, or in the way that food is described. For example, the Food Safety Act 1990, which covers England, Wales and Scotland, says that food includes:
- drink
- articles and substances of no nutritional value which are used for human consumption
- chewing gum and similar products
- ingredients used in the preparation of food.

The Act also makes it clear that food does *not* include such things as medicines, controlled drugs and animal feed or fodder.

In comparison, the American *Food Code* (the model rules for a state's own food safety legislation) describes food as raw, cooked or processed edible substances which are used, or intended for use or sale, in whole or in part, for human consumption. Ice, beverages, ingredients and chewing gum are included as food.

FOOD SAFETY DEFINED

Safe means secure from harm, injury or danger. So we could define *safety* as the condition of being free or protected from harm, injury or danger. When it comes to discussing *food safety*, it is probably useful to refine our simple definition so that it covers both *actual* harm, injury and danger and *possible* harm, injury and danger.

We can do so by considering safety in terms of hazards and risks. A *hazard* is a source of danger — any thing, condition or situation that could cause harm to the consumer — while a *risk* is a measure, or scale, of the likelihood that a hazard will actually occur. These two words have been used to discuss occupational health (health and safety at work) for some three decades, but have become increasingly important in the consideration of food safety since the 1990s. They are now central to the way that food safety is discussed, legislated and inspected, so you'll learn a great deal more about them later in the book.

For now, they help us to draw up a better working definition of food safety — the protection of human health by preventing edible substances (which are defined by law) from becoming hazardous and by minimising the risks from those hazards.

Just how safe is 'safe'?

Our definition begs the question of *how free* from hazard and risk food should be. Should it be completely free, as free as possible, free nine times out of ten, 'acceptably' free, as free as is reasonable, as free as we can get away with or free to the best of our knowledge?

British legislation does not give a direct definition of *food safety* or *safe* food in general. However, it does specify and limit the types, circumstances of use and quantities of additives that can be used. Legislation also makes clear what the law deems to be *un*safe food and what is illegal to sell. For example, food intended for people to eat must be fit for human consumption and it is illegal to add anything to food that would make it injurious to health.

There is plenty more information about the laws governing food safety in Part 3. As to the question of how safe food should be, you'll discover the answer for yourself as you read through the rest of the book.

THE SCOPE OF FOOD SAFETY

It is probably becoming clear that food safety is concerned with issues such as undesirable ingredients (contaminants) and food which is *unfit* to eat, but has nothing to do with nutrition, nutrition-related hazards (such as overeating, overdrinking or slimming diets) or animal welfare and is only partly concerned with questions of quality. What this means to someone who is charged with the responsibility for food safety is touched upon in the next chapter and developed in Part 4.

Food hygiene — a subject in retirement?

You may be wondering at this stage what happened to good old *food hygiene*. Are food safety and food hygiene the same thing? The short answer is no, but the phrases are often interchangeable so you should not worry about tripping over finer definitions. The most important thing is to understand the idea behind the

FOOD SAFETY
The protection of human health by preventing edible substances (as defined by law) from becoming hazardous and by minimising the risks from those hazards. Also, the absence of hazard and risk from food.

terms and to be able to give a definition in words that are suitable for your audience. For example, if you were talking to new employees, you might wish to say something like, "food safety involves safeguarding food from anything that could cause harm to our customers" or, "food safety is about making food free from danger to consumer health".

A wider perspective — if you want it

If you are interested in such things, there is a longer explanation about the use of the terms food safety and food hygiene. In recent years the expression food safety has tended to be used to describe the achievement of the state, or condition, of food that is safe to eat. The term covers standards, composition, labelling *and* food hygiene. In turn, food hygiene is used to refer to all the practical measures involved in keeping food safe and wholesome through all the stages of production to point of sale or consumption. So, you can see that food safety includes food hygiene, but not the other way around.

This usage is reflected in the names of some pieces of British food legislation. So the main Act of Parliament covering England, Wales and Scotland is the Food Safety Act 1990. It covers all the main principles involved in keeping food safe to eat. Regulations made under this Act include the Food Safety (General Food Hygiene) Regulations 1995 which deal with specific actions that must be taken to comply with the law.

If you work in America, you'll probably find that food *safety* is the term used for the whole subject of keeping food fit for human consumption and you may find that *hygiene* is used only to describe *personal* hygiene.

The right words in the right place

Where does this leave you? Just use the phrase that feels most comfortable to you. If you are taking an advanced-level examination in food safety/hygiene, check the title of the exam and look through the awarding body's syllabus (you should do this anyway). Make sure that you can define food safety or food hygiene, as appropriate, in your own words and can give examples of what is included.

✳ MAKING IT EASIER FOR OTHERS

- Use words that staff are most likely to understand when explaining what food safety (or food hygiene) involves.
- Point out that food safety includes drink as well as food.
- Encourage staff to define some of the criteria for safety that can be applied to food operations.
- Point out that 'a safe level' for most customers may need to be adjusted for people in the 'at risk group' such as the elderly, infants and those who are ill.

IN GOOD HANDS

It goes without saying that food safety is of concern to everyone who wants to stay alive and well, and we all hope and expect that food is safe to eat. But who exactly does food safety concern in a professional capacity? Whose real responsibility is it to look after the safety of food?

The answer to both questions is that food safety is the responsibility of everyone who works with food or whose actions or omissions could compromise the safety of food.

Every person who works with food deals with some aspect of food safety, no matter how small that aspect is in the bigger scheme of things. Even so, someone has to take overall responsibility for all the people whose work could safeguard or threaten the safety of food and for all the systems and procedures they are supposed to follow. That person is the manager, whether he or she is an owner-manager or an employee whose job is to manage.

IN YOUR CARE

You do not need to have the words *food safety* in your job title to be the person responsible for managing the production or sale of safe food.

In small and some medium-size enterprises (SMEs), the role of managing food safety may fall upon one individual. In a large company the responsibility usually starts with a supervisor or first-line manager — someone with day-to-day decision-making powers, albeit sometimes on a small scale. In medium-size and large-size food operations middle and senior managers usually have more responsibilities and a greater say in policy.

The ultimate responsibility usually rests upon a senior management team or board of directors, or upon the most senior manager or director who makes the final decisions. This is so even if the senior manager or director does not have 'hands-on' involvement in the production of food or is not based in the premises where food is produced, stored or sold.

Legally in charge

Whatever the size or type of the enterprise, legal responsibility usually lies with the person who is put in charge of food premises at any given time. You'll learn more about this in Part 3, but it is important to note here that the person with the final responsibility for food safety must ensure that the *person in charge* is adequately trained and has sufficient experience to be in charge.

AN OVERVIEW OF MANAGEMENT

So what is it that you need to manage if you are the person, or one of the people, responsible for food safety at your workplace? You'll find that everything involved is discussed in bite-size chunks throughout the book, with the chapters in Part 4 taking a highly practicable approach to everyday food safety issues. At this stage it is worth obtaining a general picture before you start to read about details.

A continuous process

One of the simplest ways to consider the job of management is as a continuous cycle (or, better still, a spiral) of planning, implementing and reviewing actions in the workplace.

Tasks involved in this process are likely to include:

- making policy and setting objectives
- communicating objectives and specific standards
- organising and implementing policies and objectives — for example, setting priorities, establishing reporting relationships and allocating resources
- monitoring, auditing and measuring performance and analysing the results and observations
- reviewing performance against objectives and standards.

A considerable role

Of course, your own responsibilities depend upon your particular job description and job specification, and to some extent upon the part of the food industry in which you work.

Nonetheless, to become an effective manager of food safety in your workplace (and to pass an accredited advanced-level food safety examination), you need to know about some aspects of food safety which you will not need to manage immediately or, perhaps, ever. For example, if you are the food and beverage manager at an hotel, you are unlikely to have to manage the canning of fish, but you still need to understand the principles involved. You need an awareness of the science underlying good practice in food safety as well as sufficient confidence and competence in your management skills.

You may find it useful as you read through the book to make a note of the aspects of food safety management that are involved in your current job. Parts 3 and 4 deal in detail with all the key aspects of food safety management. There's no doubt that this is a huge management role — and it is possible that food safety is just one part of your total management responsibilities! Part 2 sets your task in a wider business context by suggesting why it is worth the bother of attempting to manage food safety in the first place.

EXAMPLES OF BUSINESSES THAT NEED TO MANAGE FOOD SAFETY

Raw food production: farms and fisheries.

Raw food handling: abattoirs, fish processors, dairy farms, meat processors, fruit and vegetable companies.

Food processing: bakeries, dairies, breweries, canneries and manufacturers of ready-to-eat meals and frozen foods.

Transport (by road, rail, air, sea and inland waterways)**:** for livestock; raw food at ambient temperatures or in refrigerated conditions; processed food at ambient, refrigerated, frozen or high temperatures.

Packaging: bottling and boxing plants.

Storage/warehousing: at an ambient temperature or in controlled conditions.

Food sale, raw and processed: shops, supermarkets, grocers, greengrocers, fishmongers, butchers, bakers, other specialist food shops, wholesale markets, market stalls (retail), vending machines, cafeterias and sandwich bars.

Food service and consumption: public access and private facilities (such as company or members-only facilities) including cafeterias, restaurants, canteens, refectories, hotels, pubs, clubs, bars, sandwich bars, take-aways and leisure facilities; aircraft, ships and trains; institutional catering, including hospitals, care homes and the Armed Forces; retention facilities (such as prisons, remand centres and young offenders institutions); vending machines; mobile stalls and vehicles; outside catering facilities and events (such as barbecues and wedding marquees).

Catering/local food preparation: catering facilities, public hall kitchens, restaurants, cafés, canteens, hospitals, regeneration facilities, fast food outlets, mobile and outside catering facilities and domestic kitchens used for commercial food preparation.

Transport of food within buildings, sites or building complexes: including trolleys and motorised vehicles.

Serveries: including canteens, self-service facilities and vending machines.

🔷 MAKING IT EASIER FOR OTHERS

- Emphasise that every food handler has a crucial part to play in food safety.
- Explain how food safety requires full commitment from everyone.
- Ensure that people who do not handle food, but whose work could compromise food safety (such as cleaners and delivery drivers), understand the part they also play in food safety.

2 Why do we need to manage food safety?

1 What is food safety?

2 Why do we need to manage food safety?

STAYING IN BUSINESS
Customer concerns
The impact of illness
ⓕ living in dangerous times?
Safeguards through diligence
ⓕ do we really need food safety laws?
Chasing profits

Managing Food Safety

3 What do we need to manage?

4 How should we manage food safety?

"Turnover is static and our profits are down. But we haven't poisoned anybody since we started the business, so why should we use any of our precious budget on food safety?"

Just imagine how many business owners, financial directors, managing directors or production managers in the food industry have been tempted to ask themselves a version of that question at some point.

Profit margins can be tight in the food industry and the allocation of resources often involves difficult decisions between competing priorities. Why then should any food business spend any of its precious time or hard-earned profit on managing food safety? The simplest answer is: to stay in business.

Of course there are many other valid reasons for making food safety a priority. They might include a moral responsibility to protect consumers from illness, a target of winning the highest possible professional reputation and a need to operate within the law.

In this part of the book we consider aspects of these issues in a business context, so there are short chapters about business priorities, consumer expectations, food-borne illnesses and legal priorities, especially the defence of due diligence. We use the word *business* in its broadest possible sense and include not-for-profit sectors in which staying in business usually involves keeping within the food/catering budget.

Even though the management of food safety may sometimes appear to be an optional extra, we hope to persuade you by the end of Part 2 that it is an essential and integral part of any food business. Attempting to run a food business without managing food safety might be rather like trying to drive a car without gears or brakes — you might roll along quite happily for a while, but before too long you would certainly get into serious difficulty.

STAYING IN BUSINESS

🔑 KEY POINTS

Customer concerns

Customer relationship management as a key to business retention.
The value of customer loyalty.
Levels of customer awareness.
Customer expectations and perceptions.
The need to take an active approach to food scares and consumer fears.

The impact of illness

The scale of the problem.
Problems of comparing statistics.
Assessments of the true financial costs.
Personal costs of food-borne illness.

Safeguards through diligence

The general impact of legal requirements on food businesses.
The meaning of due diligence.
Due diligence as a legal defence.
What due diligence means in practice.

Chasing profits

The balance of cost-saving measures and food safety requirements.
The competitive significance of food safety.

KEY WORDS

case
one incidence of illness.

due diligence
a duty of care; a legal defence where it can be shown that all reasonable steps were taken to avoid committing a food safety offence.

food-borne illness/disease
terms used in this book to indicate *any* type of illness that is caused, or is probably caused, by the consumption of contaminated food, water or other drink.

HACCP
an abbreviation, usually pronounced 'hassup', for Hazard Analysis and Critical Control Point — a system for identifying, assessing and controlling hazards and risks associated with food and drink.

outbreak
a cluster, in time or place, of cases of illness caused by a particular organism.

CUSTOMER CONCERNS

Without customers, there can be no business, so customer relationship management is central to all businesses. Like any other successful relationship, customer relationships take time to develop and are likely to include understanding (of customer needs), appreciation (of customer expectations) and mutual trust and respect.

How can you possibly achieve this with every customer? This is a central question in any consideration of customer relationship management, but is a huge subject that we cannot examine in detail here. However, it is fair to say that a good foundation is to analyse the likely expectations of typical groups of your customers.

In this chapter we take a brief look at customer concerns and expectations within the context of food safety. As you will see, customer relationship management and food safety management often overlap in the food industry.

WHO ARE YOUR CUSTOMERS?

The head of a British trade organisation once said at an open meeting that he had a lot of customers who returned time and again to his shop. He added, however, that it was only customers he had and not consumers. On being asked to elaborate, he said that he had a great many happy, informed customers whose expectations were being met to their satisfaction, but consumers were something else altogether — they were people who were only interested in making trouble.

You do not have to agree with these tongue-in-cheek comments and we certainly do not endorse them. Even so, the comments do raise interesting points about the awareness, expectations, perceptions and satisfaction of the people who buy your products and services, and it is some of these points that we explore in this chapter.

Purchasing and consuming

What you call the people who buy your food depends to some extent on where you work. Guest, customer, client, consumer, diner and visitor are all in common use, while inmate or patient may be appropriate terms in certain sectors.

In this book we use the words customer and consumer interchangeably. However, we use the word client when we need to distinguish someone, such as a manufacturer, who buys a food or ingredient for use in a product that is then sold to someone else who eats or drinks it.

CUSTOMER AWARENESS

It is highly likely that people in the UK are more aware of food safety issues now than they ever have been. Whether from the news media, storylines in 'soaps', information from food businesses and consumer groups, school projects or the experience of friends or family, the public has had ample opportunity to hear about possible health problems from food.

In the last two decades of the twentieth century, they may have learned something about particular types of *Salmonella* in eggs and poultry; outbreaks of *E. coli* O157, the most publicised being in Scotland; *Listeria* in unpasteurised cheese; botulism in nut yoghurt; BSE ('mad cow disease') in cattle; Creutzfeldt-Jakob Disease (CJD) and its variants — the human forms of BSE; dioxins in the environment; genetically modified organisms (GMOs); irradiated food and so on.

You will probably be quick to point out that all this new awareness is not necessarily good news for the food industry and that it has to be faced that there are some customers whose awareness does not fill them with confidence. In fact, one of the reasons given for the setting up of the Food Standards Agency (FSA) in the UK in the year 2000 was to increase public confidence in food safety.

FSA ATTITUDES SURVEY

In February 2001 the Food Standards Agency published the findings of research into customer attitudes to food standards. Based upon the views of more than 3,000 people throughout the UK, the survey revealed that three-quarters of the population say they are fairly or very concerned about food safety, while less than half are confident about food safety measures. Sir John Krebs, the first chairman of the FSA, said that public confidence "may be a reflection of two decades of food crises, but it is an unacceptably low level".

However, as Sir John Krebs, the first chairman of the FSA, has said, "The responsibility for change rests with everyone involved in the food business".

Managing concern

The lack of confidence in some quarters and uncertainty in others need to be managed, not ignored. It means that as a food safety manager you need to consider how to cope with sensationalism as well as with true threats to public health — particularly how food hazards and risks affect your own particular sector or business.

GREAT EXPECTATIONS

The expectations of individual customers vary widely, but it is useful to consider some of the views that your customers might have of the public authorities, the food industry and the food they eat.

What customers might expect from politicians, government departments and food inspection services

- Laws
  - made to protect consumers
  - suitable for the current requirements
  - enforced fairly, correctly and consistently.
- Staff suitably trained and experienced for the job.
- The food safety system
  - properly funded
  - no conflict of interest
  - any shortcomings are identified and corrected
  - customer protection gets priority over the food industry if there is doubt over an issue
  - controversial issues dealt with openly and transparently.

What customers might expect from the food industry

- Safe food and packaging
  - the level of care and attention (due diligence)
  - everyone who has handled the food has treated it in the knowledge that customers are going to eat it.
- Customer relationships
  - managed with integrity and honesty
  - alert to customer expectations and requirements
  - effective complaints system in place, with recompense offered if appropriate
  - prompt product recall if there is a problem.
- Product descriptions
  - assurances about the source of the food
  - correct labelling, including for genetically modified and irradiated products
  - nutritional information provided.
- Animal welfare
  - humane treatment of animals used for food.

What customers might expect from their food

That food is:

- what it is labelled to be
- safe and will not make anyone ill
- fresh and within its shelf life, which has been established scientifically
- tasty and nutritious, with any necessary additives kept to a minimum
- good value for money.

Coping with expectations

How can you manage this range of typical customer expectations about food? Some perceptions, such as those in the first list, may be beyond your scope of influence, but others, such as those in the second two lists, can be managed in the same way as for customer awareness — by efficient and effective food safety management.

MANAGING PERCEPTIONS

It is often the case, as the following lists show, that the general public's perceptions of the dangers associated with food are in reverse order to the perceptions of specialists who work with food.

Public perception of dangers from food (in descending order)
- Pesticide residues or food additives.
- Drug residues, such as antibiotics given to animals.
- Migrating chemicals (for instance, from plasticised food wrapping).
- Natural toxicants.

Scientific evaluation of risks in food (in descending order)
- Natural toxicants.
- Pesticide residues.
- Drug residues.
- Migrating chemicals.
- Food additives.

There are many possible reasons to explain the discrepancy between the public's perceptions and scientific evaluation. They could include public mistrust of the scientific community or the government, misinformation, misinterpretation or dislike of E-numbers.

On the other hand, the discrepancy could be explained because, for example, scientists may not have got everything right in the past, done enough research into the long-term effects of additives and residues or listened sufficiently carefully to customers' concerns.

What you can do

The real point here is that it may be as difficult to deal with a *perceived* hazard or risk as it is to deal with an *actual* hazard or risk. Even so, you should never underestimate the damage that can be done by a perceived problem with a food, an ingredient or a particular sector of the food industry. But what can you do?

On the grand scale, it is a challenge for the food industry in general and you may not wish or be able to participate directly in meeting this challenge. But you can make your views known by working with, or through membership of, professional and trade organisations and by keeping in close touch with the activities of local environmental health departments, food safety and environmental health bodies and the Food Standards Agency (see pages 373 to 374 for contact details).

On a smaller scale, you may be able to do more. For example, during the height of the BSE scare in the UK in the 1990s business at many small family butchers shops increased because the public often believed that a local business would be more concerned about the source of their products than larger operations, such as supermarkets, might be. In fact, many supermarkets have schemes in place with product standards that far exceed those of smaller organisations, but there is no evidence to show that the existence of such standards always influences the public's perception.

The use or omission of additives provides another example. In the late 1970s and the 1980s the producers of diverse products, such as salad cream and tomato paste, responded to public antipathy towards E-numbers by removing additives that helped to prolong the product's shelf life. Consequently consumers were advised to refrigerate the products after opening them, whereas previously the products could be stored safely in a cupboard for quite long periods.

It would also help to have in place a plan for crisis management to deal with sudden publicity about risks, whether perceived or actual — and this is discussed in Part 4.

FROM SATISFACTION TO LOYALTY

What then is a satisfied customer? One definition of quality is the return of the customer, not the food. This suggests a way of defining a satisfied customer: one who, given a choice of different foods, shops, restaurants and so on, consistently returns for more of the same. A customer who returns indicates that all his or her reasonable expectations have been met and all perceptions have been satisfactorily dealt with.

How then can we ensure the return of the customer? A significant part of the answer is: by the efficient and effective management of all food safety issues. After all, without effective hygiene systems, you will soon lose your customers — and without customers, there can be no business.

✱ MAKING IT EASIER FOR OTHERS

- Emphasise that customers expect their food to be safe to eat. If it is not safe, custom will fall with potentially disastrous consequences for the business and for jobs.
- Encourage all food handlers to understand that they have a crucial individual part to play in producing safe food and, by so doing, in meeting customer expectations.

THE IMPACT OF ILLNESS

As we have mentioned, it was rare for many weeks to pass in the last two decades without hearing something about illnesses linked to food in the UK. But has there genuinely been an increase in the number of cases of illness linked to food or just an increase in publicity? If there has indeed been an increase, is it a worldwide problem or confined to particular countries?

USE OF TERMS
In this book we use 'food-borne illness' and 'food-borne disease' interchangeably to indicate *all* the illnesses linked to food, such as those often described as 'food poisoning' or 'food-borne infection'.

The global incidence of *food-borne illness* is notoriously difficult to calculate accurately. For a start, some countries have only rudimentary systems for collecting statistics. Then there is the problem of exactly how an illness linked to food is defined and this makes it extremely difficult to formulate meaningful comparisons between countries. Finally, as most *cases* are sporadic and may last only a short time, people may not report their illness to a doctor,so the circumstances that led to the illness may not be investigated fully.

A GROWING HEALTH PROBLEM

Nonetheless, statistics from around the world show that the incidence of food-borne disease is increasing and the World Health Organization (WHO) has reported that such illnesses are a widespread and growing public health problem in both developed and developing countries. In 1998 alone, 2.2 million people around the world, including 1.8 million children, died from diarrhoeal diseases. Many of these cases can be attributed to the contamination of food and drinking water.

Even in industrialised countries where it might be reasonable to assume that food safety systems are in place, up to 30 per cent of people are thought to suffer from food-borne diseases each year. In some developing countries the high prevalence of diarrhoeal illnesses indicates the likelihood of a higher percentage, which in turn suggests underlying food safety problems, many caused by parasites.

Examples of trends
United States of America
There are an estimated 76 million cases of food-borne diseases each year, resulting in 325,000 hospitalisations and 5,000 deaths.

MASSIVE SCALE

Although *outbreaks* of food-related illness are often fairly small and short-lived, they may also be on a massive scale. For example, in 1988 an outbreak of Hepatitis A, resulting from the consumption of contaminated clams, affected some 300,000 people in China. In 1994 an outbreak of salmonellosis from contaminated ice cream occurred in the USA, affecting an estimated 224,000 people.

While these figures are extrapolations from the actual number of cases reported, they still make depressing reading.

United Kingdom of Great Britain and Northern Ireland

As you will see from the graphs on page 20, the *general* trend in the UK has been upward since 1982, sometimes with dramatic annual leaps. It seems paradoxical that the more aware we are of food-borne disease and the more that is done to try to control it, the higher the figures seem to rise. The graphs cannot indicate the seasonal variations each year — for example, the summer barbecue season can see an upsurge in problems, such as *Salmonella* poisoning, associated with undercooked meats. Paralytic shellfish poisoning may also occur more frequently in the warmer months when toxic algae grow more profusely. In the winter months illness from small round structured viruses (such as winter vomiting disease in pre-school playgroups and infants schools) can increase.

An unseen problem?

There is a well-respected system for gathering information about food-related illnesses in the UK which dates back to the 1960s in its present form. Even so, as in many other countries, the British statistics have often been likened to an iceberg, with only the tip of the problem visible.

After extensive research in England between 1992 and 1996 the Committee on the Microbiological Safety of Food, originally chaired by Professor Mark Richmond, estimated that 20 per cent of the population of England suffered an 'infectious intestinal disease (IID)' in a year. However, only three per cent of the population went to a general practitioner (GP) — and so were recorded in official statistics. The committee's research included collecting data and stools, but did not distinguish between cases of IID that resulted from 'food poisoning' and cases from other causes. Even so, based on the research figures, there may be a staggering 9.5 million actual cases each year in England alone, compared to reported cases for England and Wales that have never reached 100,000!

A survey, which was published by the Food Standards Agency in 2001, asked people to estimate the number of times that they had suffered from food poisoning in a year, based on their own diagnosis of symptoms. The results showed that 14 per cent of people in England, 13 per cent in Scotland, 11 per cent in Wales and 10 per cent in Northern Ireland believed that they had had some form of food-borne illness in 2000. This would mean that 5 million people in the UK were ill that year from eating contaminated food.

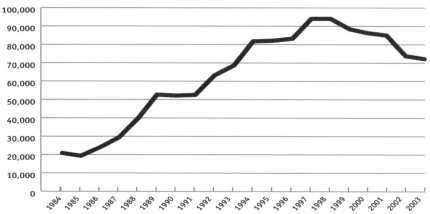

Number of notified cases of food poisoning (England and Wales)
Source: Health Protection Agency

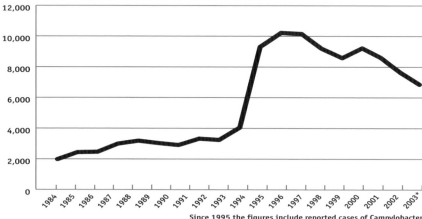

Number of notified cases of food poisoning (Scotland)
Source: Scottish Centre for Infection and Environmental Health

Since 1995 the figures include reported cases of Campylobacter
*provisional figure

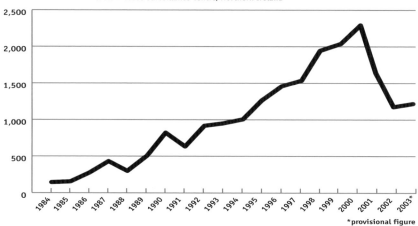

Number of notified cases of food poisoning (Northern Ireland)
Source: Communicable Disease Surveillance Centre, Northern Ireland

*provisional figure

The graphs opposite are based on figures collected by the Public Health Laboratory Service (PHLS) in England and Wales, the Scottish Centre for Infection and Environmental Health and the PHLS Northern Ireland. There are some regional differences in the sources of the figures collated which may involve statistics from various laboratories and medical reports. This makes it difficult to compare the figures in one part of the UK with those of another.

THE ECONOMIC PENALTIES OF FOOD-BORNE ILLNESS

The true economic cost of food-borne illness in any country is almost impossible to estimate. It is relatively easy to calculate the cost of medical treatment, hospitalisation, loss of working hours, investigation of the case and action to prevent a recurrence, but it is complicated and time consuming calculating the cost of lost potential business.

As for individuals, how can you put a true price on the loss of personal amenity, temporary or permanent impairment or death?

Some food-borne diseases are of short duration only and, while they may be unpleasant at the time, usually do not cause discomfort for more than a couple of days. Others however may have serious, long-term consequences which affect all aspects of a person's life, including the incalculable value of the loss of amenity to the patient, the cost of the loss of his or her earnings and possibly those of family members too.

The cost to food companies can also be extremely high and can be from many sources:
- loss of working hours and production
- loss of reputation
- loss of business
- fines
- compensation payments to customers
- product withdrawals.

Putting a figure on the cost
Despite the difficulties in calculating the true cost of food-borne illness, valid attempts can be made, as you can see from the two following examples.

England
The Committee on the Microbiological Safety of Food has estimated the average cost of infectious intestinal disease, whatever its cause, in England to be £79 per case at 1993 to 1995 prices. This amounts to a national cost of at least three-quarters of a billion pounds a year! Bearing in mind that food-borne illness is a preventable disease, this is a staggering sum of money.

The greatest financial burden, at 55 per cent, is to employers in lost production. This represents a high business cost from food-borne illness. The National Health Service shoulders the next share of the cost at about 36 per cent, with 'cases presenting to a GP' (people who go to their doctor) accounting for more than half of this figure. Direct costs to the person suffering from the illness amount to 8 per cent.

USA
With a few assumptions and some rough and ready arithmetic (and erring on the cautious side), we can gain some idea of the magnitude of the problem in the USA. Let's take the estimated figure of 76 million cases per year and assume that only half of the people were full-time workers and each had only one day off work because of the illness. If we assume that each person earned an average $30 every day, then the loss of working hours alone cost the country $1,140,000,000 per year. Of course, the true figure is likely to be far higher.

A HEAVY BURDEN

Whatever the true cost of food-borne illness around the world, it is unacceptably high. Even so, the estimates given in the examples above make it difficult to illustrate just how much it costs everyone in Britain today.

✱ MAKING IT EASIER FOR OTHERS

- Explain that food safety is about preventing people from becoming ill.
- Point out that more people around the world die from eating food and drinking water than from natural catastrophes, war or pestilence.
- Explain that statistics represent only the tip of the iceberg of actual cases of illness.
- Discuss the personal pain and suffering involved in food-borne illnesses.
- Discuss the economic consequences of food-borne illnesses, encouraging staff to consider how everyone ends up paying for cases of such illness, whether through public health care costs, higher prices for safe food or by employment uncertainty in the food industry.
- Encourage staff to consider how safe food benefits everyone — the consumer, the general public at large, the business itself and the people who work in it.
- Emphasise that food safety is an integral part of staff members' professional role, not an optional extra.

living in dangerous times?

Have you ever pondered why you have to comply with so many food safety regulations when many generations seemed to survive perfectly well without protective clothing or disinfecting their hands and with only a rudimentary understanding of temperature control?

If so, you are not alone. Many busy managers have been tempted to think that they have more red tape to deal with than their predecessors, and they may sometimes think that legal demands are tougher in the country where they work than elsewhere in the world.

In fact food hygiene rules are *not* a modern invention and forms of compliance are found worldwide.

Phoenician clay slabs dating back to 3,500 BC proclaim in neat cuneiform characters, 'You shall not poison your neighbour's fat nor shall you bewitch your neighbour's wine.'

Punishments for transgressing rules about food could be far harsher than today's penalties. In Babylon in the year 3,000 BC, for example, the adulteration of wine was punishable by death, but the offender generally had to be caught red-handed.

Early food hygiene rules were often part of religious regulations, some of which are still observed today.

Such rules might have included the prohibition of some animals, birds and fish as human food because they were regarded as 'unclean'; the separation of certain products (such as meat from milk) during preparation and storage; the use of clean and unclean sources of water and procedures for cleaning utensils after contact with animal flesh.

As many early peoples were nomadic, such rules may have helped to avoid contamination, cross-contamination and microbial multiplication in difficult conditions for food safety.

If we continued to look around the world and throughout history, we would find innumerable rules that attempt to protect communities from the unpleasant and often life-threatening effects of food-borne illnesses.

So, what, if anything, has changed about the safety of our food?

Firstly, our understanding of the causes of food-related illnesses — and subsequently the development of preventive measures enshrined in legislation — increased dramatically after Robert Koch had demonstrated at the end of the nineteenth century the connection between micro-organisms and disease.

Secondly, however, cases of food-borne disease have escalated worldwide, particularly in the two last decades of the twentieth century.

At first glance, the two developments make no sense at all. After all, it is fair to assume that a better knowledge of the causes of illnesses should *improve* food safety measures, not lead to an increase in illness. Were our ancestors getting it right after all, or are we just scaring ourselves silly with all the data that were not available in the past?

Despite frequent developments in food microbiology and technology, microbes seem always to be one step ahead of us. Recent research shows that we have badly underestimated the adaptability of micro-organisms and their ability to 'reappear' after they were believed to have been conquered — the latter are termed *re-emergent pathogens* by the World Health Organization (WHO).

One of the most worrying organisms, a strain of *E. coli* known as VTEC or *E. coli* 0157, became a public menace within just a few years in the 1980s. According to the WHO in a list published in 1997, other 'new' and 'old' pathogens which have gained significance include *Listeria monocytogenes*, *Salmonella* species (see picture, opposite), *Vibrio cholerae*, *Campylobacter jejuni*, *Yersinia enterocolitica*, *Cryptosporidium parvum* and *Clonorchis sinensis* (a parasite).

Along with the familiar symptoms of 'classic' food poisoning (such as vomiting, abdominal pain, diarrhoea and fever) may now occur symptoms with some frightening possible long-term consequences, such as arthritis, meningitis, haemolytic-uraemic syndrome, septicaemia, cancer, blindness and spontaneous abortion.

Of course, we cannot calculate how many people died in days gone by from the effects of eating contaminated food because such statistics were not collected. Some experts say that the rise in cases in recent decades can be attributed to increased reporting of symptoms, better medical diagnoses and improved microbiological detection methods. But this is certainly not the whole answer.

For example, in the last century or so Europe has seen enormous changes in public attitudes and expectations towards daily food and some radical shifts in our buying and eating habits.

These include an increased demand for meat, especially poultry, despite the increase in vegetarianism; more eating out; the extension of home deliveries of

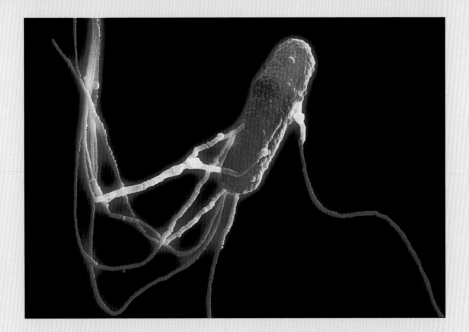

food; the demand for products all the year round regardless of the local harvesting season; the transportation of livestock and products over far greater distances and the development of a wide range of preservation methods and equipment enabling long-distance transport, long-term storage and a shift towards far more bulk buying of food for home consumption.

Another modern trend, global tourism, has enabled pathogens to spread farther and faster than was possible in the past. Typically, tourists catch infections, such as typhoid, hepatitis and cholera, in tropical countries and take them back home, often to countries where the infections were thought to be under control.

All the changes mentioned so far are well accepted, but others, which are mentioned below, are more open to debate. For instance, cheap ingredients in some imported animal feeds from tropical countries where animal infection is widespread may have led to an increased risk of introducing animal diseases into the UK, some of which affect humans.

Another possible problem is the increased resistance to antibiotics of pathogens such as *Salmonella* following the treatment of animal feed. This has resulted in the rapid development of strains of *Salmonella* which are immune to a range of antimicrobial products used to treat animals and humans. The distribution of bovine spongiform encephalopathy (BSE) is yet another example quoted of how technological changes in the processing of feeds and foods may have created new hazards within a very short time span.

It may seem that some human-created problems are like a contamination carousel, on which problems just keep coming back.

There are also issues of people in the 'at risk group'. While the number of older people increases in most industrial societies, as a result of modern medicine and better nutrition, so the number of people increases who are especially vulnerable to the symptoms of food-borne illnesses. Those with compromised immune systems as a consequence of viruses such as HIV (human immunodeficiency virus) are also in the 'at risk group'.

So, are we indeed living in more dangerous times than our ancestors as far as food safety is concerned?

All the signs are that there will always be food safety hazards, but, with newly emerging and re-emerging pathogens, it is just possible that we may be facing a greater risk than generations before us — in spite of all our knowledge and technology. What we must not forget is that the evolution of organisms has never come to an end.

Whenever we make changes, such as developing new preservation techniques, forms of transport and storage technologies, we provide new niches and possibilities for micro-organisms — they tend to adjust themselves to whatever is on offer.

So, how does someone in your job deal with constantly changing and evolving micro-organisms? You'll find many of the answers and practicable solutions throughout the book, but here we allow ourselves a little speculation about changes that may come about.

It is possible that the risks from microbiological hazards will gain significance. Principles of hazard analysis (see Part 4) will certainly help us to predict problems from microbes at various stages of the food flow and control the hazard or its risks.

Even so, we may need to acquire greater knowledge of a micro-organism than at present.

Competitive relationships between micro-organisms and interactions between microflora and packaging may become more and more important. At the same time, the demand for foods with a longer shelf life and the distances food has to travel can only be achieved by a thorough safety guarantee from the primary producer to the consumer.

Companies that deal with high risk products may have to be licensed in the future, as is already the case in the UK for butchers who handle both raw and cooked products.

Additional labelling may be needed on certain products to give consumers even clearer warnings about cross-contamination, the dangers from undercooking meat and poultry and the possible presence of allergens.

Finally, consumers themselves may need to be encouraged to meet more hygiene challenges in their homes.

This could perhaps be achieved by providing even more information and education on basic food safety principles, delivered as a standard school subject in the way it is already handled in Scotland and in some other European Union member states.

SAFEGUARDS THROUGH DILIGENCE

One powerful motivation for a business to manage food safety is that the law requires it. You will not find a clause in legislation that states anything to the effect of 'thou shalt manage food safety', but it is unlikely that a business will achieve the minimum standards demanded by legislation if food safety is simply left to chance. What's more, if something does go wrong and a business is prosecuted for breaching food safety rules, its strongest (and, possibly, its only) defence is to demonstrate that it took the greatest possible care to safeguard food — in other words, it managed food safety properly.

In Part 3 you will learn in some detail about the ways in which legislation influences the management of food safety, whether directly or indirectly. For the time being, we shall take a brief look at the principles of food safety legislation and legal compliance.

SAFETY PRINCIPLES

Every food business has legal obligations to supply the consumer with food that is:
- safe for humans to eat
- of the nature, quality and substance demanded by the consumer
- properly labelled and sold without misleading claims.

The wording of these three responsibilities is based upon British legislation, but similar basic legal obligations can be found in food safety laws throughout the world. They seem to be reasonable minimum standards that could legally be applied to any food business to protect public health and, in the case of the second and third obligations, to prevent fraudulent selling. If you are interested in a longer discussion about the reasons for controlling food safety by law, see the feature on pages 30 and 31.

LEGAL BASICS
The law expects food businesses to take all reasonable care possible to ensure that food is safe to eat, unadulterated and labelled and sold in an honest manner.

DUE DILIGENCE

Many countries have the principle of *due diligence* (or *reasonable care*) at the heart of their food legislation. In Britain, it is one of only two main types of defence for a food business accused of breaking food safety rules — that the alleged offence was committed by someone else, or that there was due diligence.

The word *diligence* comes from Latin words meaning 'to choose to be industrious', or 'to choose to be persistent in your effort or work'. The word *due* comes from Old French and Latin words meaning 'something that is owed' — in other words, something where there is little choice. So, at first glance due diligence can seem to be a bit of a contradiction — something involving persistent industriousness (because you wanted to do it), but something where you really do not have a choice (because you owe it anyway)! But do not be fooled by this apparent paradox.

It is true that the legislation does not state that food businesses must be diligent. In theory, they can be as careful or as careless as they please. However (and this is the important point), all the specific legal duties add up to the clear message that food businesses owe a *due* — a duty of care — to their customers. So, if you cannot show that you are paying your debt of care to your customers, then you are most likely be found guilty of committing the offences with which you have been charged.

There is no excuse for mistaking how a food business is expected to behave — if it does *everything* within its power to safeguard consumer health, then the law will not hold the business liable if something does go wrong.

Ensuring diligence

So how can a food business demonstrate due diligence if called upon to do so? The heart of your defence is to show that there is a management system in place and that it enables managers to identify and correct anything which may be unlawful.

This is relatively easy to show with respect to physical contaminants. Imagine, for example, that a customer has found a piece of metal in a jar of baby food. If the food processing company responsible can show that all its equipment, utensils and tools are well maintained, that it operates an efficient automatic metal detection system and that it follows an up-to-date HACCP plan, then a court may well acquit the company. Acquittal is less likely if the company cannot show that any of these measures is in place.

Even so, the existence of a system for managing due diligence is not enough in itself: the system also has to work properly. If food premises are infested with mice, or are in a filthy condition, then the mere existence of a system is unlikely to convince a court that due diligence was being exercised because the system is clearly *not* working effectively.

Working effectively

As you can imagine, it is much more difficult to have a strong defence for matters such as personal hygiene than it is for issues involving the composition, labelling or physical contamination of food, so this is where well-documented, effective training and instruction can help to establish due diligence. There is more about training and its role in food safety in Part 4. As you read through the book, you'll find many examples of policies, systems and procedures that could help a food company to ensure that it can demonstrate due diligence. The following list, although by no means comprehensive, gives an idea of some of them:

- a documented HACCP, or similar, system (see Part 4)
- evidence of supplier audits
- evidence that food has been bought from reputable sources
- cleaning and disinfection schedules
- a waste disposal policy
- a system of integrated pest management
- an accredited hygiene system
- staff training records
- policies for personal hygiene
- evidence of appropriate supervision.

As you can see, these are all management issues: legal responsibilities and the need to establish due diligence create convincing arguments for the value of *managing* food safety, and not just leaving it to chance.

MAKING IT EASIER FOR OTHERS

- Make sure that everyone who handles food, or who could have an impact upon the safety of food, understands his or her own legal responsibilities.
- Emphasise that food safety and legal compliance is a team effort and make certain that staff know how best to contribute to that team effort.
- Explain what the company does to try to ensure that food is safe to eat — for instance, ensure that the food safety policy (see Part 4) is easy for everyone to understand.
- Impress upon staff the importance of complying with the spirit and the letter of the law.
- Encourage professional pride in diligence.
- Lead by example and make sure that other senior staff do so too.

do we really need food safety laws?

Why not just let market forces determine food safety? Do we really need to control food safety by law?

In a democratic society legislation aims to achieve many things. Foremost among the objectives is the protection of society.

That protection may be from unwanted external influences, such as the importation of dangerous drugs, or from undesirable internal influences and activities, such as theft and murder.

Protection may also be from people wishing to operate outside the acceptable limits of society, for example, through terrorism. Or it could be protection from discrimination or harm directed at people who are unable, or only partly able, to protect themselves — from, for example, workplace hazards.

So where does food safety law fit into this protection?

Any state, through its government, is responsible for a great number of functions that are funded from the public purse. Some of these functions are defined by the legal system of the country. Others are part of the collective responsibility assumed by the state because 'someone has to do it' and nobody else is under any obligation to do so.

As far as food safety is concerned, a state usually assumes responsibility for the protection of public health; the suppression of fraud; the drafting, adoption and enforcement of laws; the establishment of a judiciary and a legal process; and international agreements on laws and standards.

But to what extent should a state seek to control public health and food safety?

Many people would probably agree that there should be some form of control on the causes of illnesses from food and drink. But what about nutrition? After all, bad eating habits may lie behind many illnesses and even deaths from food. Should a state seek to control an individual's diet or should it merely issue advice about it?

Most governments have restricted their function to the issuing of advice, rather than trying to control an individual's diet by legal means. Why not then merely issue advice about food safety and just leave it at that?

The simplistic answer is that diet is to a large extent a matter of individual choice (within the person's budget) and a state can usually seek to influence choice only through public education.

On the other hand, food-borne illness is often beyond an individual's control or choice — even though some people do bring about their own food-related illness because of their carelessness.

So, is it *reasonable* for a state to attempt to control the hazards and risks to public health from food? Surely the answer must be 'yes'.

After all, consumers cannot see microbes such as *Salmonella* and, even if they had daily access to powerful microscopes, most microbiological and chemical hazards, as well as physical hazards, are normally well outside their control.

What is more, although there are 'at risk groups' who are particularly vulnerable to the impact of food-borne illness, when such an illness does strike, it rarely distinguishes between the rich and the poor, the well fed and the underfed or the educated and the uneducated.

Perhaps then this gives us an idea of why most countries have introduced food safety laws — to protect, by legislation or other means, the health of the consumer in areas that are outside the consumer's normal personal control.

Of course, this does not mean that food safety education or advice is unnecessary. Indeed the opposite is true. General food safety education and specific training for people in the food industry and general food hygiene education for the public are as important as education about nutrition.

Essential though food legislation may be, laws usually lay down only the minimum standards below which something cannot fall. Recognising this, many food businesses set company standards that are in excess of the legal minimum — something that you may wish to consider.

CHASING PROFITS

Like every other commercial operation, food companies need to make a profit to survive. Even food and catering operations in non-profit-making sectors still need to keep within their budgets, so many of the issues involved in profit chasing are just as relevant to them. In the last three chapters we looked at how the need to stay in business and food safety issues impinge upon each other. In this chapter we take a brief look at some other business matters.

CONTROLLING COSTS

Every manager knows that one way to increase profit is to lower costs. But the true result of cost-lowering initiatives depends entirely on how those costs are reduced. Suppose that you decide to lower costs by reducing energy consumption. You could do this in a number of ways. However, if you were to pasteurise a product, such as milk or ham, at a temperature that was lower than the legal requirement, there would soon be an increase in costs — perhaps because of an outbreak of food-borne illness, or because the reduced shelf life would lead to food being thrown away or because of a well publicised court case and the subsequent loss of custom.

More for less

Increasing efficiency is another well-tried way to reduce costs — whether this is achieved through improved management systems, increased staff productivity, better workflow, new equipment or any other means. In the short term this may *increase* costs — for example, as a result of training staff in new ways of working, or improving the hazard analysis system. In the long term, however, you should get more benefits for less outlay, so *reducing* your costs.

Waste reduction
Yet another way to decrease costs is to reduce waste. General aspects of waste reduction — for

instance, by reducing packaging — are discussed in the CIEH's book *Environmental Management at Work*. However, in food businesses some of the most controllable waste consists of discarded ingredients or products and reworked or recalled products — all arising because of faults or customer complaints.

As you will see in Part 4, an advantage of a *HACCP* or similar system is that the cost of implementing the system can be outweighed by savings in the time and products that were previously 'wasted' because of faults and customer complaints.

The role of staff

One of your key management roles is likely to be the motivation of staff so that they can all play their full part in food safety. You need to make it clear that food safety is every individual's responsibility whether he or she is a chef, kitchen porter, quality manager, shelf-stacker, sandwich-filler, cleaner, maintenance engineer or any other jobholder in a food business. Developing a sense of individual and team responsibility should help to raise overall standards of food safety and may also reduce the need for supervision — staff may help to supervise each other.

Competitiveness

How many companies use their food safety systems and good food safety record as a marketing tool? In fact, quite a number do just that, particularly those in the manufacturing and processing sectors. If a customer or a client company (one that buys food from you but is not the consumer) is seeking a product and Company A can offer a tried and tested food safety system while Company B can offer only a wing and a prayer, who do you think is most likely to get the business?

✸ MAKING IT EASIER FOR OTHERS

- Discuss the factors of importance to food safety that help to make a profit for the business.
- Make it clear that staff should not attempt to cut corners on anything to do with food safety.
- Point out that high standards of food safety help the company to stay in business and remain an employer.

3 What do we need to manage?

1 What is food safety?

2 Why do we need to manage food safety?

3 What do we need to manage?

Managing Food Safety

HAZARDS
Hazards in context
Microbiological hazards
    Bacteria
    ⓕ *putting microbes in writing*
    Bacterial food-borne illnesses
    Viruses
    Parasites
    ⓕ *air-borne travellers*
    Fungi
  ⓠ *Management matters*
    ⓕ *microbes at our service*
Chemical hazards
    ⓕ *living with chemicals*
    Naturally occurring chemicals
    Mycotoxins
    Introduced chemicals
  ⓠ *Management matters*
Physical hazards
  ⓠ *Management matters*

LEGAL REQUIREMENTS
Food safety legislation in the UK
  ⓠ *Management matters*

4 How should we manage food safety?

34

"Waiter! There's a fly in my soup!" wails the disgruntled diner in a time-honoured British joke. "Shh. Keep your voice down sir," replies the waiter promptly, "or everybody will want one."

Even if this ludicrous scenario fails to make you smile, it certainly draws attention to consumers' expectations that the food they buy is safe to eat and that nothing about its appearance, smell, taste or ingredients will put them off eating it.

Food safety legislation supports such consumer views, insisting that all food intended for human consumption should be uncontaminated, safe to eat (so that it does not injure health) and of the nature, substance or quality that the consumer demands.

Food hazards and legal requirements are the main issues you need to manage if you are to secure the safety of the food and legal compliance. Part 3 looks at them in detail, providing the underlying knowledge for good management practice that is discussed in Part 4.

It is particularly important to understand thoroughly all the key points in Part 3 and to feel confident in using the key words listed in both sections. All these terms are explained in the relevant chapter and can also be found in the Glossary.

HAZARDS

KEY WORDS

acid/acidic
a pH of less than 7.0.

acute disease
an illness in which symptoms
develop rapidly after infection.

acute poisoning
the effect of eating food
containing a high level of a
toxic substance over a short
period.

aerobe
an organism requiring oxygen.

alkali/alkaline
a pH of more than 7.0.

allergy
a response of the body's
immune system.

anaerobe
an organism that does not
require oxygen.

at risk group
people at greatest risk from
food-borne pathogens,
including pregnant women and
unborn children, breast-fed
babies, the very young, the
elderly and people who are ill
or convalescing or who have
weakened immunity to disease.

a_w (or water activity)
the moisture available to an
organism.

bacterial growth curve
the population development of
an organism.

bacterium (pl: bacteria)
a widespread single-celled
micro-organism, some of which
are harmful.

base/basic
another word for alkaline.

binary fission
bacterial reproduction by
splitting in two.

carrier
a person who is infected by a
pathogen and can pass it on to
others, but who does not
experience symptoms.

carry-over effect
the accumulation and
transmission of a chemical.

chronic disease
an illness where symptoms last
a relatively long time and may
take some time to develop after
infection.

chronic poisoning
the effect of eating food
containing a low level of a toxic
substance over a long period.

ciguatera
the most common type of
poisoning from fish which have
been contaminated by a species
of toxic algae.

commensal
a biological relationship in
which one organism gains
benefits without harming
another; a form of symbiosis.

contaminant
any unwanted material, object
or substance in food.

contamination
the presence in food, or the
process of transferring to food,
any unwanted material, object
or substance.

core temperature
the temperature at the centre,
or in the thickest part, of food.

critical limit
in HACCP, the border between
safe and unsafe.

cross-contamination
the transfer of a contaminant from one contaminated product, such as raw meat, to another previously uncontaminated product, such as a ready-to-eat food.

danger zone
temperatures from 5°C to 63°C at which most food-borne pathogens multiply easily.

death (or decline) phase
the final stage of the bacterial growth curve.

definitive (or primary) host
the host on or in which a parasite carries out its sexual stage.

denature
a structural change in protein or nucleic acid caused by heat, chemicals or high or low pH.

DNA (deoxyribonucleic acid)
the genetic material inside every cell of an organism.

ectoparasite
a parasite living on a host's body surface.

endoparasite
a parasite living in the organs, inner tissues or blood circulation system of a host.

endospore
a survival form, or stage, of some bacteria. Usually shortened to 'spore'.

endotoxin
a toxin in a bacterial cell which is released when the cell dies.

enterotoxin
a toxin affecting the intestine.

enzyme
a type of protein that can trigger chemical reactions in an organism without itself undergoing any change.

exotoxin
a toxin released from a living bacterium into its surroundings.

extrinsic contamination
contamination from sources other than the raw food itself.

extrinsic factor
an external factor, such as temperature and atmosphere, that influences the growth and survival of a micro-organism.

facultative
a description for a microbe that can live in a variety of conditions — for instance, the presence or the absence of oxygen.

faecal coliform
an organism, such as *E. coli*, the presence of which indicates faecal contamination.

flora (microbial)/microflora
the microbial species normally found in a particular habitat, such as the intestine.

food-borne disease/illness
a general description of any illness from contaminated food. In this book the phrase covers all types of food-related illness from food or water.

food-borne infection
an infection caused by pathogens that are carried by food but are not dependent upon it.

food poisoning
an illness, caused by pathogens living on food or by chemicals, that occurs after contaminated food has been eaten. Sometimes also used as a simple general term for all kinds of illness related to food.

fungus (pl: fungi)
mushrooms/toadstools, moulds and yeasts.

gene
the smallest unit of heredity; a segment of DNA.

genus (pl: genera)
a classification of organisms; a large group of related, or similar, species sharing many characteristics.

germination
sprouting, reproducing.

halophile
a salt-loving or salt-tolerant micro-organism.

hazard
a source of danger: any thing, condition or circumstance that could cause harm to the consumer.

high risk food
a food that easily supports the multiplication of pathogenic micro-organisms.

host
an organism supporting a parasite on or in its body.

incubation
another term for 'onset'.

infection
the presence and multiplication in the body of a pathogen that produces a disease.

infective dose
the number of micro-organisms required to cause symptoms of a disease.

inherent
inbuilt.

intermediate (or secondary) host
the host in which the larval stages of endoparasites develop.

intoxication
the process or symptoms of poisoning.

intrinsic contamination
contamination associated with the food itself.

intrinsic factor
inbuilt factors, such as pH, a_w and nutrients, that influence the growth of micro-organisms.

lag phase
the first stage of bacterial growth in which an organism adapts to its surroundings and does not reproduce.

log (or logarithmic) phase
the stage of rapid bacterial multiplication.

log scale
the curve on a graph of bacterial growth.

mesophile
an organism preferring temperatures between 10°C and 55°C.

microaerophile
an organism that does not need very much oxygen.

micro-organism/microbe
an extremely small (micro) organism.

motile
capable of independent, or self-propelled, movement.

multiplication
microbial reproduction, such as by binary fission (bacteria) or budding (yeast).

mycotoxin
a type of poison produced by some moulds and yeasts.

mycotoxicosis
an illness caused by poison produced by some fungi.

neurotoxin
a toxin that acts on the nervous system.

neutral
a pH of 7.0.

nitrate
a chemical found in nature which is also used in agriculture and as a food preservative. In unsafe quantities it may cause food poisoning.

nitrite
a chemical used as a food preservative. In unsafe quantities it may cause food poisoning.

nitrosamine
a chemical compound that can cause food poisoning.

obligate
a description for a microbe that is obliged to live in particular conditions to survive — for instance, an **obligate aerobe** must have oxygen, while an **obligate anaerobe** must live in oxygen-free conditions.

onset (or incubation)
the time between infection and the first symptoms of disease.

organism
an independent life form.

pathogen
a disease-causing microbe.

pH
a scale indicating the acidity or alkalinity of a solution; a pH figure from 0 to 14.0 with 7.0 being neutral.

phagetyping
a method to identify bacteria by using viruses that attack specific bacterial strains.

potable
safe to drink.

protozoan (pl: protozoa)
single-celled animals, some of which are pathogenic.

psychrophile
an organism preferring temperatures between −5°C and 20°C.

psychrotroph
an organism that prefers temperatures between 0°C and 35°C.

scombroid poisoning
an illness from a toxin that can be formed in oily fish such as mackerel and tuna and is associated with high levels of histamine.

serotyping
a method to identify bacteria through specific antigen/antibody reactions.

spoilage
food deterioration.

spore
a reproductive cell — for instance, of fungi; a shortened version of 'endospore', the dormant, survival form of some bacteria.

sporulation
spore production.

stationary phase
the stage of bacterial growth where the population has reached its maximum.

supplier's certificate
a supplier's guarantee of the wholesomeness of a product based on criteria set by the purchasing company.

thermophile
heat-loving micro-organisms that thrive at between 40°C and 80°C.

toxic
poisonous.

toxin
a poisonous substance produced by some bacteria and fungi.

vehicle of contamination
any substance, object or living being that carries contamination from one point to another.

virus
an extremely small infective organism that can multiply only within living cells.

water activity
see a_w.

xerophile
an organism that likes dry conditions and can survive low a_w values.

HAZARDS IN CONTEXT

Hazards are central to contemporary thinking about effective food safety management and their identification, assessment and control are a significant legal requirement for food businesses. Since the 1990s all food businesses in the UK have been obliged by law to analyse the potential food hazards in their type of work and to take steps to eliminate or control those hazards.

The other chapters in Part 3 look in detail at what constitutes a food hazard — under the categories of microbiological, physical and chemical hazards — and at the main features of food safety legislation. Before reading these crucial chapters you may wish to take a brief look at what 'hazards' mean in the food industry in general and how an understanding of hazards lays a foundation for applying the best possible methods to the management of food safety.

WHAT ARE HAZARDS?

We are all familiar with the everyday conversational use of the word hazard to indicate a threat, or possibility, of danger. In Parts 1 and 2 we described food hazards simply as being any situation, thing or condition that could cause harm to the consumer. If we wanted to be more specific, we could say that a *hazard* is anything — whether microbiological, chemical or physical — that might cause harm to the consumer, or 'that is reasonably likely to cause illness or injury in the absence of its control' (*HACCP Principles and Application Guidelines*, National Advisory Committee on Microbiological Criteria for Foods, USA).

A more scientific definition, by the International Commission on Microbiological Specifications for Foods (ICMSF), explains a hazard as 'the unacceptable contamination, unacceptable growth and/or unacceptable survival by micro-organisms of concern to safety or spoilage and/or the unacceptable production or persistence in foods of products of microbiological metabolism'.

The last definition is of course restricted to microbiological hazards and ignores physical and chemical hazards. However, as you well know, there are many opportunities along the food flow from farm to fork for contamination by physical objects (sometimes called foreign bodies) and by chemicals as well as by micro-organisms.

What is clear from all these definitions, and from others we could quote, is that a hazard represents the potential for harm. As a food safety manager, you need to stop the *possibility* of harm from becoming *actual* harm, whether that harm is in the form of illness, injury or simply disgust at an objectionable extra ingredient in food.

TYPES OF HAZARD

There are many *potential* food hazards — including micro-organisms such as bacteria; chemicals such as cleaning products; and physical objects such as hair, metal staples or insects. Even so, they are *actual* hazards only when they are on food — when they have contaminated food. All forms of food *contamination* are undesirable and may cause harm to consumers. If you are to prevent illness or injury from food, you need to prevent or reduce contamination.

With micro-organisms the possibility of harm does not stop at contamination, because the *multiplication* and *survival* of micro-organisms also constitute food hazards. As you can see from the diagram opposite, microbiological hazards occur in more ways than do physical or chemical hazards. Microbiological hazards include microbiological contamination, microbiological multiplication and microbiological survival, while physical hazards are simply physical contamination and chemical hazards are simply chemical contamination.

Microbiological hazards
Potential microbiological hazards include *pathogenic* and *spoilage* bacteria, viruses, fungi and parasites.

Contamination
This can happen at many stages in the food flow including growth, harvesting or slaughtering, storage, processing and transport. Food contaminated by micro-organisms creates the *possibility* of a food safety problem. To stop the problem arising, you need to prevent or reduce contamination. So, one type of microbiological hazard is the contamination of food by micro-organisms.

Multiplication
Some micro-organisms, particularly the food poisoning bacteria, cause illness because they have experienced the right conditions in which to multiply on the food after the initial contamination. To stop this, you need to control the conditions in which the bacteria can multiply. So, another type of microbiological hazard is the multiplication of micro-organisms.

Survival
Some processes, such as heating, are designed to kill micro-organisms. If, for whatever reason, the process fails to work properly, some or all of the pathogens may survive. To prevent survival, you must ensure that such processes are effective. So, a third type of microbiological hazard is the survival of micro-organisms.

Chemical hazards
Many types of chemical can cause problems, including agricultural and industrial chemicals, cleaning products and cooking equipment. As with microbiological hazards, they are a hazard only if they are in our food, and it is this that you need

to control. Chemicals do not multiply, nor are there heat processes designed to kill them, so chemical contamination is the only type of chemical hazard.

Physical hazards

Naturally occurring materials, such as twigs, and introduced materials, such as splinters of wood from pallets, could be a hazard if found in food. It is simpler to consider the hazard not as a piece of wood but as physical contamination which needs to be controlled. Physical contamination is the only type of physical hazard.

MANAGING HAZARDS
There is more information about managing hazards throughout Part 4, particularly in the section 'Preventing food contamination' and in the chapters 'Controlling time and temperature' and 'HACCP and hazard analysis'.

CONTAMINATION, MULTIPLICATION AND SURVIVAL

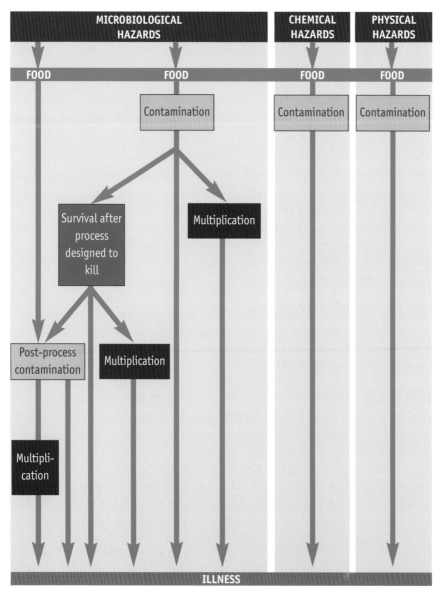

MICROBIOLOGICAL HAZARDS

Why should a manager like you need to learn anything more about micro-organisms than you know already? As your profession is to manage or supervise some aspect of a business that deals with food, even if you are not directly involved in working with the food itself, you already know that microbes can cause serious problems in a food business. So, why go further?

Microbiology — the study of microscopic life forms — underlies many of the things that your business needs to do to ensure that the food it produces is safe to eat and has an acceptable shelf life. So, it is the foundation for the main principles of food handling and for the management policies you need to develop and implement.

It goes without saying that you also need to give your full attention to other aspects of food safety management, such as the prevention and control of physical and chemical hazards, but microbiological hazards are the first among equals. Micro-organisms are responsible for most cases of food-borne disease worldwide.

Practical value

This chapter is designed to give you a far greater understanding of why micro-organisms can cause so many problems and why good housekeeping practices are essential to preventing outbreaks of food-borne illness. Later chapters discuss effective methods to prevent microbes from causing illness and the consequent loss of business reputation and profit.

Bacteria, the main cause of food-related illnesses, are discussed first, followed by the non-bacterial organisms — viruses, parasites and fungi. Problems caused by *mycotoxins*, certain poisons caused by moulds and yeasts, are discussed under chemical hazards on pages 129 to 134.

Step-by-step approach

Don't worry if you do not have a scientific background. Everything is explained in simple terms, sometimes with additional, more detailed information for those who already have a grasp of biochemistry.

In some management positions in some sectors — such as in food processing, food packaging and the development of novel foods — you may need to know a great deal more about microbiology than is covered in this chapter. If so, speak with a training adviser about additional courses of study.

Some additional reading is suggested in the Bibliography (see pages 375 to 376).

Back to basics

Before we plunge into discussion about micro-organisms, it is worth reminding ourselves of a few basics — such as what microbes are and what microbiology covers.

WHAT IS MICROBIOLOGY?

Microbiology is the study of micro-organisms. *Organisms* are independent life forms, which are sometimes referred to as 'creatures'. They are divided into various categories such as animals (which include humans), plants, fungi and bacteria.

Micro-organisms, or *microbes* for short, are extremely small (micro) life forms. Most can be seen only with the help of a powerful microscope.

Microbiology is a wide-ranging subject that incorporates many different disciplines. For example, bacteriology deals with bacteria; mycology deals with fungi (mushrooms, moulds and yeasts); and virology deals with viruses. There are also areas of study for protozoa (microscopic single-celled organisms).

Microbes form a large, varied group of organisms, but most of them are:
- extremely small — 'invisible' to the naked eye
- relatively simple in structure
- extremely adaptable to different conditions
- ubiquitous — they occur everywhere.

What they also have in common is their potential to cause either food safety problems or spoilage, or both, whatever the type of food business.

MICROBES
The study of micro-organisms helps food managers to produce safe food and prevent spoilage.

BACTERIA

There is hardly a place on Earth that is not inhabited by *bacteria*. These tiny organisms are literally all around us and are a natural, integral part of our own bodies. In fact, we cannot do without them. They help to create the air we breathe and the plants we eat. They enable us to digest and break down bodily waste products and they are responsible for foods, such as cheese and yoghurt, and medicinal drugs such as some antibiotics.

Even so, we can have trouble living with some bacteria because they can cause debilitating and life-threatening diseases. To make this love-hate relationship more complicated, some types of bacteria can be both beneficial and harmful to humans.

This chapter introduces the main bacterial characteristics of significance to food safety, while the next chapter considers specific bacteria and the illnesses they can cause. As a contrast, the feature on pages 114 and 115 takes a brief look at some of the benefits to be gained from harnessing the power of various types of microbes.

CLASSIFYING BY THE IMPACT UPON HUMANS

As you can see, bacteria are far from being just the germs or the 'bugs' of everyday conversation. One of the most convenient ways to classify them is by their impact upon humans and human activity:
- *pathogenic* bacteria are responsible for causing disease
- *spoilage* bacteria are responsible for the degradation of food (and other substances)
- *commensal* bacteria are usually harmless, may be positively beneficial — for example, for agriculture, medicine, food production and many other processes — and live in harmony with people and other host organisms.

When considering food safety we need to concentrate on *pathogenic* bacteria, because they are responsible for most cases of food-borne illness, and on *spoilage* bacteria because they can damage food and cost thousands of pounds in waste and lost business.

Some bacteria belong to more than one group, being harmless or even beneficial commensals in some contexts, but damaging pathogenic or spoilage organisms in others. For example, *Lactobacilli* are essential for the fermenting processes that produce yoghurt, certain cheeses, sausages and sauerkraut (a traditional German dish of pickled cabbage). If they get into the 'wrong' foods such as beverages, however, they may cause unwanted effects such as unpleasant, odd, or 'off', flavours. In a similar way, *Staphylococcus aureus* bacteria live harmlessly and normally as commensals in nasal mucus, but once they are transferred to food, they can have pathogenic characteristics.

CHARACTERISTICS OF BACTERIA

While humans have trillions of cells in their bodies which perform many tasks, bacteria each have a single cell. Just one little machine (the cell) is responsible for all the functions needed to stay alive, including metabolism (all the chemical changes, including combining and breaking down substances), growth and reproduction. This makes bacteria both very simple and very complicated.

Bacteria tend to be *heterotrophs* — they depend, as do humans, on consuming organic matter to continue living, growing and multiplying. In contrast, plants are *autotrophs* and make their own food by converting sunlight into energy, a process known as *photosynthesis*.

Scientists describe bacteria according to:
- morphology — the shape of the bacterial cell and other features seen under a microscope, such as the existence of organs for moving about and the way bacteria aggregate (clump together)
- anatomy — the microscopic structure of the individual bacterial cell
- physiology — the metabolism of the bacterium and the conditions that particular species favour.

We need to focus on physiology, but to understand how this impacts upon food safety, we first need to take a quick look at the morphology and anatomy of bacteria.

Morphology — shaping up

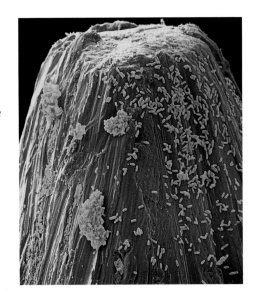

A typical bacterial cell measures between 1μm and 2μm. The symbol μ stands for micro and μm is a micrometre (or micron) — one millionth of a metre, or 10^{-6}m. (See Reference for guidance on figures expressed to the power of ten.)

It is hard to imagine 1μm or 2μm until you see the tip of the point of an ordinary household pin in this greatly magnified (x175) scanning electron micrograph. One million bacteria would fit on there quite easily!

Bacteria are tiny and colourless, so, before examining them under the microscope, scientists may stain them with a dye (see page 48). They also employ a range of other tests (see page 66) that assist them in describing and classifying bacteria.

Named after the Danish physician Hans C J Gram who developed it in 1884, the technique involves the use of crystal violet dye, iodine and alcohol (or acetone) to distinguish two groups of bacteria. The Gram reaction, or Gram stain, detects differences in the composition of the bacterial cell wall. Bacteria that stay the violet colour of the dye, such as staphylococci, are described as being Gram-positive. This is often written as Gram(+) or Gram+ve. Bacteria that go a pinkish colour, such as salmonellae, are described as being Gram-negative, often written Gram(-) or Gram-ve. There are a number of differences between Gram-positive and Gram-negative bacteria, such as the anatomy of the cell wall and the kinds of toxin they produce.

Shape

Although each bacterium merely consists of a single cell, some types can clump together, either in random clusters or in geometrical aggregates such as pairs, chains and shamrocks. Both the individual cell shape and the characteristic grouping patterns provide scientists with important clues to the identity of the bacteria in a food sample.

Rods (bacilli)

Some, such as *Salmonella* species (see pictures on pages 25 and 52) are longer than they are broad. Others, such as *E. coli* (shown below in a human intestine), can sometimes appear so short that they look almost spherical. Bacilli include Gram-positive and Gram-negative *genera*.

Spiral (helical)

These look like twisted bacilli and may, like *Campylobacter jejuni* (shown left, on the opposite page), be a spirally curved rod. Some bacteria appear like a tiny teardrop or a comma and are referred to as vibrios — for instance, *Vibrio parahaemolyticus* and *Vibrio cholerae* (see page 83).

Spherical cells (cocci)

Bacteria such as *Staphylococcus aureus* (shown right, on the opposite page) have a tendency to form clusters. Almost all cocci are Gram-positive.

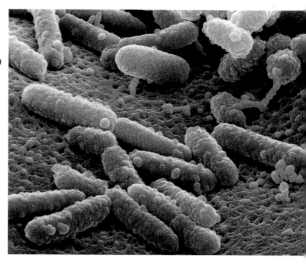

Other shapes

Some bacteria, such as actinomycetes, have a branching form that looks rather like a tree with different branches, even though they are still single cells. Even square bacteria are known to exist!

Anatomy — physical strengths and weaknesses

Close examination of bacterial anatomy has enabled scientists to discover weak points and develop other methods, such as disinfection, that can disable or destroy bacteria.

The structure of a bacterium

The *cell wall* is a strong, rigid structure that determines the characteristic shape of a particular species of bacteria. It is permeable so that the bacterium can exchange substances with the surrounding environment, allowing nutrients and waste material to pass through. The composition of the cell wall is responsible for the Gram reaction (see opposite).

Between the cell wall and the inner part of the cell is the *cell membrane*, which is also known as the *plasma membrane*. Together, the cell wall and membrane create a double organ that acts rather like a security barrier between the vital contents of the inner cell and the bacterium's immediate local environment (sometimes called the *surrounding medium*). The cell membrane is selectively permeable in both directions — it allows nutrients to pass into the cell and waste products to pass out of the cell. If the membrane is damaged — for instance, by chemical disinfectants or antibiotics — the cell is likely to die.

Some bacteria, including certain spoilage types, have a gel-like extra layer, called the *capsule*, outside the cell wall. When these bacteria contaminate food, the surface of the food becomes slimy or sticky. Chemical disinfectants can desiccate (dry out) the capsule, often damaging the cell wall and causing the bacterium to die.

Inside the cell is the *cytoplasm*, a semi-liquid containing *enzymes* (proteins that spark off other biochemical reactions), *metabolites* (proteins, fats and other products of digestion), waste products and so on. The cytoplasm surrounds

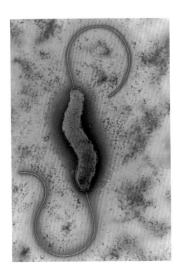 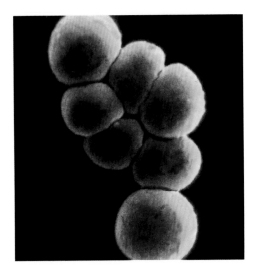

This page, left Campylobacter jejuni; *right,* Staphylococcus aureus. *Page opposite,* E. coli. *The micrographs are not magnified to the same scale.*

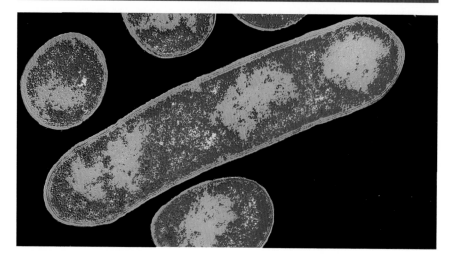

Unless you have a highly trained eye, it can be difficult to distinguish the parts of a bacterium even in a highly magnified and coloured micrograph such as this one of a *Clostridium botulinum*. The illustration opposite therefore exaggerates some key features to make them a little easier to understand. The illustration includes a flagellum, which is not present on *C. botulinum*, but you can see a micrograph on page 25 of a *Salmonella* Typhimurium that does include this structure.

essential structures such as *storage granules* (stored proteins for later use) and ribosomes (where *genes* — units of inheritance — are replicated). The genes are on a linear chromosome consisting of a strand of deoxyribonucleic acid, better known as *DNA*. The DNA determines the individual and species characteristics of the bacterium — its preferences for food and environment, for example, as well as its rate of reproduction and resilience in adverse conditions.

You might find it helpful to consider DNA as the organism's personal User's Guide to Life which contains all the information and do-it-yourself tools needed for existence, growth and reproduction. If the DNA is damaged or destroyed, the organism cannot read and follow the instructions in its User's Guide and the cell cannot function properly.

NUCLEUS FREE
Unlike many other life forms, bacteria do not have a cell nucleus.

In most life forms every cell has a *nucleus* — a structure inside the cell which protects the genetic material — but bacteria do things differently. Instead of having a nucleus, they store most of their genetic material on a circular macro-molecule (a ring-chromosome, which looks a little like a loop of the coiled cable to a telephone handset). Small pieces of DNA may form extra rings known as plasmids.

Some bacteria have an external organ called a *flagellum*, from the Latin for lash or whip, which acts rather like a boat's outboard motor, propelling them along.

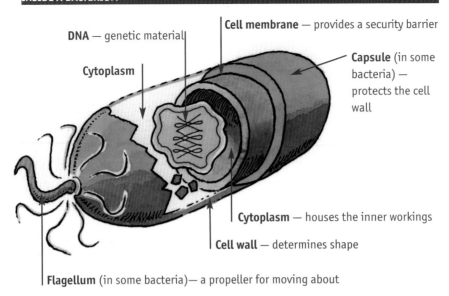

DNA — genetic material

Cell membrane — provides a security barrier

Cytoplasm

Capsule (in some bacteria) — protects the cell wall

Cytoplasm — houses the inner workings

Cell wall — determines shape

Flagellum (in some bacteria)— a propeller for moving about

Bacteria can have one, two or more flagellae to move around. Other external organs, called *pili*, are hair-like projections which help the bacterial cell to adhere to surfaces such as that of the human intestine.

Some bacterial structures, such as the capsule, parts of the cell wall, the flagellae and the pili, have *antigenic* qualities. This means that they prompt the immune system of the host to start defending itself by producing *antibodies*. Antibodies can be detected in blood, providing a useful hint about the cause of an infection (see also page 68).

Physiology — beyond the microscope
However diligently scientists examine bacteria under the microscope, they cannot discover everything in this way. Other techniques are needed to confirm identity, especially when it comes to distinguishing particular strains of a species.

Physiological tests, also called biochemical tests, are essential when the full identity of an organism has to be established beyond doubt — for example, when it is intended for use in food processing or must be eliminated to prevent food-borne disease. Physiological testing aims to identify an organism's preferred nutrients, waste products and enzyme activities.

Two immunological tests are also used:
- serotyping, based on the interaction between the bacterium and host antibodies
- phagetyping, based on identifying viruses that attack the bacterium.

For details of these and other tests see pages 66 to 68.

BACTERIAL REPRODUCTION

Understanding the way in which bacteria reproduce and the time they take to do so has helped the food industry to develop simple but effective ways to prevent food poisoning and to keep food safe and appetising to eat.

Binary fission

Bacteria are able to reproduce asexually. This means not only that they do not have sex, but also that they can reproduce without exchanging and recombining their DNA. Instead, bacteria multiply by a process called *binary fission* — which means splitting in two. As you can see from the greatly simplified diagram below, one 'mother' cell divides into two genetically identical 'daughter' cells and the 'mother' cell itself then ceases to exist. Under favourable conditions, binary fission is repeated many times, doubling the numbers every generation and creating large populations very quickly. The rate of multiplication varies from species to species, but the rule of thumb is that each cell divides in two every 10 to 20 minutes.

There are other forms of asexual reproduction (see the micrograph of yeast budding on page 110), but cell division is the only asexual bacterial method.

This Salmonella *Typhimurium bacterium is in the process of binary fission. The DNA has been replicated and the septum has been drawn in, so that two identical cells can be formed.*

The bacterial mother cell matures. (The DNA size and shape are exaggerated here.)	*The DNA is replicated.*	*The septum, a separating wall, is drawn in. (This is the stage shown in the micrograph above.)*	*There are now two separate identical cells which can repeat the process if conditions are favourable. The 'sister' cells of some species do not separate completely after fission but create cell clusters after repeated divisions.*

The bacterial growth curve

The growth rate of a bacterial population varies from species to species. It also depends on how favourable the environment is for the particular species. There is, however, a general growth pattern that bacterial populations follow.

This pattern is best shown as a graph (see page opposite), which is known as the *bacterial growth curve*. The x-axis (horizontal) is used to represent time and the y-axis (vertical) to show the number of viable cells. The curve is known as *the log scale*. To understand what happens, imagine that:

- there are a few bacteria on a high risk food that has been left in a food preparation area
- the environmental conditions of the room stay pretty much the same throughout the period we are concerned with — about five hours.

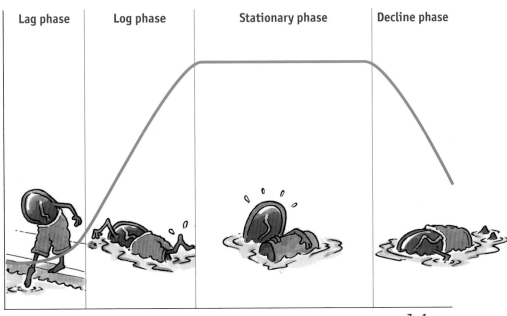

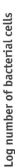

Log number of bacterial cells

| Lag phase | Log phase | Stationary phase | Decline phase |

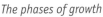

Time/hours

The phases of growth

At first there is a period, called the *lag phase*, in which nothing seems to happen. This apparent delay (or lag) is in fact a time for adjustment, while the bacteria get used to their surroundings. There is no bacterial multiplication at this stage. It may help to imagine swimmers who wade cautiously into the water and need to adjust to the temperature before starting to swim off. The duration of the lag phase depends on the species, the initial number of the bacteria and the environmental conditions in which they find themselves.

The next phase, called the *log phase* or *logarithmic phase*, is one of rapid reproduction and a steadily mounting growth curve (assuming conditions are favourable). It is as if the swimmers are gaining speed. Only a few bacteria die at this time, so the population virtually doubles every generation. The rate of increase, represented by the steepness of the curve, depends on the particular species. If you like, you can think of different species as different classes of swimmers, the advanced class racing along and the beginners striking out more slowly.

The third stage is the *stationary phase*, which, at first sight, resembles the lag phase because nothing seems to happen. In fact, the population of bacteria has reached its maximum. It is as if the swimmers have reached top speed and cannot accelerate any more. Bacteria still multiply in this phase, but the increase in numbers is balanced by cell mortality (the number of bacteria that die). The change from the log to the stationary phase happens because of the depletion of nutrients — rather as if our swimmers were using up their last reserves of energy — and the accumulation of bacterial waste products.

The final stage shows a more or less steady decline towards zero on the y-axis. The total population decreases rapidly as more and more cells die, while fewer and fewer new cells are produced. This is called the *death phase* or *decline phase*. Our swimmers become increasingly exhausted and drown.

A clue to controlling food-borne disease?

So, can an understanding of the bacterial growth curve help you to manage food safety? It may be tempting to think, if only for a moment, that the only precaution a food handler needs to take is to wait until the bacterial population has exhausted itself and died. Even if it were possible to know exactly when the food was contaminated, so that you could calculate the decline phase, the food would have lost all its nutritional value in this period. What's more, it would now also contain poisonous by-products from all the bacterial activity.

The growth curve does, however, point us towards two possible ways to help to guarantee that food is safe — we can:
- interrupt the log curve at any point by creating lethal conditions — for example, by boiling the food
- prolong the lag phase by creating inhibitory conditions — for example, by refrigerating the food, altering the pH (see page 60), removing moisture (see pages 59 to 60) or adding preservatives
- serve high risk food (see page 58) as soon as possible after preparation while any pathogenic bacteria are still in the lag phase.

A TYPICAL PATTERN OF POPULATION DEVELOPMENT				
1 cell	becomes	2 cells	after 20 minutes	(1st generation)
2 cells	become	4 cells	after 40 minutes	(2nd generation)
4 cells	become	8 cells	after 60 minutes	(3rd generation)
8 cells	become	16 cells	after 80 minutes	(4th generation)

BACTERIAL SPORES – A SURVIVAL STRATEGY

Some bacteria have the ability to produce *endospores*, often called spores for short. They should not be confused with *fungal spores* (see page 110) which are a form of propagation. Endospores are a dormant stage, or form, that a bacterium takes to enable it to survive adverse conditions. In fact, bacterial spores are one of the most resistant forms of living cell. They can survive chemical treatment, drying, freezing, normal cooking temperatures and high and low pH conditions. Only two bacterial genera produce spores — *Bacillus* and *Clostridium*. Both genera include spoilage bacteria, such as *Clostridium acetobutyricum* and *Bacillus stearothermophilus*, as well as food-borne pathogens such as *Clostridium botulinum* and *Bacillus cereus*.

When the going gets tough

When conditions become unfavourable for bacteria, those that cannot form spores start to die, while *Bacillus* and *Clostridium* species start *sporulation*, the process of forming spores (see the micrograph on the right).

The vegetative (living) cell begins to form a hard case *inside* itself. The case contains all the vital ingredients, such as its DNA, needed to continue life once the harsh conditions have passed. In the false-coloured electron micrograph (right) a *Clostridium perfringens* bacterium is completing spore formation. The spore, coloured green with a red membrane, is visible in the bottom part of the picture.

When the spore is complete, the rest of the cell degenerates, releasing a microscopic, dried-up bundle that can stay dormant, without absorbing nutrients, for many years. Spores have been detected in archaeological excavations of sites that are at least 2,000 years old, but there is considerable scientific debate about the length of time that a spore can remain viable (able to come back to life).

When conditions are favourable once more, the endospore becomes active again. It absorbs water, splits and releases a vegetative cell that restarts the normal cycle of bacterial growth and reproduction. This process of coming back to life is called *germination*.

In this greatly magnified and false-coloured electron micrograph a Clostridium perfringens bacterium is towards the end of forming a spore. The green structure with a red membrane in the lower part of the bacterium is the spore. When complete, the rest of the bacterium will dissolve, leaving a hardy survival 'capsule'.

The threat from spores

As bacteria in spore form can withstand harsh conditions and do not need water, oxygen, heat or nutrients, they can survive in almost any environment. Consequently they may be carried into food premises by various forms of 'transport', including soil on vegetables, other raw ingredients and unprocessed foods. They are often air-borne and can enter food areas in dust and dirt, particularly where windows, skylights and doors are not screened.

It is important to understand that consuming the spores themselves is not a significant risk to human health, except in the case of babies or infants, who can become ill from swallowing spores of *Clostridium botulinum*. As the example below shows, the real danger is that the spores may germinate and multiply, leading to new populations of harmful bacteria in the food.

Example

Endospores consumed in food

Food is cooked thoroughly right the way through for sufficient time at an appropriate temperature. All the bacteria which cannot form spores are killed, while the spore-forming organisms turn into their resistant dormant form. If the food is consumed immediately after cooking, nothing happens — no symptoms of illness develop and there is no threat to health.

Endospores germinate and multiply, then food is consumed

If food is cooked in the same way but left at room temperature for some time after cooking, conditions develop that are favourable to bacterial multiplication. So, the spores germinate, releasing active vegetative cells. These vegetative cells reproduce rapidly, without competition from non-spore-forming bacteria, which have been killed by the heat. By the time the food is eaten it may contain dangerous levels of pathogenic bacteria or bacterial toxins, making food poisoning very likely.

Control

Spores are very difficult to destroy so normal heat treatment, such as cooking, does not kill them. The time and temperature criteria used in canning processes (see page 290) and in autoclaving (sterilisation of medical and laboratory materials) are designed to kill them. Irradiation also destroys spores — see pages 65 and 296.

TOXINS — BY-PRODUCTS OF BACTERIAL LIFE

Toxins are poisonous substances produced by living organisms such as bacteria and some fungi and algae. They are usually complex enzymes, types of protein, and they attack other essential proteins in our bodies. The following paragraphs focus on bacterial toxins, the direct cause of most cases of food-borne disease. Some fungi also produce toxins (mycotoxins) — see pages 129 to 134.

TOXINS
In everyday speech when we say that something is toxic we just mean that it is poisonous. But in biology *toxin* has a specific meaning and refers only to poisons produced by living organisms such as bacteria and fungi.

Types of toxin

There are two sorts of bacterial toxin:
- *endotoxins*, which exist within the cell
- *exotoxins*, which are secreted as waste products.

Some bacteria, such as *Bacillus cereus*, can produce both types of toxin.

Toxins can also be classified by their effects:
- *enterotoxins* affect the intestinal system
- *neurotoxins* affect nerve functions.

You may come across a description of a bacterium that combines the type and effect of its toxin. For example, *Staphylococcus aureus* could be described as an exogenic enterotoxin-producer.

Endotoxins

Endotoxins are normally sealed in the bacterial cell and released only when the bacterium dies or sporulates. This may be either before or after the food is consumed. *Clostridium perfringens*, for example, can sporulate in the intestine.

Exotoxins

Exotoxins are poisonous substances secreted by some bacteria, either during binary fission or as digestive waste products. This means that they can contaminate food before it is eaten. Even if the bacteria themselves are killed — say by cooking — the exotoxin will still be present and able to cause illness.

Enterotoxins
Toxins that affect the intestines are known as enterotoxins. They are virulently poisonous: where it could take about 500µg per kg of body-weight to kill someone with the plant poison strychnine, just 0.1µg per kg of body-weight of bacterial enterotoxin would be needed.

Neurotoxins
These poisons attack the nervous system and are the most dangerous biotoxins on Earth. The most deadly is the toxin produced by *Clostridium botulinum*. The lethal dose is just 0.0003µg per kg of body-weight.

How bacterial toxins make you ill
Bacterial toxins may give rise to many symptoms. The most typical are vomiting and diarrhoea. Others include *chronic poisoning* and the destruction of vital organs and the nervous system. The nature of the symptoms may give a useful hint about the likely causative organism. As soon as our bodies perceive traces of unwanted matter, the intestinal system tries to get rid of them as quickly as possible. Exotoxins are usually detected early on, in the stomach. The stomach collapses and sends the food back by the quickest route — a process we call vomiting.

Endotoxins are generally detected only in the intestines. Many bacteria that produce endotoxins, such as species of *Salmonella*, would not normally survive the acidity of the stomach on their own. However, when they contaminate food, the food serves as a protective shield that allows them to pass through into the small intestine. Here they find near-neutral conditions that suit them. By then it is too late for the body to send anything back by vomiting, so our system defends itself by turning the usually slow and controlled movement of the gut (the intestinal peristalsis) into an uncontrolled, forceful process — diarrhoea.

WHAT BACTERIA NEED TO SURVIVE

When we first teach staff about illnesses linked to food, we usually tell them simply that bacteria depend upon a favourable combination of food, moisture, warmth and time. Later on, we might expand this list to include conditions such as atmosphere (oxygen and other gases) and pH (the acid-alkali scale). Whatever our choice of words, we explain that the basic conditions for bacterial survival and multiplication are a matter of the presence of favourable conditions and the absence of inhibitory factors. These are really two sides of the same coin.

As you can imagine, the biochemistry behind bacterial requirements is fairly complicated. You are not expected to study microbiology in depth but as a manager you need to understand the principles of the factors that affect the growth of bacterial populations. This will help you to appreciate how preventive measures work and, in turn, will help you to plan and monitor controls that are appropriate to your workplace:

- preventing bacteria from multiplying
- killing pathogenic and spoilage bacteria.

Essential bacterial requirements

A bacterial population grows in direct relation to the presence of favourable conditions. These conditions, or factors, can be divided into two groups — intrinsic and extrinsic.

Intrinsic factors are attributes inherent in the food and include:

- the nutrient content of the food
- moisture, expressed as water activity (a_w)
- acidity or alkalinity, expressed as hydrogen-ion concentration (pH).

Extrinsic factors are conditions of the environment and include:

- temperature
- time
- atmosphere.

Competition between micro-organisms also affects the population growth.

The next few pages look in detail at how each of these factors affects bacteria.

INTRINSIC FACTORS

These are characteristics that are part and parcel of the food itself.

Nutrient content

All foods suitable for humans also suit micro-organisms. Food-borne microbes show a marked preference for foods that are rich in protein and carbohydrates. The smallest quantities of such foodstuffs can support very large bacterial populations — a good reason for cleaning and disinfecting work surfaces, equipment and utensils thoroughly.

Some bacteria are relatively unfussy about their choice of nutrients, while others target particular foods like milk products, seafood or cereals. Some depend on the presence of certain vitamins — for example, *Staphylococcus aureus* needs thiamine (part of the vitamin B group). Foods that are particularly vulnerable to microbial multiplication are known as *high risk foods* and need to be refrigerated.

HIGH RISK FOODS

These foods tend to be rich in protein and fairly moist. They include meats and meat products, such as pies and sausages; poultry; stocks, gravies, stews and sauces; all kinds of seafood (fish and shellfish); milk, cream and dairy products; and eggs and egg products.

Some foods contain antimicrobial substances, like etheric oils, that have an inhibitory effect on bacterial growth. Other foods have biological barriers, or protective layers, against microbial growth — lobster and mussel shells, for example. The risk of bacterial contamination increases as soon as the protective layer is removed or destroyed.

The surface of meat is likely to be contaminated, so a single cut into the muscular layer increases the risk of bacterial contamination throughout the meat because microbes are transferred by the knife from the surface. The more the meat is chopped or minced, the greater the risk of bacterial contamination throughout.

Moisture

Like all living creatures, micro-organisms need water. Bacteria prefer moist foods such as meat, fish and liquid and semi-liquid products.

However, most foods do, in fact, contain quite a lot of water even when we perceive them to be 'dry' products. Items such as bread and biscuits may contain enough water to support bacterial growth. On the other hand, some foods such as jam seem to be very moist but are not high risk foods because the water is bound by dissolved agents. In other words, ingredients like salt and sugar make the moisture unavailable to bacteria.

To support bacterial multiplication, the water in the product must be actively available — there for the taking. The availability of water is known as *water activity* (a_w). It is the a_w that tells us just how likely particular foods are to support bacterial growth.

(You might see water activity expressed as $a_w = P/P_0$. The 'P' represents the vapour pressure of the food and the 'P_0' represents the vapour pressure of water at the same ambient temperature. Don't worry if this kind of information makes your eyes glaze over: the important point is to know which foods have high water activity — see below.)

The a_w of pure water is 1.0, so all foods other than water have a value below 1.0. Most fresh foods have an a_w around 0.99.

EXAMPLES OF THE a_w OF FOODS	
Meat (fresh)	0.95-0.99
Meat (cured)	0.87-0.95
Fruit & veg	0.94
Bread	0.94-0.97
Cheese (hard)	0.90
Jam	0.75-0.80
Flour	0.67-0.87
Noodles & pasta	0.2

The tolerance range of individual micro-organisms to a_w varies greatly, but most bacteria reach optimal growth at a high a_w (values at above 0.95). Pathogenic and spoilage organisms grow fastest at around 0.98. If the a_w in food is too low for bacterial growth, most bacteria become dormant. If the dry conditions are prolonged, the cells eventually die.

Gram-negative bacteria, such as *Salmonella*, are particularly vulnerable when water activity is low. Exceptions include salt-tolerant bacteria (known as *halophiles*, from the Greek for salt loving) such as *Vibrio parahaemolyticus*.

Gram-positive bacteria generally tolerate low water activity more easily, so the typical *flora* in cured meats is usually Gram-positive. Organisms growing at a low a_w are *xerophiles* (from the Greek for something that loves dry conditions). A lot of fungi are also xerophiles and this is why mould can spoil 'dry' foods which are not usually at risk from pathogenic contamination.

There are various techniques for lowering the water activity of food. They include:
- reducing the overall water content (dehydration)
- increasing the concentration of *electrolytes* — for example, by salting
- adding solutes such as sugar to bind water
- combining some of the methods mentioned above, as in pickling.

Hydrogen-ion concentration (pH)

The acidity or alkalinity of food is the key intrinsic factor in bacterial growth. The measure of whether something is *acid* or *alkali* (often called *basic*) is the *pH scale*. It runs from 0 to 14, with 7 as the neutral point (see opposite). A pH below 7 is *acidic*, while above 7 is *alkaline* or *basic*.

Most foods have a pH between 7 and 4, so they are neutral or slightly acidic. Only egg white is truly alkaline, measuring at around 8.

Microbial growth is possible within a broad range of pH values, but most bacteria grow best at or near *neutral* (pH 6-8). This means that most foods support bacterial multiplication. High and low pH values both inhibit bacterial growth.

Processing and storage usually lower the pH of food, so reducing bacterial growth. However, some other microbial growth, such as mould, may still occur at low pH. Sometimes this has the effect of increasing the pH of the food and therefore of increasing the risk of bacterial growth once more.

Bacterial spores survive at *any* pH level, but germinate only at above pH 4.5.

From a food safety point of view, pH needs to be considered in combination with other factors such as temperature. The genus *Salmonella* is a good example of how pH and other factors together affect the behaviour of pathogenic bacteria:
- *Salmonella* will usually multiply at pH as low as 4.1 if all other conditions are optimal
- at lower temperatures (below 10°C) *Salmonella* will not multiply below pH 5
- added inhibitors, such as salt and preservatives, stop *Salmonella* from multiplying below pH 5.6.

Puzzling over ways to test and control the quality of beer as it matured, Danish chemist Søren Peter Lauritz Sørensen devised a way in 1909 of measuring acidity — the pH scale. Today the scale has innumerable applications both inside and outside brewing and the food industry, including medicine, agriculture, geology, chemistry and biology. The 'p' stands for potenz, which means strength in Danish and the 'H' is the scientific symbol for hydrogen. So pH describes the concentration ('strength') of free hydrogen ions in a solution. Most solutions are within the scale of 0 to 14, with 7 as neutral, but values outside the range are also possible. Acidic foods with a pH below 4.0, such as soft drinks, fruit (like

grapefruit, above) vinegar and wine, are usually safe from bacterial multiplication (although they may be vulnerable to fungal growth) and have a long shelf life.

The chart below shows the very approximate values for some foods and other items.

Acid			Acid
	1	Gastric juices	
Lemon juice	2	Battery acid	
Vinegar	3		
Orange/tomato juice	4		
Black coffee	5	Acid rain Human skin	
	6	Saliva	
Neutral Milk	7	Pure water	**Neutral**
Egg white	8	Soap	
Baking soda	9		
	10	Detergent	
	11	Milk of magnesia	
	12		
	13	Caustic soda Household bleach	
Alkali (or base)	14		**Alkali (or base)**

EXTRINSIC FACTORS

Things that are not part of the food itself but that influence the development of microbial flora during food storage and processing are known as extrinsic factors.

Temperature

All microbial activities depend on the temperature of the environment. This is perhaps the most important extrinsic factor. Each species has only a limited temperature range within which it can grow. Within this range, there is an optimal temperature for multiplication. At temperatures _above_ the maximum for their growth range, bacteria experience thermal injury and die. At temperatures _below_ their minimum, the growth of the population stops, although individual bacteria survive and resume multiplication when the temperature rises again.

Micro-organisms in general are found at temperatures between −15°C and 80°C. However, pathogenic and spoilage bacteria are more limited in their growth range. According to their temperature requirements we distinguish three groups:
- _psychrophiles_ (from the Greek for love of the cold)
- _mesophiles_ (from the Greek for love of an intermediate temperature)
- _thermophiles_ (from the Greek for love of heat).

Between the psychrophiles and the mesophiles some scientists distinguish another group — _psychrotrophs_ (from the Greek, meaning that they can grow in the cold).

TEMPERATURE CATEGORY	RANGE	OPTIMUM
Psychrophiles	−5°C to 20°C	10°C
Psychrotrophs	0°C to 35°C	25°C
Mesophiles	10°C to 55°C	35°C
Thermophiles	40°C to 80°C	50°C

Most food pathogens are mesophiles — they grow best at room temperature. It is unfortunate for food safety that their optimal temperature is almost our average body temperature. The recommended refrigeration temperature of below 5°C stops mesophiles from multiplying but does not stop psychrophiles and psychrotrophs. Bacteria of the genus _Listeria_ are psychrotrophs and can therefore multiply in refrigerated food. Both the mesophile and the psychrophile groups contain many spoilage organisms.

As you know, the temperature range from 5°C to 63°C is often called the temperature _danger zone_ — a temperature range in which most pathogens and spoilage organisms thrive. _Most_ pathogenic bacteria do not multiply at temperatures below 5°C, which is outside the danger zone. All vegetative bacteria are killed by temperatures above 63°C — outside the danger zone. However, spores and certain toxins might not be destroyed by heat.

Do bear in mind that most of the daily routine of food preparation takes place at an ambient temperature within the danger zone which provides ideal conditions for microbial growth. This means that high risk foods (see page 58) should never be allowed to stand at room temperatures for longer than absolutely necessary.

Time

The control of time is even more crucial when it is difficult to control temperature — particularly during thawing and cooling. If these processes are allowed to take a long time, bacteria have time to multiply in the food. Remember that time determines the growth rate of a bacterial population (see page 53).

The control of time is also important during heat treatment. For example, food may reach a 'safe' temperature on the outside but, if it is not cooked for long enough, the *core temperature* may not be high enough to kill pathogens.

The rule of thumb is that bacteria provided with sufficient food, moisture and warmth divide every 20 minutes. Some species multiply much faster than the average — *Clostridium perfringens* can multiply every 9.5 minutes under favourable conditions, while *Vibrio parahaemolyticus* needs only 7 minutes.

The chart below shows what happens to a sample of food with 100,000 typical bacteria when the food is at different temperatures for different periods. (For guidance on numbers expressed to the power of ten, see Reference on page 341).

TEMPERATURE	AFTER 1HR	3 HR	6 HR	8 HR	EFFECT
4°C	100,000	100,000	100,000	<100,000	hardly any increase
22°C *	200,000	800,000	6×10^6	25×10^6	division every hour
37°C **	800,000	50×10^6	25×10^9	16×10^{10}	division every 20 min

* typical room temperature

** average body temperature

Every raw product carries its own *microflora*, which includes spoilage bacteria as well as pathogenic bacteria. With most pathogens there needs to be a considerable number of organisms (10^5 to 10^6 per gram of food) before food poisoning occurs. In raw products the number is not usually great enough to be a direct threat to health. The danger comes from keeping the food in conditions that allow the bacteria to multiply to a high concentration. Given enough time and the right environmental conditions, just one bacterium can lead to the production of one million bacteria in less than four hours — and you always have more than one bacterium on a raw product!

Atmosphere

The composition of the air — known as the atmosphere — also affects bacterial growth. Different types of bacteria have different requirements for oxygen. Some species exist only where there is oxygen. Others survive only in its absence.

Microbiologists usually distinguish between:
- *obligate aerobes*, which require oxygen
- *microaerophiles* — aerobic bacteria, such as *Lactobacillus* and *Campylobacter*, which grow better where there is a *reduced* concentration of oxygen

WITH OXYGEN
Aerobes need oxygen to survive.

- *obligate anaerobes*, which require an oxygen-free environment
- *facultative* organisms, which can survive with or without oxygen.

Each category includes pathogens and spoilage types.

Like water, oxygen may be either free or bound to other molecules. Aerobes need free oxygen (O_2) to survive, and this is present in most unprocessed foods. Preservation techniques such as canning and vacuum-packing have the effect of removing free oxygen. This kills all obligate aerobes and slows down facultative organisms, leaving perfect conditions for anaerobes. This is why it is necessary to refrigerate vacuum-packed food to inhibit the remaining microflora.

Carbon dioxide (CO_2) and ozone (O_3) slow down the growth of aerobes. Both atmospheres are used in packaging to extend the shelf life of foods such as meat and fish.

Microbial competition

Most bacteria are influenced by the presence and activities of other microbes. There are some organisms that produce substances which inhibit the actions of, or even kill, other organisms, but there are others that merely compete for nutrients and space. Either way, they are in competition, and the competition among them helps to prevent any one species taking over.

The following analogy may help: imagine the microbes as various hostile armies trying to conquer the same city (say, a morsel of food). As long as the armies fight among themselves and use up their energy in trying to defeat each other, the city has a fair chance of survival. But if one army starts to gain over the others, the situation becomes a lot more dangerous for the city. Eventually the weaker armies are destroyed and the victorious troops can launch an all-out assault on the city.

Basically, this means that it is not just the number of bacteria in food that we need to worry about, but whether or not they are all of the same kind. It is safer to have competing populations of different species than just one strong colony.

When one group of micro-organisms is destroyed or inhibited by others in the same environment, it is called *microbial interference*. When two or more groups inhibit each other, we say that there are *antagonisms* between them.

Antagonisms occur in various ways. *Staphylococcus* does not multiply in the presence of *Pseudomonas*, *E. coli* or *Streptococcus* because they consume the amino acids it needs. Aerobic bacteria suppress the growth of *Clostridium botulinum* in fresh meat by altering the pH of the food. Lactic acid bacteria create acidic conditions that inhibit or kill many pathogenic and spoilage organisms. The inhibitory effect of species, such as *Lactobacillus reuteri*, can be used to *preserve* food but they are also added to a food product as *protective* cultures.

PUTTING INTRINSIC AND EXTRINSIC FACTORS TO WORK

Food technologists manipulate the factors that are essential for bacterial survival and multiplication in order to keep food safe to eat and to prolong its shelf life. The basic idea is to put 'barriers' in the way of the bacteria by combining several unfavourable intrinsic and extrinsic conditions that slow down their growth. This is known as *hurdle technology*. For now, it is worth taking a brief look at the methods that actually destroy bacteria.

WORKPLACE WEAPONS

In most instances food businesses can only *inhibit* bacterial multiplication because there are just a few ways to *destroy* bacteria:
- heat treatment
- chemical treatment
- irradiation.

Heat treatment
High temperatures (those above the temperature danger zone of 5°C to 63°C) can kill bacteria and this thermal destruction is one of the reasons for cooking, or treating, food at high temperatures. The length of time needed at a specific temperature depends on a number of factors that you will read more about in Part 4. Thermal death is rarely instantaneous and the period involved varies with every species. Survival rates depend upon the combination of time and temperature and on the initial bacterial load — the number of bacteria on a food.

Chemical treatment
While most chemicals used for preservation purposes only *inhibit* the multiplication of bacteria and *delay* microbial spoilage, many cleaning chemicals are bactericidal, meaning they actually *destroy* bacteria in the environment. These strong chemicals cannot of course be used on food itself, but they are an essential tool in maintaining clean premises and a bacteria-unfriendly environment. The way in which the bacteria are destroyed depends on the type of chemical used. Typical lethal damage includes breaching the cell wall, coagulating the cytoplasm, disrupting the permeability of the membrane or reacting with cell constituents, such as essential proteins.

Irradiation
Electromagnetic irradiation causes cell death by destroying the genetic material (DNA) of the cell. In 1976 the World Health Organization (WHO) gave its blessing to the unrestricted use of irradiation for potatoes, wheat, various fruits and vegetables and poultry. However, there is still no uniformity in the regulations governing the use of irradiation in European Union countries. For example, in Britain irradiation is permitted for spices and certain medical diets only. There is more information about the use of irradiation as a form of preservation in Part 4.

BACTERIAL MONITORING AND ITS LIMITATIONS

Bacterial monitoring is essential in many branches of the food industry. Food packagers and processors in particular run bacteria-identifying tests regularly, both to prevent the outbreak of disease and to identify the presence of beneficial bacteria.

Identifying pathogenic and spoilage bacteria can be both time-consuming and complicated. Suspect food has to be sampled and organisms from it grown under laboratory conditions — a process that can take several days. While you are waiting for the test results, you may have to keep suspect food 'in quarantine'. You should also postpone decisions about changing or retaining food preparation and cleaning practices until test results are known. Even then, remember that the *type* of bacterium is just one of the factors to be considered and, as microbes are rarely distributed evenly on food, the result is valid only for that tested sample.

In the laboratory samples of bacteria obtained by swabbing are smeared onto a growth medium and allowed to multiply. Identification of the types and numbers of bacteria can then be carried out.

To date, none of the common methods can determine exactly how many microbes a product contains. However, they can be used to discover:
- the general amount of contamination of surfaces, equipment and utensils
- the potential contamination of food and the organisms involved
- the possibility of spoilage
- the potential shelf life of the product.

Testing methods

You need specialist advice or training to choose the right testing methods for your workplace and you need to consider:
- which foods, products and processes you deal with
- what kind of information would be the most useful
- which micro-organisms you suspect are present.

Biological techniques
These rely on being able to grow in the laboratory the microbes that are present in the sample.

Contact (or swabbing) technique
This is the oldest and most widely used method for checking food-contact surfaces. The surface is swabbed and a colony of micro-organisms grown from the swab sample. The organisms are then identified by standard methods of counting or microscopic examination, often following staining (see page 48) which makes them more visible. Swabbing is particularly useful for demonstrating the importance of food safety to staff because the micro-organisms are then visible to everybody.

Most probable number (MPN) method

This relatively simple method is useful for determining the density of *faecal coliform* bacteria, such as *E. coli*. The microbial growth in a sequence of dilutions of food samples is compared against standard MPN tables to estimate the original number of organisms.

Biochemical methods

These techniques look for indicator substances or metabolic products that show the presence of bacterial enzyme activities.

ATP bioluminescence

This method measures the emission of light by living organisms — the light emitted when a particular enzyme (luciferase) is in the presence of adenosine triphosphate (ATP), which is the main source of cellular energy in living organisms. Although this is a very sensitive method, it can be used in food premises and the results can be obtained within 15 minutes without the use of laboratory cultures. However, as food also contains ATP, the accurate interpretation of levels of contamination may be difficult. This method is best used to demonstrate the effectiveness of cleaning methods or the total level of micro-organisms in raw materials.

MUG test

Some bacteria, such as certain strains of *E. coli* and *Salmonella*, have a particular enzyme that splits the nutrient methyl-umbelliferyl-glucuronide (MUG). The MUG test detects and measures this reaction.

Physical methods

These methods use physical properties to detect bacteria.

The impedance method

Electrical resistance is used to determine the presence of bacteria. The more micro-organisms there are, the more metabolic products and the higher the electrical resistance. This method has the advantage of being quite fast, but it is unspecific about the nature of the organisms.

Microcalorimetry

This method detects the temperature change caused by microbes breaking down food.

Radiometry

This measures the speed of ingestion, usually of radioactive glucose introduced into the culture medium. The time required is inversely related to the number of micro-organisms in the sample — the fewer the organisms, the slower the process.

Immunological methods

These methods use immune responses in host cells to identify micro-organisms. Two of the most common such techniques are *serotyping* and *phagetyping*.

Serotyping

Serotyping uses known antibodies to identify unknown bacteria. Antibodies are part of a mammal's automatic defence system. They are special proteins formed in response to an invasion by foreign particles with antigenic qualities (see page 51). Antibodies react with only one component of the antigen so that when a reaction occurs it gives a clue as to which type of bacteria are present.

The test involves mixing antisera — kits of known antibodies — with bacterial samples. The results are visible, either through physical changes of affected samples on agar plates, or through colour changes of the enzymes of susceptible bacteria. The latter method is known as an ELISA (enzyme-linked immunosorbant assay) test.

Phagetyping

This test uses bacteriophages — viruses that attack bacteria. Many of these viruses attack only one bacterial strain, so when a reaction occurs the bacterium is decisively identified. Strains identified in this way are called phagetypes.

Genetic methods

These use strands of genetic material, either DNA or ribonucleic acid (RNA), to make the identification.

The PCR (polymerase chain reaction) test

This test depends on the activity of a particular enzyme involved in genetic replication and is extremely specific and expensive to carry out. It may be used more in the future because of rapid advances in molecular genetics.

✦ MAKING IT EASIER FOR OTHERS

- Emphasise that we cannot see, taste or smell pathogenic ('harmful') bacteria when they have contaminated food, so staff must follow some simple rules, such as keeping food out of the danger zone, in order to keep food safe to eat.
- Make sure that all food handlers know which are the high risk foods used in your premises and how they should take care of them.
- Link all the basic-level underlying knowledge about bacteria (and the other micro-organisms) to workplace rules and best practice.

putting microbes in writing

The proper names for microbes can appear a little daunting at first, but there are good reasons why they are named as they are. With so many creatures on Earth, we need a clear way of identifying one from another. So all living things have a two-part scientific name, such as *Salmonella enterica* (a bacterium commonly responsible for food-borne illness) or *Homo sapiens* (modern humans). All the names for organisms are Latinised. This may seem odd as Latin is a 'dead' language, but in the eighteenth century, when the

system was developed, Latin was the common language of science. Even the inventor of the system, the Swedish naturalist and physician Carl von Linné, was known then, as he is today, by the Latin form of his name — Carolus Linnaeus.

His taxonomy (system of classifying organisms), referred to today as 'the Linnaeus system' or 'binomial nomenclature', has stayed in use ever since.

This helps to avoid confusion as everyone uses the same two-part Latin name throughout the world, whatever their own everyday language.

The first part of an organism's name — such as *Salmonella* — refers to the genus, a large group of related life forms to which the organism belongs. The second part — *enterica* — refers to the species, which identifies a particular type of even more closely related organisms within the genus.

When referring to the species, you must always use the full two-part designation. Express it in *italics* or, if you are writing by hand or using a typewriter without italics, underline it instead.

The genus always takes a capital letter, the species does not, unless it is derived from a proper name. You can abbreviate the genus name — for example, *S. enterica* — after giving the name in full at least once and where there is no chance of confusion.

As scientific knowledge has increased it has become possible to make finer and

finer distinctions within species. Some of these subdivisions include varieties, strains, phagetypes, serotypes or serovars.

Rapid developments in molecular genetic techniques in the last decade have also made it possible to establish even clearer relationships between species. As a result, the classifications of some micro-organisms are being revised.

Salmonella, for example, is now recognised as having just two species, *S. enterica* and *S. Bongori*. These are then divided into more than 2,000 serotypes or serovars (subdivisions distinguished by their chemical or immunological attributes), which are commonly named after the place where they were identified or the disease they produce.

This form of identification is added to the species name in plain text beginning with a capital letter — for example, '*Salmonella enterica* serovar Typhimurium' or more simply '*Salmonella* Typhimurium'. (The latter is the style we use in this book.)

For the purposes of day-to-day food safety, the changes probably make little difference — for example, *Salmonella* Typhimurium was previously styled as *Salmonella typhimurium*, while the parasite *Trichina spiralis* was previously known as *Trichinella spiralis*.

However, as revisions to classifications are continuing, you should expect to come across other name changes as scientists gather more information using molecular techniques.

BACTERIAL FOOD-BORNE ILLNESS

There are many ways of classifying illnesses caused by pathogenic bacteria and their toxins. When talking about food-related symptoms, it is common to divide the illnesses and the bacteria that cause them into two broad categories — those caused directly by the invasion of the body by bacteria (an *infection*) and those caused by bacterial toxins produced either directly on the food, or produced in the body after ingestion (an *intoxication*).

Other classifications frequently used in the UK are *food-borne infection* and *food poisoning* and it is these that we use in this book and describe in detail on the following pages.

Avoiding confusion

Rather in the way that you are advised to use *either* imperial *or* metric measures when cooking (but not both), we strongly advise you to use just one pair of the categories — either use food-borne infection together with food poisoning, as we do in this book, or use infection together with intoxication.

In the past, you may have been accustomed to describing food-borne infection as 'food-borne disease'. There is no issue of right or wrong in this: it is simply a matter of being consistent.

REMINDER
In this book we use 'food-borne illness' or 'food-borne disease' to describe *all* the categories of food-related illness.

TWO GROUPINGS OF CATEGORIES OF COMMON FOOD-BORNE BACTERIA

Either (as used in this book)...		Or...
Food poisoning		**Intoxication**
Aeromonas hydrophila		*Bacillus cereus*
Bacillus cereus		*Clostridium botulinum*
Clostridium botulinum		*Clostridium perfringens*
Clostridium perfringens		*Escherichia coli*
Escherichia coli		*Escherichia coli 0157*
Salmonella species (except *S.* Typhi* and		*Shigella dysenteriae*
S. Paratyphi*)		*Staphylococcus aureus*
Staphylococcus aureus	**Food-borne infection**	Infection
Streptococcus species	*Brucella abortus*	*Aeromonas hydrophila*
Vibrio parahaemolyticus	*Brucella melitensis*	*Brucella abortus*
Yersinia enterocolitica	*Campylobacter jejuni*	*Brucella melitensis*
	Escherichia coli 0157	*Campylobacter jejuni*
	Listeria monocytogenes	*Listeria monocytogenes*
	Mycobacterium bovis	*Mycobacterium bovis*
	Mycobacterium tuberculosis	*Mycobacterium tuberculosis*
	Salmonella Paratyphi*	*Salmonella* species (including
	Salmonella Typhi*	*S.* Paratyphi* and *S.* Typhi*)
	Shigella dysenteriae	*Vibrio parahaemolyticus*
		Yersinia enterocolitica

* Recent name change. See page 70.

POISONING OR INTOXICATION — WHY THE DIFFERENCE?

If you are comfortable using one or other of the paired categories suggested on page 71, you may prefer to skip straight to page 73. However, if you were slightly bemused by some of the differences in categorisation and wish to know a little more about the reasons why, take a look an the explanations below.

Intoxication versus food poisoning

Intoxication simply means affected by toxin (or poison) so it is a reasonable assumption that an intoxication is the same as food poisoning. Unfortunately this is *not* the case. As you can see from the table on the previous page, some food poisonings are infections and some food-borne infections are intoxications.

In the past

The reasons for the different categories are largely a matter of convention. The first food-related illnesses to be recognised were true cases of poisoning, such as botulism. As other conditions were recognised that were being caused by bacteria that were growing on food, they were also classed as food poisoning, whether they were intoxications or infections. The important issue was that they seemed to require food for multiplication to the point where there were enough of them to cause an infection or to produce sufficient toxin to cause an intoxication.

When it was discovered that some other diseases were also related to food, because transmission could be via food, another name had to be found for them. They were generally called food-borne infections. From this arose the curious situation where some infections are in a group called 'food poisoning' and some intoxications are in a group called 'infection'.

APPROPRIATE USAGE
In everyday conversation the expression 'food poisoning' is often used to describe all types of illness from contaminated food and this may be the term you choose to use when trying to make food safety easier for some of your colleagues. This is simply a matter of *general* and appropriate *specialist* use. (See also 'Making it easier for others' on page 94.)

Category confusion

The criteria for classifications are often a compromise in the first place. Before long it is found that not everything fits neatly, so further compromises are made. As a result we can end up with classifications that are not totally logical but by now are comfortably familiar. Perhaps the good news is that modern usage tends to collect all categories together as food-borne illness (or food-borne disease)!

Distinctions — why bother?

So why bother with any categories at all? Of course, you need to recognise the terms when you read about them elsewhere. More importantly, it is useful to know which organisms fall under which group because it may help you to decide on control measures — some bacteria need to live on food before they become a food safety problem, while others use food only as a means of transport. In the end, the most important thing to remember is that you need measures in place to stop microbes getting onto food. That way, you minimise the chance of any category of food-related illness!

BACTERIAL FOOD POISONING AND FOOD-BORNE INFECTION

The main differences between bacterial food poisoning and food-borne infection can be summed up as the distinctions between the:

- number of bacteria necessary to cause symptoms of illness
- onset of symptoms
- part food plays in the whole scenario.

Food poisoning

With just a few exceptions (such as *Clostridium botulinum*), food poisoning occurs only after a very large number of bacteria (10^5 to 10^6 per gram) or a large quantity of bacterial *toxin* has been ingested. Bacteria reach such high numbers by using food as the medium for multiplication. Some bacteria, such as *Staphylococcus aureus*, can start toxin formation on the food even before it is eaten (although it takes more than one million of them to produce enough toxin to cause illness).

Most food poisoning symptoms affect the gastro-intestinal system and typical symptoms are abdominal pain, diarrhoea and vomiting. Fever, malaise and general weakness may be among other symptoms experienced.

The incubation period is relatively short: depending on the organism, people may become ill after only a few hours or days. The number of bacteria in the food influences the incubation period and the onset of symptoms is rapid if the bacteria have had time to multiply on the food. So, controlling the length of time that high risk food is left in the danger zone is essential. Most illnesses (*C. botulinum* is an exception) typically last from about six hours up to about seven days.

Food-borne infection

In sharp contrast to food poisoning, food-borne infection is caused by relatively few organisms which develop in the body of the victim over a fairly long time (days and weeks compared to the hours and days of food poisoning bacteria). With the infective dose being very small, these bacteria need not necessarily multiply in food — they are only *transmitted* or *carried* by the food. Typically they are carried by water, and this is often the source of epidemics like typhoid and cholera following a natural disaster, such as an earthquake or flood, when the supply of drinking water is one of the first things affected.

Bacteria that cause food-borne infections are also readily carried by other *vehicles of contamination* (things which pick up and move bacteria), such as hands and soil, and by air as air-borne droplets.

As bacterial multiplication does not take place on the food, the time before contaminated food is eaten is not a significant factor in the onset of illness. The symptoms can be severe, such as kidney disease, because the organism often enters the bloodstream.

FOOD POISONING
Many bacteria or lots of bacterial toxin ingested. Bacteria multiply on the food and some produce toxins on the food.
Short onset and duration of symptoms.
Time before the contaminated food is eaten is critical.

FOOD-BORNE INFECTION
Low infective dose.
Bacteria only carried by food, and multiplication takes place in the body.
Time before the contaminated food is eaten is not a significant factor in onset of symptoms.
Long incubation and long duration possible.

Common food-borne bacteria

Details of common bacteria implicated in food poisoning and food-borne infection are given later in the chapter (and summarised in Reference), together with information about some bacteria that may be of significance in the future. First, however, we look at the most common factors behind food-borne illness.

FACTORS LEADING TO ILLNESS

Food-borne illness is preventable but there is so much of it worldwide that we are forced to conclude that many things are going wrong, whether the ultimate blame is laid at the door of ineffective management, inadequate staff training, poor staff and process supervision, patchy legal enforcement, apathy, carelessness, negligence or a combination of these.

The results of research by the US Centers for Disease Control and Prevention (CDC) in Atlanta, USA, into the causal factors of food poisoning in the USA, Canada and the UK are shown below. The figures on the left show the percentage of instances in which an identified factor was at least partly responsible for an outbreak of illness. The figures do not total a hundred because there are often multiple causes identified for an outbreak.

CAUSES OF FOOD POISONING	
63%	Inadequate cooling and cold holding
29%	Preparing food ahead of planned service
27%	Inadequate hot holding
26%	Poor personal hygiene/infected persons
25%	Inadequate reheating
9%	Inadequate cleaning of equipment
7%	Use of left-over food
6%	Cross-contamination
5%	Inadequate prime cooking or heat processing
4%	Toxic chemical contamination from containers
2%	Contaminated raw ingredients
2%	Intentional chemical additives
1%	Incidental chemical additives
1%	Unsafe sources

Most common causes

Let's look at the top five causes identified. What do they have in common? With the exception of one category (poor personal hygiene and infected persons), they are all to do with temperature control.

Getting on for two-thirds (63 per cent) of outbreaks involved inadequate cooling and cold holding. We need to ask why the time and temperature control was inadequate. Was it because of the food handlers' lack of awareness, apathy, negligence or carelessness? Or had the managers failed to supply and maintain the correct equipment; provide enough refrigerators, chillers or cold cabinets; or train or supervise the staff adequately? Alternatively, had the managers accepted business that was in excess of the company's ability (equipment, premises or personnel) to deal with?

A total of 29 per cent of outbreaks was caused by preparing food too far ahead of planned service. It is highly likely that the food was left at an ambient temperature or within the temperature danger zone. Were the staff unaware of the likelihood of multiplication by food poisoning bacteria, or were they lazy or careless? Or did the managers fail to provide sufficient equipment to store prepared food, organise enough staff to work at that period, allow poor workflow or accept an order which was beyond the company's ability to fulfil?

It is impossible to give answers here for each case, but the questions highlight just how much food-borne illness is a management issue. Perhaps you should ask yourself frequently: have I provided sufficient trained staff and sufficient suitable equipment and working space for the job in hand, and can I say that none of the issues listed above will happen in my company because of poor management?

MOST VULNERABLE

Anyone could become ill with a food-borne disease after eating contaminated food, but some people are especially vulnerable if they do become ill and may even die as a result. Those in this *at risk group* include the elderly; the very young; people who are ill, convalescing or who have weakened immune systems; and pregnant women, unborn children and breast-fed babies.

PATHOGENIC FOOD-BORNE BACTERIA

Examples of the bacteria responsible for food-borne illnesses are given in alphabetical order on the following pages. Food poisoning bacteria are given first, with food-borne infection bacteria starting on page 85.

Bacteria responsible for food poisoning

These bacteria require food to multiply. They cause illness when the food they have contaminated is eaten.

Bacillus cereus

This organism has been associated with food-borne illness in Europe since the early twentieth century. Much research was carried out in the 1950s but it was not until the early 1970s that the first reported outbreak occurred in the UK.

Bacillus cereus is an aerobic, Gram-positive, spore-forming rod. While widely distributed in nature, it is typically found in soil, dust and vegetation. This bacterium can grow between 7°C and 48°C, but its optimum is between 28°C and 35°C. It has a pH tolerance between 4.9 and 9.3, although some strains can tolerate down to 4.35, and its preferred a_w is 0.912.

B. cereus produces two toxins, one of which gives rise to the diarrhoeal syndrome and the other to the emetic syndrome.

Diarrhoeal syndrome

The incubation period is normally 8 to 16 hours and the symptoms of diarrhoea, abdominal pain, nausea and some vomiting (although this is rare) usually last for one or two days. The illness is caused by the production of a toxin in the intestine, which explains why diarrhoea is a more likely symptom than vomiting and why the incubation period is longer than that for the emetic syndrome.

Emetic syndrome

This is more severe and acute than the diarrhoeal syndrome. After an incubation period of one to five hours, the symptoms may include vomiting, abdominal pains and sometimes a little diarrhoea. The symptoms last for six to 24 hours. The illness is caused by ingestion of a toxin that has already been produced on the food.

In contrast to the diarrhoeal syndrome, the toxin acts on the upper gastro-intestinal tract so the incubation time is shorter as the toxin acts quickly because it is already formed. The symptoms (mainly vomiting) are associated with the stomach rather than the intestine.

Foods implicated

As the species name *cereus* suggests, foods commonly involved in outbreaks include cereals and grains. Rice and rice-based items, cereals, soya beans and soy products, meat, fish, milk, vegetables, pasta and tofu are common sources of *B. cereus*, although it is possible to isolate it from many other foods.

A common route of infection is the cooking of boiled rice that is then stored at an ambient temperature which, given enough time, allows spores to germinate and produce a toxin. Subsequent heating of the rice will not destroy the toxin. In the case of fried rice, flash frying is insufficient to destroy either the toxin or all of the vegetative cells.

Control

Control measures are strict control of time and temperature — including cooking, cooling, storing and reheating (if reheating really must be carried out) — and the prevention of cross-contamination.

Clostridium botulinum

The name *botulinum* derives from the Latin word botulus, meaning sausage, and from the German word Botulismus which originally meant sausage poisoning. The earliest references to botulism come from Württemberg in Germany in the late eighteenth and early nineteenth centuries when outbreaks of sausage poisoning from blood-sausages caused illness and death. Originally the sausages were par-boiled, then smoked. Then it was discovered that if the sausage casings were filled loosely, so that pockets of air were left, and if the sausages were boiled thoroughly, then they did not become toxic. Without realising it, the sausage producers had established that *Clostridium botulinum* bacterium is an anaerobe.

Found in soil and water, this bacterium is an anaerobic, Gram-positive, spore-forming rod. Seven types have been identified, classified according to their toxins: five types cause disease in humans while the other two types are associated with animals.

The infection route is through raw food contaminated with **spores**. Following germination, the multiplying bacteria produce an exotoxin. The illness is caused by the ingestion of the toxin in the food.

Extremely dangerous toxin

The toxin produced by *C. botulinum* is a neurotoxin. This accounts for some of the symptoms being different to those caused by other food poisoning bacteria. The symptoms can include double vision, difficulty in speaking and swallowing, headache, nausea, fatigue, constipation, vomiting, dizziness and muscle paralysis leading to respiratory failure and death. The incubation period is eight to 72 hours, with 12 to 36 hours being typical. The illness normally lasts one to ten days, although there are reports of it lasting for much longer periods. Death can occur unless an antitoxin is given fairly early in the course of the illness. The mortality rate varies between 30 and 60 per cent and seems to be lower in Europe than in North America. There is no known carrier status for the organism.

C. BOTULINUM
Common in the environment.
Forms spores.
Produces a neurotoxin.
Almost one-third to over a half of cases lead to death.
Temperature needed for spore destruction determines a standard canning temperature.

Preferred conditions

Fortunately *C. botulinum* appears to be a poor competitor and cannot grow or produce toxin in the presence of large numbers of other micro-organisms.

The temperature range for growth varies slightly depending on the type, but 3°C is about the lowest for the types with which we are most concerned. The upper range is 50°C with an optimum between 20°C and 30°C. The spores are very heat resistant so a temperature of 121°C for three minutes is required to destroy them — hence the temperature of the 'botulinum cook' (see pages 290 to 292). The toxin, however, is not very heat stable and so can be destroyed by thorough cooking.

This bacterium is not thought to grow at a pH of below 4.5 and this is another main determining factor in a 'botulinum cook'. The a_w depends on the type: two types are inhibited at under 0.93 and the others at around 0.97.

Foods implicated

Outbreaks commonly arise in countries where home canning is popular. Canned products — typically meat, fish or vegetables which have not been heated sufficiently — are involved. There have also been outbreaks and some deaths from commercially produced foods. Inadequately processed low-acid foods, herbs in oil and vacuum-packed products have been implicated. Chopped garlic in oil, which was stored for many months at an ambient temperature, was responsible for outbreaks of botulism in the Netherlands, Canada and America in 1985.

You may also come across references to 'temperature-abused baked potatoes' which generally describes cases of botulism in America from baked potatoes that were wrapped in foil and kept unrefrigerated for several days before use.

Control

Adequate time and temperature controls are essential, especially in canning, bottling and vacuum-packing.

Infant botulism

This is a condition in infants under one year old. While an adult's intestine is not a favourable environment for spore germination, it seems that some botulinum spores can germinate in the intestine of the very young and can produce sufficient toxin to cause illness. While the symptoms in some infants are fairly mild, in others the condition is severe. Although fatalities are rare, the first and most common symptom is constipation. Other symptoms include generalised weakness, a weak cry, poor sucking reflex, lack of facial expression and poor head control.

The illness is widespread in the USA, particularly in some of the western states where there is believed to be a high incidence of botulinum spores in the soil. There are between 60 and 90 cases a year, normally associated with honey. It is therefore not recommended for food safety reasons to feed honey to children under one year old.

Clostridium perfringens

The first detailed description of the illness associated with this pathogen was by Betty C. Hobbs and others in the UK in the early 1950s (when the bacterium was named *C. welchii*), although the illness and its association with the bacterium were probably well known for at least a decade previously.

Clostridium perfringens is an anaerobic, Gram-positive, spore-forming rod and is widely distributed in nature. Five types are recognised: Type A is normally associated with food-borne illness, although Type C can cause a non-food-related disease. Sources are the human and animal intestine, soil, dust and spices.

The illness is caused by an enterotoxin which is produced when large numbers of the bacterium (usually about 10^6) sporulate in the intestine — almost always as a consequence of bad food-preparation practices.

Typically, bacterial spores form because of a survival response to the 'threat' from the heat while the food is cooking. When the food starts to cool, especially if this happens slowly, the spores can germinate and bacterial multiplication can occur. When the food, which is now heavily contaminated, is eaten the bacteria encounter unfavourable conditions in the intestine. They protect themselves once again by forming spores, in the process releasing the enterotoxin which causes illness.

The symptoms are diarrhoea and abdominal pain, which last for up to two days. Vomiting is rare. The incubation period can be six to 24 hours with the norm being around eight to 18 hours. Fatalities are rare but do occur in the elderly and in people with compromised immune systems.

It is believed that the toxin can sometimes be produced on the food itself, which would account for the shorter onset times that are sometimes encountered.

C. PERFRINGENS
Forms spores.
Toxin released during sporulation in the intestine. Poor temperature control is a common cause of problems.

Preferred conditions
C. perfringens is a mesophile, growing at between 20°C and 50°C, with 37°C to 45°C as the optimum. The ideal pH is between 5.5 and 8.0. The a_w for spore *germination* and growth has been reported at as low as 0.93, with spore formation requiring a higher value.

Foods implicated
Foods commonly include foods and ingredients that have been cooled too slowly after cooking is complete, such as cooked meat and poultry, gravy, sauces and spices.

Control
Measures include strict time and temperature control in cooking, cooling and reheating; only reheating once (if absolutely necessary); separation of cooked and raw foods; and thorough cleaning and disinfection routines.

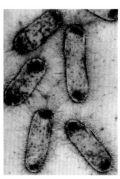

Escherichia coli

This bacterium is a normal inhabitant of healthy human and animal intestines where it lives in large populations as a harmless commensal. In fact, most strains of this aerobic rod-shaped bacterium are harmless, but certain strains are pathogenic and can cause severe abdominal pains and diarrhoea, the latter being especially dangerous and even fatal for young children.

The serotype ETEC (enterotoxic *E. coli*) is the causative agent for traveller's diarrhoea (also known by a range of more colourful names, including Montezuma's revenge and la tourista) because the bacterial strains involved are not usually found in the traveller's home country and are, in a sense, in the wrong place at the wrong time. The strain of *E. coli* that has been in the news for several years — *E. coli* 0157 — is classed as a food-borne infection (see page 88).

Food poisoning from *E. coli* is caused by an enterotoxin and usually starts between 12 and 72 hours after eating contaminated food. The symptoms usually include abdominal pain, fever, diarrhoea and vomiting and last from one to 14 days.

Sources and foods implicated
Human and animal intestines are the major source of *E. coli*, together with meat and sewage. As large numbers of the bacterium inevitably end up in sewage, it has long been used as an indicator organism for faecal contamination (faecal coliform) of food or water. Meat is sometimes contaminated by *E. coli* during slaughter. Foods commonly involved are raw meat, undercooked meat products, gravy and raw milk.

Preferred conditions
This Gram-negative mesophile can multiply at temperatures as low as 7°C to 10°C. Research suggests that it may even be able to multiply at a temperature as low as 4°C as it can survive refrigeration. Its optimal multiplication temperature is around 37°C — average human body temperature. It needs a minimum a_w of 0.95 and prefers a neutral pH, although multiplication is possible as low as 4.4.

Control
The safe disposal of sewage is essential, together with the strict separation of raw and cooked foods, adequate cooking and effective personal hygiene.

Salmonella species

Salmonella is the organism which most clearly demonstrates that bacterial evolution is continuing. Not only are new strains identified and described every year, but the bacterium also reveals how a relatively harmless initial inhabitant of the gut has developed new and dangerous representatives and occupied new niches, such as the ovaries of poultry.

As with some other pathogenic bacteria, *Salmonella* have also developed antibiotic-resistant strains.

Named after Daniel Elmer Salmon, an American vet who lived in the late nineteenth and early twentieth centuries, *Salmonella* is a genus of facultative anaerobic, Gram-negative rods which are widely distributed in the environment. The main reservoirs are humans and animals. In terms of severity their effects can vary from mild discomfort to death.

Categorising the bacterium
With nearly 3,000 known serotypes, not all of which are true food poisoning organisms, the *Salmonella* bacteria are in a league of their own — and their taxonomy (biological classification) is complicated and often revised (see page 70). For epidemiological purposes (the study of the causes and spread of disease), they can be divided into three groups:
- those that infect humans only and can be transmitted by food, such as *S.* Typhi and *S.* Paratyphi (previously *S. typhi* and *S. paratyphi*)
- host-adapted strains, some of which — for example, *S.* Dublin (formerly *S. dublin*) in cattle — are human pathogens and can be transmitted by food
- strains with no preferred host, which can be pathogenic for humans and animals — this group contains most of the strains responsible for food-borne illnesses.

Salmonella Typhimurium (formerly *S. typhimurium*) — pictured on pages 25 and 52 — and *S.* Enteritidis (formerly *S. enteritidis*) are the most common causes of food poisoning.

The illness is caused by the invasion of the body by a large number of bacteria, which have multiplied on the food. The infective dose is thought to be about 10^5 per gram. The incubation period is between six and 96 hours, typically 12 to 48 hours.

The symptoms of salmonellosis are diarrhoea, vomiting, fever and abdominal pain, which usually last up to seven days. The mortality rate varies according to the age of the person affected, with high rates among the 'at risk group' (see page 75). The serotype reported to have the highest mortality rate is *S.* Choleraesuis (formerly *S. choleraesuis*). Normally the intestine is clear of the organism fairly quickly after the symptoms disappear, but up to five per cent of patients become *carriers*.

Preferred conditions
Salmonella multiply quite readily between 7°C and 45°C. Their minimum pH tolerance is between 4.05 and 5.5 depending on the *type* of acid in a food. The optimal growth range is between 6.6 and 8.2. The a_w tolerance depends on the pH, but multiplication is believed to be inhibited at about 0.94 when pH is neutral.

Sources and foods implicated
The primary sources of *Salmonella* are human and animal intestinal tracts and faeces. The infection route is via raw animal products such as raw meat, eggs and egg products, milk and poultry. Another infection route is via faeces and fertilisers,

SALMONELLA
Multiply in food. Eggs, poultry, raw milk and raw meat are commonly implicated.

CARRIER
Someone who is infected by a particular pathogen, does not develop symptoms of the illness but can pass on the pathogen to others.

for example, on vegetables. Insects, birds, pets, rodents, terrapins, sewage and water can also be sources. Foods commonly involved in outbreaks include meat and meat products, poultry, raw milk, eggs and egg products, dairy products and seafood.

Control
High standards of personal hygiene, avoidance of cross-contamination, thorough cleaning and disinfection routines, effective pest management and strict control of time and temperature are the main weapons against this bacterium.

Staphylococcus aureus
This bacterium and its associated illness were first studied at the end of the eighteenth century but its full mechanisms were not fully understood for some considerable time.

S. AUREUS
Found on the human body and in the throat, nose and boils and cuts.
Short onset and duration.
Toxin-producer.
Toxin fairly heat resistant.
Grows at low a_w.

Staphylococcus aureus bacteria, which are pictured on page 49, are facultative anaerobic, Gram-positive cocci and are mostly resident in humans. They are found in the nose, throat and hair and on skin and hands, as well as in boils, pimples, sties, septic lesions, burns and wounds.

In moist habitats, such as the nose, the numbers per square centimetre can be as high as 10^3 to 10^6. They can also be found in animals — for example in cows or goats with mastitis — and can lead to a direct infection in humans as a result of drinking raw milk.

S. aureus is an exotoxin producer, but not every bacterium produces toxin. There need to be about 10^6 (one million) bacteria for there to be enough toxin-producers present to produce sufficient toxin in the food to cause illness when the food is eaten. The toxin is fairly heat resistant and can survive for 30 minutes at 100°C.

The symptoms of illness include diarrhoea, acute vomiting, nausea, abdominal pain and sometimes collapse. A fall in body temperature may sometimes occur. The onset time is one to six hours and about four hours is typical. Symptoms normally last for 12 to 48 hours. The mortality rate is very low.

Preferred conditions
The growth range is usually between 7°C and 48°C, with toxin being produced at between 10°C and 46°C. While the bacterium can grow over a pH range of 4.0 to 9.8, its optimal range is 6.0 to 7.0. Even though it is not salt tolerant, *S. aureus* can grow at the rather low a_w of 0.83, but 0.86 is regarded as typical.

Sources and foods implicated
Foods commonly involved in outbreaks include ham, poultry, egg products, dairy products, potato salads and raw milk from cows and goats.

The infection route is via humans and bad hygiene practices and, on occasion, from raw milk. The contamination results from any one or a combination of factors: infected food handlers contaminating the food as a result of bad personal hygiene; poor temperature control; preparation of food too far in advance of serving; inadequate heating and so on.

Control

Control measures are strict personal hygiene, especially with regard to hand washing, 'excluding' food handlers with skin infections or colds (see page 234), effective temperature control and avoiding the use of raw milk.

Vibrio parahaemolyticus

Vibrio parahaemolyticus is unique among pathogens connected to food because its source is almost exclusively fish or seafood. Identified in the early 1950s in Japan, it remains the major food poisoning problem in that country.

A Gram-positive, facultative anaerobe, the bacterium is a halophile found in coastal sea waters. Illness is caused by the invasion of the body by a large number of this bacterium. The infective dose is not accurately known but is thought to be about 10^4 per gram. Carrier status is possible.

The symptoms are diarrhoea, vomiting, abdominal pain, fever and dehydration and can last for up to seven days.

The onset time is four to 96 hours with 12 to 24 hours being typical. The infection can be fatal to those in the 'at risk group'.

Preferred conditions

Multiplication is possible between 10°C and 44°C, with the optimum being 37°C. The organism is pH tolerant between 4.8 and 11.0 with an optimal growth range of 7.6 to 8.6. The a_w is 0.99.

Foods implicated

The primary sources are fish and seafood, especially those from warmer waters or polluted water, although cross-contamination can cause a problem in other foods.

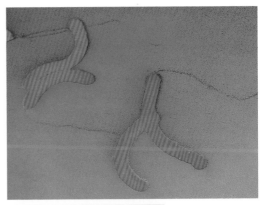

AN UGLY DEATH

A mid-nineteenth century illustration depicts cholera as a sinister shrouded figure rising from a river while the figure of Science, shown as a Roman soldier, nods off to sleep. The micrograph above is the bacterium now known to be responsible for cholera, *Vibrio cholerae*, which is often water borne. Death can follow rapidly after violent vomiting, diarrhoea, muscle spasms and dehydration, which can make the victim's face look black. There were epidemics in Peru and in most countries of South and central America in 1991. More than a thousand people died from the disease in eastern India and Bangladesh in 1992.

VIBRIO
PARAHAEMO-
LYTICUS
Aquatic.
Illness usually
associated with
fish or seafood.

Foods commonly involved in outbreaks include clams, oysters, crabs, shrimps and lobsters.

Control
Measures are buying seafood only from known and approved sources, strict time and temperature controls and avoiding the serving of raw or lightly cooked seafood to 'at risk groups'.

Yersinia enterocolitica
Yersinia enterocolitica is from a family of facultative anaerobic, Gram-negative rods with 11 species that include *Yersinia pestis*, the organism responsible for outbreaks of plague, such as the Black Death (1348) in Britain and The Great Plague of London (1665-6). The genus is named in honour of the pioneering Swiss bacteriologist Alexandre Yersin who produced an antiserum and cured several plague victims in Hong Kong in 1896.

The symptoms of *Yersinia enterocolitica* are mainly diarrhoea, fever, headache and abdominal pain, but it has been associated with much more serious conditions such as reactive arthritis, mesenteric lymphadenitis, terminal ileitis and pseudo-appendicitis.

The incubation period is usually one to 14 days and the bacterium can persist in the patient's stools for some considerable time. The infective dose has not yet been confirmed.

Preferred conditions

YERSINIA
ENTEROCOLITICA
Multiplies under
refrigeration.
Often spread by
faecal-oral routes.

Widely distributed in the environment, both on land and in water, *Y. enterocolitica* can multiply at temperatures as low as 0°C or as high as 44°C, but its optimal range is between 32°C and 34°C.

Its pH range is from 4.6 to 9.0 with an optimum between 7.0 and 8.0. Of particular concern is the ability of this bacterium to multiply at refrigerator temperatures.

Foods implicated
It is commonly associated with milk, milk products, egg products, raw meat (especially raw pork), poultry and vegetables. The route of infection is faecal-oral and contaminated food or water.

Control
Control measures include proper heat treatment.

Emerging food poisoning pathogens
Streptococcus species
S. viridans and *S. faecalis* have been suspected of involvement in food poisoning but as yet no firm evidence has been established.

Aeromonas hydrophila

This is an aquatic organism associated with fish and frogs. It is a facultative anaerobic, Gram-negative rod and is a toxin producer. As well as diarrhoea, it has also been associated with endocarditis, meningitis, soft tissue infections and bacteraemia.

Bacteria responsible for food-borne infections

Although food poisoning bacteria are probably the best known pathogens in the food industry, it is the bacteria which cause food-borne infections that often have the most dangerous consequences. In many cases — for instance, *E. coli* 0157 — scientists and food handlers have had to develop new strategies to fight these constantly developing sources of microbiological hazard.

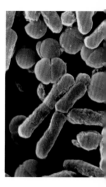

Normal inhabitants of the human gut can include Streptococcus *and* Escherichia coli.

However, you will also find under this heading some bacteria that rarely cause infection through the food-borne route: tuberculosis (TB) is a case in point.

Pasteurisation, the heating process for milk, was originally based on the destruction of the bacteria *Mycobacterium tuberculosis* (responsible for TB) and *Brucella abortus* and it is often forgotten that this method was designed to combat one of the main scourges of humans that still causes deaths in many parts of the world.

Information about tuberculosis and brucellosis is included in this book because they are still prevalent food-borne infections in many places. (TB is also re-emerging via routes other than food, but these are not discussed here.)

General controls

Establishing a *general* preventive approach to food-borne infection through your company's hazard analysis or HACCP system will help, even though some *special* measures may be needed to deal with particular organisms. A combination of the following methods will help to control almost all bacteria implicated in food-borne infections:

- ensure the safety of all water supplies
- make certain that sewage is disposed of safely
- take special care that milk and milk products, including ice-cream, are subject to the correct and appropriate heat treatment, such as pasteurisation
- do not use or sell shellfish from polluted waters
- train staff in all aspects of food hygiene
- supervise staff to maintain the highest possible standards of personal hygiene
- identify suspected carriers (see also page 234)
- supervise and monitor standards of hygiene through all stages of production, storage, distribution and sale
- avoid contact with animals: if contact is necessary, make sure that staff observe strict personal hygiene
- maintain effective systems of pest control.

Brucella

Brucellosis is a typical zoonosis, an illness which can be transmitted from animal to human and from human to animal. It is known under many names, including undulant fever, Malta fever (*Brucella melitensis*), Mediterranean fever or Bang's disease (*B. abortus*).

The natural reservoirs are sheep, goats and cattle but the bacteria may also be found in deer, caribou and dogs. The sources of infection vary according to the geographic area — the disease occurs worldwide but especially in Mediterranean countries, central and South America and central Asia. Sporadic outbreaks often occur following the consumption of raw cow's, sheep's or goat's milk or products made from the milk.

BRUCELLA
Transmitted by
raw milk, contact
with animal
tissue or blood,
or by air-borne
droplets.

One mode of transmission is by contact with animal tissue or blood, so the people most at risk are those working with infected animals or their hides and tissues, such as farm workers, abattoir workers, shepherds and vets. There is also the possibility of airborne (droplet) transmission by both animals and humans, for example by inhaling *Brucella*-infected dust from manure.

The bacteria multiply only in the host but can persist for long periods in dried dung or tissue. Laboratory personnel dealing with *Brucella* must take special safety precautions.

The symptoms include fever, headache, weakness, depression and generalised aching after an incubation period of between five and 30 days.

The common hosts of *B. melitensis* are sheep and goats in Mediterranean countries and in Mexico and central America where up to 90 per cent of herds of goats can be infected. As a consequence, Malta fever is largely an occupational disease.

The name of *B. abortus* hints that the bacterium is often responsible for stillborn calves.

Brucella in raw milk survive in milk products which are not heat treated. The cream of the infected milk is usually more heavily affected than the other components. The organism is not heat tolerant and will die at standard pasteurisation temperatures. The deliberate souring of milk inhibits the organism but does not eliminate it. Brucella can tolerate pH levels of 4 to 5.

Control

The control of milk-borne brucellosis depends on its eradication from dairy animals, which may involve slaughtering every animal in the infected herd or flock, and on adequate heat treatment of milk and dairy products. Other necessary preventive measures are thorough hygiene measures in the slaughterhouse and throughout the food flow, including strict personal hygiene after dealing with farm animals.

Campylobacter jejuni

The name *Campylobacter* comes from the Greek word campyle, meaning crosier or Bishop's crook, and under the microscope the bacterium appears as a spirally curved rod (see page 49). *Campylobacter* is a microaerophilic Gram-negative bacterium, which can survive vacuum-packing.

The genus *Campylobacter* contains about 14 different species. Before the 1970s it was implicated in abortion in cattle and sheep and reduced fertility in cattle — it was originally named *Vibrio foetus* — as well as with a multitude of different clinical symptoms in animals. For a long time the human pathogenic potential of the genus was of no interest, but it is now of special concern to the food industry. The infective dose can be under 500 cells.

Campylobacter jejuni is the most commonly reported species and causes sporadic gastro-enteritis and acute infectious bacterial diarrhoea. The symptoms also include headache, fever, abdominal pain and nausea. The usual onset time is between two and five days, but is sometimes longer.

C. JEJUNI
Can survive vacuum-packing. Destroyed by normal cooking temperatures.

The normal duration of illness is between two and seven days, but a subsequent stage can follow.

The potential complications are meningitis or septicaemia. Occasionally, *C. jejuni* is implicated in serious conditions that can follow the food-borne infection. These include Reiter's syndrome (polyarthritis enterica), Guillain-Barré syndrome (a form of acute polyneuritis) and Miller-Fisher syndrome (ophthalmoplegia; face paralysis).

Patients are typically aged from 10 to 29 years, but predisposition plays a special part — for example, the incidence of infection among AIDS patients is almost 40 times as high as that in the general population.

The optimum temperature for *C. jejuni* multiplication is 42°C, which is also the point of maximum toxin production. The organism produces a heat-labile enterotoxin. Normal cooking temperature will destroy *Campylobacter*.

Wild birds, such as seagulls, crows and feral pigeons, are a natural reservoir and often contaminate surface water. Poultry, sheep, pigs and cattle can also harbour the organism in their intestines, so turning farm animals into potential carriers.

C. jejuni is commonly found on raw poultry, raw meat, raw milk, offal and sewage. Person-to-pet and pet-to-person transmission is also frequent, while person-to-person transmission is probably of minor significance.

The major causative factors are undercooking by time or temperature, or both, and contact with animals.

Correct pasteurisation temperatures and the prevention of cross-contamination are major tools to control the organism.

Escherichia coli 0157

This is an extremely tough organism. It has been shown to survive for 60 days on a stainless steel surface and can persist for a long time in the environment — in cattle dung, contaminated water and soil. So far it has been detected in cattle, pigs and sheep.

Its full name is *Escherichia coli* serotype 0157:H7. This may be shortened to the more manageable *E. coli* 0157. You may also find references to this serotype as VTEC or EHEC — abbreviations that refer to their pathogenic characteristics.

Symptoms and duration

The infective dose is even lower than that for *Campylobacter* and less than ten organisms can cause symptoms. The onset of symptoms varies widely, but 48 hours is typical. The illness can last for one to eight days.

The bacterium produces a dangerous toxin that has been likened to the Shiga toxin (see page 93). Infection is accompanied by bloody diarrhoea (haemorrhagic colitis) and haemolytic uraemic syndrome (HUS), the latter resulting in kidney failure. About two per cent of cases result in death.

Foods implicated

The serotype has been recognised since 1982 when it became established in Canada and the USA. It is sometimes known as 'barbecue disease', or by similar such nicknames, because of its association with undercooked beefburgers. It hit the headlines in Britain in November 1996 (see panel), the same year in which there was a serious outbreak in Japan. Several deaths in Germany since 1996 have been attributed to *E. coli* 0157.

As well as undercooked beefburgers, foods linked to the bacterium include raw meat, gravy, raw and incorrectly pasteurised milk, some raw fish and unpasteurised apple cider.

Control

The separation of raw and cooked foods and strict personal hygiene are among the current control measures. New controls may become evident as knowledge increases of this relatively new threat to public health.

LANARKSHIRE OUTBREAK

A delivery of meat products for a senior citizens' event in Lanarkshire, Scotland, was at the centre of an outbreak in 1996 that made around 500 people ill, many of them seriously, and resulted in 21 deaths. The outbreak prompted public calls for stricter food safety controls and the government appointed an eminent professor to investigate. His resulting findings, popularly known as the Pennington Report, made many recommendations, particularly for butchers shops, including the strict separation of raw and cooked products (see page 163 for additional information).

USING A LETTER
Serotypes start with a capital letter, so write 0157 with a capital letter 'o' and *not* with a zero.

SEROTYPE 0157
Toxin producer. Associated with undercooked meat and meat products.

Listeria monocytogenes

The genus *Listeria* consists of six species of Gram-positive, facultative anaerobic rods. *Listeria* and the resulting illness, listeriosis, have been well documented for many decades. The species of major concern in food safety is *L. monocytogenes* which is widely distributed in the environment in soil, water and sewage. It can be excreted by human and animal carriers and there are many cases of cross-infection. Any product of animal or plant origin may harbour the bacterium.

Listeria bacteria are often found in chilled or delicatessen products — hence the common nickname 'the delicatessen bug' — such as soft cheeses made from raw (unpasteurised) milk, pâté, cook-chill meals, coleslaw, sausages and prepared salads, but it has also been detected on fruits and vegetables.

Characteristics and preferred conditions

Although it does not form spores, *L. monocytogenes* is in many ways an exemplary survivor: it is a halophile (copes with salt), tolerates an a_w of 0.93 and can multiply at a pH level between 5.0 and 9.5.

More importantly, the bacterium is psychrotrophic and can grow and multiply at cool temperatures, between 1°C and 3°C. This poses special problems for food handling and storage, as standard refrigeration temperatures will not inhibit multiplication and the cells are able to survive for long periods, even in unfavourable conditions. Ideal conditions and a combination of extrinsic factors are usually found during the production, storage and maturing of soft cheeses.

Symptoms

The incubation period is from just one day up to 70 days, with an average typical onset period of up to 21 days.

Symptoms include fever, septicaemia and meningitis. Healthy adults who are not pregnant are highly resistant to listeriosis and may only suffer from mild, flu-like symptoms after contracting the infection. However, people in the 'at risk group' are far more vulnerable — pregnant women and foetuses, the elderly and people with suppressed immune systems, such as those recovering from illness and those with AIDS, diabetes or alcoholism.

RECALLS AND EPIDEMICS

When *L. monocytogenes* bacteria were detected in a raw milk product — a soft cheese of the Vacherin Mont d'Or brand — a massive product recall started that stretched from 1983 to 1987. In that period there were 122 cases and 34 deaths associated with the cheese.

Vacuum-packed ham and pâté were the subject of product recalls in Britain between 1989 and 1990 when high levels of the bacterium were revealed. After a government warning to pregnant women to avoid soft cheeses, the number of cases of listeriosis decreased in England and Wales.

Contaminated coleslaw killed 15 unborn or newborn babies in Canada in 1981. Raw milk and cheese caused an outbreak in the USA between 1983 and 1985 in which there were 142 cases and 48 deaths.

When pregnant women are infected, listeriosis may result in premature birth or stillbirth, or the baby may be born with meningitis. The duration of the illness depends upon the symptoms and the predisposition of the victim.

Listeria monocytogenes invades both body tissue and the bloodstream, producing the substance listeriolysin which prompts changes in the red blood cells. In response, the body increases its production of monocytes, white blood cells which fight foreign or antigenic bodies. The increased level of monocytes is conspicuous in blood samples of those infected and gives the species its name.

Control

In the USA it is estimated that the financial damage attributable to *Listeria monocytogenes* is approximately $500 million each year! Many American states have issued special restrictions on the 'acceptable' level of the bacterium in food by declaring it 'an adulterant' and there must be no *L. monocytogenes* in any 25g sample of food. This means that ready-to-eat foods containing the organism are considered 'adulterated' — in other words, not fit for human consumption.

In the UK, however, where soft cheeses, for example, carry a health warning for those in the 'at risk group', the presence of *L. monocytogenes* may not always be regarded as a measure of unfitness. In the mid-1990s a Scottish court ruled that a particular cheese was fit for human consumption, even though more than one laboratory reported that the cheese had high levels of the bacterium.

Given the symptoms, thorough hygiene measures are nonetheless essential from primary production (slaughterhouse, dairy) to the very last process step. As a psychrotrophic organism, *Listeria* is a special hazard for every product stored under refrigerated conditions for long periods (for instance, many dairy products).

The best general methods of control take particular account of the risk for specific groups of people as well as time and temperature. Avoid serving raw (unpasteurised) milk and milk products, such as some soft cheeses, to those in the 'at risk group'. Make certain that milk is correctly pasteurised (see 283) and cook thoroughly foods that are implicated in *Listeria* infections. Where foods are served raw, such as some vegetables and salad ingredients, ensure that they are washed thoroughly.

Mycobacterium tuberculosis and Mycobacterium bovis

Tuberculosis (TB) is a chronic bacterial disease caused either by *Mycobacterium tuberculosis* or by *M. bovis*. The infection is detected by special tuberculin testing — the tuberculin sensitivity appears after a few weeks and usually the initial infection goes unnoticed.

The primary reservoir is now humans but there is also a variety of animal hosts, particularly cattle, which gives *M. bovis* its species name, from the Latin word *bovis* meaning cattle. In the UK the badger is reported to be a host, in New Zealand this niche is occupied by the opossum and in the USA (among other countries) it has been reported in wild deer. Because of its ability to jump species, bovine TB could theoretically find almost any animal species to be a suitable host.

MYCOBACTERIUM
Milk-borne.
Controlled by
heat treatment.

The occurrence is worldwide, and infants, children and adolescents are most at risk. The transmission is often air-borne (droplet infection), via direct contact (direct invasion through the skin) or food-borne (especially raw milk and dairy products).

Symptoms and long-term consequences
The average incubation period is between four and 12 weeks. Whereas young children are highly susceptible, it usually takes a high dose of the organism (more than 10^6) to infect healthy adults, the exception being direct infection of the lung which can be caused by inhaling only very few bacterial cells.

Tuberculosis is a progressive disease characterised by the permanent destruction of lung tissue. Chemotherapy (chemical treatment) is usually necessary for one to two years as the organism is able to encyst in human lungs and survive for many decades. This bacterial survival ability caused problems before chemotherapy was available: in many cases a cured person still harboured the organism and unwittingly infected other people or cattle many years after convalescence, so that *Mycobacterium* became active again.

Mycobacterium bovis infection (primarily from cattle) is slightly milder in human beings than is *M. tuberculosis* and spontaneous healing processes are possible. The transmission route works mainly via raw milk as well as via milk infected by cattle manure.

Control
The main preventive measure for food-borne transmission is the correct heat treatment of milk and dairy products.

Salmonella Typhi and Salmonella Paratyphi
Typhoid fever
Typhoid fever (also called typhoid, enteric fever or *Typhus abdominalis*, but *not* typhus) is caused by *Salmonella* Typhi (formerly *S. typhi*). It is the most severe of all the diseases caused by the *Salmonella* species. It occurs worldwide and some strains have become multi-resistant to standard antibiotics. It is human-specific and has carrier status.

TYPHOID FEVER
Human specific
with carrier
status. Long
incubation. High
mortality rate.

S. Typhi is in many ways an organism of superlatives among the food-borne infections: it has the longest incubation time (from three to 56 days), produces the highest body temperature and causes the highest mortality rate.

Foods implicated and routes of infection
Water and milk are typical foods that are affected by this bacterium, which can be

Early in the twentieth century an American army doctor, Major George Roper, investigated an outbreak of typhoid in the New York area. Six of the eleven members of a household were ill at the summer residence of a wealthy New York banker. Roper discovered that the family's cook, Mary Mallon, had joined the household a couple of weeks before the outbreak and left shortly afterwards. He then linked her to seven other outbreaks in eight of the families for whom she had worked in the previous decade.

By the time the authorities caught up with her, she was linked to even more outbreaks of illness. Mary was a classic typhoid carrier.

As a public health measure, Mary was forcibly held in state hospitals for a number of years — while the public viewed her either as a poisoner or as an ageing woman unjustly persecuted by the authorities. She was eventually released and, after changing her name to gain work, caused further outbreaks.

Mary was described as being uncommunicative but a superb cook who loved cooking, and it was never established whether she really understood the danger she posed or whether she was driven to ignore it because of her need to earn a living. Whichever was correct, Mary was forced to live out the rest of her life in a state hospital — a perfectly healthy, inadvertent biological weapon.

transmitted by food or sewage-contaminated water. Drinking water can be contaminated by sewage, or polluted water can contaminate food. Shellfish taken from beds contaminated by sewage, as well as raw fruits, vegetables, milk and milk products contaminated by carriers are important vehicles of contamination. Flies are also thought to be significant in the spread of the disease because they can easily transmit the organism from faeces onto food.

The organism is excreted in the faeces of patients and carriers. Up to five per cent of persons affected become permanent carriers, a symptom which is also typical for many other *Salmonella* species.

Symptoms and impact
The incubation period depends on the number of bacteria on the food, but it is usually between 12 and 20 days. The symptoms include fever, spleen enlargement, rose-coloured spots on the body and severe diarrhoea. Relapses are likely to occur. Typhoid fever is fatal in two to ten per cent of cases.

Paratyphoid
Paratyphoid, caused by *S.* Paratyphi (formerly *S. paratyphi*) is less severe than typhoid fever and, unlike *S.* Typhi which is human specific, can also affect animals. While the two illnesses are clinically similar, fatalities from paratyphoid are fewer than for typhoid fever and the occurrence is sporadic or in limited outbreaks.

Control
The preventive measures for both *S.* Typhi and *S.* Paratyphi are:
• ensuring that water used in all food processes is potable and that used water is disposed of safely
• avoiding cross-contamination between water supplies and sewer systems

- proper disposal of human faeces
- high standards of personal hygiene
- strict cleanliness in handling and preparing food (for example, cleaning surfaces and equipment thoroughly)
- thorough time and temperature control in all processes and stages
- obtaining shellfish only from an approved source
- 'excluding' infected persons from handling food (see 234)
- effective pest control.

Remember that apart from their typical symptoms and that they use food only as a vehicle, *S.* Typhi and *S.* Paratyphi are just like other species of *Salmonella* and the control measures depend on the same intrinsic and extrinsic factors.

Shigella dysenteriae (bacillary dysentery)

The genus *Shigella* consists of four species — *S. dysenteriae, S. sonnei, S. flexneri* and *S. boydii* — all of which are human pathogens. Unlike the closely related *Salmonellae* and *Escherichiae*, the *Shigellae* have no known animal reservoir. Infection is usually by the route of human-to-human transmission with outbreaks therefore caused by human carriers. Food and water, however, can play an important part as vehicles in the infection chain.

DYSENTERY
This is a general term for bloody diarrhoea.

Of the four species, *S. dysenteriae* causes the most serious symptoms — the fatality rate among hospitalised cases has been recorded at as high as 20 per cent. A total of two-thirds of cases are infants and children under ten years. The occurrence is worldwide and typical outbreaks occur under conditions of poor hygiene and sanitation.

Preferred conditions

These Gram-negative rods easily tolerate low pH: in one case lasting for an entire week in stewed fruit with a pH level of 3.2. The organism grows and multiplies best at between 10°C and 48°C. The survival rate correlates with the ambient temperature. For example, *S. sonnei* and *S. flexneri* can survive in flour, milk, eggs and seafood at 25°C for 50 days: at a lower temperature they can live for even longer.

Infection and impact

The infection is initiated by very low doses (just 10 to 100) of the pathogen and this may account for the fact that the organism is hard to detect in foods that have caused illness. The incubation time varies between one and three days.

The cause of illness from *S. dysenteriae, S. sonnei* and *S. boydii* is the Shiga toxin (named after Kiyoshi Shiga, the Japanese bacteriologist who first isolated it). The toxin is a bacterial enzyme that inhibits protein synthesis in the victim's body. (*S. flexneri* lacks the Shiga toxin, but behaves rather like the ETEC strains of *E. coli*.) Shigellosis, which is also known as dysentery, is spread through the faecal-oral

SHIGELLA
Low infective dose. Tolerates low pH. High fatality rate.

route from an infected person or by consumption of contaminated food. Food handlers primarily responsible for transmission are often those who do not pay attention to thorough hand hygiene.

Dysentery often occurs in countries with poor or insufficient water sanitation. Cockroach- and fly-borne transmission may also occur as a result of direct faecal contamination.

After infection, the bacterial cells penetrate the mucous membrane of the victim's colon where they start to multiply, causing parts of the tissue to die and resulting in severe diarrhoea. The stools often contain blood and mucus and the symptoms also involve fever and sometimes vomiting.

Foods implicated
Food-borne infections caused by *S. dysenteriae* have involved milk, water, vegetables, fruits and shellfish as well as salads and egg dishes.

Control
The preventive measures are the same as those listed under *Salmonella* Typhi, in particular:
- good personal hygiene and training
- controlled water supplies and disposal
- good sanitary hygiene
- avoiding direct or indirect faecal contamination (for example, flies).

✿ MAKING IT EASIER FOR OTHERS

- It is *not* crucial for beginners to know the difference between food poisoning and food-borne infections, although it can often be helpful for managers to distinguish them when considering control measures.
- You may also find it useful to characterise individual genera or species of bacteria to make them more interesting and easier to remember. For example, *Salmonella* — the ubiquitous one (it is found almost everywhere and often), *Listeria* — likes it cold, *Bacillus cereus* — the two-faced one (because it produces two sorts of illness), or *Yersinia* — the one with a sting in the tail (because it may cause dangerous side-effects like arthritis).
- Make sure that all food handlers have a good idea of the most typical transmission routes and the typical symptoms of illness (such as abdominal pain, nausea, vomiting and diarrhoea).
- Emphasise the measures that food handlers should take every day to stop or reduce the likelihood of causing illness.
- Remind food handlers of the unpleasantness of food-borne illness and that some pathogens are life threatening.
- Emphasise the benefits to them, their colleagues, consumers and the general public of high standards of food safety.

VIRUSES

Extremely small and highly infectious, *viruses* defy easy categorisation. They do not have a complete cell structure and they cannot reproduce themselves independently. Some scientists have even questioned whether they can be described as being truly alive and some do not list them among the micro-organisms (tiny independent life forms). What is certain, however, is that viruses are responsible for causing increasing numbers of cases of illness linked to food.

About 2,000 cases were reported through official channels in the UK in 1999, but research funded by the Department of Health suggests that, as the illnesses caused by viruses often last only a day or so, most cases go unreported. The researchers estimate that the true figure may be far closer to three million cases a year! Food-borne illnesses from viruses also receive far less publicity than those from bacteria, but, as you can see, they are a more serious and prevalent problem than was previously thought.

To date, however, only three viruses or viral groups have been shown to be significantly associated with food for human consumption. These are Hepatitis A, Norovirus and Rotavirus which are discussed in this chapter. We do not discuss those viruses, such as the one responsible for foot and mouth disease (FMD), that are not *food*-borne human health problems.

IMPACT AND RANGE
Viruses are a greater food-borne problem than commonly realised. However, the problems seem to be limited to a few viruses and a restricted range of foods and contaminated water supplies.

Foods implicated

Viruses are typical examples of a cause of food-borne disease — illnesses caused by infectious agents that are *carried* by food or water, rather than living in it or needing it to multiply. Theoretically any food could be involved in carrying and transmitting a virus, but in practice viruses are typically water-borne and may affect shellfish from polluted waters. Raw foods, including milk and vegetables, are also common viral carriers.

CHARACTERISTICS OF VIRUSES

Viruses are measured in nanometres (nm) — one billionth of a metre — and are between 20nm and 300nm in diameter. This makes them about one-hundredth to one-third the size of bacteria! (See page 47 for comparison.) Their structure is very simple: a single strand of nucleic acid (genetic material) is surrounded by a protein coat which acts as a protective shell and enables them to link to the surface of a host cell. Host cells are needed because viruses can multiply only *within* living cells — they do so by hijacking the cells of bacteria, animals and plants.

Multiplication

As soon as a specific surface structure of the viral protein coat becomes attached to a corresponding structure on the surface of the host cell, rather like a lock and key,

BACTERIAL
HOSTS
Viruses are
obligate
parasites. Those
which infect
bacteria are
known as
bacteriophages.

the viral nucleic acid is injected into the host cell where it immediately starts using the nucleic material of the host to prompt the formation of new virus particles. New viruses are released gradually from the host cell, which may go back to its normal cellular functions. Viral illness occurs when infected host cells do *not* perform their normal functions.

As viruses can multiply only in living tissue, the virus-contaminated food we eat must be regarded as a form of transport into the human body. The food carries the virus but the virus does not need the food as nutrition.

Contamination and general controls
Viral contamination can occur in two ways:
- at source — foods intended to be eaten raw, such as oysters
- by handling.

The first route of contamination indicates the need for an integrated approach to food safety, from primary production right through to consumption — for example, strict control of sewage emissions, control of irrigation water and the testing of water from which shellfish are harvested (see the paragraph on testing, opposite). The general bacterial control measures of time and temperature are also effective against viruses because they can be destroyed by normal cooking processes. This helps to explain why viruses are generally associated with *raw* foods such as salads and uncooked seafood. Viruses can, however, withstand a number of chemical disinfectants.

The second route of contamination can be controlled by effective personal hygiene, as with other forms of microbiological contamination.

VIRAL FOOD-BORNE ILLNESS

It may take only one virus to turn a host cell into a virus-producing factory, so the infective dose is usually very small. Viral infections are very contagious and person-to-person spread among family members, close friends or employees working in the same workplace is common. The spread of a virus often occurs by the faecal-oral route where personal hygiene standards are poor. The onset of illness is often 'explosive', with projectile vomiting and diarrhoea.

Hepatitis A (HAV)
This organism, which belongs to the genus *Hepatovirus,* has only one serotype. If you are infected by it, you gain life-long immunity. To date it is the only food-borne virus for which a vaccine is available.

The symptoms of HAV infection are fever, nausea, vomiting, abdominal pain, liver disease and jaundice and can last from seven days to several months. The incubation period can be 15 to 50 days, although patients tend to be infectious for a week before the symptoms show. The routes of infection are often difficult to ascertain, but it is generally accepted that the faecal-oral route is significant. The human intestinal tract is the usual source, although urine and blood may also be infected.

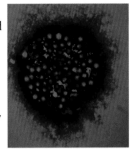

Foods commonly involved are sewage-contaminated water, raw shellfish, raw vegetables, salads and any foods, such as sandwiches, that are prepared by bare hand.

Testing
Shellfish are usually infected after being too close to a sewage outlet and it is difficult, if not impossible, to cleanse the shellfish by *depuration*. (This involves keeping shellfish in clean (unpolluted) water for several days. The shellfish will flush out any bacterial contamination but cannot cleanse themselves of viruses.)

Although the European Union shellfish directive requires all sorts of control on bacterial contamination of water, it ignores viruses which are, arguably, the greater cause of problems. In the case of raw vegetables, the contamination comes from irrigation by contaminated water. Inadequate hand washing can lead to the infection of food that is prepared by bare hand.

Control
Control measures include adequate hand washing, correct heat treatment, ensuring that irrigation water is free from contamination and buying shellfish from reliable sources — that is from classified waters. (In fact, it is a legal requirement to use shellfish only from classified waters.)

Norovirus (previously known as Norwalk and Norwalk-like viruses)

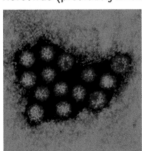

Norovirus are a group of small round structured viruses (srsv) that are named after an outbreak in Norwalk, USA, in 1968. They were first described by the American paediatrician Zahorsky in 1929 as being associated with winter vomiting disease. The source is the human intestinal tract and water contaminated by sewage. The foods most commonly involved are raw shellfish, raw vegetables, salads and water. The incubation is one to two days and illness usually lasts between one and three days. The symptoms are nausea, vomiting, diarrhoea and abdominal pain, although fever and headaches are also possible.

Control
As with Hepatitis A, the control measures are scrupulous hand washing, correct heat treatment, buying shellfish from reliable sources and ensuring the wholesomeness of irrigation water.

Rotavirus

Rotaviruses cause between 500,000 and one million deaths worldwide each year. They cause several types of gastro-enteritis and frequently cause severe diarrhoea in young children which can lead to serious dehydration. The source is humans and sewage-contaminated water and the symptoms are diarrhoea, vomiting and some fever. The onset period is one to three days and the duration is four to eight days. As with the other viruses, the foods most commonly involved are raw shellfish, raw vegetables, salads and infected waters.

Control

Again, the control measures are hand washing, correct heat treatment, buying shellfish from reliable sources and ensuring that irrigation water is free from contamination.

MAKING IT EASIER FOR OTHERS

It is not important for everyday food hygiene activities to discuss with staff whether viruses are to be counted as living organisms or active particles. However, explaining the characteristics listed below may help staff to understand why they are asked to do, or not to do, certain things when working with food.

- Viruses are food-borne but do not need food as nutrition.
- Viruses multiply only within living cells and this means that viruses need other living organisms in order to multiply.
- The infective dose is usually very small because it takes only one virus to turn a host cell into a virus-producing factory.
- Some viruses can be transmitted by water and food. The typical high risk products are shellfish from polluted waters and raw foods such as unpasteurised milk and uncooked vegetables.
- Viral infections are very contagious and person-to-person spread among family or staff members is fairly common.
- The spread of the virus often occurs by the faecal-oral route when general hygiene rules are not obeyed properly.
- Viruses can be destroyed by normal cooking processes.

PRIONS

Proteinaceous infectious particles, or prions (pronounced 'pree-ons'), are rogue forms of normal proteins in mammals, such as humans and cattle, which are found in the brain, for instance. They may be the infective agents behind brain-wasting diseases such as scrapie in sheep, bovine spongiform encephalopathy (BSE) in cattle (commonly known as mad cow disease) and variant Creutzfeldt-Jakob Disease (vCJD) in humans, although there are also many other theories for these illnesses. Prions are *not* viruses, although their impact was sometimes associated with them in the past, sometimes as *virions*. As a public health precaution in the European Union specified bovine offal, such as brain and spinal cord, is banned from the human food chain.

PARASITES

There are many close relationships in nature where two species profit from living together. This is known as symbiosis. Parasitism, in contrast, is an exploitative relationship.

The parasitic organism, which may be a micro-organism, plant or animal, lives on or inside another organism — the host — at the host's expense. It may be a little like having inconsiderate, illegal tenants in occupation. Although parasites can cause injury to, or even the death of, their host, this is a rare and accidental consequence of everyday parasitic activity. After all, why would a parasite aim to destroy its home and food store? Sometimes a host dies simply because a developing stage of a parasite, which usually has a complicated life cycle involving moving home several times, ends up in the wrong host.

A problem worldwide

Many of our foodstuffs enable a variety of 'unwanted guests' to take up human occupation. Foods of animal origin, such as beef, lamb, pork, fish and shellfish, are most frequently involved, but leafy vegetables can also become contaminated by the infective forms of parasites.

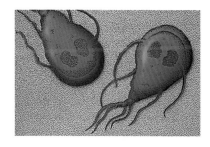

Sewage-polluted water often carries parasites, such as this protozoan Giardia lamblia, *that become uninvited guests in the human body.*

Dealing with them can require specialist training, but all managers and chefs throughout the food industry need to know something about parasites, particularly as some, such as *Chlonorchis sinensis,* are listed by the World Health Organization as a cause for increasing concern (see page 24).

Making a practical difference

It has to be acknowledged that the life cycles of many parasites can seem a bit complicated at first. However, unless you work in a sector of the food industry where specialist knowledge is essential, it is not usually necessary to memorise the names of all the different stages of parasitic life cycles. Just concentrate on how contamination occurs, which foods or products are most affected and suitable preventive methods. Use the summary charts in the Reference section as a reminder.

COMPLICATED SPECIALISTS

For the purposes of nourishment and propagation, parasites are selective specialists living permanently or temporarily on or in another organism:
- *ectoparasites* live on the surface of the host's body
- *endoparasites* live in the inner organs, tissue or blood circulation system of the host.

Ectoparasites, which include fleas and lice, are outside the scope of this book, but endoparasites include three groups of food-borne organism that can infect humans and so are significant to the management of food safety. They are:

- protozoa
- flatworms, including tapeworms and flukes
- roundworms.

CHARACTERISTICS OF PARASITES

Parasites do not live and reproduce themselves on foodstuffs. They always need a *living* host where they can develop from the 'egg' stage into a mature adult form. Development usually takes place in several stages and may involve one or more *intermediate host* which may be potential human food sources, such as cattle and pigs. The *definitive host* (sometimes known as the *primary* host) is the one in which the adult parasite carries out its sexual cycle.

The development cycle

Before you read about the life cycles of a number of parasites, you may find it helpful to obtain a general view of the stages involved in just one life cycle, in this case, *Taenia saginata* — the beef tapeworm.

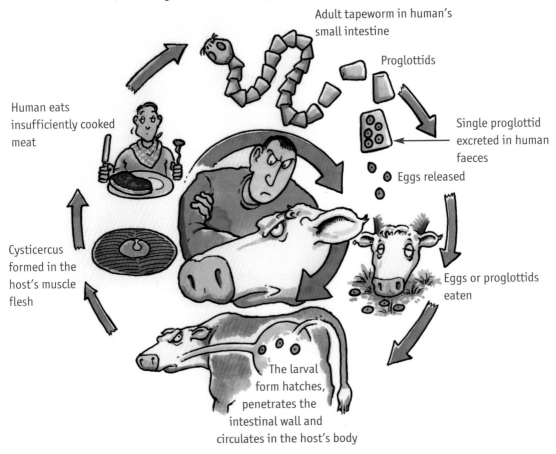

Adult tapeworm in human's small intestine

Proglottids

Human eats insufficiently cooked meat

Single proglottid excreted in human faeces

Eggs released

Cysticercus formed in the host's muscle flesh

Eggs or proglottids eaten

The larval form hatches, penetrates the intestinal wall and circulates in the host's body

LIFE CYCLES AND ILLNESSES

Protozoa

The name *protozoa* (singular: *protozoan*) means first creature and many scientists believe protozoa to have been among the first organisms on Earth.

They are unicellular (single-celled), as are bacteria. However, they have a cell nucleus to protect their genetic material (DNA), so in this respect protozoa are more like microscopic animals than like bacteria. Many protozoa have highly developed organs, such as flagella, lashes and undulating membranes, to help them to move. Some types can form cysts — tough, inactive forms which can survive without food.

Cryptosporidium parvum

This protozoan has a two-stage life cycle in one host. The first stage is in the form of thick-walled *oocysts* (types of cyst) which start the infection when ingested. The second stage is in the form of *sporozoites* (active, mobile cysts) which invade the host's body cells and produce new oocysts which are excreted in the host's faeces.

Cryptosporidium parvum oocysts are found in environmental water, such as rivers, lakes, ponds and even puddles, and they can survive chlorination, one of the purification processes involved in making water safe to drink (*potable*). The transmission of cysts is usually by drinking untreated water or by drinking water that has become contaminated. They can also be spread by food, animals such as cattle, faecal-oral routes and from person to person. To date the minimum infective dose has not been established, but it has been known to be as few as ten cysts.

On the right are Cryptosporidium parvum oocysts. On the left are hatching vegetative organisms, the sporozoites.

After an onset period of about ten days, symptoms of cryptosporidiosis — the illness from *Cryptosporidium parvum* — appear. They include diarrhoea, vomiting, abdominal pains and loss of weight. Healthy people may get away with a little diarrhoea but those who are immuno-compromised — such as those recovering from debilitating illnesses or with damage to their immune systems (for instance, AIDS patients) — can suffer severely. It often becomes difficult to maintain the balance of body fluids and it has been known for an infected person to lose 17 litres of fluid a day. Symptoms occur six to 14 days after ingestion and symptoms typically last between about nine and 23 days.

Giardia lamblia

Like *Cryptosporidium parvum,* this flagellated protozoan also exists in environmental water, usually in the form of microscopic, pear-shaped cysts. The cysts reach the water in the faeces of wild animals, such as rats and beavers, or in the faeces of people who have already played host to the parasite.

When a human host ingests a cyst, the acidic stomach environment prompts the organism to turn into another form — an active, *motile* form known as a

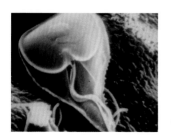

trophozoite, which means feeding cell. At this stage the cell is aggressive and invades the intestinal tissues where it obtains its nutrients by absorption. Between about five and 25 days after consuming *G. lamblia*, a human host usually experiences nausea, foul-smelling and often explosive flatulence and watery diarrhoea. Subsequent weight loss is common. About three to four weeks later the host excretes cysts in his or her stools.

The Giardia lamblia *trophozoite 'feeds' by absorbing nutrients from the human intestine.*

One infected person can shed up to nine hundred million cysts per day and the cysts can survive for up to three months in sewage sludge. As a result, giardiasis, the illness caused by *Giardia lamblia*, is common in countries, regions and institutions with bad sanitary systems.

Giardia cysts can be transmitted by:
- contaminated water
- vegetables that have been washed or grown in contaminated water
- hands washed in contaminated water
- rodent faeces
- human faeces, via the faecal-oral route of poor personal hygiene
- human sewage
- hand-to-hand contact, via the hand-oral route.

The *infective dose* is very low — a single cyst can lead to giardiasis — and the illness is highly contagious. Symptoms can last from several months to a year or more.

Preventing giardiasis and cryptosporidiosis

Many of the measures to prevent these illnesses need to be taken at the source of water (for example, by the water supply company) or by the food grower, but you should also ensure, as part of good practice, that your workplace takes the following preventive steps:
- use only potable water supplies: this may mean using portable purification equipment and chemicals for outdoor catering events and military 'field' catering
- alert food handlers to the hazards of using private water sources, such as wells or bore holes
- teach food handlers about symptoms to watch out for after returning to work from taking part in outdoor activities such as wilderness walking and inland boating
- train all food-contact staff (and others whose work could affect food safety) in effective personal hygiene, especially with respect to hand washing
- monitor hand washing
- avoid the possibility of cross-contamination by enforcing strict measures for personal hygiene if your staff have contact with pets, for farm or wild animals
- ban animals from food areas
- ensure that an effective pest control programme is carried out (see Part 4)
- make certain that food premises are kept scrupulously clean.

Other food-related protozoa

These include:

- *Entamoeba histolytica*, which causes amoebic dysentery
- *Toxoplasma gondii*, an organism mostly spread by domestic cats
- *Sarcocystis* species, parasites derived from cattle (*S. hominis*) and pigs (*S. suihominis*).

Proper cooking — for example, cooking meat to a minimum *core temperature* of 70°C — should destroy these organisms. However, freezing may not always help because the oocysts are highly resistant. Undercooked meats present the greatest risk of infection from *Toxoplasma gondii* or *Sarcocystis*, while poor personal hygiene can lead to contamination of foods by *Entamoeba histolytica*.

Flatworms

Flatworms have simple, flattened bodies without blood vessels. They include free-living flatworms and parasitic flukes and tapeworms.

Tapeworms

The tapeworm's taxonomical category is *Cestodes*, from the Greek for girdle, and aptly describes the adult worm which looks like a girdle of many links. This parasite develops in several stages and may have more than one intermediate host.

The adult tapeworm develops in the intestines of its definitive host. Single proglottids, each containing many eggs, are excreted in the faeces of the definitive host. Back in the natural environment, the released eggs can be taken up by an intermediate host which harbours the development of the larval stages.

The larvae travel through the intestinal layers of the intermediate host into the bloodstream and lymph system, from where they proceed into the muscle tissue or other organs, or both. A larval cyst is then formed — a form containing several new potential 'buds' from which new tapeworms can emerge. It is the swollen larval cyst that gives immature tapeworms the common name of *bladderworm*, because the cyst looks rather like a miniature worm-filled balloon.

While adult tapeworms are usually easily treated with medicines, the larval cyst can 'hide' in vital human organs and cause serious illness or death.

Food-borne tapeworms of special concern are:

- *Taenia saginata* (beef tapeworm)
- *Taenia solium* (pork tapeworm)
- *Diphyllobothrium latum* (fish tapeworm)
- *Echinococcus granulosus* (dog tapeworm).

The first three of these organisms are named after their intermediate host, even though the definitive hosts are humans.

Taenia saginata

The beef tapeworm is widely distributed throughout the world wherever beef is eaten. The adult worm can reach up to ten metres long! The adult attaches itself to the intestinal wall of the definitive host — humans — and the terminal proglottids, which contain eggs, are passed in the faeces. About eight or nine proglottids are excreted every day, each of them containing up to 80,000 eggs.

The proglottids, or the released eggs they contain, are eaten by grazing cattle (intermediate host). The eggs hatch in the cattle and develop into the first larval form which moves through the body and ends up as a bladderworm in muscle tissue, such as the heart, which may be eaten by humans. The life cycle restarts when the adult form develops in a human (the definitive host) after raw or undercooked infected tissue has been eaten.

METRES OF WORM IN THE HUMAN INTESTINE

The body of an adult tapeworm is divided into a head-like structure (the scolex) and thousands of thin, flat body-segments. To think about these parts as head and body is, however, rather misleading as the scolex is mainly a contact organ, the hooks and suckers of which allow tapeworms to attach themselves firmly to the layers of the intestinal tract. Two of the suckers are visible  in the top of this micrograph of a *Taenia saginata* — at this angle they look a little like eyes. The suckers of a *Taenia solium* (shown at a more conventional angle at the top of the page opposite) appear as four circles. The scolex narrows into body-segments (proglottids) which each contain complete 'male' and 'female' sexual apparatus (tapeworms are hermaphrodites).

The chain of proglottids can reach several metres, so a host harbouring several tapeworms may have a gut literally stuffed with metres and metres of worm segments! The mature segments, which are the last third of the chain of proglottids, contain thousands of eggs.

Taenia solium

The pork tapeworm also occurs worldwide wherever pork is eaten. The adult superficially resembles *T. saginata* except for the scolex which is armed with a double row of hooklets that provide firm fastening to the intestinal wall.

The life cycle is also very similar except that pigs are the intermediate hosts and harbour the bladderworms which can give pork a speckled appearance, often referred to as 'measly' pork.

Bladderworms (the larval cysts) are found not only in the muscular tissue but also in various organs such as the lungs, liver, heart and brain. Pigs often become infected on land contaminated by outflow from septic tanks, which are common in farming districts, or from faeces of other farm animals.

It is usual for people harbouring the adult tapeworm (as definitive hosts) to need to undergo chemotherapy treatment.

However, humans can also become the intermediate host if eggs are accidentally ingested (for instance, via hands contaminated by polluted soil). When this happens, the bladderworm can grow in human muscle tissue or in vital organs — a condition known as human cysticercosis. When the brain is infected (cerebral cysticercosis) symptoms similar to those of a brain tumour occur — and the condition is inoperable.

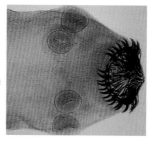

Infection by Taenia solium (left) can lead to inoperable conditions of the human brain. Cooking meat thoroughly or freezing it can destroy Taenia cysts.

The safe collection and treatment of sewage play an important part in the prevention of *Taenia* infections. By law beef and pork are checked for, among other things, traces of tapeworm infection at the abattoir. However, there are important preventive steps that can be taken farther up the food flow, including cooking pork and beef thoroughly — to a minimum core temperature of 70°C — or freezing the meats, both of which destroy the cysts.

Diphyllobothrium latum

The fish tapeworm lives in the intestines of humans and other mammals such as dogs, cats, pigs and bears. Infection in humans is usually caused by eating raw or underprocessed freshwater fish from sewage-contaminated ponds and lakes. Just three weeks after being ingested, the worm reaches its characteristic final length of ten metres. One fish tapeworm can have as many as 4,000 proglottids and the host's faeces can contain as many as a million eggs.

Diphyllobothrium has at least two intermediate hosts and four stages of development. The first larval form, a free-swimming organism, hatches in water where it is ingested by the first intermediate host, which is usually a crustacean. A second larval stage develops in this first intermediate host. Then the food chain takes its usual course and the first intermediate host is eaten by a second intermediate host, which is usually a freshwater fish. The third stage of development takes place in the muscle tissue of the fish.

Before it is the turn of humans, the second intermediate host can be devoured by a bigger species. As big fish eat little fish and even bigger fish eat the big fish, the hosting can be repeated several times until this third larval form is eaten by a human or another mammal — the definitive host. Only then does the adult tapeworm develop.

Avoid serving or selling raw or very lightly cooked fish. Thorough cooking or freezing will kill the organism.

Echinococcus granulosus

Unlike the parasites we have discussed so far, the definitive hosts of *Echinococcus granulosus* are not humans but dogs. However, humans can become infected when they consume vegetables contaminated with dog faeces containing dog tapeworm eggs or when dogs lick humans — just consider for a moment how dogs clean themselves. Once a person is infected, the cyst develops in the inner organs, such as the liver, lungs or brain — often with fatal consequences. Treating a dog regularly with worming treatments minimises the risk, but food handlers should be made aware of the hazards of keeping pet dogs, particularly in or near kitchens or other food areas.

The fox tapeworm (*E. multilocularis*) has similar dangerous symptoms as those of *E. granulosus*. Foxes can contaminate wild berries, which are often eaten raw.

Flukes
Fasciola hepatica
The liver fluke has a complicated life cycle of several stages which may involve more than one intermediate host. It is widely distributed in areas where sheep and cattle are raised. The major definitive hosts of *Fasciola hepatica* are humans, cattle and sheep. It has also been found in goats, pigs and deer.

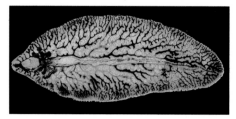

The adult fluke lives in the definitive host's bile duct (which is reached via the liver), where it causes inflammation.

Eggs released by the fluke are passed out in the host's faeces, often ending up in environmental water. After a few days in the water, the first larval stage (the miracidium) develops. This motile organism infects its first intermediate host — a water snail. Inside the snail the miracidium turns into a *sporocyst*, which produces a 'mother cell' (the redia). In turn, the redia turns into another free-swimming larval stage (the cercaria) that leaves the snail and attaches to water plants.

Adult liver fluke, Fasciola hepatica, at the stage where it ingests blood and tissue debris from its host's bile duct.

The definitive host usually eats the cercaria (the infectious stage) on plants such as watercress or weeds that grow in water. Symptoms occur about 30 days after ingestion and include pain in the area of the liver, loss of appetite and fatigue. It is also possible to develop a throat infection (pharyngeal fascioliasis) from eating raw, or undercooked, infected liver. Painful hoarseness and coughing may lead to difficulty in breathing and swallowing.

Farmers can use antiparasitic medication to treat cattle and sheep. Freezing or cooking meat thoroughly prevents infection. Food businesses should ensure that they buy vegetables that are grown in water, such as watercress, from reputable sources. Freezing or cooking vegetables will also kill flukes.

Roundworms
Belonging to the taxonomical category of *Nematodes*, roundworms have slender, unsegmented, cylindrical bodies and are found in abundance in soil and water. Many are parasitic.

Trichina spiralis (formerly Trichinella spiralis)

This roundworm affects pigs, horses, domestic mammals, rats and more than 40 other species of wild animal around the world. The life cycle is simple: the larvae and adult form live within the same host, although in different organs and tissues. *Trichina* are not hermaphrodite, but have both male and female forms.

When infected muscle tissue from a host animal (such as a pig or rat) is eaten, the larvae, which are in cyst form in the muscle, are released into the host's stomach. They mature in the intestines, often without giving rise to symptoms in the host. The male worms die, while the females each produce up to 2,000 new larvae which travel through the lymphatic system towards the muscles where they encyst, remaining viable and infectious for many years. For further development the encysted larvae need to enter a new host which usually happens when infected muscle tissue is consumed.

The dark green oval is a cyst of Trichina spiralis in human muscle tissue. The cyst contains one coiled larva, stained in purple.

When people eat infected pork, the first symptoms are usually nausea, abdominal pain, diarrhoea and sometimes vomiting. These symptoms pass and the next stage — invasion of the muscle tissue — may happen almost unnoticed at first. Serious muscle pain, fever and difficulty with breathing, chewing and swallowing may follow, sometimes leading to death. The muscle pains indicate that 1,000 or more *Trichina* larvae per gram of tissue have been deposited.

Trichinosis (or trichinellosis), the illness cause by *Trichina*, can be prevented by ensuring that pigs are not fed with infected meat, game or uncooked waste food. Pigs are omnivorous and often become infected by feeding on rat carcasses containing the encysted organism.

The disease can be prevented by cooking pork thoroughly to a minimum core temperature of 70°C. The use of microwave ovens for heating pork has been shown to be unreliable, unless steps are taken to ensure that the meat is cooked thoroughly throughout. Freezing pork kills the encysted larvae only after 15 days of frozen storage! Pickling and salting is also a preventive measure, but do note that the meat is safe only four months after processing.

MAKING IT EASIER FOR OTHERS

Emphasise the importance of preventive measures that are appropriate within your sector of the food industry. For instance, if you manage a catering company, stress the importance of proper cooking or freezing to kill parasites.

air-borne travellers

For many people the word fungi suggests strange growths on a rotting woodland tree stump or, in a food context, tray after tray of button mushrooms in a supermarket. But this is like thinking of animals as being just large furry mammals and forgetting about the birds, fish, insects and other creatures that make up by far the greater number of animal species. As well as the familiar woodland varieties and edible mushrooms, fungi include *microscopic* organisms — the single-celled yeasts and the thread-like moulds.

Originally considered as part of the plant kingdom, fungi are now recognised as being in a separate biological category of their own.

Unlike plants, fungi cannot make their own food through photosynthesis. Instead they live by absorbing nutrients from their environment, which may be soil, water or — as with the treestump varieties — dead organic matter.

Fungi also grow on living plants, sometimes causing severe crop damage. A few types can live on humans — for example, athlete's foot and thrush (*Candida albertans*).

Fungi that grow on plant and animal matter survive by breaking down the tissue of their host so that they can feed on dissolved nutrients.

As specialists in decomposition, they have both beneficial and harmful effects on our food. For instance, the process of fermentation — which is a specialisation of certain yeasts that can turn carbohydrate into alcohol and carbon dioxide — has given us beer, wine and leavened bread. Without moulds we would have no Camembert, no Stilton, no soya sauce, and not even chocolate.

On the other hand, fungi can destroy living material, spoil food and leave a product that is not of the nature, substance or quality that the consumer expects (see page 154).

Fungi have a varied repertoire of reproductive techniques but it is often through air-borne spores that they manage to reach food, seemingly out of nowhere.

There is no biological difference between mushrooms and toadstools. They are the fruiting bodies of certain types of fungus.

When you pick a mushroom, you are picking just the fruit, not the whole organism. The main part lives in the soil sending out long fibres that produce mushroom bodies when conditions are favourable.

Anyone who picks or purchases wild mushrooms must learn to identify dangerous varieties, such as the destroying angel and deathcap (see page 123). As moulds can produce spores, even storing toxic varieties with edible ones could lead to illness.

Most yeasts grow as colourful colonies ranging from creamy white to pink to red. The powdery bloom on grapes, plums and other fruit is a form of wild yeast. These fungi will not make you ill but they can spoil food, making it inedible — in fact they are one of the few micro-organisms to affect acidic foods such as pickles. Yeasts usually reproduce by budding. The round brownish pink structures you can see in the greatly magnified colour scanning micrograph (below) are budding yeast cells on the skin of a melon.

Moulds consist of tubular cells called hyphae which collectively form a growth known as a mycelium. The most familiar types are the green-grey growth on stale bread and the white down on fruit and vegetables. In the micrograph, air-borne mould spores have germinated and penetrated the skin of the melon. The long green structures are mould hyphae, and you can just see the fruiting bodies on the tips of some of them.

Mouldy food should always be thrown away as mould can produce poisonous substances known as mycotoxins (see page 129).

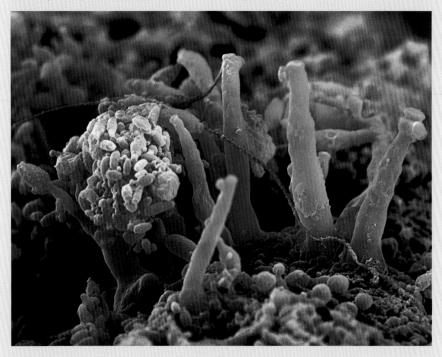

FUNGI

Fungi play an important part in our culinary traditions but they can also cause illness and spoil food. Some mushrooms — types of *fungus* that are visible to the naked eye — are poisonous and these are discussed in 'Chemical hazards'. This chapter discusses the *microscopic* fungi — the yeasts and moulds.

YEASTS

Yeasts are microscopic unicellular fungi. They can be distinguished from bacteria by their larger cell size — from 5μm to 8μm in diameter — and their typical oval or elliptical cell shape.

Most yeast species reproduce by budding. As you can see from the greatly magnified micrograph below, a small bud gradually grows from the 'mother' cell

(the larger structure) of *Saccharomyces cerevisiae*, also known as baker's or brewer's yeast. When the 'daughter' cell is about the same size as the 'mother', it separates as a new, but genetically identical, individual. The circular areas on the 'mother' cell are scars from earlier buds.

Some yeasts also produce spores, known as ascospores or basidiospores. These should not be confused with bacterial spores (endospores), which are a survival mechanism.

Yeast spores can spread by many contamination routes, but air-borne contamination is typical. Foods contaminated by yeasts may have a fruity smell.

Preferred conditions
Yeasts are fairly heat resistant and can multiply over a wide temperature range. Many are psychrophilic and can grow at a temperature as low as −15°C. They prefer an a_w range of 0.90 to 0.94 and grow best in slightly acidic conditions, with a pH between 4 and 4.5, in foods with a high sugar content.

A problem of spoilage
Yeasts do *not* cause food poisoning but there are some species that are capable of causing considerable spoilage. As they prefer acidic food with a high sugar content, foods such as fruit, fruit juice, wine and pickled food are especially vulnerable to yeast spoilage.

Yeast cells need a lot of sugar to maintain their adenosine triphosphate (ATP) level (the primary source of energy for living organisms). Fruit contains high amounts of both glucose and fructose (types of sugar) which are broken down by the yeast enzymes. If there is only a little or no oxygen available, the sugars are broken down into alcohol. Yeasts have been hailed as a possible source of cheap, abundant energy in the form of fuel-alcohol for motor vehicles.

MOULDS

Moulds are filamentous (thread-like) fungi. Their tubular cells, called hyphae, are about $30\mu m$ to $100\mu m$ in diameter. They extend, sometimes forming branches, into a mass known as a mycelium. Many moulds reproduce by both asexual and sexually formed spores, and the identification of moulds is based primarily on the structure of these reproductive bodies.

Preferred conditions

Although they prefer neutral conditions, moulds can also tolerate a pH range from 2 to 8, so they have a considerable advantage over most bacteria which have a more limited range of tolerance. Moulds prefer ambient temperatures but, like yeasts, continue to grow at temperatures below $0°C$. Some species can tolerate low water activity at below a_w 6.0 and this is why many dry foods such as biscuits, cheeses and nuts may be spoiled by mould.

Moulds are strictly aerobic and will grow only on the *surface* of foods. Food spoilage is often visible as white, black or blue-green mildew.

 MAKING IT EASIER FOR OTHERS

- Explain that as mould spores can be carried in the air, they can settle anywhere and colonise a wide variety of foods.
- Encourage staff to think of preventive measures as being common sense or plain good housekeeping practices:
  - rotate stock in storage, making sure that food is used before the expiry of *use by* or *best before* date marks
  - check for signs of mould or yeast before using or selling the product
  - store the food in dry conditions
  - keep containers and cupboards clean.

🏅 MANAGEMENT MATTERS

At first there may seem to be a lot to learn about microbiology at this level of study. However, knowledge means power when you have to deal with microbes and you could compare this aspect of food safety to military defence. First you need to get to know your enemy as closely as possible by studying the weak and strong points, then you can use that information to make the conditions for your attack as favourable as possible. Armed with this information, you will be in a far stronger position to carry out a hazard analysis (see pages 314 to 325) and to formulate and implement effective management controls. In short, the information will help you to become a better manager.

A knowledge of intrinsic and extrinsic factors is a key to food safety in general and to food preservation in particular. Sometimes a single factor can control an organism, but most of the time you have to deal with several factors, the most important of which is usually the time and temperature combination.

Distinctions between types of illness

It is necessary to get to grips with the technical differences between food poisoning and food-borne infections, a task not made easy by the different historical, geographical and industrial uses of different terms in the same context. You might find it helpful to use the mnemonic FIN to check the main differences between food poisoning and food-borne infection:

- *f*ood (a medium for multiplication or merely a vehicle of contamination)
- *i*ncubation time (short or long)
- *n*umbers (small or large).

Characteristics of bacterial species

Don't worry if it is difficult at first to remember details like the incubation time, temperature ranges, pH levels and so on for a particular organism: after all, unless you are working with such information every day, it is the kind of thing you can look up when you need to. If you are following a course of study, your trainer or tutor will give you invaluable guidance about the level of detail you need to remember. Rereading and making notes will help to make things easier, of course, as will the summary charts in the Reference section. You should find that the marginal notes provide useful reminders and they may be a great revision boon if you are about to take an advanced-level examination.

The information about any pathogen is like a logic puzzle — know one or two pieces of information and the rest become apparent by association or by a process of elimination. For example, think of the symptoms, as they give a clue to the nature of the pathogen. Ask yourself whether vomiting is involved. If so, then the stomach must be affected and therefore the onset time of the illness is probably quick as the stomach is near the beginning of the alimentary tract. Conversely, if vomiting is not involved, then the onset time may be a bit longer. There again, if the onset time is very quick, your first thought should be of toxins as they acutely affect the stomach before the rest of the alimentary tract. This type of exercise can be done for most of the symptoms.

Spores and toxins
It is easy to remember which bacteria are spore-formers or toxin-producers or both.
- *Spore-formers* are all members of the genera *Bacillus* and *Clostridium*. None of the other food poisoning genera are spore-formers.
- All the spore-formers are toxin producers. So too is *Staphylococcus aureus* (which does *not* form spores).

Controls
When you are thinking about how you can apply all this information to your workplace, it may be helpful in the first instance to compare the preventive measures of *protect-prevent-destroy*, which work against food poisoning organisms, with the options you have for food-borne infections:
- *protect* food from contamination — this will always work
- *destroy* bacteria (heat treatment) — this will also be important
BUT
- *prevent* multiplication — this will be useful only with food poisoning organisms where illness arises from the ingestion of large numbers of bacteria; in contrast, bacteria responsible for food-borne infection can cause disease in very small numbers (sometimes fewer than 100) and *do not* depend on multiplying in the food.

What about other control measures? Again, this is fairly easy as almost all of them include proper time and temperature management, good personal hygiene, prevention of cross-contamination, good cleaning, disinfection and so on.

microbes at our service

When you are in charge of producing safe food it is easy to feel besieged by armies of lethal microbes just waiting to break through your defences and wreak havoc among your customers.

Microbes can indeed be very dangerous, as you have seen in Part 3. But these humble life forms are in fact powerhouses of complex chemical reactions that can be harnessed to promote health and cure disease in dozens of different ways.

Fungi and bacteria have given us antibiotic drugs such as penicillin and streptomycin, used to treat a host of killer diseases including tuberculosis and septicaemia; cyclosporin, used against eczema and to prevent the rejection of transplant organs; and gliotoxin, a potential weapon against cancer.

Vitamin C (ascorbic acid) no longer has to be extracted from foods but can be manufactured, thanks to the oxidising properties of the bacterium *Acetobacter suboxydans*.

Vitamin B_2 is produced from yeasts while B_{12}, once extracted from animal liver in order to treat pernicious anaemia, is now created in large quantities by the same bacteria that are used to ferment sewage. Carotene, a close relation of Vitamin A, can be produced industrially from fungi.

Then there is the amazing story of steroids — drugs such as cortisone, used to relieve the crippling pain of arthritis, and progesterone, a key ingredient of the contraceptive pill.

Until the 1950s many steroids could be made only through enormously complex and expensive chemical processing: cortisone initially cost more than £300 a gram and required 37 different steps to create. Then scientists discovered that a simple mould could do most of the work for them simply by being

The Scottish bacteriologist Alexander Fleming discovered penicillin in 1928, allegedly through sheer untidiness. He left a culture of bacteria growing uncovered long after he should have disposed of it from the laboratory of St Mary's Hospital, London, where he worked. (The picture shows him there, in the foreground, as a young man in 1909.) One day Fleming noticed that a colony of the mould *Penicillium notatum* had started to grow alongside the bacteria — not in itself surprising as mould spores are common in the air. Around the mould, however, the bacterial culture was dissolving — medicine's first glimpse of the power of antibiotics, strange chemicals that are made by some microbes but destroy others. By the 1940s antibiotics were in medical use and they now help to save lives every day all around the world.

allowed to grow on the right chemical mixture. Now cortisone is an everyday prescription drug.

These are just a few of the uses to which scientists have put micro-organisms in a bid to improve health, cure illnesses and alleviate symptoms. There are many other uses, including the production of artificial blood plasma, the creation of antisera (given after exposure to infectious diseases) and the making of vaccines.

Of course, this is not the end of the story. As scientists look for new ways to put these miniature chemical factories to work, the list lengthens on the benefits side of the microbiological balance sheet.

CHEMICAL HAZARDS

Perhaps there is a curious twist to the way in which chemical threats to food are perceived. On the one hand, the media frequently raise concern about 'chemicals, poisons and toxins' in food. On the other hand, chemical hazards are sometimes nudged aside in professional discussion about food safety management — and may receive scant consideration when a food hazard analysis is carried out. We cannot debate here whether there really is a gap between the genuine and perceived threat from chemicals. Instead, we outline the potential chemical hazards to food so that you can start to consider what *you* should be doing in your workplace to ensure that the food you produce is safe from harmful chemicals. There is more information and advice about prevention in Part 4.

THE LEVEL OF RISK IN YOUR BUSINESS

Serious contamination of food by chemicals is, as you know, less common than bacterial contamination. What's more, it is not always possible to point to one product as the culprit, because some types of poisoning take a considerable time to develop in the body. So, it may be tempting to think that your main forms of control of chemical hazards are *suppliers' certificates* and the prevention of the careless use of chemicals, such as cleaning products, in your workplace. Needless to say, these measures are essential, but you also need to manage *all* the food-borne chemicals that put human health at risk. As chemical hazards can arise at *any* stage in the production and sale of food, you also need to be aware of problems that might occur *outside* your premises — including environmental pollution, the use of pesticides and the inclusion of food additives, such as preservatives, in some products.

Practical management

Although chemicals and chemical reactions are complicated — perhaps reason enough for a busy food manager to try to avoid the subject — we focus on the essential, basic information that you need for your work. This and the following three chapters look at particular types of chemical in greater detail, while Part 4 provides additional useful information about eliminating, or reducing the impact from, chemical hazards.

A PLACE IN HISTORY

The deliberate use of slow gradual poisons earns chronic poisoning its own place in history. During the European Renaissance, for example, poisoning was often chosen as a discreet and effective way to get rid of hostile spouses, political rivals, and those blocking the route to a throne. Symptoms of such poisoning included kidney disease, anaemia and skin discoloration.

TYPES OF CHEMICAL

Before we go any farther, you may wish to check exactly what we mean when we talk about *chemicals* by reading the feature on pages 121 to 122. Most chemicals are harmless and necessary, while many give our lives considerable benefits. However, just as a few types of bacteria can cause immense human harm, a few food-borne chemicals can also cause illness and even death. For our purposes here, the easiest way to discuss these harmful chemicals is to classify them as *poisons*.

Harmful substances

A poison is any substance that harms or kills living *organisms*. Poisons do not affect inanimate things — you cannot poison a machine or a piece of equipment. If people talk about poisoned containers or utensils, they mean that these objects contain, or are coated with, a substance that is poisonous when it comes into contact with a person or other living thing. Poisonous substances are usually described as being *toxic* and chemical poisoning arises by means of a *toxic agent* (a chemical poison).

Practical divisions

You will readily appreciate that chemical hazards are a wide-ranging, rather untidy collection of threats to food safety. To make this unwieldy subject a little easier, we have divided them into two main categories — naturally occurring chemicals and introduced chemicals. This division should help you to identify potential *sources* of chemical contamination and the *products* that are most likely to be affected by chemical hazards. Both categories must be taken into account during a hazard analysis (see part 4).

Naturally occurring chemicals

These are poisonous substances (toxins) that are formed naturally in foods. The toxins are *inherent* — they are a part of the food. Naturally occurring chemicals include some types of:
- plant
- fungus
- animal, including fish and shellfish.

Some fungi produce poisons known as *mycotoxins*. As these pose a particular threat to food safety, they are discussed in a chapter of their own (see page 129).

Introduced chemicals

This heading covers a wide variety of hazards.

Residues

These are chemicals which are deliberately or accidentally added to, or brought into contact with, the product as it grows. They include:

TOXIC AND TOXIN
Toxic means poisonous. But a toxin is a biological poison. Toxic can be used to describe the effects of toxins *and* chemical poisons (also called *toxic agents* or *toxicants*).

- veterinary drugs given to animals to treat disease, to improve their resistance to disease or to increase their growth rate
- animal feed additives that can be *carried over* into human food
- pesticides, herbicides and insecticides used to treat crops.

Environmental contaminants

These are chemicals that can accumulate in food as a consequence of environmental pollution, such as by leaching (filtering through) from batteries in rubbish tips into the soil and water. Substances involved include:
- heavy metals, such as lead and mercury
- radio nuclides
- by-products of industrial and commercial processes, such as the creation of dioxins when fossil fuels (like coal) or plastics are burned in the presence of chlorine.

Additives

These chemicals are ingredients which are deliberately added to food to enhance its flavour, appearance or shelf life. They include flavourings, colourants and preservatives.

Inappropriate practices

Under this heading comes a wide range of actions, omissions and conditions, including:
- contact reactions, such as the use of unsuitable containers or packaging
- careless use of chemicals, such as cleaning products and disinfectants.

SYMPTOMS AND CONSEQUENCES

Before we discuss all these different types of chemical hazard in detail in the following chapters, it is important to understand the general effects of poisons on human health.

TWO TYPES OF REACTION
Symptoms caused by eating chemically contaminated food can occur immediately after eating or a short time later (acute symptoms), or months or even years later (chronic symptoms).

Acute or chronic

Unlike many cases of bacterial food-borne illness, in which symptoms start within a few hours of eating contaminated food (acute symptoms), the effects of chemical poisoning can be either acute or chronic. A food containing a high level of a toxic substance could cause *acute poisoning* if eaten just once or a few times — for example, symptoms of chemical poisoning usually start between six and 24 hours after eating toadstools containing the toxin amanitin.

In contrast, *chronic poisoning* develops over a long period as a result of eating food that contains a low level of a toxic substance. Although the intake of the toxic substance may be more or less continuous, the symptoms show only after a considerable time has passed. For example, lead poisoning from old lead water pipes usually takes a long time to develop.

A healthy and fit person can tolerate a higher exposure to a toxic substance than someone who is unfit or weakened by illness. This fact is taken into account in a standard measure — the acceptable daily intake (ADI) — which classifies the toxicity of substances. The ADI represents the amount of a chemical which is believed to be safe to consume every day for a lifetime.

Chemicals in our bodies — various ways to become ill
Dangerous levels of poison in our food can make us ill by:
- causing symptoms similar to those of food-borne disease
- overwhelming the body's natural defence mechanisms
- competing with other similar chemicals that are naturally in our bodies
- inhibiting some essential body functions
- exaggerating the effects of chemicals in our bodies
- causing allergies.

Similar to food poisoning
Some symptoms of chemical poisoning are similar to those of many types of food-borne disease, including vomiting, diarrhoea and stomach pains. The victim may also experience dizziness, headaches and loss of muscular power. The kidneys and liver are often affected.

Overwhelming natural defences
The body's self-defence mechanisms are often overloaded by poisons. The body's immune system, which fights 'intruders' that have antigenic properties (see page 51), cannot cope with an overload of chemicals. Instead of fighting off the invading chemicals, the body starts to incorporate and accumulate them. This does not necessarily result in immediate damage because the accumulation of poisons is usually a long-term process. The toxicity of a chemical depends on the state of health of the person who consumes the poison and the impact is increased when someone is undernourished.

Competing with the body's chemicals
Some toxicants can compete with other chemicals in the body and try to replace them. This usually occurs when the poison belongs to the same chemical group as a beneficial compound in the body. In the case of cadmium poisoning, for example, calcium, which is vital for our bone structure, is slowly replaced by cadmium. This leads to a condition known as glass bones in which the skeleton becomes so fragile that bones splinter, sometimes fatally piercing vital body organs.

Inhibiting and exaggerating body functions
Some poisons inhibit the body's usual absorption of essential nutrients, others
amplify the effects of various chemicals which occur naturally in the body.

TACKLING ALLERGIES

Certain chemicals in some foods can cause allergies. A food *allergy* is an
immunological response (what the body's defence system does) that is triggered by
food or food additives.

An allergy is *not* a form of food-borne illness, even though some symptoms, such as
vomiting, gastro-enteritis and skin rashes, may resemble those of some types of
bacterial food-borne illness.

Allergic responses are specific to individuals and the symptoms range from mild,
through severe, to life threatening.

True allergies are experienced by a tiny percentage of the population, but the
number of people affected seems to be growing.

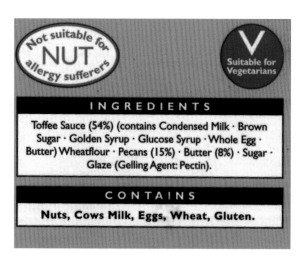

A food business cannot prevent allergies, but
it can alert allergy-sufferers by, for example,
labelling foods and menu items clearly with
their ingredients, displaying allergy warning
signs and ensuring that waiting and sales
staff can give correct information about
ingredients.

The packaging for this toffee pecan tart, for
example, includes a clear *symbol* warning
consumers that the product is unsuitable for
people with a nut allergy. In addition there is
a *list* of ingredients that have commonly been
linked to allergies — nuts, cow's milk, eggs,
wheat and gluten.

🌐 MAKING IT EASIER FOR OTHERS

- Discuss the potential chemical hazards that could be encountered in your type of
  food operation.
- Ensure that staff understand the steps they should take to prevent chemical
  food poisoning.

living with chemicals

We all recognise cleaning products and pesticides as chemicals, but we might not immediately think of substances such as sugar, salt, fats, perfume and even alcohol as chemicals. It is also easy to forget that there are chemical reactions going on inside our bodies all the time and that these are perfectly natural and necessary processes. So what exactly are chemicals?

Most definitions relate to something that is a part of, related to, or made by chemistry. So, to understand what a chemical is, we need to understand a little about the study of chemistry.

The science is divided into organic and inorganic chemistry. Organic chemistry deals with carbon compounds (which form the basis of all living things), whether natural or synthesised, while inorganic chemistry deals with elements other than carbon.

Chemistry deals with the *composition* of substances, their *combinations* and their *changes* under various conditions — how one substance can be generated or transformed into another.

A familiar example makes the point. When water (H_2O) turns to steam or ice, these are *physical* reactions (the water is still water but in a different state). Water that turns into a *different* substance — for instance, in the formation of alcohols — is however a *chemical* process. Whereas physical criteria deal with alterations or variations in the state of a substance, chemical criteria deal mainly with the structure of compounds and changes in compounds or elements.

For simplicity, we could just say that a chemical is a substance involved in a chemical process. This process is generated or produced by the interaction between different factors in the environment, inside a living organism (such as a bacterium, protozoan, plant, fungus, animal or human) or in a laboratory or factory.

Residues of harmful chemicals can accumulate along the food chain. The build-up may start with low levels of chemical contamination of plants that are eaten by cattle, sheep, pigs and poultry. As the chemicals gradually accumulate in the animals' fat tissue and organs, they become even more concentrated in animal-derived foods (such as meat, milk and eggs) that are often eaten by humans.

Although our bodies have detoxifying mechanisms that can deal with some harmful chemical residues, a life-long exposure to, or intake of, a poisonous chemical increases the number of milligrams of unwanted chemical to each kilogram of body-weight. In the final link of the food chain, a human baby can take in a harmful concentrated dose of chemicals from its mother's breast-milk.

NATURALLY OCCURRING CHEMICALS

People have learned from painful experience to differentiate between the plants, fungi and animals that are safe to eat and those which are not. Even so, many people throughout the world are harmed or killed each year by eating foods that are poisonous to humans. The natural toxins in some plants, fungi and animals are so dangerous that the food should *never* be eaten. But there are also foods containing natural toxins which can be eaten without any ill effect, provided they are prepared in a way that eliminates the hazard.

POISONOUS PLANTS AND FUNGI

With increased public interest in food from the wild and 'naturally' grown produce, it is possible that cases of food poisoning could increase if people accidentally eat toxic plants and mushrooms.

Cases of mistaken identity

Children are often attracted by the berries of a wide range of poisonous plants, including yew, holly, lily-of-the-valley and members of the nightshade family. However, even adults often poison themselves by mistaking an edible food for a toxic one — typically wild mushrooms.

Wild mushrooms

Eating just one small part of the death cap mushroom *Amanita phalloides* can cause death and it is responsible for up to 95 per cent of deaths from mushrooms. Death cap has some close cousins, such as the destroying angel *A. virosa*, that are also highly toxic. The toxic agent responsible, *amanitine*, binds rapidly to body tissue and about 12 to 24 hours after eating the mushroom, severe nausea and vomiting start. Diarrhoea, headache, mental confusion and jaundice follow. The liver, kidneys, brain and heart are particularly affected. Although treatment with penicillin has reduced the death rate, about half of all people poisoned do die from the symptoms.

Looking a little like the field mushroom (Agaricus campestris) to the unwary, these death cap mushrooms (Amanita phalloides) live up to their common name. Every part of the mushroom, including its spores, is extremely toxic and often causes death.

The striking red and white spotted mushroom fly agaric (*Amanita muscaria*) is not necessarily deadly, but contains substances which cause narcosis, convulsions and hallucinations. Sometimes referred to as the witches' mushroom and frequently depicted in children's book illustrations, the fungus has long been associated with magic, shamanistic rituals and the hallucinogenic sensation of flying.

Plants

Hemlock (*Conium maculatum*), which caused Socrates' death, is a member of the otherwise relatively harmless parsley family. It contains several substances which cause muscular paralysis. The symptoms start with nausea, vomiting and fever and proceed to increasing muscular failure followed by respiratory failure and death.

Yew (*Taxus baccata*), an evergreen tree that can be used as hedging, is frequently involved in food poisoning. Although all parts of the yew are poisonous, it is mostly the fruit — a red cup-like berry — which looks edible. After a rapid onset of about six hours, the symptoms are nausea, abdominal pain and possible heart failure.

Nightshades, including bittersweet (*Solanum dulcamara*), black nightshade (*Solanum nigrum*) and deadly nightshade (*Atropa belladonna*), grow wild in many parts of Europe. Poisoning usually results from eating the shiny berries, but other parts of the plant are also toxic. As few as three berries of deadly nightshade can be fatal. The symptoms include a dry mouth, rapid heartbeat and pupil dilation.

The castor bean plant (*Ricinus communis*) is often grown for ornamental purposes. Eating just one castor bean can cause fatal poisoning when the bean is chewed. (If the beans are swallowed whole, poisoning is unlikely to occur because the hard seed coat prevents rapid absorption of the toxic agent, ricin.) Symptoms start from two hours to several days after ingestion with a burning sensation in the mouth, nausea, vomiting, diarrhoea, abdominal pain, drowsiness and disorientation, finally leading to circulatory collapse and convulsions.

Keeping them off the menu
Most cases of mistaken identity are, of course, a matter of public awareness and outside your control. But you should consider the possibility of contaminated supplies when you undertake a hazard analysis (see Part 4).

Prepared for safe eating
Some familiar foods can be poisonous under certain circumstances and food preparation staff need to be clear about the preparation methods they should follow to make such foods safe to eat.

Potatoes
Every day millions of people eat potatoes (the tubers of *Solanum tuberosum*) in one form or another, most of them without knowing that this member of the nightshade family can be toxic.

When potatoes sprout they produce a natural chemical, solanine. If green or sprouting potatoes are eaten without first boiling them in water, solanine can cause a burning sensation in the mouth and throat, as well as general weakness, nausea, dizziness, delirium and convulsions. The fatal dose is 25mg of solanine for adults: a serving of 100g of green or sprouting potatoes could contain about 8mg of solanine. The chemical is water-soluble, which means that potatoes with partly green skins should be safe after boiling in water, but the water should not be consumed, for instance as stock or gravy. The greatest risk is if green or sprouting potatoes are used as jacket potatoes — potatoes baked in their skins — because the solanine is not destroyed.

Red kidney beans

These beans (*Vicia faba*) contain a toxic protein, haemagglutinin, which is heat labile (changeable by heat), so can be destroyed by boiling the beans for about ten minutes. If the beans are eaten without this treatment, they can cause nausea, vomiting, abdominal pain and diarrhoea. Most problems occur when beans are undercooked or when they are cooked slowly — perhaps in a 'slow cooker' — without first boiling them for ten minutes. If red kidney beans are ingredients in products such as vegetable burgers, the beans must still be boiled first. One possible control is to buy canned beans, because the canning process destroys the haemagglutinin.

Rhubarb

The cooked stalks of the rhubarb plant (*Rheum rhaponticum*) are edible, but the leaves and buds are toxic due to their high content of oxalic acid. (Raw stalks also contain very low concentrations and may be toxic.) The symptoms are nausea, vomiting, diarrhoea, abdominal pain and haemorrhages.

Nutmeg

Consumed in small quantities as a flavouring, nutmeg (*Myristica fragrans*) is safe. But eating large quantities can cause hallucinations and delirium accompanied by abdominal pain, headache and dizziness. Several car accidents in America have been attributed to intoxication from eggnogs which have been generously sprinkled with nutmeg. The responsible chemical is myristicine, which is said to produce hallucinatory effects.

Common ink cap

This mushroom (*Coprinus atrementarius*) is poisonous if it is consumed with alcohol or within about 48 hours of drinking alcohol. Fortunately this type of poisoning is not fatal, but you may suffer from severe abdominal pain.

POISONOUS ANIMALS

Some animals are *inherently* poisonous to people. Others become poisonous as a result of chemical reactions during decomposition, or because they have eaten substances which are harmless to them but can poison humans — a kind of second-hand poisoning that occurs at the top of the food chain.

Poisonous fish and shellfish

Poisoning from fish mainly affects the peripheral nervous system, those parts of the nervous system that carry information from the sensory organs and carry out involuntary functions such as breathing, digesting and sweating.

Inherently poisonous fish

The roe of some freshwater fish, such as sturgeon and catfish, are toxic during their reproductive season. Eels, sea lampreys and elephant fish are among the fish also known to produce *neurotoxins* — toxins that affect the nervous system. Symptoms of poisoning have also been recorded from the consumption of shark and ray. Some neurotoxins are destroyed by temperatures above 60°C.

Fugu (puffer fish)

In Japan, where puffer fish (*Arothron hispidus*) is known as *fugu,* the fish is eaten raw. As it has tetrodotoxin, a neurotoxin, in its intestines and gonads, all traces of these parts must be removed before the fish is safe to eat. The effects of the toxin are rapid — symptoms start 10 to 45 minutes after eating — and include unco-ordinated movement, numbness, weakness, nausea, vomiting, diarrhoea, abdominal pain, convulsions and paralysis. The mortality rate is more than 60 per cent. Tetraodon poisoning (the illness caused by tetrodotoxin) occurs throughout the tropical Pacific, Atlantic and Indian Oceans.

This elegant presentation of the Japanese delicacy of fugu fish has an invisible danger. If the fish has not been prepared properly, toxic poisoning will follow, with a high likelihood of death — about 20 a year. Chefs in Japan must have a special diploma to be permitted to prepare this dish.

Problems from spoilage — scombroid poisoning

Scombroid poisoning occurs after eating improperly stored dark-fleshed fish such as tuna, mackerel, herring, sardines and bonito. Proteins start to be destroyed by normal ageing processes soon after fish have been caught. If the fish are not refrigerated, frozen, canned or smoked immediately after being caught, spoilage bacteria, such as *Proteus* species, can turn usually harmless chemical compounds in the decaying tissue into highly toxic agents (scombrotoxins).

The toxin is found where there are high levels of histamine present in the fish. (Histamine is a substance released from damaged cells and associated with allergic reactions.) The histamine is produced by an enzyme reaction (decarboxylase) that converts the amino acid histidine, which is naturally present in the fish, into histamine. The enzyme is produced by spoilage bacteria: their multiplication is inhibited by storing the fish on ice or immediate processing. So, although the histamine itself is not the causative agent, controlling its formation seems to prevent the toxin from being produced.

The reaction to scombroid fish poisoning is like an allergic shock. After just a few minutes, symptoms can include a headache, nausea, cramp, vomiting, facial flushing and dryness, and burning sensations in the mouth. Characteristic red and itchy welts may develop. Difficulty in swallowing follows the initial symptoms and death from shock may occur.

Poisonous at the top of the food chain

Many types of marine fish that have fed on certain types of *alga* and other organisms are poisonous as human food. Some fish such as puffers, trigger fish and parrot fish are poisonous for most of the year, while others, such as moray eel, surgeonfish, moonfish and porcupine fish, are toxic only in certain seasons. Sometimes it depends on the part of the ocean where these fish live — so, poisonous fish in one locality may be completely harmless elsewhere. More than 300 species have been reported to cause fish poisoning.

Ciguatera poisoning

The most common type of fish poisoning, known as *ciguatera*, occurs with fish usually considered to be safe, such as mackerel, snapper, sea bass, perch, grouper, surgeonfish, barracuda, pompano and butterfly fish. These fish are not necessarily related but they all live in narrow stretches of coral reef. Ciguatera is a form of secondary toxicity brought about when algae that are toxic to humans enter the food chain — small fish eat algae, big fish eat small fish and humans eat the big fish. The toxin is mainly concentrated in the viscera (internal organs such as the intestine) and may not be completely removed by evisceration (removal of the organs). The toxin is heat stable and therefore cannot be destroyed by normal cooking processes.

Symptoms of acute poisoning begin between 30 minutes and four hours after ingestion and include numbness, tingling of the face and lips, nausea, vomiting, diarrhoea, dizziness, abdominal pain and muscular weakness. These symptoms can progress to a second stage of muscular paralysis or convulsions. Death from convulsions or respiratory arrest can occur within one to 24 hours. Patients who survive retain some of the first-stage symptoms for many weeks. They tend to sense temperature in reverse to normal, so that ice feels hot and heat seems cold. Cold objects can cause pain resembling that from an electric shock — a response known as electric shock syndrome.

Poisonous shellfish

Mussels, clams, oysters and other shellfish can become temporarily poisonous during the warm season after feeding on certain *dinoflagellates*, which are small protozoa in plankton. The toxins, which are thought to be a by-product of the protozoa or bacteria associated with them, accumulate in the digestive glands and gills of the shellfish without harming them. However, the shellfish may have become so poisonous to humans that eating just one contaminated mussel, clam or oyster could, in the case of paralytic shellfish poisoning (see page 128), result in death.

Two types of illness may result, depending on the kind of toxin involved:
- PSP — *paralytic shellfish poisoning*, which involves a neurotoxin, starts with tingling sensations or numbness in the mouth and spreads to the arms and legs within four to six hours
- DSP — *diarrhoeic* (or diarrhetic in American English) *shellfish poisoning*, which has symptoms of chills, nausea, abdominal pain, vomiting and diarrhoea within one to two hours.

If the patient survives the first 12 hours after eating the contaminated shellfish, recovery is likely. The fatality rate is between one and ten per cent.

Toxins associated with shellfish poisoning are usually heat stable, so are not destroyed by cooking. As the limiting growth temperature is between 8°C and 10°C, the usual recommendation is not to eat shellfish in the warm seasons: in the UK the rule of thumb is not to eat marine shellfish during months without a letter 'r' in their name — the summer months of May, June, July and August.

Poisonous mammals

Toxic mammals are not usually a problem for the British food industry, but some mammals from cold climates, such as sledge dogs (huskies), sea lions and polar bears, have been reported as being poisonous to humans. Most of the evidence stems from early polar expeditions.

Desperate measures

In 1912, faced with dwindling supplies and a 500km journey to their Antarctic base camp, Australian explorer Dr Douglas Mawson and his Swiss companion Xavier Mertz gritted their teeth against temperatures down to −30°C and winds up to 300km an hour. They were forced to eat their sledge dogs, one by one, little knowing that they were slowly poisoning themselves with an excessive intake of vitamin A from the dogs' livers. Mertz did not survive, but Mawson just made it back to camp alive. He was later knighted and is credited with significant discovery, mapping and scientific achievements.

⚙ MAKING IT EASIER FOR OTHERS

- Create clear rules for staff who purchase raw foods and ingredients that might contain naturally occurring chemicals.
- Establish clear rules for staff who deal with such foods.
- Consider banning staff from bringing foods and ingredients into the food premises that have been collected from the wild or obtained from sources other than your approved suppliers.

MYCOTOXINS

A large number of moulds produce toxic substances — *mycotoxins* — that can cause a range of serious illnesses and even death. These toxins are from a different chemical group to those produced by mushrooms and are sometimes considered as adulterants rather than as 'naturally occurring poisons'. As far as day-to-day food safety is concerned, it really does not matter how you categorise them and you should not be surprised to come across mycotoxins described as biological hazards rather than as chemical hazards. From a practical point of view and to avoid academic hair-splitting, you may simply prefer to think of mycotoxins as agents of 'non-bacterial food poisoning'.

AN UNDERESTIMATED PUBLIC HEALTH HAZARD

In the past, food contaminated by mould was often regarded as an economic nuisance rather than a health issue and spoiled, or 'rotten', crops were sometimes used as animal feed because they were considered to be harmless. Now, however, it is known that exposure to mould spores or the consumption of mycotoxins can lead to serious illnesses in both people and animals. Cereals (especially rye), nuts and dried fruit are among the foods most likely to be affected.

Although research continues into the degree of risk that mycotoxins pose generally to humans, it is known that mycotoxin-producing moulds can cause food-borne illness and that long-term exposure to mycotoxins can lead to cancer, organ damage and a number of other life-threatening conditions.

Preferred conditions

Mycotoxin-producing moulds tolerate a wide range of acidic and alkaline conditions and can be found in low pH products, such as fruit juice, in which bacteria have no chance of multiplication. The moulds tolerate low water activity down to 0.80 a_w, so can colonise 'dry' foods, giving them another advantage over bacteria.

BEYOND BACTERIA Moulds that produce mycotoxins can thrive in conditions where bacteria can rarely survive.

Moulds are aerobes and their preferred temperature range is from −7°C to 35°C. However, mycotoxins are heat resistant and can withstand pasteurisation and even sterilisation. At the other end of the temperature scale, the ability of moulds that produce mycotoxins to grow at a temperature below 0°C can be observed in many cold-stores and walk-in refrigerators in the form of black patches in moist, inadequately cleaned corners.

General control measures

As many preservation techniques have no significant impact upon mycotoxins, the most effective measures are at source, on the farm, and include preventive measures that minimise or eliminate the growth of mycotoxin-formers as well as rapid drying processes after harvesting. Also crucial are storage and transport under controlled anaerobic (sealed) conditions or frozen storage at very low temperatures (such as −18°C). Water activity is best kept at above 0.8 with a pH at below 3 or above 6.5.

There are several electronic sorting and detection methods using fluorescence under ultraviolet light for aflatoxins (see below). Any company using foods that are vulnerable to mycotoxin-producing moulds must not overlook them when carrying out a hazard analysis (see Part 4).

TYPES OF MYCOTOXIN

The following examples are those that are likely to be the most significant for food safety in food businesses in Europe.

Aflatoxins

In 1960 turkeys in a number of flocks in the south and east of England died without apparent reason and the illness was dubbed *turkey X disease*. Investigation showed that the causative agent was peanut meal imported from Brazil. This led to the first identification of *mycotoxicosis*, the general term for any illness caused by mycotoxins. Subsequently many samples of foodstuffs and peanut meal were tested for toxicity and a considerable number of samples from some 14 peanut-producing countries were found to be contaminated.

The fungus responsible was eventually identified as *Aspergillus flavus* and the type of toxin it produced was named *aflatoxin* after the species name — a(spergillus) fla(vus) toxin. Other types of fungus were also investigated and it was established that several moulds from the genera *Aspergillus* and *Penicillium* produce types of mycotoxin, all of which are referred to as aflatoxins.

Foods implicated
The foods which are most commonly contaminated by aflatoxins are:
- nuts
- cereals, including rice
- dried fruits.

Carry over
Research also shows that cows fed on foods containing aflatoxins excrete toxic milk. This phenomenon, which is typical for mycotoxins in general, is often described as *carry over* or the *carry-over effect* (see also page 122).

What happens is that toxins (in this case, aflatoxins) in the primary foodstuff (in this case, cattle feed) are carried over into the next link in the food chain (the cattle). The toxins accumulate in the body fat tissue of the organism (the cattle) and therefore in any food product, such as meat or milk for human consumption, that is gained from the organism.

LURKING DANGER
Mycotoxins can persist throughout the food chain and accumulate in animals used as human food.

Every link in the food chain must therefore be regarded as being at risk from a carry-over effect, because there is no technical process to eliminate mycotoxins once they have been ingested and incorporated into body tissue.

Symptoms
Aflatoxins are carcinogenic (can cause cancer tumours) and toxic to the liver. The illnesses that result can be *acute* or *chronic*. Acute symptoms include cramp, jaundice-like mucous membranes, loss of appetite and loss of body-weight.

Causes and preventive measures
Aflatoxins often form because of inappropriate food storage conditions and prolonged storage periods. The two most important factors influencing the formation of aflatoxins are high levels of moisture and the temperature.

Patulin
Several fungi of the genera *Aspergillus* and *Penicillium* can produce *patulin* in rotten fruit and other foods. The presence of patulin in food products usually indicates the use of mouldy raw materials.

Foods implicated
The foods which are most commonly contaminated by patulin are:
- fruit, including apples, bananas, pears, grapes, pineapples and peaches
- fruit juices
- bread.

Symptoms
Patulin is considered to be carcinogenic. High concentrations of patulin (levels as high as 440mg per litre) can cause acute symptoms like haemorrhage (severe bleeding) and oedema (internal swelling caused by fluid).

Preferred conditions
Some moulds can form the mycotoxin at temperatures below 2°C, so creating a particular risk to fruit and fruit juices kept in chilled storage for prolonged periods.

Ochratoxin
In the 1960s scientists first managed to isolate an unknown mycotoxin from South African cereals and vegetables infested by the organism *Aspergillus ochraceus*. The mycotoxin proved to be highly nephrotoxic (the cause of permanent kidney damage). Since then more than seven closely related substances of the ochratoxin group have been detected, of which Ochratoxin A is the best known and the most toxic.

Hazard to staple foods
Ochratoxin is particularly hazardous to food safety because it can affect so many staple foods (the major foods in the diet of a community), such as cereals,

cornflour and bakery products. When ochratoxin is present in animal feed, it has a carry-over effect like that of aflatoxins and accumulates in the animal carcass as well as in animal products. Some countries have legal limits for levels of ochratoxin. For instance, Denmark declares pork to be unfit for human consumption if pig kidneys contain more than 25mg of ochratoxin per kg of meat.

Foods implicated
This mycotoxin has been found in:
• cereals
• sweetcorn (maize)
• dried beans
• cocoa beans
• coffee beans
• soy (or soya) beans
• citrus fruits
• nuts, such as peanuts
• cured hams and other cured products.

Symptoms
The main symptom is kidney damage.

Control
The best way to deal with ochratoxin is at source, such as quick-drying processes, and storage under controlled dry conditions.

Ergot
St Anthony's fire was the name given, centuries ago, to symptoms caused by eating bread made from diseased grain. Victims, who suffered fire-like pain from gangrene in the fingers and toes, believed that they would be cured by a pilgrimage to the shrine of St Anthony. Today we know that these symptoms are caused by *ergot*, a toxin produced by the mould *Claviceps purpurea* which forms a hard black spur on ears of grain. The illness is now called *ergotism*, a form of *mycotoxicosis* (an illness from a mould toxin).

Ergotism is caused by a number of *alkaloids* — a group of chemical substances produced by plants and fungi — which are derivatives of lysergic acid, the main ingredient of the hallucinogenic drug LSD.

Some alkaloids — such as caffeine, which is found in tea, coffee and cola-based soft drinks — are relatively harmless. Others have modern medicinal uses — for example, low controlled doses of ergometrine, a constituent of ergot, are often administered towards the end of childbirth. However, some alkaloids — including nicotine, cocaine, morphine, atropine and alkaloids found in nightshades, such as bittersweet and deadly nightshade — can cause serious intoxication or death when digested in high or uncontrolled doses.

In its chronic form ergotism occurred in frequent and widespread epidemics causing many deaths in Europe throughout the Middle Ages. Even scientific advances have not totally eradicated it and an epidemic occurred in England as recently as the 1920s. Ergot is still an economic problem in many areas around the world that grow sorghum (Indian millet or 'Guinea corn') and there were outbreaks of ergot poisoning in the Russian Federation in 1997.

Foods implicated

The foods which are most commonly contaminated by ergot are:

- rye
- other grains.

Symptoms

High doses of ergot cause gangrene, the gradual mortifying (death) of tissue and limbs. Convulsions may also occur.

Preventive measures

The supplier's guarantee and checks on deliveries of cereals provide the best controls.

POSSESSION, RITUAL AND MIDWIFERY

Perfectly preserved for more than 2,000 years, the body of this man discovered in a peat bog in Grauballe, Denmark, in 1951 revealed that his last meal had included many ergot-contaminated grains. His throat had been cut from ear to ear, suggesting a ritual slaughter that may have included the use of ergot as part of the ritual or may have been prompted by fear at the man's symptoms — convulsions, or changes in his appearance because of gangrene. The hallucinogenic properties of ergot may be behind claims of possession and bewitchment in many countries in centuries past, including the events leading to the Salem Witch Trials in Massachusetts in 1692. Often used by medieval midwives in very small doses to ease childbirth, ergot was also used to abort unwanted pregnancies — a practice that probably contributed to the decision to burn many midwives as witches.

 **MAKING IT EASIER FOR OTHERS**

It is often easiest to explain a food safety problem, such as that from mycotoxins, by relating it to products that staff are likely to have in their own homes. So, ask staff for suggestions about products that are vulnerable to the growth of mould. They are likely to suggest nuts, cereals, bread, fruit, fruit juices, stewed fruits, cooked vegetables, jams and meat products. Most people have encountered mould on one of these at some time.

- Remind staff members about the health dangers posed by mycotoxins.
- Encourage them to consider changing any inappropriate old habits — for example, cutting off the mould 'beard' from bread and cheese or scraping off the mouldy layer of jam before using, serving or selling the rest of the product.
- Point out the risk to consumers' health of doing such things at work.
- Remind staff of their legal obligations and emphasise the importance of prevention as the best course of action.

INTRODUCED CHEMICALS

Chemicals used on crops have protected food from attack by fungi and insects while chemicals used on the land have helped to boost the number of harvests and increase their yields. Even so, there is a great deal of public concern about the long-term consequences for the safety of food and the environment from chemicals that were first hailed as wholly beneficial poisons.

PESTICIDES

The term *pesticide* covers several groups of substances designed to kill pests and weeds and to protect crops and stored products. Pesticides include:

- insecticides — insect control
- acaricides — mite control
- rodenticides — rodent control
- herbicides — plant protection
- fungicides — mainly for mould control.

Pesticides have helped to control diseases, such as malaria, protect sources of human food (such as the apple trees shown here) and increase crop yields, but the overuse, or careless use, of them can poison land, water and the food chain.

Pesticides can get into a human food product as a result of controlled and traceable measures, such as treating animal pens with insecticide to eliminate flies, or through less controllable environmental sources, such as water, soil and the air. Some pesticides can accumulate in the environment and join the food chain, becoming increasingly concentrated as they are moved along the links to the top of the chain.

Benefit or harm?

Although pesticides have been designed to protect sources of food for humans and the human environment, it should not be forgotten that they are intended to kill living organisms — a purpose which may create dangers to human health.

Many modern pesticides are now in the third or fourth generation of their chemical formulation and the scientists developing them take into account possible close encounters between people and pesticides. In the past, however, some substances threatened environmental havoc — for example, the organochloric compound DDT (dichlorodiphenyltrichloroethane) was found in the 1960s to persist and accumulate in the environment and the food chain, threatening to make some species of birds of prey extinct because their eggshells became thinner. This led to worldwide restrictions on the use and distribution of the chemical.

Of course, the potential benefits of applying pesticides need to be weighed against the potential hazards to human health.

In most cases, basic precautions and proper application of the chemical reduce the risk of chemical contamination to a level that is generally considered to be safe.

Public awareness of the possible damage from pesticides in farming may also have helped to curb any excessive or irresponsible use. Nonetheless, 'safe' pesticides can quickly become unsafe if they are stored in an inappropriate way or used in any way other than that specified by the manufacturer, such as spraying crops with an incorrect dilution of the chemical.

Control
An effective integrated pest management programme (see Part 4) should ensure that:
• pesticides do not come into direct contact with foodstuffs
• food contact surfaces that have been contaminated by pesticides must be decontaminated before re-use.

Nitrite, nitrate and nitrosamine
These chemicals are derivatives of nitrogen, which is represented by the chemical symbol N.

The nitrogen cycle
Nitrogen is a vital constituent of life on Earth. While animals obtain the nitrogen they need by eating plants or other animals, plants must extract it from the soil, mainly from derivatives of nitrogen such as ammonia (NH_3) and nitrates. With the help of bacteria — which, for example, release nitrogen from animal waste and from dead animals and plants — nitrogen is continuously recycled and re-used in processes known as the nitrogen cycle.

As nitrogen is a key to plant productivity, farmers use various methods to help the nitrogen cycle along, including:
• leaving fields fallow to enable nature to take its gradual course
• planting legumes (peas and beans) to provide a suitable habitat for billions of bacteria (various species of the genus *Rhizobium*) that live on the roots and 'fix' nitrogen
• spreading fertilisers to replace nitrogen and other chemicals rapidly.

There are practically no nitrate-free foodstuffs of *plant* origin whereas milk, fresh meat, fresh fish and eggs are *virtually free* of nitrates.

Nitrites and nitrates
Nitrites (NO_2^-) and *nitrates* (NO_3^-) are ubiquitous and necessary in the environment, but can also occur as environmental contaminants.

In the food industry the application of nitrite/nitrate combinations is a long-established method of meat preservation, which helps to retain the colour of meat in pickling and salting processes.

The chemicals must be used in controlled measures — the allowable residue of nitrite in food is just 0.01 per cent — as an overdose can result in *acute poisoning*, with symptoms including a fall in blood pressure, collapse, cyanosis (turning blue), coma and respiratory paralysis. Death follows if emergency measures are not taken. *Chronic poisoning* depends on the level of exposure.

Nitrates can cause problems in canned products which result in the breakdown of the lacquer used to coat the inside of the can, so allowing tin to leach into the food. Poisoning can also occur as a result of drinking water from a well where nitrates have leached in. The nitrates in the water can be converted to nitrite by the action of intestinal bacteria. This is especially dangerous if the water is used for reconstituting dried baby milk or baby food.

Nitrosamines
Nitrosamines are highly carcinogenic. They can be formed in foods from reactions between nitrites or nitrates with other compounds, or the presence of certain spices, such as pepper, which react with the nitrate and nitrate salts during the pickling process.

With fresh meat of reliable origin and flawless pickling methods (the addition of ascorbic acid to the pickling process counteracts the formation of nitrosamines), there should not be a problem at all. However, in meat which is less than fresh, a degradation of biochemical substances starts and secondary compounds form. If such meat is then pickled, nitrosamines can be formed. Also, if pickled products are exposed to temperatures above 160°C — for example, on a fierce barbecue — nitrosamines can form.

Polyaromatic hydrocarbons
Polyaromatic hydrocarbons (PAHs) are derivatives of phenol which are often used as antiseptics, disinfectants and germicides (you may know these as carbolic acid) and preservatives. Tar and creosotes are mixtures of phenolic compounds and other compounds produced by burning wood or coal— either in uncontrolled conditions, such as forest fires, or in intentional incineration processes, such as metallurgy, or in tobacco smoking. PAHs are widespread environmental residues. Many polyaromatic hydrocarbons are highly carcinogenic. They can be formed unintentionally when sausages, ham or other meat products are fried, barbecued or smoked, or when the cooking temperature is too high.

Dioxins
The word dioxin covers a group of chemicals that are organochlorine compounds. Among past uses of dioxins were the powerful insecticide DDT (see page 135) and the defoliant spray Agent Orange which was used by the American air force during the Vietnam War and subsequently linked to birth defects. Liver and heart defects, intestinal damage, chloracne (a form of eczema), neurological problems and cancer have all also been attributed to dioxins, while some experimental studies suggest that dioxins may be mutagenic (cause genetic alteration) in humans at extremely low doses.

In an accident at a chemical factory in Seveso, Italy, in 1976 dioxins contaminated a wide area, prompting major health concerns. In the late 1990s there was a scandal in Belgium about levels of dioxins in food when it was alleged, among other things, that chickens were given feed containing high levels of dioxin.

The World Health Organization has defined a level of intake of dioxins considered to be tolerable, and dioxins exist in small quantities in many foods including vegetables, meat, milk, eggs and fish.

Dioxins can be formed when organic substances smoulder or burn in the presence of chlorine. This may happen in the burning of fossil fuels, such as during the production of steel and aluminium, during industrial bleaching of cellulose such as paper production, and also in crematoria.

METALS

Metals are common elements distributed in nature in varying quantities around the Earth. They can enter food by a number of routes — for example, direct contact with unsuitable food containers, industrial pollution of soil used for growing crops and contamination of water from agricultural chemicals.

High levels
All our food contains tiny traces of metals. Usually this is not a reason for concern, but there is a genuine danger to human health if high levels of heavy metals are present. They have caused some dramatic cases of poisoning and heavy metals are banned from use as food containers or food-contact surfaces.

Heavy
Heavy metals are those with a high atomic mass, such as cadmium, lead, mercury and zinc. They are pure elements that are more likely to combine with other compounds. In low pH environments in particular they pass into their ionized form which prepares them to bind with inorganic or organic substances. They can attach themselves to proteins and change the character of the original compound. If the protein is a functional agent, such as an enzyme, and its original function is altered or blocked, a cascade of toxic reactions can occur.

The next three pages outline the problems to food safety caused by some metals.

Lead
Lead in the environment is almost impossible to avoid. Lead was used for many years in typesetting, batteries, paint, toys, solder, electric cable covering, pottery glaze, water pipes and brass alloys. Some of these, such as paint, no longer contain lead but there are still other sources, including fumes from motor vehicles, ashes and fumes from burning, and lead in water despite extensive programmes of lead-pipe replacement.

The most serious toxic effects in humans arise from damage to the brain and the peripheral nervous system. The accumulation of levels of lead in the brain and the liver can be five to ten times the level in blood. Lead is deposited in the skeleton where it accumulates and remains for life. The symptoms are tiredness, loss of appetite, pallor and headaches. Lead poisoning is usually chronic.

Dangers in the food chain

Cattle may be poisoned by lead — for instance, if they feed from contaminated soil or from food or water containers in which red lead (minium) is used as a rust preventative. Minium poisoning leads to acute neurotoxic symptoms. The livestock cannot be used for beef for human consumption because there is no process for reducing the lead content in meats. In 1989 milk from cows on about a thousand British farms was contaminated by lead from feed pellets that had been in contact with lead sulphate during transport.

Food preparation and storage

Lead poisoning can occur through the misuse of ceramic containers glazed with lead oxides. *Acute* symptoms include a metallic taste remaining in the mouth, abdominal pain, vomiting, diarrhoea and characteristic black stools. In the past, a common cause of lead poisoning was the action of soft water on lead water pipes but most such pipes have now been replaced.

Most national regulations in the European Union have *critical limits* for the permitted lead content of various foods. Precautions can include using meat, and especially offal, only from young animals because the lead content accumulates with age.

Cadmium

Cadmium is used for plating metals and in the manufacture of bearing alloys, batteries and silver solders. It can carry yellow and orange pigments, so is widely used in the colour, varnish and plastics industries. Cadmium plating is soluble in acid foods such as fruit juices and vinegar, and it is banned for food contact under British food regulations.

Cadmium can get into the atmosphere, water and soil as smoke which is created when products containing cadmium are heated above the metal's melting point, for example, during ore smelting or industrial waste disposal.

However, cadmium is mainly accumulated in plants. The uptake occurs via the root system, from where it spreads into other plant organs.

CADMIUM DAMAGES HUMAN CELLS

The toxic potential of cadmium was revealed fully after the investigations into the itai-itai disease in Japan. The Japanese word itai means 'it hurts' or 'ouch'. Farmers and their families had been living for several years on rice which had been grown in waste water from smelting works that was contaminated with cadmium. The victims had pathological alterations to their bone structures, resulting in 'glass bones' and collapsing spines.

Animals feeding from cadmium-contaminated plants then accumulate the metal in their livers and kidneys and other organs eaten by humans as offal. Wild mushrooms can also absorb high levels of the metal.

Mercury

Mercury and its salts are used in the manufacture of thermometers, felt, cellulose, paints, explosives, lamps, electrical appliances and batteries. The burning of coal around the world emits about 3,000 tons of mercury into the atmosphere every year. The main influence that mercury has on foodstuffs arises from waste water and exhaust fumes from combustion engines. The accumulation of mercury in environmental water is much higher than in agricultural food chains. Ingestion of mercuric salts can cause acute poisoning which affects the intestines and kidneys. Chronic poisoning leads to accumulation in the body — for instance, in the hair — and in permanent damage to the central nervous system.

Toxic seed coating

Some mercury compounds are used to treat cereal seeds to delay spoilage during storage. In sporadic incidents, starving people in famine-affected areas of Iraq, Pakistan and Guatemala ate such seeds rather than planting them and were poisoned.

As mad as a hatter

In the past, hatters treated the felt, from which many hats were made, with a mould inhibitor made from mercury salt solutions. During their professional lives hatters working with felt were constantly exposed to mercury vapours. Inhalation and skin contact often led to chronic poisoning which manifested itself as, among other symptoms, depression, hallucinations and mental deterioration.

This may be the origin of the saying 'as mad as a hatter'. Some people suggest that the character of Lewis Carroll's hatter in 'A Mad Tea-Party' in *Alice's Adventures in Wonderland* may be explained in this way.

'MINAMATA DISEASE'

Between 1953 and 1960 more than 100 people in Minamata Bay, Japan, were suffering from unidentified, serious nervous complaints and 45 people died. (Some environmentalists say that several hundred people died.) Eventually, the symptoms were traced to methyl mercury compounds which had drained into the sea from a chemical factory. Mercury had been accumulating in local marine fish on which the local fishing community were more or less living. The Minamata victims had about 70mg to 100 mg of mercury to every kilogram of their body-weight.

Other toxic metals

Acute poisoning can arise from ingesting aluminium, copper, tin and zinc. Symptoms include burning pain in the mouth and throat, vomiting and retching, watery or bloody diarrhoea, tenesmus (a disorder of the rectum), haemolysis (destruction of red blood cells), anuria (kidney failure), liver damage with jaundice, hypotension, collapse and convulsions.

Copper

All copper salts are highly toxic. Copper poisoning typically occurs when antique copper and novelty souvenirs, such as copper kettles, are used for the preparation or decorative display of *acidic* foods. In these circumstances copper ions will migrate from the container into the product and cause poisoning.

Arsenic

Used in ant poisons, insecticides, weed killers, paint, ceramics and glass, arsenic is not only a strong poison but is also carcinogenic. The initial symptoms of acute poisoning from ingestion include those of gastro-enteritis, burning sensation in the throat, vomiting and bloody or watery diarrhoea. Later the skin becomes cold and clammy, the blood pressure falls and death may follow from circulatory failure. If the victim survives, there may be jaundice. Chronic poisoning from ingestion or inhalation includes symptoms of polyneuritis (disorder of the peripheral nervous system), burning pain in the hands and feet, changes in skin colour and texture, weight loss, liver damage, cancer and cardiac failure.

Thallium

Once used as a rodenticide and an ant killer, thallium is now prohibited as a pesticide. Poisoning resulted most frequently from accidental ingestion of bait.

Aluminium

Aluminium can leach from old, worn kitchen utensils and containers. Some herbs, such as leaf tea, are known to accumulate aluminium in high doses as they grow.

Zinc

This is a natural component of many enzymes, so many foodstuffs contain zinc in small concentrations. In industry, base zinc is used in welding, metal cutting and smelting galvanised iron. Zinc salts are water soluble and can be formed by reaction with acidic foods on galvanised utensils. As zinc can become corroded by aggressive sanitizers, zinc surfaces should not come into contact with food at all. Fatalities have been reported following the ingestion of 10g of zinc sulphate.

Tin

Contamination can occur when tin-plated cans are used for the long-term storage of acidic foods, such as stewed fruit, causing the tin to leach. This is why it is good practice to store canned food in a non-metallic container once the can has been opened. The Food and Agriculture Organization and the World Health Organization have recommended a critical limit of 250mg of tin to every kg of food.

CLEANING CHEMICALS

Chemical poisoning from substances such as lubricants, glue and cleaning chemicals used in a food room usually results from careless handling or a lack of know-how.

The cleaning process

The use of products may involve diluting the chemical to the correct concentration specified, then using a dosing container such as a spray. Normally the process involves rinsing to remove any chemical residues from surfaces. While most traces of residue from cleaning chemicals will only taint food products, so that they may smell or taste unpleasant, or both, there are some cleaning chemicals which should never be used in food premises as they contain toxic components. Examples are phenolic substances and aldehyde compounds.

The disinfection process

Chemical disinfectants are designed and formulated to kill micro-organisms by interrupting essential metabolic actions or by *denaturing* vital cell components (changing the protein or nucleic acid structure). It is, of course, important to ensure that these effects are not transmitted to the food or to humans because the chemicals cannot distinguish between micro-organisms and other types of cell. As many disinfectants contain substances such as chlordioxide, iodine, sulphuric acid, formaldehyde, fluoride and nitric acid, which can poison humans in certain doses, their application needs to be controlled with considerable care.

Advice to hand

Reputable manufacturers of chemical cleaning and disinfection substances offer ample advice and training information for the use of their products in every branch of the food industry. Their expertise should be sought and implemented. Legal requirements, such as the Control of Substances Hazardous to Health Regulations 1999 (COSHH) require the correct application, storage and use of chemicals. You will also find more information on the control of chemical hazards in Part 4.

 MAKING IT EASIER FOR OTHERS

- Ban the use of equipment that is unfit for food contact, such as zinc or lead containers.
- Ensure that staff use work surfaces, containers and equipment only for their approved and designated purposes.
- Ban the use of utensils and equipment that have not been bought from approved suppliers.
- Encourage staff to report flaking equipment and utensils, such as special or protective coatings, to their manager or supervisor.
- Make certain that cleaning chemicals will not cause corrosion.
- Train staff how to use and store cleaning chemicals safely.
- Supervise the use of cleaning chemicals with care.
- Remind staff regularly that cleaning chemicals are carefully formulated to do particular jobs and that using more of the chemical than recommended by the manufacturer is unlikely to improve their effectiveness but may cause food poisoning.

⦿ MANAGEMENT MATTERS

Chemical contamination of food is much less common than bacterial contamination and occurs in various forms — naturally occurring, mycotoxins and introduced — which may require slightly different preventive measures. From a management perspective perhaps the most important questions to ask yourself are:

- which chemical hazards can appear in which products used in my workplace?
- why could the contamination happen — for example, because of pollution, contamination of raw materials or improper handling of introduced chemicals during production?
- what is the likely effect on the consumer?
- how can I influence and/or control this hazard?

More information about answering these questions and on dealing with chemical hazards is given in Part 4, but it is always important to remember that chemical contamination can occur at any stage of the production chain — from the growing of the raw materials through to the finished product. When chemical contamination happens in food premises it is usually due to carelessness in handling introduced chemicals. Nonetheless, managers must also be aware of the possibility of chemically contaminated foods entering their food premises. The following points are suggestions for your consideration.

- Nominate approved suppliers and consider banning from the premises any foods and ingredients from other sources.
- Develop appropriate buying policies for foods and ingredients that might be vulnerable to chemical contamination, such as cereals.
- If your company purchases cereals directly from the primary producer, make certain that staff have been adequately trained to check the appearance of the grains, or ears of grain, and to recognise ergot contamination.
- Ensure that checks for signs of mould are made before purchase, but ensure that staff are also trained to make thorough checks on deliveries to your premises.
- Provide adequate suitable storage, such as dry goods stores with dry conditions.
- Make regular checks on food in storage.
- Provide separate storage areas for cleaning chemicals and cleaning equipment and emphasise the importance of segregating such materials and equipment to prevent contamination.
- Make sure that containers, cupboards, stores, refrigerators, freezers and utensils are kept clean.
- Emphasise the importance of stock control and of using food before it goes past its *use by* or *best before* date.

PHYSICAL HAZARDS

Have you ever found a hair or a fingernail in your food or even the proverbial fly in your soup? How did it make you feel? Probably reluctant to continue eating. Perhaps you complained. If so, you were not alone. Physical contaminants in food cause many customer complaints simply because — unlike microbes and most forms of chemical contamination — they are so obvious. They do not always cause injury, but they are still completely unacceptable to consumers — and to the law. What's more, they are clear evidence that something has gone wrong in the management of food safety.

This chapter outlines the kinds of physical hazard that affect food. Additional advice about detecting and controlling physical hazards is given in Part 4.

WHAT IS A PHYSICAL HAZARD?

You will recall that a food hazard is anything that might cause harm to a consumer. Physical hazards are simply physical contaminants, which are sometimes called 'foreign bodies'. Physical hazards fall into two main categories:
- objects that could cause physical injury — such as splinters, buttons or glass or metal fragments
- objects that are offensive but not necessarily dangerous — such as hair, caterpillars, plasters or dirt.

Medically, the first kind is more serious. The objects may cut the skin, obstruct the respiratory or digestive system, or lodge inside the body causing tearing. They can also create a hazard to general health and well-being. However, the second category of object is just as damaging for a food business — perhaps even more so, because of the strong emotional reaction that objects in food can provoke in customers.

Disgust — the power of the mind

People vary enormously in what they find disgusting in food. Some like to think of themselves as tough and claim not to be put off by anything. Others, perhaps the majority, feel there should be no possibility of anything offensive entering their food. Disgust also depends on culture and society: in some parts of the world insects and larvae, such as termites and maggots, are gourmet food, while in other regions cheese is regarded as rotten milk.

If everyone has a different idea of what is disgusting, why should we bother about the concept at all? Consider a situation in which you bite into a cockroach in your bread roll. You are unlikely to be physically injured and, strictly speaking, you have not been exposed to a health hazard because the poor insect has been thoroughly baked and is microbiologically sterile. Still, you will probably not regard a cockroach as welcome extra nutrition but as a cause for disgust and a reason to complain. If you are really horrified you may vomit. Perhaps you will never be able to eat a roll again or may suffer nightmares about cockroaches.

Hackney LBC won fines and costs of £700 after the [redacted] Bakery of Stoke Newington, London admitted a food safety offence. A customer complained that a bread roll contained a cockroach, and an EHO inspection found cockroaches beneath ovens and on a table used for making confectionery.

Remember that a hazard is anything with the potential to harm a consumer. Clearly for some people the reaction to a cockroach will be so strong that it falls into this category.

Unseen hazards

An interesting question arises here that is worth a brief diversion: is the cockroach a hazard only because people notice it and are revolted by it? After all, many other things could theoretically happen behind the scenes that would disgust consumers if only they knew about them.

Imagine for a moment that, even though your roll was free from cockroach, it had been mixed, kneaded and baked by staff with unwashed hands in a filthy bakery, full of mould, dirt and pest excretions. The baking process would have killed the pathogens in the bread and, even if the filth and mould recontaminated the bread, there would be nothing visible to upset you. However, if you came to know about the conditions under which the food had been produced, you would quite probably feel nauseous. So there is still a theoretical potential for harm, just as when the evidence is there for all to see.

OBJECTIONABLE
Food that consumers find disgusting can be classed as hazardous.

Food safety law, as you will see in the next chapter, is as much concerned with the potential for harm as it is with actual, visible contaminants. By law food premises must be kept clean and maintained in good repair and condition, employees must work in hygienic ways and businesses must identify the hazards in their own workplaces then adopt measures to prevent the *potential for harm* from becoming *actual harm*.

THE SOURCE OF THE PROBLEM

As far as preventive management is concerned, it is helpful to consider the sources of physical hazards in two main categories — those:
- associated with the food itself (*intrinsic contamination*)
- introduced from external sources (*extrinsic contamination*).

Intrinsic contamination

Intrinsic contaminants were part of the original plant or animal and are inedible or undesirable, or both. Plants used as food or ingredients may include twigs, pits, stones or kernels, while meat may have bones, gristle or skin that consumers expect to have been removed before service or sale. In either case, the problem lies at the start of the food processing chain.

Extrinsic contamination

Wood, glass, cardboard, insects, hairs and dozens of other objects can be introduced into food during storage, processing, transport, display or almost any other stage between harvesting or slaughter and the consumer's point of purchase. Such incidents are serious as they can cause severe injuries and give rise to extremely damaging publicity.

Prevention is therefore vital and if lapses do occur, they must always be investigated thoroughly and a fresh hazard analysis must be conducted (see Part 4).

The following paragraphs suggest some of the most typical extrinsic contaminants in food.

NOT IN THE RECIPE

Some of the items that have found their way into food can be difficult to credit. In 1983 a researcher reported coming across objects including a rubber boot, an umbrella handle, a hat, half a Bible, pieces of farm machinery and a typewriter.

Metal
Nuts, bolts, swarf and other metal hazards usually come from machinery and equipment.

Glass and other brittle materials
Fragments of glass, plastic, porcelain or other brittle materials can cause serious injuries and must be prevented from entering food products at all costs. There are many potential sources of sharp fragments, such as lamps and light tubes, bottles and jars, crockery and windows.

Packaging materials
Staples, strings, cardboard, soft plastic and polythene can enter food when deliveries are unpacked or during the packaging and dispatching of finished products.

Rubber and plastic
Small rubber and plastic items such as utensils, disposable gloves, vending machine cups and rubber bands can all find their way into food.

Home-made patches and repairs
Staff are often very creative in finding ways to patch up utensils and equipment with tape, wire and other inappropriate means. This must be discouraged as all such materials represent a potential source of physical contamination.

Wood
Containers, pallets and surfaces made of wood can all produce splinters that may contaminate food.

Animal pests
Insects, birds, rodents and other animals can all introduce physical contamination. The problem is not just the animals themselves, which sometimes end up in food

products, but also their hair, droppings, feathers, eggs, pupae, larvae and skins.

Personal items
Cigarette butts, sweet wrappers, chewing gum, jewellery and other small personal objects show that somebody has not understood the rules about eating, smoking and personal hygiene.

Building materials
Sometimes the building structure itself can cause contamination. Broken tiles, flaking paint and rust from old pipes can all find their way into food.

Tools and clothing
Pens, pencils, pen caps, screwdrivers and other small tools — even pagers — can easily slip out of a breast pocket. Insufficient or unsuitable protective clothing can also be a source of contaminants, adding hairs, buttons, fibres and other odds and ends to the list of potential problems.

The deliberate contamination of food is known as malicious tampering. It is sometimes done by blackmailers outside the company but it may also happen on the premises if employees are disaffected. The type of physical contaminant involved depends to some extent on the opportunities for tampering without raising suspicion.

 ## MAKING IT EASIER FOR OTHERS

Teaching people about physical hazards is easier than explaining microbiological or chemical contamination. Offending items such as hairs, insects and glass can be seen and there is no complex theory to explain.

- Encourage staff to identify and categorise likely physical hazards in their own workplace.
- Consider teaching prevention in terms of five key factors:
    - good housekeeping
    - buildings and equipment
    - personal hygiene
    - awareness and hazard spotting
    - pest control.

⊛ MANAGEMENT MATTERS

Compared to microbiological hazards, physical hazards are in many ways much easier to deal with — they do not, for example, breed and multiply, so problems are more readily identifiable and containable. On the other hand, processes such as heat, chemical treatment and irradiation that kill bacteria are absolutely useless when it comes to physical objects. While standardised measures can deal with microbiological hazards, preventing 'foreign bodies' from entering food depends on a host of factors to do with the individual nature of the premises and processes involved.

Preventing physical hazards calls for a two-pronged approach aimed firstly at the physical environment (building materials, equipment, packaging, fittings) and secondly at people and their attitudes. Often the second aspect is overlooked even though the personal aspect is usually far more significant to food safety than the objects that members of staff work with. The issues involved are discussed in greater detail in Part 4.

LEGAL REQUIREMENTS

♔ KEY POINTS

Food safety legislation in the UK 151

The relationship between British and European Union food safety legislation.
The application of European directives to member states.
The main requirements of legislation in the UK dealing with food safety.
The role of industry guides, codes of practice and guidance on food safety.
How legislation is enforced and the actions that can be taken by enforcement officers.
The consequences of legal non-compliance.
Legislation as a guide to effective management practice.

KEY WORDS

ambient shelf stable
products that do not readily support the multiplication of pathogens and spoilage organisms, so can be stored in their packaging without refrigeration or freezing during storage or transport.

authorised officer
a qualified person authorised by a food authority to take action on food safety matters.

due diligence
a defence that every possible precaution was taken to avoid breaching food safety legislation.

emergency prohibition order/notice
legal documents authorising the closure of a food business which is considered to be an imminent risk to health.

improvement notice
a legal document requiring improvements to be made in food premises.

nature or substance or quality
a legal requirement to sell food that is constituted as the consumer expects.

unfit food
food that is not suitable for human consumption.

ready-to-eat
food produced for immediate consumption, without further treatment (except perhaps for heating).

FOOD SAFETY LEGISLATION IN THE UK

The list of legislation connected with food is long and comprehensive, covering broad issues of food safety and hygiene, composition, quality, labelling, standards and packaging as well as product-specific issues, such as those affecting meat, poultry, shellfish and dairy foods. In this chapter we concentrate on the legislation covering the *general* issues of food safety and hygiene in the United Kingdom, which covers England, Wales, Scotland and Northern Ireland.

UK LAW IN CONTEXT

The separate legal systems of Scotland and Northern Ireland vary slightly from that of England and Wales for historical reasons. Until 1990 food legislation differed throughout the UK. Now the *main* food legislation is the same throughout the UK, although there is still some separate provision for Scotland and Northern Ireland. There were two main reasons for the change in 1990. The first was the need to have legislative consistency throughout member states of what is now the European Union (EU) and the second was to enable the British food industry to operate to consistent legal standards throughout the UK.

European legislation

British laws are aligned with and formed by European Union legislation, of which three types are relevant to food safety — regulations, directives and decisions.

Regulations

These are legally binding in member states as soon as they have been agreed by the Council of Ministers. Member states have no option but to enforce them word for word. There are currently no European regulations in force with respect to food safety, although this could change in the future.

Directives

Almost all national food safety legislation in member states has its origin in an EU directive. The wording of a directive is to some extent open to interpretation in each member country and, unlike an European regulation, must be re-enacted in the country's own legislation.

There are two types of directive. *Horizontal directives* apply right across the food industry. Typical examples are the General Food Hygiene Directive and directives dealing with labelling, articles and materials in contact with food and food additives. *Vertical directives* apply to an industry sector such as meat and meat products, milk and milk products, game, eggs, fish and fish products or shellfish.

Decisions

These are applied either to a particular product, or to a particular country, whether an EU member or not. For example, decisions have been used to ban the importation of products into the European Union from a country which has a particular food safety problem or to ban the export of a product from an EU country where there has been a problem — there was a ban on exporting British beef, for example, in the wake of BSE. Decisions are legally binding on relevant member states.

British legislation

There are two types of law in the UK which are important to food safety — primary and secondary legislation.

Primary legislation

This is an Act of Parliament which must be presented to Parliament as a Bill, debated in both the House of Commons and the House of Lords and voted upon before it is enacted.

In the case of food safety, the primary legislation in England, Wales and Scotland is the Food Safety Act 1990. This is an *enabling* Act. It deals with the general provisions, such as powers, offences and defences, that are necessary to establish and maintain a food control system and it enables ministers to make regulations that cover more specific matters. The Act covers, among other issues, definitions of food and food that is unfit for human consumption, powers of entry for *authorised officers*, offences, defences, improvement notices, emergency prohibition orders and notices and the seizure and condemnation of unfit food.

In Northern Ireland the Food Safety (Northern Ireland) Order 1991 is the enabling legislation.

Secondary legislation

This covers such things as regulations made under the primary legislation. There are regulations to cover all the horizontal and vertical directives. Regulations are generally much more detailed and prescriptive than Acts. An analogy would be of the Act as a skeleton and the regulations as the muscles attached to the bones.

OUTLINE OF MAJOR BRITISH FOOD SAFETY LEGISLATION

The following pages in this chapter outline the main provisions of the Food Safety Act 1990 and the general requirements of some of the regulations made under it. While the greatest care has been taken in compiling the information, you should be aware that the chapter does not claim to be a comprehensive or authoritative interpretation of food safety legislation in the UK. The writers, editors and publishers cannot be held responsible for actions or omissions taken on the basis of this general guidance which is provided in good faith.

Food managers should always have to hand a copy of the current relevant legislation (including sector-specific or product-specific legislation, where relevant), keep themselves up to date and take qualified specialist and/or legal advice on legal matters.

FOOD SAFETY ACT 1990

The Food Safety Act 1990, which covers England, Wales and Scotland, deals with the safety of food from primary production through all possible stages to sale or service to the consumer. Similar provision is made under the Food Safety (Northern Ireland) Order 1991.

THE 1990 ACT
It is divided into four parts.

The legislation places duties on government ministers, food authorities (effectively environmental health departments or trading standards departments) and food businesses.

Duties and powers of ministers

The Act allows ministers to make regulations and imposes certain duties or powers. Ministers can, for example, issue an *emergency control order* covering commercial operations where something is considered to pose an imminent risk of injury to health. They can also remove powers from a food authority which is considered to be failing to carry out its duties properly. Ministers also have powers to issue *codes of practice* (see page 164) to food authorities to provide guidance on enforcing the Act and its regulations. There is a long list of such codes, including separate ones for many of the regulations and some dealing with topics such as improvement notices, the seizure of food and food hygiene inspections.

Duties of food businesses

The legal responsibility for offences by a food business under this Act and its regulations normally lies with the *proprietor* of the business. This is usually the owner, the most senior manager or person in charge or, in the case of a limited company, the company secretary.

A court may also prohibit a proprietor or manager from working in a food business following a conviction.

The duties of food businesses can be divided roughly into two categories — obligations with regard to the food being sold and obligations to co-operate with enforcement officers.

Landlord fined over filthy pub

HEALTH inspectors found crawling insects, dried blood, out-of-date food and conditions were 'appalling'

By JOHN MANNING

Obligations concerning food to be sold

This group of duties goes right to the heart of food safety responsibilities.

NATURE,
SUBSTANCE,
QUALITY
Section 14.

Nature or substance or quality

All food sold must be 'of the *nature or substance or quality* demanded by the purchaser'. While the meaning of these three terms is straightforward in the context of food safety, people are often confused by them.

Nature deals with type or variety and is concerned with authenticity. So, you should not sell Golden Delicious apples as if they were Granny Smith's, or whiting fillets as haddock, and you should not say that something was produced in Scotland when in fact it originated in Argentina.

Trading standards act on allergy meal

A █████ restaurant owner was fined £2,000 and ordered to pay £625 costs after a university student suffered a severe allergic reaction to a chicken korma containing peanut.

The case was brought at ████ magistrates court last ██████away staff if ██ trading standards con-tain██ neanuts, saying she was allergic to them.

...that there was confusion in the

quest, which was disregarded.
█mple of the meal for peanut pro-
█ccounted for seven per cent of the
██ was prosecuted under Section
safety Act 1990.
██ity to selling to the purchaser's
██ korma which was not of the substance ██████ded.

The case led to an allergy awareness campaign by TSOs throughout Yorkshire and Humberside.

Substance refers to the composition of food, which should have the proper ingredients. If it is stated that a food contains x, y and z but actually contains only x and y, then the food is clearly not what the customer reasonably expected. Although this could be considered to be a labelling infringement, it is a matter of the substance of the food.

sold mouldy milkshake

A mouldy milkshake, 10 days past its sell-by date, has led to a £6,500 fine for ████ ███ Stores. In August 1999, a customer bought a four-pack Friji Fr███ ███████ Wharf.

████ milkshake, when he discovered mould growth. He complained to Tower Hamlets LBC's food safety team, which carried out an investigation into ████ safety systems.

It was considered appropriate to prosecute, under Section 8 (1) of the Food Safety Act, for selling con-taminated food, when it was discovered that the

been missed by 30 safety checks
August.
█████ guilty to the offence, but appealed
against the £6,500 fine with £3,500 costs, which was
imposed by Thames Magistrates Court. Southwark
Crown Court dismissed the appeal, awarding a further £600 in costs to the council. The Southwark
recorder said that the fine was appropriate because
██ was a large company and had pleaded guilty to
the offence. It also appeared that there had been a
"relatively high degree of negligence" by the
company, because the milkshake had gone through 30
checks and had not been picked up.

Quality, although a hard concept to define generally, is relatively easy to understand in this context. The customer expects a certain quality, such as firm but ripe fruit, and should not therefore receive something inferior, such as bruised mouldy fruit.

Unfit food

A food business is obliged to sell food that is *fit for human consumption*. This is a common sense statement but how does the law actually define 'fit for human consumption'? As is often the case in law, the meaning is not defined, but its opposite — in this case *unfit* — is made clear. The Act stipulates that food offered for sale should meet 'food safety requirements' and specifies that food does *not* meet those requirements if it:

FOOD SAFETY
REQUIREMENTS
Section 8.

- has been rendered injurious to health — in other words, someone has done something to the food which has made it unfit
- is unfit for human consumption — the most common example of this is food that has gone off
- is so contaminated, whether by extraneous matter or otherwise, that it would not be reasonable to expect someone to eat it in that state.

If food intended for sale is treated in a way that it becomes injurious to health, the law also takes into account the cumulative effect of eating such a food over a long period. The clause about contamination (the last in the list above) is interesting because the food involved does not necessarily have to be harmful to health. Similar clauses appear in food safety law in many countries. For example, in

Germany it is nicknamed the 'loathsome' clause, as most people would find it loathsome, or objectionable, to eat such food even though it may be harmless.

On page 145 we gave the example of a cockroach baked into a bread roll. Eating the cockroach would do no harm to health, but it would make most people's flesh creep even to imagine eating such a roll. Interestingly, if someone were to eat such a roll, discover the cockroach and subsequently vomit, the offence could change to that of selling food that was injurious to health — even though the vomiting results from a psychological reaction.

Properly labelled
While there are detailed regulations covering labelling, the Act itself also makes it an offence to misleadingly label food or to describe food falsely.

Obligations to co-operate with enforcement officers
This group of requirements are administrative and procedural.

Compliance with regulations
An obvious but important duty imposed on food businesses is to comply with the provisions of the Act and with any regulations made under it.

Obstruction
Authorised officers of the food authority have legal powers of entry into food premises (see below). It is an offence to obstruct an authorised officer in any way. Obstruction covers the barring of entry, failing to provide information and supplying false information.

OBSTRUCTION
Section 33.

Duties and powers of enforcement officers and food authorities
The Act places a number of duties on the food authority (usually the local authority) and its enforcement officers who are usually environmental health officers (EHOs). The first and foremost duty is to enforce the provisions of the Act and the regulations made under it in the local authority's geographical area. There are also other duties such as appointing a public analyst, who usually carries out chemical analyses of food, and food examiners, who usually carry out microbiological analyses of food.

Power of entry
An authorised officer of the food authority has the power of entry into food premises at all reasonable hours and, after giving 24 hours' notice, may also enter a private dwelling house. If there is resistance to the right of entry, a warrant may be issued by a Justice of the Peace (JP) at short notice to authorise entry, by force if necessary. Authorised officers may also inspect any records, including computer records, and seize them if they are required as evidence.

POWER OF ENTRY
Section 32.

Improvement notices
An authorised officer may serve an improvement notice on the proprietor of a food

business requiring work to be done to comply with the Act or regulations made under the Act. The notice must specify which regulation has been contravened, the work to be done and the time in which the work must be carried out. Failure to comply with such a notice is an offence. These notices can be used for many things including processes, structure, equipment and methods, but cannot be used for something ongoing, such as keeping something clean.

Emergency prohibition notices and orders

If an authorised officer believes there to be an imminent risk to health, then he or she can issue an *emergency prohibition notice*. This notice, which can apply to the whole business or to any part of it, must be ratified by a Magistrates' or Sheriff court within three days. Provided that the court is satisfied that the notice was served justly, it will issue an *emergency prohibition order* which remains in force until a certificate that lifts the order is issued by the local enforcement authority. The order and notice must be displayed conspicuously on the premises.

Examples of an imminent risk to health include severe pest infestation, sewage disposal problems and outbreaks of food poisoning or food-borne infection.

Seizure of unfit food

An authorised officer can seize food which appears to be unfit for human consumption and take it before a JP who may issue an order to have it condemned. However, the owner of a food business may make representation to the court to have the request for such an order refused. If the court refuses to condemn the food, compensation may be granted to the owner of the food for unjust seizure of the food.

Defences, offences and penalties

As discussed in Part 2, there are only two main defences under this Act:
- that the offence was the fault of another person
- *due diligence*.

Upon conviction, the penalties for offences under the Act and its regulations can be severe. In addition to fines or imprisonment or both, courts may serve a *prohibition order*, which has an effect broadly similar to that of an emergency prohibition notice, and can even prohibit the owner or manager from working in a food business.

Summary of the main sections

The following paragraphs provide a quick guide to some of the most important sections of the Food Safety Act 1990. Please note that the information is for guidance only and should not be used as a substitute for proper reading of, and reference to, the Act itself.

Part I

This contains six sections dealing with definitions and requirements for food authorities (mainly local authorities) to enforce the Act.

Authorised officer: any person authorised by a food authority to act in matters relating to the Food Safety Act 1990.

Commercial operation: in relation to food (or contact material), includes selling, possessing, preparing, advertising, labelling, storing or transporting for the purposes of sale, importing and exporting.

Food: 'drink, articles and substances which are of no nutritional value which are used for human consumption; chewing gum and other products of a like nature and use; and articles and substances used as ingredients in the preparation of food...' The definition does not include 'live animals or birds, or live fish which are not used for human consumption while they are alive; fodder or feeding stuffs for animals, birds or fish; controlled drugs within the meaning of the Misuse of Drugs Act 1971...' or medicinal products or any other exceptions which may be made by the Ministers.

Food premises: 'any premises used for the purposes of a food business', including any place, vehicle, stall or moveable structure.

Food source: 'any growing crop or live animal, bird or fish from which food is intended to be derived (whether by harvesting, slaughtering, milking, collecting eggs or otherwise)'.

Part II

This contains the 'teeth' of the Act in that it lays down the main offences and deals with the serving of notices and orders on food businesses.

Section 7

This section makes it an offence to treat food in a way that makes it injurious to health if it is intended that the food be sold in that state. The cumulative effect over a long time is also to be taken into account.

Section 8

This is an important section dealing with the fitness of food for human consumption. All food which is sold has to meet 'food safety requirements' (see page 154).

Section 9

This section allows an authorised officer to seize or detain foods which are thought to contravene Section 8 and to bring them before a Justice of the Peace who decides whether or not the food should be condemned.

Section 10
Improvement notices (see pages 155 and 156) are dealt with in this section of the Act. Failure to comply with the improvement notice is an offence. Until the summer of 2001 environmental health officers (EHOs) were required to give a warning of their *intention* to issue an improvement notice in a document known as a 'minded to serve' notice, but this requirement has no longer in force.

Section 11
This is arguably the toughest section in the Act. Where there has been a conviction under the Act or regulations and the court is convinced that there is a risk of injury to health, the Act gives power to the courts to issue a prohibition order on a process/treatment, the premises or equipment. This type of order is similar to an emergency prohibition notice or order served under Section 12, but there is a sting in the tail because the court can also impose a prohibition order on the proprietor or manager of a food business. This bans a proprietor or manager from any involvement in the management of a food business for a specified period.

Section 12
Emergency prohibition notices and orders are the subject of this section which details how, when and under what conditions such action can be taken.

Section 13
This is the section that allows Ministers to make emergency control orders.

Section 14
The terms and the legal impact of 'nature or substance or quality' are covered here.

Section 15
Misleading labelling and false descriptions are offences under this section.

Section 20
This covers the defence that an alleged offence was the fault of another person.

Section 21
This is the section that deals with the defence of due diligence.

Part III
This deals with administration and enforcement.

Sections 29 and 30
These sections give powers to authorised officers to take samples and submit them for analysis.

Section 32
Authorised officers are given powers of entry into food businesses under this section. They are also given the power to inspect, seize and detain any records including computer records.

Section 33
Under this section it is an offence to obstruct authorised officers in the execution of their duty.

Section 35
Penalties are laid down in this section. These depend on the offence but can involve up to two years' imprisonment and fines of up to £20,000.00 for each offence on indictment.

CRIMINAL MATTER

Offences under the Act are criminal matters and therefore create a criminal record on conviction.

Under civil proceedings, a court may order a food business to pay compensation — for example, to someone who suffered a severe food-borne infection.

REGULATIONS

There are a large number of regulations made under this Act. They cover areas such as registration, administration, general food hygiene, temperature control, labelling, composition, additives, colourants, imported food and materials in contact with food. The following pages in this chapter look in broad terms at what the regulations dealing with hygiene and temperature are trying to achieve.

Hygiene
The fundamental aim of any hygiene regulation is to create conditions in a food business that will lead to the safe production of food. There are quite a number of regulations in this area. The Food Safety (General Food Hygiene) Regulations 1995 are the most commonly used by environmental health officers in England, Wales and Scotland because the legislative scope is the widest. The Food Safety (General Food Hygiene) Regulations (Northern Ireland) 1995 have similar provision.

Other hygiene regulations deal with specific products such as milk and milk products, meat and meat products, fish and shellfish.

Generally speaking, the regulations take a two-pronged approach:
- the management and control of the structure of food premises and the equipment used
- the management and control over what happens in food premises.

Management and control of the structure of food premises and equipment
These requirements aim to create the correct hygienic environment from which food can be produced, processed, cooked, served, stored or transported. As may be expected, there are provisions for the structure of the building itself and the design of equipment.

Premises
The food premises, whatever their purpose or construction, should be:
- constructed in such a way that prevents contamination of the food
- easy to clean
- designed in such a way that prevents pests getting in
- large enough and suitably designed and equipped for the purpose to which the premises are being put.

Also covered are certain social welfare issues such as the provision of toilet facilities, changing rooms and so on. There are slightly different requirements for different types of premises because of differing hazards and risks.

Equipment
The regulations state that equipment should also be constructed so that it can be cleaned easily and positioned so that it is easy to clean under and around it.

Management and control over what happens in food premises
While the basic structure of food premises and equipment are very important, it is recognised that it is far more important to *manage* and *control* people and processes in order to eliminate food hazards and reduce the risk of food-borne illness. These requirements therefore deal with such matters as hazard analysis, hygiene training, supervision, personal hygiene, microbial sampling and analysis, cleaning methods and pest control.

The main thrust is therefore towards what actually happens in a food business and how those activities can be managed to minimise risk. These *general* regulations stop short of requiring a full HACCP system for all food businesses (see pages 314 to 323), but they require the principles of hazard analysis to be employed (see pages 323 to 324). Some *product-specific* regulations do, however, require a full HACCP system to be in place (see page 163).

The *detailed* requirements are usually contained in schedules, which are part of the regulations, and can be quite specific, particularly in terms of structural requirements. In the regulations dealing with milk and milk products, for example, they are also specific about microbiological standards.

Temperature control
The Food Safety (Temperature Control) Regulations 1995 cover England, Wales and Scotland. Regulations 4 to 12 cover England and Wales only, while regulations 13 to 16 apply to Scotland only. Similar rules to regulations 4 to 12 are covered by The Food Safety (Temperature Control) Regulations (Northern Ireland) 1995.

The main thrust of the regulations is to ensure that, subject to certain exemptions, food which is likely to support the growth of pathogenic micro-organisms or the formation of toxins is kept at a temperature below 8°C or above 63°C. This requirement applies to foods, including raw materials and ingredients, at all stages of transport, preparation, processing, storage and display for sale during manufacture, retail and catering.

If a food authority decides to take legal proceedings under these regulations, then the burden of proof lies with the food authority to show that the food concerned is likely to support the growth of pathogenic micro-organisms or the formation of toxins.

Foods requiring chilled storage
Dairy products
In the main, these are soft and semi-hard cheeses and dairy-based desserts with a pH of above 4.5 when it is offered for sale.

Cooked products
These include cooked products — such as meat, fish, eggs (or substitutes for them), milk, hard and soft cheese, cereals (including rice), pulses and vegetables — as well as *ready-to-eat* products, such as sandwiches that contain fillings and toppings prepared with these foods.

Smoked or cured fish and meat
Some meats are *ambient shelf-stable*, so that they can safely be stored at ordinary room temperature, but smoked or cured fish and meat products usually require chilled storage.

Prepared ready-to-eat foods
These are items that are prepared for consumption without additional preparation or treatment, such as cooking. They include prepared vegetables and vegetable salads.

Uncooked or partly cooked pastry and dough products
Typical examples are pizzas, sausage rolls and fresh pasta that contains meat, fish or vegetables or substitutes for meat or fish.

Exemptions from chill control requirements
Some foods are exempted because they are intended for processing in a way that should eliminate pathogenic micro-organisms or toxins.

There are also exemptions for some other foods, even though it is possible for them to support the growth of pathogenic micro-organisms or the formation of toxins. The justification for these exemptions is that firstly, a limited period outside chill control will not have adverse consequences for human health and secondly, that some foods are stable, even for long periods, if they are kept at ambient temperatures for their prescribed shelf life. The exemptions are given on page 162.

Food which, for the duration of its shelf life, may be kept at ambient temperatures with no risk to health

Some examples would be certain pickles or jams, dried and air-cured hams with low water activity, bakery products and sandwiches which are produced or prepared and sold on the same premises within a short period, certain types of cake and pasteurised milk (although this is usually kept chilled in retail premises to maintain its quality).

Food which is being subjected, or has been subjected, to a process, such as dehydration or canning, intended to prevent the growth of pathogenic micro-organisms at ambient temperatures

This covers anything canned or dried.

Food which must be ripened or matured at ambient temperatures

This exemption, which does *not* apply once the ripening or maturation is completed, is intended to allow foods such as soft or mould-ripened cheeses to ripen at ambient temperatures. The exemption applies only where the cheese is unable to ripen at or below 8°C.

Raw food intended for further processing (including cooking) where the process will ensure that the food is fit for human consumption

This applies only when it is expected that the food will be subsequently thoroughly cooked. Examples of food where the exemption does not apply are meat intended for steak tartare or fish intended for sushi, because they are eaten raw.

Food sent to a consumer as part of a mail-order transaction

An exemption is given, but there is a requirement that any such food will be supplied at a safe temperature.

Hot holding

The hot holding temperature stated is at least 63°C for specified time limits. The requirement applies to cooked or reheated food being held for service or on display for sale which would allow the multiplication of bacteria or the formation of toxins if it were not kept at a temperature of 63°C or above.

Separate Scottish requirements

There are differences in some temperature requirements in Scotland — for example, covering cold holding, reheating and gelatine.

There is no specific cold holding temperature stated for Scotland. With certain exclusions, high risk food should be kept in a refrigerator or cool ventilated space. Food that is reheated should be brought to a temperature of at least 82°C unless it can be proven that to do so would result in a deterioration of the food. There is a requirement that gelatine should be boiled then kept at a temperature of at least 71°C for 30 minutes.

Butchers' licensing regulations

In 1996, following a serious outbreak of *E. coli* 0157 linked to meat in Lanarkshire, Scotland, Professor Hugh Pennington was asked to chair an expert group to look at ways of reducing the risk from this organism. Among other things, the group recommended the introduction of licensing for food businesses, other than catering premises, that handle both cooked and raw meat. The regulations that were implemented in 2000 are broadly similar throughout the UK but there are some differences in Scotland.

The legislation is:
- in England and Wales — The Food Safety (General Food Hygiene) (Butchers' Shops) Amendment Regulations 2000 and, in Wales only, The Food Safety (General Food Hygiene) (Butchers' Shops) (Amendment) (Wales) Regulations 2000
- in Scotland — The Food Safety (General Food Hygiene) (Butchers' Shops) Amendment (Scotland) Regulations 2000
- in Northern Ireland — The Food Safety (General Food Hygiene) (Amendment) Regulations (Northern Ireland) 2001.

In England and Wales a licence is issued provided that:
- the business complies with the regulations
- the staff have received satisfactory training
- at least one person is trained to a level that enables proper supervision of the premises with regard to compliance with the regulations and HACCP procedures
- HACCP procedures are in place.

In Scotland certain prescriptive requirements can be met as an alternative to having a HACCP system in place.

HACCP
The licensing regulations require full HACCP (see pages 314 to 323), not merely hazard analysis as required under the general food hygiene regulations.

Other regulations

There are many other regulations concerned with food safety. If you work with animal products, such as meat or milk, find out about the specific regulations for the product.

Industry guides

Guidance has been developed for several food sectors on how to comply with the regulations — for instance, The Catering Guide to Good Hygiene Practice. The guides tend to go beyond simple legal compliance and deal with what is good practice even if it is not a legal requirement.

The guides have no defined legal standing, but in practice EHOs and the courts do pay attention to them when making judgements about compliance.

Codes of practice

Ministers have the power under Section 40 of the Food Safety Act 1990 to issue codes of practice. They cover a wide range of topics including the qualifications required of enforcement officers, the issuing of notices such as improvement notices and emergency prohibition notices, and details of how a food hygiene inspection should be carried out.

The Food Standards Agency (FSA) monitors the work of the local authorities (LAs) — usually local councils. Among the criteria against which the LAs' performance is measured are these codes. This means that enforcement officers should be fully conversant with the codes and should carry out their work in accordance with them.

✴ MAKING IT EASIER FOR OTHERS

It is not necessary for every food handler to have a detailed knowledge of food safety legislation or to memorise the title of Acts and regulations. Even so, it is important to ensure that every member of staff has a good general awareness of how food safety legislation affects food handlers' daily activities and the general operation of the company.

- Emphasise that everyone who works with food has a legal responsibility to work in a way that safeguards the health of consumers.
- Make sure that all food handlers understand that they *must*:
  - keep themselves clean
  - keep their workplace clean
  - wear clean and suitable protective clothing
  - do everything possible to protect food from contamination
  - store, prepare and display food at safe temperatures
  - tell you, or another senior staff member, if they have any symptom of food-borne illness or certain other conditions or illnesses (see page 234).
- Emphasise that food handlers *must not:*
  - do anything that would expose food to contamination
  - serve or sell food that is unfit for human consumption
  - sell food with an expired date mark
  - work with food if they have symptoms of a food-borne illness or until they have been cleared as safe to do so.

⚙ MANAGEMENT MATTERS

Food safety legislation has a simple aim — to prevent consumers from becoming ill and perhaps dying. The manager's role is to ensure that the letter and the spirit of the law are observed. To achieve this, managers need to ensure a mixture of legal compliance and good practice so that:

- the premises are registered with the local enforcement authority, in England, Wales and Scotland, under The Food Premises (Registration) Regulations 1991, which were amended in 1993; and in Northern Ireland, The Food Premises (Registration) Regulations (Northern Ireland) 1992, which were amended in 1997
- the business is properly designed and equipped for the kind of food operation being carried out to prevent contamination and food-borne illness or injury — bear in mind that staff cannot be expected to work within the law if they are not, for instance, provided with adequate and appropriate protective clothing
- there are adequate washing facilities and arrangements for personal hygiene
- staff are trained on appropriate hygiene subjects and to a level that is in line with the kind of work they do and the responsibilities they have
- staff who are not food handlers but whose work could affect food safety are also given appropriate training in basic food safety
- everyone knows exactly what is expected of them
- the manager and senior staff set an excellent example
- there is adequate supervision
- food hazards are analysed and appropriate systems put in place to eliminate them or to minimise the risks from them.

You may decide that legislation states only the minimum standards that you wish your staff to achieve and you may establish higher standards or stricter performance criteria than are required by law. For example, many companies have house rules for cooking and reheating times and temperatures.

There is plenty of practicable advice on food safety available to you, whether in the form of free publications, advice from your local EHO or independent food safety adviser, or from one of the professional food safety bodies or trade associations listed in the Reference section.

4 How should we manage food safety?

1 What is food safety?

2 Why do we need to manage food safety?

Managing Food Safety

3 What do we need to manage?

4 How should we manage food safety?

PREVENTING FOOD CONTAMINATION
Contamination and its consequences
    Microbiological contamination
    Chemical contamination
    Physical contamination
    Management matters

MANAGING RESOURCES
    from the ground up
Under a suitable roof
    food on the move
Developing staff competence
    Making learning easier
Fit to work with food
    Management matters

MANAGING SYSTEMS
Clean enough for food
Pests under control
Safe food at its best
    Controlling time and temperature
    Maintaining quality over time
    finding the energy
    Storing food for safety and profit
    beyond your control?
Risk management
    HACCP and hazard analysis
    Turning a crisis to advantage
    Management matters
Integrated management

Managers need to understand the principles behind the details involved in their particular business and, at the same time, to be able to see the bigger picture of the operation so that they can formulate appropriate standards and procedures. This is true for all managers in all types of business.

It is particularly important for managers of food establishments, because a failure to see the bigger picture or to take account of a microscopic detail could result in the death of a customer.

Parts 1 and 2 gave you an overview of the food industry and the impact of food-borne illness upon food businesses and their customers. Part 3 examined the hazards to food safety.

In Part 4 we outline the management issues involved in making food safe to eat. In doing so, we appreciate that *you* may not be directly responsible for every aspect of management that we mention. You may not, for example, be directly responsible for cleaning, maintenance, pest control or training. Even so, you need to consider such aspects of food safety and to be able to communicate effectively with the manager who does have the direct responsibility for such matters.

A book of this size can deal only with the principles of management. So, when you have finished reading each chapter, it is worth considering how the issues discussed are significant in the operation that you manage. Ask yourself questions such as: is this procedure already in place in my company and how does it contribute to the safety of the food we produce; if it is not in place and implemented, would it help to improve food safety standards; what do I, as the manager, need to do about each of the issues raised in the chapter; which one thing could I do or change in my company that could improve food safety standards; how can I make it easier for staff to produce safe food; what do need to discuss with senior colleagues to improve standards of food safety?

By the end of the book, we hope that you will have a short list of points to put into action in your workplace.

PREVENTING FOOD CONTAMINATION

🔑 KEY POINTS

ambient temperature
the environmental temperature, often used to describe 'normal' room temperature.

carrier
a person who is infected by a pathogen and can pass it on to others, but who does not experience symptoms.

contaminant
any unwanted material, object or substance in food.

contamination
the presence in food, or the process of transferring to food, any unwanted material, object or substance.

critical control point
in HACCP, a stage in the process of handling food at which food businesses can exercise controls which could prevent a hazard or minimise the risk from it.

critical limit
in HACCP, a border between what is safe and unsafe.

cross-contamination
the transfer of a contaminant from one contaminated product, such as raw meat, to another previously uncontaminated product, such as a ready-to-eat food.

direct contamination
the route directly from the source of contamination to a food.

due diligence
a legal defence where it can be shown that all reasonable steps were taken to avoid committing a food safety offence.

extrinsic contamination
contamination from sources other than the raw food itself.

faecal coliform
an organism, such as *E. coli*, the presence of which indicates faecal contamination.

hazard
anything, whether microbiological, chemical or physical, that might cause harm to the consumer.

hazard analysis
the systematic identification of hazards and the estimation of the degree of risk from them.

high risk food
a food that easily supports the multiplication of pathogenic micro-organisms.

hurdle technology/concept
the controlled manipulation of factors essential to bacterial survival and multiplication.

indirect contamination
contamination due to the action of a vehicle of contamination or a vector.

infective dose
the number of micro-organisms required to cause symptoms of a disease.

inherent
inbuilt.

intrinsic contamination
contamination associated with the food itself.

microbiological flora
the microbial species normally found in a particular habitat, such as the intestine.

multiplication
microbial reproduction, such as by binary fission (bacteria) or budding (yeast).

mycotoxin
a toxin produced by some fungi.

potable
safe to drink.

product specification
a customer's detailed description of the content, design, composition and intended use of the product to be supplied.

ready-to-eat
food that is either eaten raw, or is not prepared or treated (such as by cooking) in a way that would kill any pathogens present immediately before it is eaten.

source of contamination
where a contaminant has its origin.

sterile
a condition in which all living organisms have been destroyed.

supplier's certificate
a supplier's guarantee of the wholesomeness of a product based on criteria set by the purchasing company.

vector
animals, insects, birds serving as vehicles of contamination.

vehicle of contamination
any substance, object or living being that carries contamination from A to B. Vehicles are factors in indirect contamination.

CONTAMINATION AND ITS CONSEQUENCES

What is the common feature in the way that microbiological, chemical and physical hazards move from being *potential* threats to food safety to become *actual* threats of harm? Contamination is the simple answer, as you can see in the diagram on page 43.

Tracing the origins and routes of that contamination might, however, seem far from simple at first and could appear rather like a whodunit where the detective has justifiable suspicions about the identity of a culprit but forms only a confused picture of the way the culprit reached the victim. The good news is that careful detection over the years has revealed regular patterns of clues to contamination — clues that can place you in a good position to prevent harm to your customers.

UNDERSTANDING CONTAMINATION

The word *contamination* derives from the Latin verb contaminare, meaning to soil, spoil or make impure. In current usage contamination indicates the presence in food of, or the process of transferring to food, a *contaminant* — any unwanted material, object or substance. In short, contamination is anything in food that should not be there. (The word contamination is sometimes muddled with the word contagion, which means the transmission of a disease from one person to another by direct contact, but the words are *not* interchangeable.)

Contamination can involve an unwanted ingredient that is fairly easy to see, such as a slug in a salad, or something invisible to the unaided human eye such as a bacterial toxin. All types of contamination — whether easily visible or not and whether they cause illness, injury or just disgust — make food unfit for human consumption and it is illegal to sell contaminated products.

Starting out
It may help you to think of the process of contamination as a journey. The starting point is the *source of contamination* — where the contaminant has its origin. The destination is food, often high risk food.

Routes
If the route of contamination is straight from the source to a food, we call the process *direct contamination*. Examples include raw food touching a high risk product in a display cabinet, blood dripping onto a cooked *ready-to-eat* food in a refrigerator and a screw from overhead ducting falling into unpackaged food on a conveyor belt below. More often — and this is especially so for microbiological contamination — contaminants are carried or transmitted by a *vehicle of*

contamination. This is a substance, object or living thing which moves the contaminant away from its source and on to food. An example is when a knife used for cutting raw poultry is then used for slicing a quiche without cleaning and disinfecting the knife between tasks. The route taken is not straight from the source, so the process is called *indirect contamination*.

If the vehicle of contamination is an animal, insect or bird, then it is properly termed a *vector*. The difference between a vehicle of contamination and a vector is that a vector moves under its own power.

Another form of contamination is *cross-contamination*, which usually refers only to microbiological contamination. It occurs when a contaminant is moved from one contaminated product, such as raw meat, on to another as yet uncontaminated product, such as a ready-to-eat product like cold ham. Cross-contamination creates a high level of risk of illness when it involves products which do not receive any additional treatment, such as heating, immediately before they are consumed.

MANAGING CONTAMINATION

To start to manage contamination you should be able to answer the following questions, which are similar to those suggested by HACCP and other systems of *hazard analysis* (see Part 4):
- which *contaminants* am I likely to encounter in my workplace?
- which are the potential *sources* of contamination of foods in my workplace?
- what are the potential *routes* of contamination in food in my workplace?

It may help you at the outset to consider the hazards which are associated with:
- specific ingredients and products
- specific processes or forms of preparation
- specific types of food business.

CONTAMINANTS	POTENTIAL SOURCES	POTENTIAL ROUTES
Usually depend on specific:	**Usually depend on specific:**	**Usually depend on specific:**
ingredients and products	ingredients and products	
processes or forms of preparation	processes or forms of preparation	processes or forms of preparation
types of food business.		types of food business.

Examples of contaminants are given on the following three pages. Potential sources and routes are discussed later in this chapter.

EXAMPLES OF CONTAMINATION

FOOD	CONTAMINANT
PLANTS	
Cereals	unwanted plant material
	insects and larvae
	insecticide residues
	fertiliser residues
	rodenticides
	rodent droppings
	moulds and other micro-organisms
	mycotoxins
Fruit (including fruit concentrates and preserves) and nuts	insects and larvae
	twigs
	unwanted plant material
	insecticide residues
	wax coating on fruit skin
	fertiliser residues
	moulds and other micro-organisms
	mycotoxins
Herbs	soil
	unwanted plant material
	insects and larvae
	small stones
	insecticide residues
	fertiliser residues
	micro-organisms
Spices	soil
	insects and larvae
	insecticide residues
	rodenticides
	rodent droppings
	micro-organisms
Vegetables — cooked	insecticide residues
	fertiliser residues
	micro-organisms
Vegetables — prepared	insecticide residues
	fertiliser residues
	micro-organisms
	small stones
	unwanted plant material

Vegetables — raw	soil
	unwanted plant material
	insects and larvae
	small stones
	insecticide residues
	fertiliser residues
	micro-organisms

DAIRY

Eggs	veterinary medicine residues
	micro-organisms
	chemicals

Raw milk	veterinary medicine residues
	cleaning chemicals
	micro-organisms
	heavy metals

Pasteurised, UHT or sterilised milk	veterinary medicine residues
	cleaning chemicals
	heavy metals

Dairy products made from raw milk	veterinary medicine residues
	cleaning chemicals
	micro-organisms
	heavy metals

Dairy products made from heat-treated milk	veterinary medicine residues
	cleaning chemicals
	micro-organisms
	heavy metals

MEAT

| Meat — cooked | veterinary medicine residues |
| | micro-organisms and toxins |

Meat — raw	veterinary medicine residues
	parasites
	other micro-organisms
	faeces

FISH

Fish — farmed	parasites
	other micro-organisms
	veterinary medicine residues

Fish — freshwater and marine	heavy metals
	toxins
	parasites
	bacteria
	mycotoxins
Shellfish and crustaceans	pieces of shell
	heavy metals
	toxins
	parasites
	viruses
	bacteria
LIQUIDS	
Liquids other than water	chemicals
	toxins
	micro-organisms
Water	plant material
	soil
	pieces of metal, wood and rubbish
	small crustaceans
	naturally occurring chemicals
	chemicals added during purification
	micro-organisms, including bacteria, viruses and parasites
	faeces

HAZARDS AND CONTAMINATION

MULTIPLY
Most food poisoning organisms must multiply before they can cause food poisoning, but most of the organisms that cause food-borne infections do not need to do so.

In the rest of this section we look at contamination in some detail, using the familiar food hazard categories — microbiological, chemical and physical.

You may find it helpful at this stage to refresh your memory about hazards and contamination by reviewing the flow chart on page 43 which shows the typical routes from contamination to illness. Bear in mind that microbiological hazards include *multiplication* and survival, as well as contamination. Although not all pathogens need to multiply before causing illness, you might find it helpful to remember this word equation:

microbiological contamination + time = microbiological multiplication.

We refer at times to *hazard analysis*, *critical control points* and *critical limits*. These are explained later, in the chapter 'HACCP and hazard analysis' (pages 314 to 327). When you have read that chapter, you may find it helpful to reread this section.

MICROBIOLOGICAL CONTAMINATION

In a laboratory that breeds pure monocultures (colonies of identical individual micro-organisms) everyone has to take special precautions to prevent microbiological contamination and cross-contamination. Laboratory staff often have to work in *sterile* conditions where even the air flow is controlled. Sterile conditions are certainly not possible, or even necessary, in most food businesses. But we must never forget that micro-organisms are ubiquitous — they are here, there and everywhere — and that many of their sources, such as the air, humans, animals, food, water and the environment, are unavoidable.

TYPICAL SOURCES — THE START OF THE PROBLEM

Food managers need a thorough understanding of potential microbial sources in order to carry out a hazard analysis, as required by law, and to establish procedures designed to prevent contamination. The following paragraphs consider the main sources in detail.

Raw food

There is no such thing as sterile food. We have to live with the fact that we deal with potentially contaminated materials from the very beginning. Raw food can contain between 100,000 and 200,000 bacteria per gram of food. These may not all be pathogens, but we still need to instigate measures to keep the bacteria at levels that will not accelerate spoilage.

Examples of typical pathogens that may be present in raw food are:
* *Campylobacter jejuni*
* *Clostridium perfringens*
* *Listeria monocytogenes*
* *Salmonella* species
* *Staphylococcus aureus*
* *Vibrio parahaemolyticus*
* *Yersinia enterocolitica*.

As we saw in Part 3, we need to eliminate bacteria — either by heat or chemical treatment, or by employing temperature control and preservation methods — in order to keep the bacterial population in its lag phase for as long as possible.

With the continual spread and evolution of micro-organisms (see pages 23 to 26) the work of food managers has not become any easier. Food preparation techniques that seemed to have produced safe food in the past may need to be reviewed and adjusted to combat emergent pathogens such as *E. coli* O157 and deal with concerns about residual veterinary drugs, such as antibiotics, in foods of animal origin.

Dust and soil

The soil is probably one of the most important sources of initial microbial contamination. Depending on the amount of vegetable mould and other organic substances that make up the earth, soil can contain billions of microbes in every gram. Anaerobic spore-formers, psychrotrophs and fungi are the dominant organisms in soil, but there may also be faecal organisms from manure used to increase plant yields and from sewage that has contaminated groundwater and soil.

Leafy vegetables, cereals, fruit and especially root vegetables are contaminated by soil particles. Washing is the first step to get rid of this microbiological and physical contamination. Soil organisms can also get into food premises in dust particles.

Vegetables and fruit

Most soil and water organisms can contaminate plants, so the surfaces of fruit and vegetables can be loaded with micro-organisms.

The types of microbiological organism on land-grown fruit and vegetables are usually those of the soils in which these foods are grown. *Faecal coliforms* may survive in some manure that is spread on the soil and may contaminate plants.

Spoilage organisms that persist on plant products because of their special adherence to surfaces are lactic acid bacteria and some yeasts and moulds.

Microbiological surface contamination is best controlled by washing raw fruit and vegetables thoroughly before use, whether they are cooked or eaten raw.

HIGH RISK FOODS

Certain foods support microbiological multiplication more easily than others, so they create a greater risk of causing food-borne illness than other types of product. These *high risk foods* are characterised by all, or most, of the following:

- high levels of protein
- intrinsic factors (such as pH and a_w) that easily support multiplication
- strict temperature control required to keep the food wholesome and safe to eat
- usually intended for immediate consumption without further heat treatment or any preservation method that would destroy or control the growth of micro-organisms.

If we consider two different foods, such as an apple and minced meat, we know that both products have a reasonable amount of moisture. However, the minced meat beats the apple by the level of protein it contains. This makes the crucial difference to a food being a high risk one or not. All foods with high levels of protein (especially protein of animal origin) need to be handled, stored and processed with special care as they easily support microbiological multiplication.

Ready-to-eat high risk foods pose special problems for food safety because they are consumed without treatment immediately before eating that would destroy micro-organisms acquired by re-contamination or cross-contamination. Products that come under this category include processed foods, such as cooked meat that is eaten cold, and raw and ready-to-eat products, such as minced meat served as beef tartare.

Rice and cereals

The *microbiological flora* of wheat, rye, corn, rice and related products are also heavily influenced by the soil in which they were grown. As these foods are often stored for quite long periods, the condition of their storage environments can make them vulnerable to further contamination as well as to microbial multiplication. Usually the level of micro-organisms is fairly low as the relatively low water activity (a_w) of these foods inhibits the growth of micro-organisms. Aerobic spore-formers such as *Bacillus cereus* and moulds such as *Claviceps purpurea* and *Aspergillus* species are the main organisms.

Herbs and spices

Although spices do not suffer from microbiological spoilage as much as some other products, all spices and herbs may be contaminated by soil organisms such as those of the *Clostridium* genus. These products are not always cleaned thoroughly after harvesting, so spores can easily survive in *dried* herbs and can germinate under favourable conditions when they are added to protein-rich foods.

Water

This is one of the most overlooked sources of food-borne pathogens and is often neglected in a hazard analysis. Many pathogenic organisms can be transmitted by water. Typical ones include:

- *Campylobacter jejuni*
- *Cryptosporidium parvum*
- *Entamoeba histolytica*
- *Escherichia coli*
- *Giardia lamblia*
- Hepatitis A
- Norovirus
- Rotaviruses
- *Salmonella* species
- *Shigella* species
- *Vibrio cholerae*
- *Vibrio parahaemolyticus*.

USE OF WATER

Bear in mind how many different tasks water is used for in a food business. For example, it may be used as an ingredient, for personal hygiene (for instance, washing hands), cleaning food and for cleaning food-handling equipment and food-contact surfaces. There are many methods for controlling pathogenic micro-organisms in potable water, including filtering, ultraviolet irradiation, addition of biocides and temperature control.

Most of these water-borne pathogens are strong survivors in the environment and are highly infectious even in small numbers.

Many food handlers in Britain are convinced that water must be safe if it comes out of a tap. This is largely true, but even controlled supplies of *potable* water are occasionally contaminated at source or may become contaminated by leaking sewage pipes or seepage from slurry. Potable water can also become contaminated by using unsuitable construction materials and water fittings which may not only affect the taste, odour or chemical composition of the water, but may also support the growth of micro-organisms such as fungi. In drought years water companies have sometimes drawn water from a source such as a bore hole that has been contaminated by *Cryptosporidium parvum*. Additional problems may be caused by water drawn from storage tanks which have not been maintained properly or covered adequately, so that bird faeces and air-borne contaminants have got into the water.

Outdoor activities, such as walking, camping and watersports, may bring food handlers into contact with contaminated water in their leisure time and they need to be made aware of water-borne organisms, such as the parasites *Giardia lamblia* (see page 101) and *Leptospira interrogans* (which causes leptospirosis — Weil's disease), that could affect food safety.

Humans

Everyone is a universe of living micro-organisms. Most relationships between humans and our microbiological guests are simply a quiet co-existence, and some micro-organisms, such as our intestinal *flora*, are essential for our well-being. As we know, however, other micro-organisms are pathogenic and can cause diseases when present in critical numbers — the *infective dose*. Typical micro-organisms associated with, and distributed by, humans are:

- *Escherichia coli*
- Hepatitis A
- Norovirus
- *Salmonella* species
- *Shigella* species
- *Staphylococcus aureus*.

Some pathogens are carried by humans who do not themselves experience symptoms of illness but who nonetheless pass on the pathogen to others. Even healthy people carry bacteria like *Staphylococcus aureus* and *E. coli* and may spread them if special precautions are not in place. When people who work with food are infected with certain bacteria, or are *carriers* of certain pathogens such as *Salmonella* species, the law prohibits them from working with uncovered food and there are strict rules governing when they may return to working with food (see page 234). There needs to be a 'hygiene barrier' between food and food handlers, so you must establish and supervise rules covering such issues as personal hygiene, protective clothing, the washing of hands and general good hygiene practice. (There is more information about these topics later in Part 4.)

Animals

Animals, insects and birds may carry and spread a wide range of pathogenic micro-organisms, which tend to be specific to the type of animal, and include:

- *Brucella* species
- *Campylobacter jejuni*
- *Clostridium perfringens*
- *Cryptosporidium parvum*
- *Escherichia coli* 0157

- *Giardia lamblia*
- *Mycobacterium tuberculosis*
- parasites such as tapeworms
- *Salmonella* species
- *Toxoplasma gondii*.

Food can be contaminated in the abattoir by direct contact between an uncontaminated and contaminated animal or carcass. Raw milk may contain some of the udder flora, while the intestinal flora of slaughtered animals may contaminate the meat in the abattoir, the hands of the staff, the storage containers and the general abattoir environment. Pests and pets can also carry pathogens and cause contamination. It makes good sense to exclude all animals, birds and insects from food areas, but, as this may not be possible at the point of primary production of foodstuffs of animal origin, there may be a high risk of contamination from animals if proper hygiene procedures are not in place.

Beloved family pets can also create food safety problems if they are allowed into food areas. Managers of small family businesses often need to take a firm line on pets and to make sure that all family members and staff wash their hands after handling pets.

Refuse

Rubbish and waste, especially when it contains food waste, is also a source of contamination and at an ambient temperature is obviously an ideal growth medium for bacteria. The contamination caused can be either *direct*, by spilling or contact, or *indirect* via the hands of food handlers. In addition, food waste can attract pests which in turn can cause contamination. Bins need to be emptied frequently and you should consider how much encouragement and supervision staff will need to do so — a small bin in a food preparation area, for example, needs to be emptied more frequently than a large one.

VEHICLES OF CONTAMINATION — A DETECTIVE'S TASK

Cross-contamination occurs when microbes (or other contaminants) from one food, usually a raw one, are transferred to another food, usually a cooked or ready-to-eat one. This may happen directly. Examples are when pathogens are transferred from the viscera (such as the gut) and the hides of one animal carcass in a slaughterhouse directly to another if the carcasses touch one another, or when frozen raw meat left to thaw in a multi-purpose refrigerator drips onto cooked meat stored below it. Most cross-contamination is, however, caused by vehicles or vectors, of which the most common are:
- hands
- hand-contact surfaces, including utensils and handles (of cupboards, refrigerators and so on)
- food-contact surfaces, including work surfaces and cutting boards; storage containers; crockery; mixers, cooking pans and other cooking equipment; knives and other utensils
- wiping cloths, dishcloths and other cleaning equipment
- clothing
- pests.

The routes, vehicles and vectors involved may be as difficult to track down as a criminal in a detective novel, as many of the vehicles and vectors are long gone, thrown away, or cleaned and disinfected once the 'crime' (contamination) is discovered. But an understanding of the principles involved will help you to investigate so that you can prevent a recurrence. Although we cannot *see* the routes that micro-organisms take, it needs only a little imagination to sketch a map of the way they travelled.

Hands

We use our hands to manipulate various food utensils, operate food equipment and to shape, divide and arrange food. Without deliberation, we also scratch our heads, either to relieve an itch or to help us to think. Every hand movement we make can imitate a pick-up truck — our hands load up with micro-organisms, dump off some at the next stop and collect others, then drop off more as we continue our rounds. Small wonder, then, that managers need to emphasise the importance of washing hands properly (see pages 231 to 232) and supervise it as far as they can.

Hand-contact surfaces

These are the surfaces that are often forgotten when it comes to cleaning and disinfecting. As a result, an inconspicuous refrigerator or tap handle can develop into a contamination storage area, just waiting for the next pick-up truck — our hands — to load up and move the microbes on to the next food or surface.

Food-contact surfaces

All foods, especially raw ones, can leave micro-organisms on any surface they touch. They can also easily pick up micro-organisms when a surface has not been cleaned and disinfected between processes. This is why food managers must emphasise both the importance of cleaning and disinfecting food contact surfaces regularly (see pages 243 to 259), and the importance of cleaning and disinfecting surfaces between use for different products, or for raw then cooked food.

Colour-coded equipment and utensils may help staff to separate types of use, but effective cleaning procedures are still essential.

The equipment you choose for food preparation and storage should be designed to minimise cross-contamination. Cleaning and maintenance should be carried out in a way that avoids contaminating ingredients, products or packaging materials and also ensures that equipment is microbiologically safe before it is used again. If food processing equipment has 'dead ends' that are difficult to clean, a microbiological flora can build up on the food residue that remains and can cross-contaminate the product.

Key questions to ask yourself when evaluating the risk posed by equipment include:
- can effective cleaning be carried out?
- can the equipment and its construction provide additional hazards?

Wiping cloths, other cleaning equipment and utensils

Cloths and other items of cleaning equipment are unobtrusive and can be easy to forget when it comes to food safety.

A dishcloth or wiping cloth, or even a tea towel, could be used for almost any task: to wipe down a work table, to absorb liquid from a food preparation surface, to remove dirt and grease from a piece of equipment and to dry a food handler's hands.

You might object that *your* staff would never use a cloth in a sequence such as this one. But can you be certain that they *always* use a fresh cloth when they need to use one — and if not, how do they know about its true recent past? The same question can be posed for other utensils and equipment that come into contact with different products during the course of the day. Colour coding is one way to help to restrict the use of these items to a certain area, process or product.

Clothing

You need to ensure that the people who work with food understand that protective clothing is not there to protect their own clothes from becoming soiled but to protect the food from contamination from human sources.

Even the most suitable protective clothing can become a contamination vehicle if it is not properly cleaned or is worn in the wrong places. Protective clothing should be restricted to the food production or preparation and storage areas only, and should *not* be worn outside the workplace or during breaks.

If personal clothing, such as T-shirts or sweatshirts, are worn, their use should also be restricted to the workplace. Of course, it may be necessary to put on a different protective garment, such as an apron, when starting a different task or when a garment becomes soiled.

Pests

Rodents, insects and birds carry a wide range of pathogenic micro-organisms as well as creating a physical hazard and should be kept out of food premises at every stage. A well-functioning pest management system is essential (see pages 260 to 274). Pests can load and unload pathogens everywhere, just as human hands can.

THE MICROBIOLOGICAL CHAIN

There is usually a sequence of events, not just one activity, that leads to food-borne illness and it is common to describe that sequence as a chain of contamination or a microbiological chain. A typical chain of events is shown in the top diagram opposite. To make better sense of it, consider this example of actions that are likely to lead to *Salmonella* food poisoning. The numbers correspond with those in the diagram.

Example
1. Raw meat contaminated with *Salmonella* is cut up on a chopping board with a cook's knife.
2. Immediately after, a hot roast joint of meat is placed on the same chopping board and cut in half (to speed up the cooling time) with the same cook's knife.
3. The roast meat is left on the board to cool before it is stored in a refrigerator.
4. Later, the cold roast meat is sliced then very briefly reheated just before it is served.
5. A consumer eats the food and becomes ill with *Salmonella* food poisoning.

Breaking the links in the chain
The bottom diagram opposite indicates how the chain can be broken.

Contamination
As microbiological *contamination* is an ordinary part of the natural world, the only way to break this part of the chain is to *protect* food from contamination.

Multiplication
Microbiological *multiplication* can occur rapidly. For example, bacteria can multiply when:
- high risk food is left at an *ambient temperature*
- hot food is cooled over a prolonged period
- hot food is kept hot (or warm) at a temperature below 63°C
- food is not preserved adequately (for instance, if the pH level or the salt concentration is inappropriate)
- there is no, or little, microbial competition.

The way to break this part of the chain is to *prevent* multiplication.

Survival
Microbiological *survival* occurs whenever a process that is designed to kill pathogens is not carried out in the right way. This could occur, for example, as a result of:
- the wrong time and temperature combination during cooking or reheating
- the wrong combination of factors (such as a_w and pH) during preservation.

The way to break this part of the chain is to *destroy* microbes in the food.

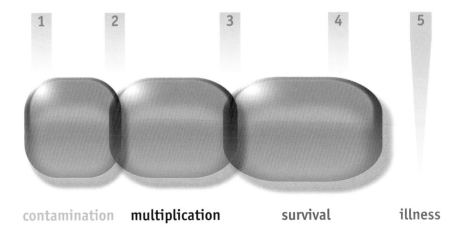

1	2	3	4	5

contamination **multiplication** survival illness

The first link in the chain (see the top two paragraphs opposite) forms between actions 1 and 2: contamination occurs. The second link in the chain is between actions 2 and 3: a suitable combination of time and temperature allows microbes to multiply. The third link in the chain occurs between actions 3 and 4: the temperature does not become hot enough for long enough to destroy the microbes, so they survive in sufficient numbers to cause a food-borne illness. The three links in the chain — contamination, multiplication and survival — lead to illness.

WHERE TO BREAK THE CHAIN

contamination **multiplication** survival

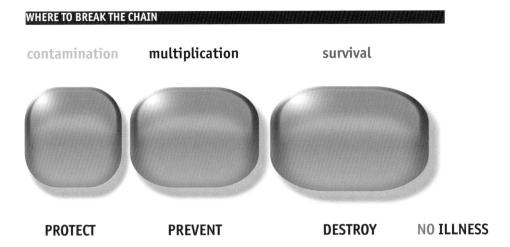

PROTECT **PREVENT** **DESTROY** NO **ILLNESS**

There are three points at which you can break the microbiological chain — by protecting food from contamination, preventing microbiological multiplication or destroying microbes.

*BREAK THE
CHAIN*
Protect food from
contamination.
Prevent
multiplication.
Destroy microbes
present in food.

PROTECT, PREVENT, DESTROY

To control microbiological hazards you must ensure that all your food safety systems work in line with the principle of *protect, prevent, destroy*. Staff who work with food need to understand why the principle works and what they must do to follow it.

The chances of preventing a food-borne illness become more and more limited the longer the microbiological chain becomes. Once food has been contaminated, depending on the type of pathogen present, the level of contamination may still be below the critical level that causes illness.

This may be the case with organisms like *Salmonella*, *Staphylococcus aureus* and *Clostridium perfringens* which cause problems only when they are present in high numbers. However, many organisms that cause food-borne infection, such as *Campylobacter* or *Shigella*, can cause harm even in very small numbers.

As there are only limited opportunities for destroying such organisms and the techniques, such as cooking, may not be suitable for every product, the most important word to remember is *protect*. If you limit the opportunities for contamination, you improve the chances of preventing multiplication and destroying those bacteria that survive.

Protection
Protection generally involves:
- removing the sources of contamination
- putting barriers between sources and vehicles of contamination
- putting barriers between sources and products.

Removing sources
Actions include:
- effective pest control
- thorough cleaning and disinfection
- effective personal hygiene and habits
- proper waste management.

Creating barriers
These can be:
- physical, such as covering food before storing it
- spatial, such as separating raw food from cooked food and ready-to-eat food.

Separation
Separation is one of the simplest but most effective ways of protecting food against microbial and other forms of contamination. It includes:
- separating raw food from cooked food and ready-to-eat food

- separating preparation areas for dirty products and processes from preparation areas for clean products and processes (see pages 202 to 214)
- providing different sets of utensils and equipment for the preparation of different products
- providing separate cleaning facilities, such as basins for hand washing only and sinks for cleaning foods and washing up.

Protection checklist
Premises and equipment
- Make sure that work areas are properly designed and constructed.
- Choose equipment made from appropriate materials.
- Choose equipment that can be cleaned and, if appropriate, disinfected properly.
- Ban the use of dirty or damaged equipment.
- Consider providing colour-coded utensils or colour coding for food preparation and storage areas.
- Schedule regular maintenance and servicing of equipment to prevent the build-up of microbial colonies.
- Consider buying disposable wiping cloths.
- Try implementing the principle of separation by *time* if space constraints prevent physical separation — so, if food rooms are too small to have separate areas for the preparation of raw and cooked foods, try, for example, organising timetables and workflows so that raw food is dealt with before 9.30 in the morning and cooked food is prepared after this time when all equipment, utensils and surfaces have been thoroughly cleaned and disinfected.

Cleaning and disinfection
- Instigate effective cleaning and disinfection procedures, including cleaning schedules and a clean-as-you-go policy (see pages 255 to 258).
- Monitor the results of cleaning and implement remedial steps if necessary.
- Ensure that there is an efficient system for waste disposal.

Pests
- Deny pests access to the premises and shelter within or around them.
- Store food in pest-proof containers.
- Implement a pest management programme (see pages 260 to 274).

Food
- Keep food covered.
- Separate raw and cooked products during transport, storage and display.
- Separate raw and ready-to-eat products.
- Use separate, clean and disinfected utensils, such as boards and knives, when preparing raw and cooked products.

Poorly constructed and inadequately cleaned premises can easily contaminate and recontaminate food. The mould in this bakery makes the premises unsafe for food production.

Food handlers

- Ensure the highest possible standards of personal hygiene.
- Ensure that staff wear appropriate protective clothing.
- Follow recommended good practice for your industry sector.
- Work with other managers, such as chefs, food and beverage managers and sales managers, to develop ways to minimise hand contact with food.

Prevention and destruction

Although protection against contamination is the crucial first part of the food safety armoury, the prevention of multiplication and the destruction of micro-organisms are also important alternative ways to break the microbiological chain.

Aspects of prevention and destruction are discussed throughout the rest of Part 4 and in particular in 'Controlling time and temperature' (see pages 277 to 284) and 'Clean enough for food' (see pages 243 to 259).

❄ MAKING IT EASIER FOR OTHERS

A good and enjoyable way to help food handlers to understand the typical routes and consequences of microbiological contamination is to give them an informal case study. They could, for example, trace how *Salmonella* contaminated a salad in a salad bar that offered salads made from raw and cooked vegetables, fruits, rice and mixed foods as well as cold sauces such as mayonnaise.

- Establish clear and simple rules that staff can follow to protect food from microbiological contamination, prevent multiplication and destroy micro-organisms.
- Ensure that senior staff set an excellent example.
- Provide suitable training.
- Reinforce the rules covering personal hygiene and habits.
- Supervise food handlers.
- Monitor hygiene practices and adjust rules and procedures if necessary.

CHEMICAL CONTAMINATION

Chemical *hazards* are wide-ranging and include naturally occurring chemicals, which are *inherent* in the product; *mycotoxins* produced by some fungi; and introduced chemicals such as residues of veterinary drugs, pesticides, food additives used in unsafe quantities, contact reactions from inappropriate food containers and the careless use of cleaning products. Chemical contamination can be *direct* or *indirect* and the route of contamination can start inside or outside food premises.

ROUTES OF CONTAMINATION

The careless use or storage of pesticides on a farm could directly contaminate cereals, vegetables or fruit, or could cause indirect contamination by contaminating containers or packaging used for food. In food preparation areas the use of the wrong concentration of a cleaning product or the careless application of a machine lubricant could splash or drip directly onto food.

Contamination risks increase if chemicals are stored in containers that are not purpose-made because they may leak. If they are kept in unmarked containers, such as soft drinks bottles, the contents may be mistaken for food, with potentially fatal consequences. Purpose-made containers that have been recycled for food storage without full decontamination have also caused food poisoning outbreaks.

Poisoning can occur from contact reactions when food touches inappropriate materials — for example, zinc poisoning from galvanised containers — or as a result of the leaching or migration of toxic substances into food — for example, acid foods carried through pipes or containers made from metals such as antimony, copper, cadmium or lead.

DETECTION

Although all food deliveries should be checked for contamination, detecting chemical contaminants is complicated or even impossible because many residues, such as heavy metals, can be detected only by laboratory methods. This is a point at which your controls may be obliged to depend upon those of your supplier, whose *supplier's certificate* should guarantee that your *product specification* has been fulfilled to the letter. Even so, you should consider arranging regular audits (see pages 307 to 308) and random tests. Whenever you undertake a hazard analysis (see pages 314 to 324), include possible chemical residues, as well as potential contamination on your premises.

Transport
Delivery vehicles used for transporting food should be used only for food. Other products which are transported with food or are carried on the vehicle during a

previous delivery can contaminate food by spilling or as a result of evaporation. As consignments of goods may pass through the hands of several transport companies and be loaded on and off several vehicles before the products reach your premises, you need written assurances from your immediate supplier about the steps taken to protect food from contamination.

CONTROLS

As you can see, although some measures can be controlled on your premises, many others that you need to put in place are indirect or at arm's length. You must however ensure that you do establish appropriate systems of control.

Before receipt
- Create a product specification.
- Obtain a supplier's certificate.
- Arrange product sampling.

Before use
- Ensure that a supervisor or manager has checked that the chemical is of the right kind and strength and that it is correctly labelled.
- Ensure that staff check the purpose and function of chemicals.
- Establish and supervise the rules for the dosing and dilution of chemicals.

Storage and transport
- Label all chemical containers if substances must be decanted from the manufacturer's containers.
- Use only purpose-designed containers.
- Store chemicals in labelled storage areas away from food and food equipment.
- Inspect and control stocks regularly.

In general
- Use only non-toxic food-grade substances (such as food-safe machinery oil) where there is a risk of direct contact with a product.
- Keep an inventory of all chemicals used and stored on the premises.
- Consider documenting the *application* of chemicals.
- Train and supervise staff in the safe use of chemicals.

⊕ MAKING IT EASIER FOR OTHERS

- Outline the measures that your company puts in place to protect food from contamination that could occur outside the premises.
- Explain the importance of using cleaning and other chemicals on the premises in a way that does not cause contamination.
- Remind staff of personal safety when using chemicals.

PHYSICAL CONTAMINATION

Is it better to concentrate on *preventing* physical contamination in the first place or to accept that it will happen and put your main effort into *detecting* it when it does? The only correct answer is that you must do both.

Physical *contaminants*, such as pieces of glass or splinters of wood, must be prevented at all costs. Not only can they cause serious injury, but they are also extremely difficult to detect. Other forms of physical contamination, such as stones, pits and soil in raw foods including fruit and grain, may not be completely preventable and must be detected instead. The problem is that detection is never one hundred per cent effective, so it should be seen as the last line of defence, never a main strategy.

SOURCES

As we have seen in Part 3, *intrinsic* physical contaminants are part of the original raw food and include leaves, twigs, scales and bones. They may be present in deliveries of raw ingredients and may remain during production or preparation. *Extrinsic* contaminants can enter the food flow at any stage. Some may be a severe *hazard*, causing major injury or even death. Others may be unpleasant but physically harmless. Even so, a food business can be prosecuted for the presence of any contaminant in food simply because the product is not of the nature, quality or substance expected by the consumer.

TYPICAL CONTAMINANTS AND THEIR SOURCES	
Contaminants	Likely source
Wood	Wooden pallets, packing cases, wooden surfaces, wooden utensils
Bolts, nuts, wire, staples, swarf	Equipment, machinery, utensils, blades, maintenance staff, packaging materials
Cardboard, string, plastic, rubber bands, tape	Packaging materials, staff
Insects, larvae, eggs, pupae	Raw products and ingredients or through infestation of food premises
Animals, fur/hair, feathers, droppings	Raw products and ingredients or through infestation of food premises
Glass	Lights, windows, auxiliary items (such as stop watches and manometers), bottles, jewellery (especially watches)
Fragments of paint, rust, enamel	Equipment and premises
Personal items: hair, fingernails, pieces of jewellery, hair clips, plasters, cigarette ends	Staff, visitors

PREVENTION

Every food business can use various forms of barrier to prevent physical contamination and cross-contamination. These barriers may be:

- physical — for example, the use of lids on containers of food in storage or the use of filters and sieves during food preparation
- spatial — for example, the separation of 'clean' and 'unclean' materials and processes.

Some barriers are obvious, but others may be identified only through a hazard analysis of products, processes and management controls such as waste disposal and pest control.

Contamination that comes from food

It is important to sort out intrinsic contaminants at an early stage because processing and preparation can reduce the size of, and disguise, the food and the contaminant so making it more difficult to detect and remove the contaminant at a later stage.

It may not be a pleasant thought, but it is a sad fact that primary producers often have to deal with a high level of organic material that counts as physical contaminants, such as insects and little vertebrates that are picked up by harvesting machines. Washing and floating loose items such as fruit and vegetables can be a first step to sorting out these 'foreign bodies'.

Agreeing responsibility and standards

The key to ensuring that intrinsic contaminants are removed lies in establishing and implementing effective controls, either with your supplier, or within your own premises, or both. Sometimes the main responsibility is with the supplier. However, your company still needs to check the condition of food on delivery and to keep an eye open for problems during processing or preparation.

Wherever the responsibility lies, it needs to be clearly spelled out. Bear in mind that while external measures may save you time and effort, in-house checks, where they are practicable, may give you greater confidence and control over standards.

Specifying

When you contract with a supplier to provide a product or ingredient you need to state as precisely as possible in the *product specification* the nature, type and quality of the product you require. This should protect you from having to accept inferior or unsafe goods. If you expect suppliers to provide you with food from which some parts have been removed, this must be clearly set out in your product specification. You also need to agree with the supplier on the exact controls and standards to be applied. Should salad vegetables be washed before delivery? Will you accept a small amount of soil on carrots, but not cakes of mud, or must they be entirely free from visible contaminants?

Contamination introduced during processing

Non-food items (extrinsic contaminants) can be accidentally introduced into food at almost any stage of the food flow, with the possible consequence of serious injuries or damaging publicity, or both. So prevention is your company's first line of defence. If lapses do occur, despite your best intentions, you must carry out a thorough investigation and a fresh hazard analysis (see pages 314 to 327).

There is not a single, universal method of prevention. Instead, you need to tackle potential contaminants one by one, as revealed by your hazard analysis. The following paragraphs suggest some *general* controls that may be appropriate to consider for your workplace. In each case it is important to:

- establish proper procedures for checking food
- train staff to understand the importance of following the workplace procedures
- ensure that all incoming deliveries are checked carefully — this involves special training for the staff who are given the responsibility for checking deliveries
- establish procedures for reporting contamination and encourage staff to do so
- establish procedures for dealing with contaminated products, including lines of responsibility
- keep the premises clean, tidy and in good repair
- set a good example.

Pests
- Keep the premises pest-free and implement a rigorous pest control programme (see pages 360 to 374).
- Get professional advice on the positioning of insect traps and electrical fly-killers. Ensure that staff understand how to deal with rodent bait boxes and why they are positioned as they are.
- Deal immediately with any signs of pests in a food processing or storage area.
- Destroy damaged or part-consumed products and call in expert assistance.
- Reject any infested incoming material before it enters the storage area.
- Set up a quarantine zone for contaminated goods.
- Establish a safe disposal method for contaminated food.
- Train and encourage staff to spot and report signs of infestation.

Building materials
- Maintain the premises in good condition.
- Encourage staff to report defects.

Food packaging materials
- Keep packing and unpacking processes away from areas where food is handled.
- Ensure that the unpacking area is kept clean and tidy.

- Provide suitable containers for packaging refuse.
- Train staff to look out for pieces of plastic wrapping adhering to frozen food.
- Avoid using metal staples in cardboard cartons containing food.

Glass and other brittle materials
- Use unbreakable, shatter-proof or splinter-proof materials whenever possible.
- Protect breakable light fittings with diffusers or shatter-proof sleeves.
- Prohibit the use of glass bottles, jars and other such utensils in food areas except where they are an unavoidable part of the production or preparation process.
- Establish breakage control and disposal procedures where breakable materials have to be used and ensure that staff are fully trained in them.

Home-made patches and repairs
- Establish procedures for reporting defects and problems with machinery and equipment, including lines of responsibility.
- Encourage staff to report problems or suspected problems and ban attempts at do-it-yourself repairs, however well intentioned they may be.
- Make sure that proper maintenance help is available and that staff know who to call on.
- Provide good supplies of new utensils and insist that broken items be thrown away.
- Service equipment regularly, rather than having to deal with emergency repairs, and keep spare parts in stock.

Metal
- Position equipment and machinery in such a way that loose pieces cannot fall into food on a work surface, conveyor belt, mixer, cutter or filling hopper.
- Train maintenance personnel not to leave screws, nuts and machine parts lying around after a job or between tasks.
- Insist that maintenance staff check machinery and conduct a trial run after adjustment, repairs or moving. (If there is friction between moving parts metal swarf may sheer off and contaminate food.)
- Ensure that every engineering task is rounded off by a check that includes ensuring that there are no loose parts.
- Establish clear rules for employees and for contract, or off-site, personnel who maintain, service or repair any kind of machinery. Do not forget to include vending machines and refrigerators under this heading.
- Ban the use of company packaging such as jars, buckets, cups and bottles for any use other than for food in case the container is accidentally filled with food later.

Personal items and non-food items
- Provide staff facilities for relaxation, eating and smoking. Ensure they are pleasant and well maintained. If people are not using them, find out why.

- Make certain that staff are aware of the rules for personal hygiene and personal habits, such as not wearing jewellery (see page 235). Put up notices to remind everyone and make sure that refresher training is carried out on a regular basis and whenever problems of physical contamination occur.
- Ensure that plastic cups, sweet wrappers, chewing gum and so on are not brought into food areas.
- Consider banning the use of rubber bands, paper clips, pens, personal stereos, pagers, screwdrivers and other such non-food items in food areas.
- Consider motivational factors if things go wrong. Deal with any issues such as stress or examples of poor supervision that might prevent rules being taken seriously.
- Provide suitable protective clothing and check that it is appropriate and in good repair so that fibres, buttons and so on do not fall off.
- Consider sewing name labels and badges securely on to protective clothing.
- Consider providing sealed boxes, or similar containers, for carrying small tools and equipment through food areas.
- Ensure that supervisors and managers set a good example.

Wood
- Whenever possible, replace wooden items with stainless steel or hard plastic.
- Consider banning wooden pallets from food areas. Alternatively, consider transferring goods to plastic pallets before they enter these zones.
- Handle wooden crates and pallets with care and introduce a pallet policy to identify and dispose of defective ones.
- Take special care when wood is part of the finished product, such as cocktail sticks in rollmop herrings or sticks in lollipops or iced lollies. Ensure that the wood is close-grained and splinter-free and is kept in suitable containers.

DETECTION

Even when you have taken every possible care to prevent contamination, there may still be scope for contaminants to get into food and remain there. Every food business therefore has a responsibility to detect contaminants that could remain. Exactly what you do and how you do it depends on the type of food business and its size. Small businesses, for example, may need to contract, where possible, to place the main responsibility for removing physical contaminants on suppliers. This may be the only realistic way that some small and medium-size enterprises (SMEs) can deal with some kinds of contamination as it may not be reasonable to expect them to install X-ray machines or metal detectors. Even so, the smallest, one-person food business still has a legal responsibility to protect its consumers from harm, if only by staying alert to what is in food.

Routes
There is just one good thing about physical hazards: usually they tell a story. While it may be immensely difficult to trace the contamination routes of microbiological

hazards, by comparison, physical contaminants provide hard evidence — and you can use that evidence to discover what went wrong. For example, if you find a metal screw, you may suspect that a piece of equipment has been poorly maintained, whereas a false eyelash will point you in a rather different direction.

Methods of detection

Even so, you may find yourself involved in something akin to hide-and-seek as physical contaminants do not always turn up in the most obvious places. Detection methods for physical contaminants include:

- visual inspection
- metal detectors
- base and side scanners of bottles
- X-raying.

Visual inspection

This form of detection can take place in most food businesses during many stages of food handling. It is the first-line control during the receipt of deliveries to your premises and should include random spot-checks when staff open some of the packaged goods. Visual inspection can also be carried out, for example, during manual sorting from a conveyor belt when unwanted plant material can be separated from fruit and vegetables, and it is an essential part of general stock and pest control.

Do bear in mind that where staff are involved in on-line inspection or sorting processes, they may lose concentration at times, so additional methods may also be desirable where they are feasible. Staff must know what they should do if they discover physical contaminants, and supervisors or managers should monitor visual inspections to ensure that the control deals adequately with any *critical control points* (see pages 318 to 320) that are designed to prevent harm to consumers.

Automated processes

Detection equipment is designed to distinguish differences between the physical properties of the food or food product and the contaminant. Criteria for detection may be shape, size, colour, density, magnetic properties or opacity to X-rays. It is good practice to make a note of incidents of contamination in a log book for automatic detection devices. The log could also include details of checks on equipment and calibration records. You could also run *dummy tests* with identifiable batches of food to ensure that the devices are working properly.

Magnetic devices and metal detectors

Magnets can detect and remove most metallic contaminants. Even so, the force by which magnetic materials are attracted is proportional to their size, and smaller particles, such as staples or swarf, are harder to detect than larger ones such as nails. The strength of the magnetic device also decreases with distance.

Magnetic devices detect and extract metal contaminants from products such as soup. In contrast, metal detectors detect metal in products such as bread and reject the entire contaminated item. As a consequence, metal detectors are usually positioned towards the end of a production process, often at the packaging stage. The crucial factors are not only the diameter of the metal particles, but also the speed of the conveyor belt — detectors can, for example, fail to detect contaminants if the conveyor belt goes too fast.

Bottle scanners

These work by sending beams of light through the bottles onto a photo-electric cell as the bottles proceed along a conveyor system. Dirt or other physical contaminants interrupt the light beam, triggering the machine to remove the bottle from the conveyor. This not only prevents possible physical contamination but also allows returnable glass containers to be cleaned thoroughly and re-used.

However, scanners cannot usually detect contaminants through the base of a bottle, which is usually thicker than the rest of the glass, unless it has top and bottom light beams in addition to the side beams. The efficiency of scanners must be checked regularly by sending through a contaminated dummy bottle.

X-raying

This method is especially useful for detecting material such as bone, glass, plastic and aluminium which are not magnetic. X-raying is practicable only for large-scale production and preparation and is often used in the production of supermarket convenience meals.

Procedures after detecting physical contamination

Ensure that everyone knows what to do if physical contaminants are discovered. Include the responsibilities and reporting procedures as well as the specific steps to be taken. Bear in mind that detection devices may not reveal every particle of a contaminant like glass and there may still be shards in the food.

Your procedures are likely to need to include the following actions:
- stop production
- discard the whole batch of food that was under production or preparation
- identify and remove the *source* of the contamination
- clean and service any food equipment and utensils involved
- resume the process or preparation only after a supervisor or manager has checked that every possible action has been taken to avoid a recurrence

- record the incident, possibly in a log book
- review the system, critical control points and critical limits (see pages 314 to 337)
- instigate any appropriate measures to prevent the contamination from happening again.

🧩 MAKING IT EASIER FOR OTHERS

- Explain how physical contaminants are a cause of considerable customer dissatisfaction and distress.
- Point out that physical contaminants make food unfit for human consumption, even if they have done no physical harm.
- Emphasise the role that staff have in spotting physical contaminants in food.
- Encourage staff to report any situation that they feel could lead to physical contamination.
- Encourage staff to watch out for signs of pest infestation and to report it to their supervisor or manager.

⊛ MANAGEMENT MATTERS

Contamination marks the start of the route from hazard — the possibility of harm — to food-borne illness. As a consequence, all your food safety systems must be geared to preventing contamination in the first place. To do so, you must establish and maintain systems and controls that PROTECT food from contamination. Where microbiological contamination is possible, you must also establish and maintain procedures that PREVENT microbiological multiplication and DESTROY any pathogenic and spoilage micro-organisms that could survive in food. There are various ways to establish such systems and to monitor their effectiveness and these are discussed in detail in the rest of Part 4.

As a manager, you must make yourself aware of the potential sources, routes and vehicles of contamination both within your premises and before food is delivered there. Knowledge of these factors will help you to implement the key controls for protecting food from contamination. To assess the risk of the multiplication of pathogens you also need to consider product attributes (intrinsic factors) and process qualities (extrinsic factors). Additional knowledge about the total composition of the microbiological flora may also help you to assess whether pathogenic organisms are supported or inhibited.

The prevention of contamination and the minimising of its consequences when it does occur depend upon dedicated teamwork throughout the company. Make sure that you:

- provide the right equipment for every task
- provide suitable protective clothing
- set clear rules for personal hygiene and habits
- build a culture that values doing things the right way
- organise appropriate supervision
- ensure that premises and equipment are kept clean and are maintained and serviced regularly so that they do not deteriorate
- do not expect people to follow rules unless they have been trained properly to carry out their jobs
- ensure that all food handlers understand the impact of their actions and omissions
- ensure that staff who do *not* handle food are also aware that they could cause contamination if they fail to follow company procedures
- make certain that managers and visitors do not break the rules
- set a good example yourself.

MANAGING RESOURCES

🔑 KEY POINTS

Criteria for the selection of a site for food premises.
Why workflow is so important to food safety.
The significance of 'clean' and 'dirty' processes.
How the design and construction of food premises can contribute to the prevention of contamination and cross-contamination.
Why foods and processes must be segregated.
What to bear in mind for essential services and facilities.
Why separate facilities are required for personal hygiene.
Suitable materials for the construction of food premises.
Suitable materials for food-contact surfaces, equipment and utensils.
Factors affecting food safety in the design of food equipment.
What to consider in planning the safe storage and disposal of rubbish and food waste.
The part that the design and construction of premises plays in pest control.
The importance of an easy-to-access and easy-to-clean layout.
How design and construction affects transport vehicles, temporary and movable food premises, vending machines and the use of domestic premises for commercial food production.

Why food safety training and development are essential in a food business.
The benefits of effective training.
The management role in staff training in food safety.
The principles of training.
Who needs to be trained.
How to evaluate the training needs in food safety and to draw up a training needs assessment.
Determining an appropriate training strategy.
Implementing, monitoring and evaluating the training strategy in comparison to food safety practice in the workplace.
Keeping training records.
Continuing the professional development of food safety managers.

KEY WORDS

ambient temperature
the environmental
temperature, often used to
describe normal room
temperature.

carrier
an infected person showing no
symptoms of an infectious
disease, who may transmit it to
others.

contaminant
any unwanted material, object
or substance in food.

contamination
the presence in food, or the
process of transferring to food,
any unwanted material, object
or substance.

cross-contamination
the transfer of a contaminant
from one contaminated
product, such as raw meat, to
another previously
uncontaminated product, such
as a ready-to-eat food.

direct contamination
the route directly from the
source of contamination to a
food.

due diligence
a legal defence where it can be
shown that all reasonable steps

were taken to avoid committing
a food safety offence.

extrinsic contamination
contamination from sources
other than the raw food itself.

flora (microbial)
the microbial species normally
found in a particular habitat,
such as the intestine.

food safety policy
a company's written statement
of its commitment to meeting
its obligations towards
customers and to producing
safe and legal products.

hazard
anything, whether
microbiological, chemical or
physical, that might cause
harm to the consumer.

high risk food
a food that easily supports the
multiplication of pathogenic
micro-organisms.

indirect contamination
contamination due to the
action of a vehicle of
contamination or a vector.

intrinsic contamination
contamination associated with
the food itself.

multiplication
microbial reproduction, such as
by binary fission (bacteria) or
budding (yeast).

potable
safe to drink.

ready-to-eat food
a food that is either eaten raw,
or is not prepared or treated
(such as by cooking) in a way
that would kill any pathogens
present immediately before the
food is eaten.

risk
a measure, or scale, of the
likelihood that a hazard will
occur.

source of contamination
where a contaminant has its
origin.

vehicle of contamination
any substance, object or living
being that carries
contamination from A to B; a
factor in indirect
contamination.

workflow
the logical route organised
through food premises for
food, food handlers, equipment
and waste throughout each
stage of production.

from the ground up

Designing your own new premises is the ideal situation. Right from the choice of location to the last details of fixtures, fittings and decoration, you can plan for food safety every step of the way.

Even if you do not have this luxury, most of the principles are the same whether you are moving into an existing building or converting or refurbishing premises.

There are three main stages in the process: planning, design and construction.

The first consideration in the planning stage is the identification of a suitable site — a process that can involve feasibility studies and research into planning legislation and zoning requirements, transport links, environmental impact, market factors and financing.

Planning then boils down to four main aspects: access for delivery, distribution, market and customers; workforce availability; raw materials availability; and the 'orientation' of the site — that is, the potential effects of

Food premises must comply with laws governing construction, occupational health and safety and food safety. Bodies such as English Heritage and Cadw can influence plans likely to affect historic buildings and locations, while local authorities can impose restrictions in designated conservation areas. Building legislation includes: the Town and Country Planning Act (1990) which controls the volume of development and the appearance and layout of buildings; the Public Health Acts (1936 to 1961) which impose restrictions on noise, pollution and public nuisance; the Highways Act (1980), dealing with roads and pavements; the Building Act (1984), the main construction legislation; and The Building Regulations (1991) which set out material and design standards.

external pollution or contamination from the surrounding environment. The order of importance of these factors depends on the nature of the business — access to bulk agricultural products, for instance, is not important to a small restaurant, whereas good access is vital for both workforce and customers, as well as for the delivery and distribution of products.

If the premises are sited within the business's main market or customer catchment area, you must take into account the food safety implications of walk-in customers.

In addition to general staffing, you may need to look at the availability of specialists. Will the area attract the people you want? What about suitable housing for your workforce? Will the commuting of staff create a nuisance or have an adverse environmental impact? Are raw materials readily available in the vicinity? If not, can they be easily obtained via road, rail, sea or air links? Will their delivery have consequences for food safety or the environment?

Pollution or contamination from the surrounding environment must also be considered. For example, care must be taken to ensure that air intakes are not downwind of likely contaminants, such as silage pits or landfill sites.

Finally, the provision of essential services (water, gas, electricity, waste removal) and the addressing of any potential food safety hazards, such as smoke, chemicals or flooding, also come into the planning stage.

At the design stage, you and the architect decide on the form of the building, its internal layout and the materials and finishes that will be used. After detailed consultation with you, the architect makes drawings of the building and suggests the layout of equipment and fittings.

This is also the stage at which pest prevention measures and facilities for controlling the internal environment — through lighting, noise reduction, heating, cooling and air conditioning systems — are designed to suit your kind of business.

At last all the paperwork turns into reality — from the substructure right through to the installation of equipment and the application of surface materials, finishes and colour.

UNDER A SUITABLE ROOF

Imagine it is your job to turn a derelict warehouse on a trendy waterfront into a state-of-the-art restaurant. As the walls are currently decorated with cobwebs and there are pipes hanging from the ceiling, it does not look as if food could ever be prepared there, let alone hygienically.

Alternatively, imagine that after years of happily running a small convenience store cum sandwich bar from a Tudor-beamed building, you have been quietly advised to improve your workflow and install food-safe work surfaces. Nothing has actually gone wrong, so you are loathe to spend hard-earned profit unless it is really essential.

Or, there again, imagine yourself in the position of a newly appointed food safety adviser to the designers of a new canning plant: you have your best chance ever to influence food safety.

Knowing what to do

But would *you* know where to start in each of these three very different situations? What would be important and how would you create and maintain premises that are fit for food?

THE BASICS

Despite initial appearances, the principles are the same whether you are building from scratch, or renovating or improving existing premises. They apply equally, no matter which food sector you are dealing with, whatever the type, size or location of the food business, or age of the building.

The principles are the same because the main aim in any food operation is to eliminate food *hazards*, or at the very least to minimise the *risks* from them. This involves:
- *protecting* food against microbiological, chemical and physical *contamination*
- *preventing* microbial multiplication
- *destroying micro-organisms*, their spores and toxins.

This chapter outlines the ways in which the design and construction of premises play a major part in:
- protecting food from contamination and cross-contamination
- helping staff to prevent microbiological survival and multiplication
- enabling staff to destroy micro-organisms.

What is involved

Of course, *you* may not have much of a say, if any, in where food premises are located, and you may not be the person with the final responsibility for service and maintenance contracts for the building. Even so, as a manager with responsibility for food safety, you need to know:

- which materials are the most suitable for the structure of food areas
- which materials are the most suitable for food-contact surfaces
- which services (such as water, light and ventilation) and facilities (such as toilets and rubbish areas) should be provided
- how the design and construction can help you to keep pests out of the premises
- what to consider when purchasing and installing food equipment
- how easy, or otherwise, it is to clean the premises and its equipment to standards that are suitable for food preparation and storage
- how a linear *workflow* can contribute to the elimination of food hazards or can help to minimise the risks from them.

WHAT MIGHT IT COST?

Time, effort and money invested in getting your premises up to scratch, and keeping them that way, will pay you back many times over. Some food hazards, such as dust from utensils hanging over food (see the picture right), could be eliminated, while others, such as cross-contamination, could become easier to control. What's more, an orderly work environment gives customers and clients greater confidence in your company and may improve staff morale by making some tasks, such as cleaning, more straightforward. There is also the matter of legal compliance (see page 160): after all, a food hygiene inspection is *not* the time to discover that mice are running riot in your dry goods store or that your famous old copper kettle could be slowly poisoning your regular afternoon tea drinkers.

In the end, perhaps the real issue is whether you can afford *not* to provide suitable premises and equipment. Although complete refurbishment may not be cheap, even making a few minor changes or re-organising your workflow could help you to enhance your operational efficiency, avoid an outbreak of food-borne illness and keep your company well within the law.

HOW SAFE FOR FOOD?

Throughout the book we use the word construction in the usual way to mean either the process of erecting a building or the physical structure of a building. The word design is used in a broader-than-usual sense to cover the shape and external appearance (including landscaping) of the premises, as well as the internal layout, installations and fittings.

PREVENTION
Effective design
and construction
help to eliminate
contact between
high risk foods
and between
high risk and
other foods. They
also help to stop
food from making
contact with dirt,
waste and
rubbish, unfit
food and toxic
materials.

DESIGNED TO AVOID CONTAMINATION

Needless to say, premises need to be suitable for the kind of food operation you are running, but they must also help you to prevent food hazards from leading to food-borne illness — see the diagram on page 43. Effective design and construction of food premises can help to:

- prevent direct contamination by the:
  - use of appropriate construction methods
  - provision of appropriate surfaces and finishing materials
- prevent cross-contamination through:
  - a linear workflow (a logical way of working)
  - the separation of raw and other foods and the separation of various functions such as 'clean' and 'dirty' processes.

On the following five pages we outline each of these guiding principles in turn, then discuss some specific points in greater detail. Before we do so, it may help to outline what we mean by 'clean' and 'dirty' in the context of design.

Clean and dirty

There are designated 'clean' and 'dirty' areas in many food premises. This does not mean that the clean area is never dirty, or that the dirty area is never cleaned. The descriptions refer to the state of the food or processes carried out in that particular area. So, anywhere that raw food is handled or prepared is considered 'dirty' because of the possibility of contamination from the food, while a 'clean' area is one where foods are being processed or packaged, or finished foods are handled.

With this explanation in mind, you will easily see why it makes sense for the air circulation and drainage flow to move from clean to dirty areas, and for the workflow (see page 206) to prevent taking staff or food, or both, from clean areas or processes back to dirty areas or processes. Staff in large food premises often wear different coloured protective clothing according to the area where they should be working: they are then easily spotted if they stray into the 'wrong' area.

APPROPRIATE CONSTRUCTION METHODS

LEGAL DEMANDS
By law, food
premises must be
suitable for their
use and easy to
clean. They must
be designed and
constructed in
ways that
prevent
contamination
and access by
pests.

Whether you are designing a building from scratch or converting or refurbishing existing premises, the following principles of construction should be observed to help maintain food safety. Premises should be:

- windproof and waterproof
- equipped to prevent access by pests
- designed to make cleaning easy
- constructed from durable, impervious and easily cleaned materials (floors, walls and ceilings in food areas)
- designed to allow for a workflow that progresses from 'dirty' to 'clean', allowing for efficient working.

Outside the building

Circulation

Vehicles can include incoming deliveries of food and ingredients, incoming staff and customers and outgoing products, waste and rubbish. Ideally the incoming and outgoing routes should be separated: at the very least, they should be controlled.

Entrances

It is not always necessary or practicable to have separate entrances for staff who handle food and for those who do not, such as administrative workers. However, you might be able to provide separate corridors or routes through the building.

Delivery and loading areas

Although in many cases the same dock and entrance may be used for both delivery and loading, it is preferable to have segregated delivery and dispatch areas. For example, in abattoirs the fresh meat should not be loaded onto lorries in the same place where live animals are brought in. A double-entry system can help — food is unloaded and taken to a designated unpacking area before being moved to a temperature-controlled area, if appropriate.

Landscaping

Landscaping around food premises should:

- be easy to keep clean
- not encourage rubbish dumping or dirt collection
- not encourage or harbour pests.

There should be a strip of hardstanding, such as concrete or tarmac, around the building, directly against the outside wall, to discourage pests from nesting near, or gaining access to, the building. This has the added benefit of making obvious any hole in the building that might allow pests to get in.

Exterior waste storage and disposal

Food premises tend to produce a wide variety of food waste and other rubbish, including dry (such as packaging), liquid (such as drinks and waste water used for cleaning), food (including, possibly, food suitable for composting) and chemicals.

Waste has to be stored outside until collection for disposal. If it is not removed immediately or automatically, then it should be kept separate from any incoming or outgoing deliveries of food. Controlled conditions, including refrigeration for some food waste, may be necessary to prevent microbial multiplication.

Disabled access

You should ensure that there is adequate access for disabled staff and visitors, according to the appropriate regulations.

Inside the building

The internal layout may be predetermined if you are taking over premises rather than building from scratch. Ideally, however, the internal layout should take into account the:

- circulation of people within the building — food handlers, other staff, customers and visitors
- workflow
- waste storage and disposal.

Customers and visitors should have their own entrances and separate circulation routes that keep them away from food processing areas. Areas to which customers have access should be designed to minimise contamination.

Circulation

Wherever possible, the paths of food handlers and other staff should not cross. This may be a matter of designating areas where individuals have authority to go and not to go, or it may entail structural separation. Visitors, such as delivery drivers, and customers should be kept away from food processing areas.

Workflow

The flow of people and food through the building, and from activity to activity, must be planned with as few cross-over points as possible. See below for more information about workflow.

Waste storage within the building

Prior to its disposal, waste and rubbish must be collected and stored, initially inside the building. At no time should it come into contact with food products — for example, waste and rubbish should not travel through the building by the same route as fresh food, including movement by lifts, hoists, trolleys or vehicles.

PROVISION OF APPROPRIATE SURFACES AND FINISHING MATERIALS

All surfaces that come into contact with food should:
- be easy to maintain, clean and disinfect
- be made from a non-toxic material
- prevent the migration of chemicals onto food.

Surfaces that are *not* expected to come into contact with food should also be selected with care — for example, wall paint should be non-toxic and washable. The chart opposite suggests suitable materials for surfaces and finishes.

LINEAR WORKFLOW

Workflow is the sequence of stages or processes involved in creating a product. In the food industry the term usually refers to the various routes travelled by food, food handlers, equipment and rubbish during food production from the delivery of raw food right through to the dispatch, sale or service of the finished products. *Linear* workflow is the ideal: you should aim to organise a clear and logical progression of tasks that safeguards food through all the process stages. Wherever

CHARACTERISTICS	EXAMPLES OF IDEAL MATERIALS
Work surfaces	
Non-porous	Stainless steel
Non-scratch	
Easy-to-clean	
Equipment and utensils	
Easy-to-clean	Stainless steel, polypropylene and other
Smooth finish	synthetics
Non-porous	
Shelving	
Easy-to-clean	Stainless steel or plastic
High-strength	
Walls	
Light-coloured to show up dirt	Glazed tiles, smooth painted plaster
Grease-resistant	
Heat-resistant	
Coved at base and top	
Floors	
Non-slip	Epoxy resin, concrete with granite chips,
Easy-to-clean	vinyl sheet, non-slip ceramic or quarry
Weight-bearing	tiles
Hard-wearing	
Sloped for drainage	
Water and chemical resistant if	
necessary	
Ceilings	
Smooth	Metal, plaster
Easy-to-clean	
Coved	
Light-coloured to show dirt	
Fire-resistant	
Non-flaking	

possible, avoid points where people, food and equipment cross paths. The more cross-over points that exist, the more opportunities there are for contamination.

SEPARATION OF FOODS AND PROCESSES

In addition to a linear workflow, it is an advantage to separate different foods, functions and processes to prevent contamination. For example, it would be unwise to prepare raw meat in the same area as salads.

Providing separate work areas

It is common in larger food businesses to have several preparation areas designated for particular foods or processes, each area with its own facilities and equipment. Dishwashing and laundry should be carried out away from food areas.

Keeping foods apart

Different groups of food need to be kept apart — root vegetables, for example, could contaminate cheese if stored in close proximity. You need to ensure that there is appropriate and separate storage for all the products and ingredients your company uses — for example, refrigerated, dry and frozen.

It may also be necessary to provide suitable storage areas at different stages of the workflow — for example, to store raw materials or finished products.

The most important points are to:
- provide suitable storage conditions, such as ambient, refrigerated and frozen
- keep raw foods apart from cooked and *ready-to-eat foods*
- segregate *high risk foods* from each other and from cooked and ready-to-eat products.

Every effort should be made to ensure that these groups do not come into contact with each other, either when in storage, or in transit between storage and other areas of the premises.

Other storage requirements

As well as keeping different types of food segregated, it is essential to separate food and non-food items. Cleaning materials and any other potentially toxic materials must be stored safely and separately, well away from food. More information on storage is provided on pages 301 to 306.

FROM OUTLINE TO DETAIL

Now that we have covered the basic underlying principles for avoiding food contamination through the effective design and construction of food premises, we examine certain aspects of the design of food premises in greater detail.

DOMESTIC PREMISES

Just as with vending machines and mobile premises, commercial catering done from a home kitchen must comply with the same principles of food safety. The only difference is one of scale.

IN POSITION FOR CLEANING AND MAINTENANCE

According to the law, all food premises must permit adequate cleaning or disinfection or both. This means that the floors, walls, ceilings and work surfaces must be made from materials that can be cleaned and disinfected easily.

Avoiding dirt traps

The design, layout and location of equipment must avoid inaccessible nooks and crannies in rooms where dirt can collect unnoticed or where only microbe-sized staff could possibly reach to clean. Similarly, equipment should not have sharp-angled internal corners which are difficult to penetrate for cleaning.

Pipes and ducts

As everyone who has ever tried to clean behind a toilet knows, badly positioned pipes can easily become a dirt trap. Pipework and ducts in food premises need to be accessible for maintenance but should also be incorporated into the structure in such a way that surfaces are smooth and continuous for easy cleaning.

MACHINE SERVICE

Vending machines and other stand-alone facilities are subject to the same regulations governing the rest of the food industry. The law assumes that the food going into a vending machine has been prepared in food premises that meet all the relevant food safety and construction standards. In addition, the law views the vending machine itself as a food establishment, albeit on a miniature scale.

The mobile solution

Movable, rather than fitted, equipment gives better access for cleaning on all sides and underneath. The degree of mobility depends on the size and weight of the item, how much space there is for moving equipment, the services — such as water, electricity or gas — to which it is connected, and health and safety considerations for the staff who must move the equipment.

KEEPING PESTS OUT

The design, layout and equipping of food premises should ensure that pests cannot simply walk or fly in. Insects and birds can get in through unprotected open windows or doors that are opened frequently. Birds may roost on unprotected window ledges, canopies and architectural features outside, while insects and some rodents may be attracted to 'dead spaces' behind refrigerators and other equipment, or may find comfortable homes in ducting, cracks and crevices.

Waste or refuse, such as packaging and pallets, that could attract or harbour pests should not be stored against the building. Outside drains should be sealed and not left open, as in the photograph (right). Interceptor chambers can also be installed which include a vertical baffle to obstruct swimming rodents. Any

Drains and gulleys must be covered to prevent contamination and access by pests.

windows that can be opened should be fitted with fly screens. External doors should be fitted with closers and, where deemed necessary, with fly screens. Traps, baits or fly killers within the building should be used and positioned with great care so that dead pests do not contaminate food.

UTILITIES AND PERSONAL HYGIENE

Food preparation cannot take place without access to water and the means to heat and chill food.

A safe water supply

Water that is safe to drink is described as being *potable*. By law all food premises must have an adequate supply of potable water. Food hygiene regulations (see page 159) also stipulate that 'potable water must be used whenever necessary to ensure foodstuffs are not contaminated'.

Direct contact with food

Many recipes and drinks call for the direct addition of water. Water for this purpose should come from a drinking-water supply that meets legislated standards. When a product needs to include carbonated, flavoured, distilled, iced or cold vapourised water, you should ensure that it is prepared from drinking-quality water. To comply with the law and to protect food from contamination, make sure that only potable water is used for washing raw food.

Indirect contact with food

Because of the risk of indirect contamination and cross-contamination, only potable water should be used for cleaning food-contact surfaces and equipment and for supplying wash-hand basins.

ICE AND STEAM

Water is not always used in a liquid state — it may also be used as ice or steam. If there is any chance of contact with food, only potable water must be used. This rule applies whether the ice or steam is added to food or drink directly — as crushed ice in a cocktail or as steamed milk in a cappuccino, for example — or whether it is used indirectly as in a chilled display, such as a fishmonger's slab. Ice and steam machines should be treated like all food-contact equipment and kept free of contamination.

Separating potable and unclean water

You must ensure that potable water cannot come into contact with non-potable water, for instance waste water in the drainage system, rain, water that is part of a heating or cooling system or is kept at hand for fire fighting. Where possible, stop staff from having access to water that is not of drinking quality. If this is not feasible, with fire-fighting supplies for instance, make sure that the water is labelled clearly and that staff training sessions include warnings and explanations about the hazard to food.

Drains

Drains must have sufficient fall to allow all liquid and solid waste to be removed. The direction of the flow should be away from 'clean' areas. Where toilets are flushed into the same drainage system, the entry points must be *after* the food areas.

Gas and electricity

All food premises need a source of energy, usually electricity or gas. This energy supplies not only ancillary systems such as light, heat and computer power but also the energy for processing the food. This is mostly in the form of mains supplies but often food factories have an emergency back-up of bottled gas or electricity generators.

Facilities for personal hygiene

Food operations must provide adequate facilities for the staff's personal hygiene, and there should be wash-hand basins in toilet areas and also in strategic points that are readily accessible to food handlers from food areas.

Basins

In deciding where washing facilities are necessary, take into account the activity being carried out, the probable frequency of hand washing needed at that point or stage in the food flow, how close the next wash-hand basin is and how many people work in the vicinity. Delicatessen counters, butchers' counters, various preparation areas in kitchens and between dirty and clean areas, are some of the places where hand washing facilities may be thought to be essential. Some businesses also place basins between the staff changing rooms and the food area to prompt staff to wash their hands before starting work.

Staff should *not* use food preparation or washing-up *sinks* for the purposes of personal hygiene because of the risk of contaminating food or food-contact surfaces.

Wash-hand *basins* must have a good supply of hot and cold water. In some premises that handle animal products, the use of hand-operated taps is forbidden because of the risk of contamination and cross-contamination from hands. Consider whether food safety in your company might benefit from having taps which can be operated only by knee, foot or elbow.

Toilets

You must provide adequate toilets for the number of staff employed, with separate toilets provided for visitors or customers. The 'suitable' number is set out in legislation covering buildings and health and safety. There are restrictions on where toilets are placed and how they are maintained. Toilets may not open directly onto a room in which food is processed and need to be separated by a ventilated space from any food handling area. To prevent food being contaminated by the air from the

Hard though it may be to believe, this toilet was discovered by EHOs during an inspection of food premises. All personal hygiene facilities must be kept scrupulously clean to help to prevent indirect food contamination.

toilets they must be ventilated, mechanically or naturally, to legislated standards (six to eight air changes per hour). Toilets must also be connected to a sealed drainage system though an effective trap. Facilities for women must include a hygienic means of disposing of sanitary towels and tampons.

Changing rooms and lockers

Food handlers should have one clothes locker for street clothes and another for protective work gear to prevent hygienic wear being contaminated by items from outside. Once staff have changed into protective clothing, the layout should avoid putting them in contact with staff working in 'dirty' areas or making them enter areas that are not hygienically controlled.

A COMFORTABLE WORKING ENVIRONMENT

Food safety occasionally comes into conflict with staff and customer comfort. For example, some foods must be kept at below 8°C, but this temperature leaves most people feeling rather chilly. So, the provision of heating, cooling, lighting and ventilation needs to take both food and people into account. You should also remember that both lighting and ventilation can affect the ambient temperature.

Lighting

Badly lit premises not only make working more difficult, but also make it harder to stay alert and active, so increasing the risk of mistakes. Where food is being prepared there can be numerous extra hazards — dirt could be overlooked, cleaning could be less thorough and the colour and general appearance of the product may be hard to gauge. For all these reasons good lighting is crucial.

TYPICAL ILLUMINATION LEVELS	
Offices	
500 lux	
General inspection	
1000 lux	
Corridors	
100 lux	
Emergency	
0.1-1.0 lux	

Natural and artificial

There are two main kinds of lighting needed inside food premises:

- general background lighting to create a bright, pleasant environment without making people feel they are under a permanent spotlight
- task lighting to provide high and focused illumination for specific jobs.

There needs to be a balance between, on the one hand, the detrimental effects of direct sunlight on equipment, materials and food, and on the other hand, the well-being of staff who generally feel more comfortable when there is some natural light.

Direct sunlight also increases room temperatures, particularly where there are many windows, and therefore increases both the demand on, and the cost of, running the ventilation system.

Where artificial lighting is provided, the light fixtures (including emergency lighting) must be:

- protected by shatterproof diffusers or shrouds so that there is little risk of physical contamination if a bulb breaks
- mounted in such a way — by incorporation into a sealed ceiling system, for instance — that there are no dirt-collecting spaces
- easy to clean.

What colour of light?

There is a surprising amount of variation, known as 'colour temperature', in what we generally regard as white light. It is crucial to get this right where processes require control of food colour. For accurate colour matching, choose 1A or 1B on the colour rendering index or 100 or 90 on the colour rendering groups specified by the CIE (from the French for International Commission on Illumination).

Ventilation

A good flow of air through the building is, of course, necessary to keep people breathing easily, carry away odours and prevent the build-up of condensation. In addition, dust, fumes, chemicals, odours, bacteria and other lightweight (often invisible) hazards can all reach food from the air, whether blown in from outside or wafted around the building through air conditioning and ventilation ducts.

The air circulation should be controlled — after all, there is little point in having clean and disinfected areas if the air itself recontaminates them. Airflow in food premises should always be from 'clean' to 'dirty'. In many factory environments high risk areas are put under positive pressure so that the airflow is forced towards the outside or 'dirty' areas.

REGULAR CHANGES OF AIR
The number of air changes required varies according to the use of the space.
Restaurants and canteens
8-12 air changes per hour
Industrial kitchens
20 to 60 changes per hour
Toilets
6-8 air changes per hour

While natural ventilation may reduce energy consumption and contribute to staff well-being, it often conflicts with the need to prevent contamination. Many food premises control the air temperature, humidity, air quality and number of air changes by mechanical means so that only purified air is supplied to 'clean' areas where food is being processed. All filter systems in a mechanical ventilation or air conditioning system must be accessible for cleaning and replacement.

Air quality control

An air change does not mean merely recirculating the same old air. The law requires a steady supply of fresh air, but your ventilation system is only as good as the air that goes into it and how it is filtered before being circulated around the building. It is important to ensure that the air inlet is not positioned where it could draw in air from the building's air outlet or from any other potentially polluted source.

Removal of hot or impure air from sensitive areas

There may be places where direct, local extraction is required to draw heat, smoke or polluted air away from a particular activity or piece of equipment. This usually means fitting a hood with an extractor fan.

Environmental temperature

In every food facility there are likely to be areas, such as kitchens, that generate heat and may need cooling and others, such as offices, that need to be heated for staff comfort. A good layout will keep these areas separate from each other: a poor layout that locates them close together can make fuel bills soar. You may need some local temperature control — for example, ventilation and extraction to dissipate heat generated by an oven or the back of a refrigerator.

RECOMMENDED AMBIENT WORKING TEMPERATURES	
Dining rooms and restaurants	18°to 21°C
Factories	
sedentary work	19°C
light work	16°C
heavy work	13°C
Toilets and cloakrooms	18°C
General offices	20°C
Warehouses	13°to 16°C

Keeping food hot and cold

To meet legal requirements all food premises must have enough suitable equipment to cook, heat, hot hold and refrigerate food, according to what is appropriate for the foods and processes at each workplace. The equipment must be able to hold high risk foods at the temperatures specified — below 8°C or above 63°C — not only to meet legal obligations, but also because effective temperature control is a major weapon in the battle to prevent microbial multiplication and to destroy pathogens (see also pages 275 to 298).

✤ MAKING IT EASIER FOR OTHERS

- Ensure that the premises are designed, constructed, equipped and laid out to make it as straightforward as possible for staff to produce food that is safe to eat.
- Train the staff how to use the facilities and equipment.
- Formulate company policies for dealing with malfunctioning equipment.
- Encourage staff to report defects in the building and equipment to their manager or supervisor.
- Supervise and review the workflow as part of your hazard analysis.

food on the move

Whether you are catering for a society wedding in a grand marquee, selling burgers and hot dogs from a van at a sports ground or serving afternoon teas in a church hall, the highest standards of food safety are still a legal requirement. The best way to consider such temporary and movable premises and transport is as if they were just another food facility.

Many temporary and mobile premises need a permit from the local council. Although there are some separate regulations — covering market stalls, for instance — the basic requirements for personal and food hygiene are the same as for permanent facilities.

The way in which you meet those requirements may, of course, vary. For example, you may need to install water tanks and hoses, ensure that they are filled from a potable supply — ideally the mains — and arrange for the tanks to be cleaned and disinfected regularly.

You may, however, be permitted such things as covered plastic buckets and plastic bags for waste and rubbish disposal — provided there is no risk of food contamination or environmental pollution.

Even so, safe food storage, the separation of raw and cooked food, temperature control, pest control and general cleanliness must all follow approved good practice if you are to avoid causing food-borne illness.

DEVELOPING STAFF COMPETENCE

Staff can be a company's most valuable resource. But if they are in the wrong place at the wrong time, or if they do not do what they should be doing, staff can also be a shocking drain on company profit. Of course, people make mistakes for many reasons. Sometimes it is because they are under stress, feel insecure in their job or are not motivated, but usually it is because they do not know enough about identifying hazards, minimising risks and setting priorities — in short, because they are poorly trained.

WHY TRAINING COUNTS

As you might expect, there are *statutory* requirements for food safety supervision and training, but from a *business* point of view, it is impossible to rate the importance of staff training and development too highly.

TRAIN FOR
SUCCESS
Training gives
staff the
competence and
confidence to
carry out their
work to the
highest
professional
standards.

Time and time again it has been shown that, besides making fewer mistakes, well-trained employees usually do a better job. On a personal level, they tend to get more out of their work, have more confidence and greater motivation. They may well take on more responsibility, encourage others to achieve even higher standards and may need less supervision. This all counts towards the bottom line.

So, appropriate training in food safety helps a food business to:
- assure the fitness of food for human consumption
- prevent food contamination, microbial multiplication and survival
- prevent food-borne illness
- reassure customers and clients (if they see the evidence of effective food hygiene measures)
- demonstrate *due diligence* (particularly if training records are kept).

Why then are some food handlers poorly trained or not given any training at all? The short answer is: poor management.

Who is responsible for training?

It may be that *you* do not have the word training in your jobtitle, or there may be someone else in your company whose role it is to take care of all forms of occupational training. Even so, if you have any kind of management responsibility for food safety, you are likely to have a responsibility for some aspect of food safety training. This could simply be to liaise with training staff within the company on food safety topics, to make reports to the board of directors, or to make the contractual arrangements with outside training consultants.

However, your role could also involve assessing the type and level of training required, arranging and running training courses and monitoring the effectiveness of all training activities within the workplace.

What you need to know

This chapter covers the main areas of management responsibility for food safety training and development. You may not be responsible for carrying out all the activities mentioned, but you need to know about them and consider how they fit in with your other responsibilities. The chapter is *not* designed to help you to train as a trainer, even though you may find some useful advice here. If you are going to run training sessions yourself, we strongly advise you to enrol on a course that deals specifically with training techniques and, perhaps, to study for a qualification such as the Professional Trainer Certificate (see Reference section for awarding bodies).

WHAT DO WE MEAN BY TRAINING?

Most definitions of training talk about preparing someone to achieve a desired level of skill or competence by the means of instruction and practice. Sometimes the development of certain attitudes and habits is also mentioned. As you read through the rest of this chapter, you might wish to include some of the following words somewhere in your own definition — learning, understanding, confidence, responsibility, teamwork and professionalism. Let's take a brief look at two aspects of dictionary definitions of training — desired level of skill or competence and instruction and practice.

Desired level

Effective training starts with clear goals. It is essential to know what you want staff to achieve by the end of any food safety training activity ('the outcomes') and that the goals are indeed achievable and are measurable. The expected outcomes should be easy to understand and should be as precise as possible, whether they are a change in behaviour (such as more frequent hand-washing) or a demonstration of knowledge (such as being able to state the causes of food poisoning).

A vital part of food safety training is to ensure that staff are shown and told what to do in their own workplace.

Putting it into practice

Training usually needs to include information that helps staff to understand *why* they must do things in certain ways — the chain of contamination and the ideal conditions for microbial multiplication, for example — and firm guidance on *what* to do, *when* to do it and *how* to carry out the task. Formal, classroom-type training is just one possible step, however. Any new knowledge needs to be constantly reinforced in the workplace by a manager or supervisor — perhaps by you.

It does not end there: after all, the best training in the world will be useless if staff are not given the materials and support required to work hygienically. If, for example, there are too few wash-hand basins, or the liquid soap runs out, or the hand towels are fabric ones that are replaced only once a week, how can staff implement all they have learned about the importance of hand hygiene? Similarly, if there are too few staff on duty at peak times or managers set a bad example, it is foolish to expect staff to achieve high standards.

THE SCOPE OF RESPONSIBILITY

The management of food safety training encompasses action to:
- identify all the jobholders in the organisation whose actions or inaction could affect the safety of food
- evaluate the *training needs* for each jobholder
- create a written *training needs assessment*
- devise a strategy for delivering training
- ensure that the strategy is implemented effectively
- monitor and evaluate the training programme
- keep training records
- stay abreast of the company's training requirements.

IDENTIFYING THE JOBHOLDERS WHO COULD AFFECT FOOD SAFETY

Employers in the food industry have a legal responsibility to ensure that everyone who works with food has adequate preparation. The European Union *Directive 93/43 Annex X* states, 'Food business operators shall ensure that food handlers are supervised and instructed and/or trained in food hygiene matters commensurate with their work activity'. British food safety regulations closely follow this wording.

What does this rather vague requirement mean in practice? Simply that food handlers must be competent to work hygienically with food. There is not a standard syllabus: instead it is up to every organisation to determine what kind, and what level, of training is required by each individual to achieve that competence.

The expression *food handler* should not be taken to refer just to people like butchers, bakers and chefs who have direct contact with food, but to anyone who

MATCHING THE JOB
Anyone whose actions, or inactions, could affect consumer health must receive food safety training that matches their tasks and responsibilities.

works with food or whose actions or inactions could affect food. This list gives
examples of the range of jobholders who may need food safety training:

- administration and secretarial staff
- cleaners
- delivery drivers
- food preparation staff
- food retail staff
- kitchen porters
- maintenance engineers
- marketing and public relations staff
- packaging staff
- senior managers and directors
- supervisors
- waiting staff
- warehouse staff.

EVALUATING TRAINING NEEDS

Training needs describes what people need to learn and to carry out in order to do
their jobs properly. Determining training needs is not always straightforward and
you may need to draw on various sources of help.

Written job descriptions and job specifications should provide a good framework for
defining what a particular job involves. Separate interviews with staff and
managers or a round-table discussion with the people who are doing a particular
job should help to reveal what actually happens day to day. It should also give staff
a chance to take an interest in their own professional development and to avoid any
concern they may have that training is a disguised form of criticism of their
personal professional performance.

Finding out what people know and still need to learn

The staff in your organisation probably come from many cultural, social, ethnic and
educational backgrounds, with a variety of experience of the food industry. Some
will have had formal training away from their workplace while others may have
learned everything on the job. Some training activities will have covered hygiene
comprehensively, while others will have done the bare minimum — and it may all
have been a long time ago.

Before you can plan specific training programmes, you need to know people's
training history. There may be company records you can consult and you may need
to ask people to describe the training they have had, including the level — basic,
intermediate, advanced. You can find out a lot by talking to people and making
your own observations. Do this sensitively — people often find it difficult to admit
to gaps in their knowledge, especially if they are professionals with many years'
service under their belt. And nobody likes to feel watched. Some ground rules are:

PROOF
Staff should be
able to prove
that they have
undertaken
training by
producing an
attendance or an
examination
certificate.

- talk about training as a wonderful opportunity, never a judgement on someone's ability
- emphasise that everyone needs to be involved in the training programme, including the managers, and that no one is being singled out
- ask for staff opinions before you present your own ideas
- make observations discreetly — don't walk around with a clipboard.

Commensurate — measuring up to the job

Food safety training needs to match what staff actually do as closely as possible. It is most likely that the people who prepare or serve food need to understand more food safety topics and practise a wider range of food hygiene activities than those who transport food in sealed containers. Some people will need thorough general training, whereas others may be well served by one or two short sessions on clearly defined subjects.

It is worth repeating how vital it is for *everybody* who could influence the safety of a product — whether by practical action or inaction, or by management decisions or advice — to take part in food safety training. This could even include administrative staff if they enter the production area — for example, a secretary who delivers a sales note. Supervisors and managers are not exempt as they need broad training in all aspects of food safety so that they can make sure that the rules are implemented correctly throughout the organisation.

At the right moment

WHEN TO TRAIN
New staff, new responsibilities, hygiene problems and changes in legislation, machinery or procedures all warrant some form of training session.

In broad terms, some kind of food safety training needs to take place whenever:
- new staff join the company — staff must be aware of the most basic food safety dos and don'ts from day one and such training must be included in their general induction training, even if they have been trained by a previous employer
- staff have new responsibilities — the topics and level depend upon the particular job and should equip staff to do their jobs professionally
- there has been a lapse in food hygiene standards or a new food hazard is identified — the topics and level could be new, or could be designed to refresh jaded memories
- procedures or systems change or new machinery, equipment or products are introduced
- food safety legislation changes or new rules are introduced.

As you can see, training is not a one-off exercise but needs to take place continuously — to motivate and develop staff, to maintain desired standards and to comply with the law.

DRAFTING A TRAINING NEEDS ASSESSMENT

All the information you collect about training requirements for different tasks in the organisation should be recorded in a document that is usually described as a *training needs assessment.* The assessment should be circulated throughout the organisation to encourage comments from staff and managers and to ensure that the senior management team (and the board of directors, if there is one) endorse it formally. This endorsement commits the organisation to providing and supporting the necessary training.

Provided that the training does actually take place, the endorsement could be used as legal evidence that the organisation has taken its safety responsibilities seriously — a point worth making to any management team that seems reluctant to give food safety the priority it deserves.

The assessment is not a once-and-forever activity and the training needs analysis should be reviewed regularly and updated in the light of changing circumstances.

DEVISING A TRAINING STRATEGY

The next step is to plan and implement a programme that fulfils the requirements you have identified: in the jargon of trainers, this is often described as delivering the needs or delivering the training. Depending on the nature and size of the organisation, the training needs you have identified and the resources to which you have access, there are many different ways in which training can be 'delivered'.

It is likely that you will need to use several methods. If, for example, there are a number of new staff who need basic-level training and a few who would benefit from a refresher course in the near future, you might decide to book the new staff right away onto a one-day external course, then discuss the running of refresher training with in-house trainers or external consultants. How can you decide what is best? Some options are outlined below and on the next two pages.

Learning in the workplace

Learning by copying skilled and experienced people is a time-honoured and highly effective method that almost everybody uses at some time in their life, whether deliberately or not. Skills and attitudes can be shaped by structured on-the-job training, such as a demonstration, or by ad hoc advice or simply by following what others do.

Although this is an inexpensive method of training, it is unwise to rely on this alone, as staff could pick up some bad habits and there is no guarantee that the underlying knowledge — the reason why the rules are as they are — will be grasped without some formal instruction.

In-house courses

If your company employs suitably qualified staff, you can organise your own training courses within the organisation. Provided there is space enough to run the theory part of the course, there is likely to be less disruption than when staff

INFORMAL WORKPLACE LEARNING
Practical and related directly to the workplace. May be unthreatening to nervous learners. Inexpensive. Likely to be incomplete. May pass on bad habits. Little quality control. May disrupt production.

IN-HOUSE
COURSES
May be truly
commensurate
with activities.
May be cheaper
than external
courses.
Possible quality
control issues
without any
external
accreditation or
validation.

attend an external course. An in-house trainer can tailor the course precisely to people's jobs and may be able to assist with follow-up — for instance, by monitoring and assessing the outcomes.

Despite the cost of the trainers' salaries, an in-house programme may be cheaper than sending staff on an external course. However, staff may miss out on hearing about the experiences of employees in other organisations if they do not attend an open external course. If the trainers are not accredited by an awarding body and the staff do not take an externally validated exam, it may be difficult to monitor and control the quality of the training that they receive.

Using external providers

Some organisations rely on consultants to deliver the bulk of their formal training, whether on the premises or outside. The consultants may be local environmental health officers, employees of independent companies or one-person consultancies.

Experienced consultants can train large numbers of people quickly and can offer a variety of tried and tested courses. Particularly where an organisation's training needs vary greatly over time, making it difficult to provide all the in-house instruction required, external courses may offer a cost-effective solution even though the cost of staff travel and meals may need to be added to their time away from the workplace. Some consultants offer to shape courses to your company's own requirements and they may provide a follow-up service in the workplace. If not, you will need to ensure that the training translates into behaviour at work.

EXTERNAL
PROVIDERS
May have
wide-ranging
experience.
May offer tailored
courses and
workplace
follow-up.
Could provide a
more objective
view of training
needs.
May be inflexible.
May cost more
than in-house
solutions.
Possible quality
control issues.

Making some basic checks

Before you sign a contract it may be a good idea to interview two or three consultants and to compare them. Here are some questions to consider.

- Do they seem interested in your organisation and its specific needs?
- Will they visit your premises to see what you do and will they adapt their material and delivery accordingly?
- Can you see some of their teaching aids? Do you find them easy to understand, and will your staff?
- Do they offer to provide follow-up and implementation, or must their involvement end with the last training session?
- Will they put on a sample session or let you sit in on one?
- What qualifications do the trainers have themselves?
- Is the consultancy an accredited training centre?
- What do previous clients say about them?

Open learning material

Open (or distance) learning packs aim to provide a self-contained programme. They are usually cost-effective in comparison to face-to-face taught courses and, as they are not dependent upon the varied skills and experience of particular trainers, can provide a consistent message in a consistent way.

Staff can learn at their own pace, so high-flyers can get ahead while those who take longer than average to absorb information can take all the time *they* need. Open learning material is also often beneficial to people with low self-confidence who do not wish to be seen making mistakes.

Curious though it may seem at first, some people whose first language is not English also get on better with open learning materials than with courses taught in English, because friends or family can translate for them.

Open learning may not, however, always be suitable as a stand-alone method because most people benefit from being able to ask questions and obtain specific work-related advice. Not all open learning materials are recognised by awarding bodies as a suitable necessary preparation for their exams, so staff may not be able to sit a nationally accredited exam.

IMPLEMENTING THE STRATEGY

To be successful, training cannot be a one-off event. As well as dealing with immediate needs, your strategy should incorporate plans for regular follow-up sessions and annual refresher courses. Some staff may need or want more advanced instruction or instruction on particular aspects of their job.

Make sure everyone knows what training opportunities are available. Often people battle on, without realising that training could make their working lives more straightforward. You need to encourage an open, non-blaming company culture where people feel free to speak out about any difficulty they are having and to report any concern they have about food safety hazards or hygiene practices. If people cannot tell you what's wrong, you have little chance of designing training to improve the situation.

Management commitment
Keep the rest of the management team up to date with activities and progress. If necessary, remind them that all the effort, time and money spent on training will be wasted if staff cannot act on what they learn, or if managers set a bad example.

MONITORING AND EVALUATING SUCCESS

There is little point in running any kind of training if you do not check how successful it has been in helping staff to work hygienically — how well, for example, it helps to prevent food-borne illness, comply with the law, avoid court cases, prevent food from being wasted and create a favourable impression among customers. The basic questions you need to ask are:
- what evidence is there that staff have met the training objectives?
- are the outcomes appropriate to your company?
- what, if anything, in the training programme needs to be changed?

OPEN LEARNING Usually inexpensive. Provides consistent quality. Allows learning at a suitable personal pace and 'in private'. Unthreatening. May help those with poor English. May not be related to the workplace. May not be recognised by awarding bodies.

Feedback

You will probably have your own ideas about answers to these questions (see page 223) from observing the way in which staff carry out their work, but it is also important to know what the staff feel about a course and what their supervisors perceive as the benefits or failures. It is good practice to ask for comments immediately or shortly after any structured training and at about six monthly intervals, if not more often. This allows for the so-called halo effect of a course to wear off and for staff to put the training into practice.

Questionnaires

Questionnaires are a popular way to obtain comments because they provide a written record, allow for anonymity and, provided they are written in simple language, are quick and easy to complete. You can use either open questions, where staff have plenty of space to write comments, or multiple-choice answers where staff tick their choice of answer or respond according to a scale of satisfaction, or a mixture of the two. In either case it is always a good idea to leave a blank space for comments not covered by the questions. Although questionnaires can provide a great deal of insight, they do not provide objective standards or enable water-tight comparisons between teaching methods or practitioners.

Verbal comments

You can ask people, either singly or in a group, for verbal feedback. If you do, bear in mind this advice:

- let a speaker finish, however long-winded or tortuous
- encourage everyone to have their say
- explain, but avoid becoming defensive
- thank people for their comments
- remember that you don't have to accept every piece of advice.

Management feedback to staff

You need to keep other managers and supervisors informed of what staff have learned and to make sure they recognise the efforts staff have made. Managers who notice and comment positively on improved practices reinforce the training message and increase motivation: those who do not can rapidly destroy the investment of time and money. Some managers and supervisors will do this without thinking, but it is still a good idea to make it explicit as it is all too easily overlooked in the daily rush of work. You may be able to give encouragement by paying regular visits to ex-trainees, listening to their comments, helping to resolve any problems and praising their efforts.

KEEPING TRAINING RECORDS

There is no legal requirement to keep records of training but it makes legal and business sense to do so. Records can hold information that, once analysed, can help you to plan, review and revise your company's training activities. If the worst happens, they can be produced as written evidence that appropriate food safety training has been given.

The information you write down is likely to include information about the:
- names of people who have received training
- date of the training (day/month/year)
- type and level of the training
- duration and phasing (for instance, 36 hours' trainer-led training over seven days)
- training subjects covered and practical activities undertaken
- form of training (such as, trainer presentation, group discussion, workshop, case study, demonstration)
- use of training aids and media (such as books, acetates, slides and videos)
- formal outcome (such as the name of any qualification achieved and the results of tests, exams or work-based assessments).

You may also wish to include the name(s) and qualifications of the person (or people) responsible for the training content, the training schedule and the training review.

CHECKING
During a food safety inspection EHOs may ask to see training records, exam certificates or course attendance documents. They may also question staff to check how much they understand about food safety.

STAYING ABREAST OF REQUIREMENTS

Managers also need to keep up to date. There are many ways of doing this, including joining one of the professional organisations listed on pages 373 to 374, subscribing to food safety journals or magazines and attending seminars.

⚙ MAKING IT EASIER FOR OTHERS

- Lead by example, and ensure that other managers do too.
- Create conditions in which it is easy for staff to learn.
- Shape training programmes to your workplace and to the jobs that staff do.
- Remember that people learn in different ways.
- Provide the right equipment, so staff can practise what they have learned.
- Supervise and follow up training — it is a continuous process.

MAKING LEARNING EASIER

Whether your role is to run training courses yourself or is limited to choosing consultants or outside courses, it is worth understanding the principle training methods for food safety, their possible advantages and disadvantages and the circumstances in which they are most suitable.

THE LEARNING PROCESS

Adults do not learn like children — they are usually more self-directing and independent, and they may demand to know why they need to know certain things.

Learning happens in a number of distinct steps and a good training course takes account of this. First comes the stage of receiving new knowledge, whether through observation, words or practice. Then the knowledge needs to be discussed with others and interpreted in the context of the workplace. Finally it needs to be applied in practice and, if the outcome is good, passed on to others. Remember, though, that bad experiences as well as good ones are shared. Poor training can be worse than no training at all, undermining key messages and perhaps prompting staff to lose interest.

DIFFERENT METHODS OF TRAINING

There are many different methods available to trainers. Suitability depends on the subject and time available and on the people receiving the training. Good trainers recognise that different people respond to different methods and try to use a variety of approaches, which can range from a formal presentation to a highly informal discussion or role-playing activity.

SCHEDULING TRAINING
Tired people make poor students. Try to schedule training at the beginning, rather than at the end, of a work shift.

All methods have advantages and disadvantages, but people usually learn better when they see something as well as hear about it, better still when they have the chance to discuss it, and best of all when they are required to tackle a task themselves. Most good trainers use a mix of methods so that staff do some listening, watching, discussing and hands-on practical work. This helps to vary the pace and maintain interest, as well as improving the learning process.

Presentation

In a presentation the trainer gives information to those being trained. The interaction is essentially one-way, with the trainer doing most of the talking and the students taking notes and asking questions. The technique is useful for communicating complex or abstract material that needs the full attention of the audience. It works best when combined with more participatory methods, such as a demonstration or discussion, and when followed by some kind of student activity such as an exercise, question and answer session or case study.

The possible advantages are that:

- a lot of information can be conveyed in a short time
- the presentation and its timing can be prepared thoroughly in advance.

Among the possible disadvantages are that:

- students may need to be prompted to ask questions, otherwise there may be little feedback, making it hard to gauge just how much they have understood
- it may be difficult to get the pace right for all the students
- students may not have time to formulate their own thoughts
- the material may not be remembered.

A Message from the Bored

We, the long-suffering business men and women of Britain, are fed up with boring, badly prepared presentations that send us to sleep. High on our list of bad marks are poorly laid-out rooms.

Next comes waffling (why can't presenters get to the point quickly and stick to it?)

Followed by unfunny or embarrassing jokes. Who needs them?

Equally unpopular are presenters who waste time apologising for being 'no good at presenting'.

And who likes to sit there while a speaker sweats, stammers and dries-up?

Or, speaking of which, who raises their voice? Droners, whisperers and squeakers all have a hard time holding our attention. Knowing how to speak is one thing. Knowing when to shut up is another.

Why should we stay put for a moment longer than scheduled? Of course, punctual ending begins with prompt starts. (Take note all presenters who like to learn how the equipment works in front of the audience.)

Discussion

Discussion is a good technique for encouraging people to develop their thoughts and find solutions to problems. Discussion methods include the formal 'platform' approach in which the trainer encourages individuals to speak; the informal, open discussion in which everyone contributes as they wish; and the unstructured, free session (sometimes referred to as a brainstorm) in which the only rule is not to criticise anyone else's idea. The subject, composition and size of the group, and the goals of the training session all have a bearing on which is most appropriate in any given situation.

Among the possible advantages are that:

- participants are active and involved
- everyone is encouraged to make their own suggestions
- individual suggestions and solutions may make the topic more meaningful (staff may 'take ownership' of the issue), so they are more likely to remember what they ought to be doing in their daily tasks
- communication and understanding are promoted, which may improve workplace co-operation.

The possible disadvantages are that:

- the method is time consuming
- discussions may degenerate into disputes, if the trainer is inexperienced
- contributions may wander off the point, unless the trainer guides the group gently
- less assertive people may not have a fair say.

Demonstration

Most skills or techniques benefit from a practical demonstration. This could be in the workplace if time, space, hygiene and health and safety considerations permit, or it could be a classroom mock-up of a real situation, or it could be on a video.

A simple demonstration in the workplace can help staff to relate theory to everyday good practice.

The possible advantages are that:

- the students get information by both seeing and hearing, so they are more likely to remember what they have witnessed
- it is easy, particularly with a live demonstration, to explain details and answer questions as they arise.

Possible disadvantages are that:

- the preparation may be time consuming
- the demonstration may not be suitable for large groups, unless you have a camera and screen
- the students may lose concentration because it is a passive experience.

Case study

In a case study the trainer presents the group with a story, or scenario, that raises some important food safety issues. The story can be taken from real life, made up, or a combination of the two. If good real-life material is available this is often most interesting — though if it is a well-known incident, the details should be disguised so that students do not recognise the case immediately.

Among the possible advantages are that:

- the students can imagine themselves in a real situation instead of a hypothetical one
- the focus is on facts and causes
- independent thinking is encouraged.

Possible disadvantages are that:
- good, ready-made, appropriate cases can be hard to find
- preparation can be time consuming, as solutions must not be too easy or too difficult
- the case study may be suitable only for small groups, to give everybody a role, and where a larger group is divided into smaller groups, the feedback in the plenary session may be time consuming
- some students may take an inflexible stance, creating group tension.

CHECKING THE QUALITY OF COURSES

Before you authorise training, it is a good idea to discuss with the trainer which approaches will be used. A variety usually works best. Trainers should be able to explain why they consider their techniques appropriate for the audience, the designated outcomes and the time and facilities available.

It can also be useful to see the training aids and materials that the trainer will be using, such as books, handouts, acetates, computer-based presentations or videos. These should have clear learning benefits and be of a professional standard.

Finally, it is reasonable to ask trainers specific questions. How will they relate their teaching to the actual workplace experience of the students? What will they do to make sure students understand and that everyone keeps up? How will they keep students interested? What will they do to help students to put their new knowledge into practice? What goals will the training have and how will they be measured?

FIT TO WORK WITH FOOD

Is your workforce clean, tidy and well groomed at all times? Do staff take pride in their appearance and in high standards of personal hygiene? These things may sound trivial, but few issues can be more important in the food industry where so many processes are literally hands-on and lapses in personal hygiene can lead to cases of severe food-borne illness.

In contrast, a smartly turned-out, hygiene-conscious workforce is one of the best insurance policies you can have. As well as safeguarding food from contamination, it sends out a powerful message of professionalism and trustworthiness to customers, clients and the general public. In turn, this maintains your company's business standing and may help to boost the team spirit and morale of employees. Perhaps best of all from your viewpoint, it helps to make the manager's job easier!

THE MANAGEMENT CHALLENGE

Personal hygiene is not a difficult subject. There is no complex theory to learn and no long list of facts to remember. Managing it is quite another matter, however.

People can be extremely resistant to changing their behaviour, especially when it means giving up long-standing habits. Some employees may find it difficult, embarrassing or offensive to discuss aspects of personal hygiene. *You* may find it difficult too. As everyone comes to the subject with different attitudes and standards, you need to respect these differences while ensuring that everyone lives up to the same high standards at work. So, even though this is the most personal of all the topics involved in food safety, you need to ensure that the subject does not appear to be aimed at a single particular individual but applies equally to all — staff and managers alike — and is seen to do so.

Your four-point plan

Despite the difficulties, personal hygiene can be managed successfully. There are four key things you need to do:
- implement a personal hygiene policy as part of your general food safety policy (see page 338)
- provide suitable and effective training
- create a hygiene-focused working environment
- monitor personal hygiene.

The personal hygiene policy

Your organisation should have a clear written statement setting out the standards it expects of its staff with regard to personal hygiene and habits. Such statements are usually included in a document known as the company *food safety policy* or the company food hygiene policy. The document should be as detailed and unambiguous as possible and should be circulated to everyone. Once you have a general policy, you can draw up simple, specific rules based upon it and post these in appropriate places to remind people about issues such as washing their hands before entering a food preparation area. When such notices identify the instructions as company policy, they tend to carry extra weight.

Training

Do *you* follow instructions blindly? Probably not. So why should your staff? Training should *explain* the reasons for the rules — a much more effective means of getting people to comply than lecturing or threatening them.

A hygiene-focused workplace

Clean toilets and basins; a good supply of hot water, soap and hand-drying equipment; hats, hairnets and other protective clothing; and sticking plasters readily available — all these things make a difference by making it easier for staff to maintain high personal standards. After all, rules that are hard to follow are hardly ever followed.

Monitoring

Not all aspects of personal hygiene are on show! But many can be observed and managers and supervisors should stay alert to ensuring that rules are being followed. The ideal, however, is to promote self-monitoring by encouraging people to take a pride in their own and one another's hygiene habits and personal presentation. Part of the written policy might be that each employee is expected to take responsibility for his or her own health and hygiene.

KEY ASPECTS OF A PERSONAL HYGIENE POLICY

There are a number of crucial subjects that should be covered in the personal hygiene section of your food safety policy. Firstly, there are factors relating directly to the human body: hands, skin, mouth, nose and throat, and infectious diseases. Then there are body adornments and applied products, such as jewellery, toiletries and sticking plasters. The rest of this chapter discusses each of these in turn.

Hands

Of all bodily parts, the hands are most likely to come into direct contact with food. How many processes can you think of in your business that require someone to touch food with their hands? Not even the most automated of industrial processes is likely to be completely hands-free. Unsavoury though the thought may be, just consider what people might do with their hands regularly every day. These are just a few possible answers:

- handle non-food items, waste and bins
- scratch their head or rearrange their hair
- stroke their chin, scratch an itch or wipe their mouth

Ooh, those aching feet! But after a quick restorative massage, does the waitress wash her hands?

- stifle a cough or sneeze, or blow their nose
- massage aching feet
- handle money
- open doors
- shake hands with others
- use toilet paper
- touch their genital area
- handle raw and cooked food.

Each of these actions has the potential to contaminate the hands and consequently any food that is handled. As any textbook will tell you, there is a simple solution: hands must be washed after each of these actions, before entering a food room and before handling food. Real life, however, is not quite so straightforward.

Solving the great hand-washing mystery

Surveys show that almost everyone knows that they ought to wash their hands after going to the toilet, but that surprisingly few actually do so. One possible reason for this discrepancy comes from PhD research carried out by Lisa Ackerley in the 1990s into what she calls 'health benefit analysis'. Her findings suggest that people will do something only if they are convinced it brings a direct health benefit. In other words, unless people believe that dirty hands really do cause disease, there is very little chance of encouraging a hand-washing habit.

In a way this is good news because it means that you can use information about food-borne illness to change behaviour, perhaps by discussing or pinning up dramatic stories of real incidents of disease caused by poor hand hygiene. The downside, however, is that you will probably not get far just by sticking up more and more lists of rules or by introducing fines and penalties.

Teaching good technique

Even if your workforce is thoroughly convinced of the need for hand washing and is committed to doing so at every appropriate moment, individuals might still not be washing their hands thoroughly. You can supply water at the correct temperature (usually 45°C to 50°C), copious amounts of an approved unscented soap, nailbrushes and hygienic methods of hand drying — but there is no guarantee that all parts of the hands will be washed properly.

Might a visitor to your workplace from another planet be forgiven for thinking that the process more or less involved showing the hands to water, stroking them together once and wiping them down the front of clothing? It may seem petty and tedious, but even adults often need to be helped to understand that the soap and hot water do only part of the work and that rubbing hands together vigorously and using a nailbrush really do help to prise microbes from the skin surface. As for wiping hands down clothing, staff often need to be reminded of the source of microbes and the possibility of cross-contamination and recontamination.

Skin complaints

Cuts, boils, septic sores and other skin problems and infections can all harbour pathogenic bacteria, such as *Staphylococcus aureus*, which can cause food poisoning. In a way, these problems are easier to manage than hand washing because they are often easily visible.

Treating skin conditions

People may continue working with minor cuts, sores and so on, provided that the skin condition is covered with a brightly coloured waterproof dressing. The rule about dressings should apply to both visible areas of the body, such as the face or forearm, and to covered areas, such as the torso — although in the latter case you will have to rely on staff co-operation since you will seldom know about the problem. Even if you do know, you may not ask to monitor treatment as this could be an infringement of personal liberty.

Mouth, nose and throat

The mouth, nose and throat can all harbour pathogens, particularly *Staphylococcus aureus*. When people sneeze or cough, they spray out tiny water droplets which can land on food, utensils or preparation surfaces, so transferring pathogens. Another route of transmission is, as already mentioned, via the hands when people touch their mouth or nose, then handle food without first washing their hands.

What managers can do

There are two things you need to do to prevent contamination from the mouth and nose: keep people with coughs and colds away from food and stop people scratching or picking their nose or touching their mouth.

Dealing with coughs and colds

Coughs and colds are minor infections in themselves, which is part of the problem because people still come to work. In the food industry, however, they are a serious issue and need to be dealt with in a similar way to that of reporting infectious diseases (see page 234).

Preventing contact with hands

It is extremely difficult to stop people from touching their mouth or nose, since it is usually a completely unconscious action. Even when people do become aware of what they are doing, you still need to persuade them to wash their hands after doing it.

Hair

Apart from touching the hair, which we have already mentioned, the main problem of contamination is from loose strands that may fall out and contaminate food.

What managers can do

Hats and hairnets are the best way of preventing stray hairs from entering food, so ensure a good supply is always available. If possible, find a style that people are happy with. Include instructions on headgear in the written hygiene policy and give training so that people understand why the policy is as it is.

Monitoring and enforcement are relatively easy, since few things are more obvious than wearing or not wearing something on your head.

Infectious diseases

It is illegal to allow people to work with food when they are suffering from, or are suspected of suffering from, a disease which could be transmitted through food or which makes it likely that they could cause microbiological contamination. The illnesses that fall into this category, and the requirements for returning to work, are set out in the code of practice document *Food Handling – Fitness to Work*.

SEEING A DOCTOR

Many management policies require employees to seek medical advice for any severe or long-lasting health problem. The advice may be from a company doctor, if there is one, or the person's own general practitioner. The policy may also require the doctor to state that the person is fit to work as a food handler before he or she is allowed back to work after illness. This can make the manager's job easier and prevent the need to ask intrusive questions that could infringe rights to personal privacy.

Carriers

Food handlers who are, or may be, suffering from a food-borne illness and those who have been in contact with them are obliged to report this to their manager or supervisor. This, however, is only one part of the story as many people are *carriers* of disease — they do not suffer symptoms themselves but can pass the disease on to others. The role of these carriers in causing outbreaks is still not fully understood because, unlike Typhoid Mary (see page 92), not all carriers excrete the organisms responsible for the illness.

What managers can do

Juggling the issue of illness can be difficult. The manager's primary responsibility is, of course, to ensure that anyone who could genuinely pose a hazard to health is either excluded from the premises altogether or is given work well away from any food handling operations. Some managers take the view that the risk from a carrier who works with food may be too great to permit, even if the person is not excreting the organism.

Managers must also ensure that staff do not report an 'upset stomach' every time they want a day off work. As with hand washing, there is a certain degree of trust involved. You need to be confident that people will report symptoms of a food-borne illness when they have them and that they will not fake symptoms. Some companies analyse their sickness records and if people consistently take Mondays or Fridays off for 'diarrhoea', they may, as a matter of routine, ask the company doctor or the employee's doctor to investigate.

Checking it out

If a food handler suspects symptoms of food-borne illness, advise him or her to consult a doctor and explain that he or she may need to provide a faecal sample. If an infectious illness is confirmed, the health service will inform the Consultant in Communicable Disease Control (CCDC) which, in turn, informs local authorities if it is a notifiable disease or food-borne infection.

Absence and return to work

Food handlers with a food-borne illness or certain other conditions (such as skin infections and other septic and bronchial conditions which could contaminate food) can be excluded from work by the local authority. If this happens, the employee may apply to the local authority for compensation for loss of wages.

The big question is how long do they need to be excluded from work? The Department of Health guidelines issued in 1995, together with the Public Health Laboratory Service's Salmonella Subcommittee's recommendations of the same year, recommend in most cases that there should be no return to work until at least 48 hours after the last episode of vomiting and diarrhoea and even then only if the strictest observance is paid to personal hygiene. The table in the Reference section (on page 358) outlines the criteria for when a sufferer or a contact may return to work after he or she has become free from symptoms.

Jewellery

Most organisations prohibit food workers from wearing jewellery because of the hazard from bacterial and physical contamination. While most customers would probably not mind finding a diamond ring in their breakfast cereal, the hard gemstone could cause physical injury — and you can imagine how many pathogens might be lurking in the gem setting.

Protective clothing may need to extend to beard snoods as well as hair restraints.

Sometimes exceptions are made for a plain wedding ring and some companies permit staff to wear sleeper earrings, nose studs or religious jewellery only if they are fully covered by coloured sticking plasters. You should assess such hazards and their risk in your business, formulate an appropriate policy and make clear it clear to all.

Clothing

Some items of protective clothing are designed to protect the wearer from burns, scalds and knife or impact injuries, but most items, such as overalls, hats, hair nets, footwear, gloves and aprons, are to protect food from contamination. However, many food handlers mistakenly believe that the purpose of protective clothing is to protect their own clothes from food. Training should correct this misconception. Most management policies insist on protective clothing being worn by everyone who works directly with food. Garments are usually supplied by the company: light colours are preferable because they show dirt more easily, prompting staff to to put on fresh clothing. Sometimes garments are colour-coded by work area to help to maintain the separation of staff working with raw and cooked food, for example. All protective clothing should be either washable or disposable. There should be no pockets or only internal pockets (to prevent items falling out of them and into food). Fastenings should take the form of studs, hook-and-loop strips or secure buttons. Ideally, name labels should be sewn into uniforms rather than pinned on.

Toiletries

Some foods — especially milk, milk products and tea — are particularly susceptible to taint by strong-smelling substances. For this reason you may wish to ban food handlers from using perfumed toiletries and personal grooming products, or to encourage restraint in their application. Problems could be caused by chemical contamination from perfume, aftershave, deodorant, soap, hand cream, ointments, powders or medicines such as strong-smelling ointments.

Bandages and plasters

Sticking plasters and other dressings should be waterproof to prevent leakage. They should also be brightly coloured (usually blue) so that they can be seen and retrieved if they come off, and appropriate further action taken (such as disposing of that batch of food). Some types of sticking plaster also contain a thin metal strip so that they can be picked out by a metal detector if they fall into food.

MAKING IT EASIER FOR OTHERS

- Lead by example. If you break the personal hygiene rules, no one else will respect them either.
- Apply the rules equally to all, including top management and visitors. When it comes to hygiene, everyone is an equal risk.
- Explain carefully and sensitively. Don't just issue an order. People won't change their behaviour unless they know there is a good reason for doing so.
- Keep the explanations simple. Whether it is in a training session or on notices on the wall, all messages should be unambiguous, easy to understand and easy to remember.
- Repeat messages often but in different ways. We all have our own ways of learning, so varying your techniques will get through to more people. Try notices, cartoons, videos, refresher training and so on.
- Consider asking everyone to sign a copy of the hygiene rules. It is common policy to print a booklet of hygiene rules and to ask each member of staff to sign that they have read and understood it. This prevents people saying later that they were not told or did not understand the rules.

⬤ MANAGEMENT MATTERS

If you have ever worked in a badly planned building or one that has been poorly maintained, you will know what a difference it can make to your attitude and your ability to do your job. A well designed building makes professional activities more straightforward and may help to promote feelings of pride, self worth and well-being among staff, while a poor design may sap energy and lead to demotivation, absenteeism and a range of complaints, such as the so-called sick-building syndrome. Bear in mind that the working environment your company provides may influence the standard of the finished product that staff produce. Of course, many companies have to make compromises to the ideal, but those should never be compromises to the safety of food. Deficiencies that are often highlighted during inspections include inadequate working space for the processes being undertaken, inappropriate workflow and insufficient contamination control because of poor separation of foods and tasks.

When it comes to staff training, we make no apology for repeating that the process is a continuous one and not a one-off event. When you run a car, you expect to have to put in fuel and to take the car to for regular servicing. Intermediate-level and advanced-level training sessions, as well as regular refresher training for everyone, including you and the other senior members of staff, help to ensure that the food safety 'tank' stays topped up. Supervision and motivation help to ensure that the food safety 'engine' is properly tuned.

Acknowledge staff's work experience and always give credit where it is due. Make connections to familiar experiences to make food safety more meaningful — for example, mention domestic situations or reminding staff that what happens in a food business can also have consequences for partners, children and friends. The message that everyone is a customer can also prove to be helpful.

Sometimes even the words you use can help to nurture the corporate food safety culture. Use 'we' and 'our' rather than always saying 'the company'. Try to make everyone feel part of the team: your hygiene standards are only as good as the team members who support it, and every team is only as good as its weakest member.

Consider whether motivational awards or rewards might help. Well-tried possibilities include in-house certificates or shields, bonus systems, commendations in the house newspaper or on the news board and proposal systems which reward staff who propose helpful ideas. Watch out for local and national cookery competitions which include points awarded for hygienic practices and knowledge of food safety. What simpler route into tackling the sometimes tricky matter of managing standards of personal hygiene?

MANAGING SYSTEMS

⚷ KEY POINTS

Continued over page

ambient shelf stable
a description for foods that can safely be stored at ordinary room temperatures for a specified period.

ambient temperature
the environmental temperature, often used to describe 'normal' room temperature.

best before
a date that indicates the period within which food is at its best.

botulinum cook
a method of high temperature preservation designed to kill the spores of *Clostridium botulinum* and to reduce the spores of spoilage organisms to a level accepted as being safe for human health.

carrier
a person who is infected by a pathogen and can pass it on to others, but who does not experience symptoms.

case
one incidence of illness.

catalyst
a chemical that initiates or accelerates a chemical reaction without changing itself in the process.

clean
free from dirt, marks or soiling.

clean as you go
the recognised good practice of cleaning up throughout food preparation tasks and immediately after completing the task.

cleaning
the process of making something clean; usually a combination of mechanical, chemical and thermal energy.

cleaning schedule
a management plan for effective cleaning and, where appropriate, disinfection, detailing what, how and when something is to be cleaned.

commercial freezing
the rapid freezing and storage of foods at temperatures below $-18\,°C$, typically at $-22\,°C$ or colder.

commercial sterilisation
a method of high temperature preservation, also known as appertizing, in which no viable organisms can be detected by recognised methods, or the number of surviving organisms is so low as to be insignificant. See also STERILISATION.

contact time
the period when a disinfectant must remain on, or must surround, a surface in order to achieve disinfection.

core temperature
the temperature measured at the centre or the thickest part of the food, or close to the bone.

critical control point (CCP)
in HACCP, a stage in the process of handling food at which a food business can eliminate a hazard or minimise the risk from it.

critical limit
in HACCP, the border between safe and unsafe.

danger zone
a description of the temperature range ($5\,°C$ to $63\,°C$) at which most food-borne pathogenic and spoilage micro-organisms multiply easily; the temperature range to be avoided for high risk foods.

date mark
a date or code indicating the period within which food should be consumed. Legally recognised date marks include *use by* and *best before* dates.

detergent
a chemical formulation that helps to dissolve grease and remove food particles or other soiling.

disinfectant
a chemical formulation or the application of heat (as steam or hot water) to achieve disinfection.

disinfection
the reduction of micro-organisms to a level accepted as being safe for human health.

due diligence
a defence that every practicable measure was taken to avoid breaching food safety legislation.

enzyme
proteins (chemicals) produced by cells; they act as catalysts in essential biochemical reactions.

food safety
the protection of human health by preventing edible substances, which are defined by law, from becoming hazardous and by minimising the risks from those hazards. Also used to indicate the *absence* of harm to people from food.

food safety policy
a company's written statement of its commitment to meeting its obligations towards customers and to producing safe and legal products.

hazard (food)
a source of danger: anything microbiological, chemical or physical, or any condition or circumstance that could cause harm to the consumer.

hazard analysis
a systematic process for identifying, assessing and controlling hazards and risks associated with food and drink; a simplified system of HACCP.

Hazard Analysis and Critical Control Point (HACCP)
a system for identifying, assessing and controlling hazards associated with food and drink.

high risk food
a food that easily supports the multiplication of pathogenic micro-organisms.

infestation
the presence of food pests, usually in large numbers, in any kind of food or domestic premises.

integrated pest management
a style of pest management based on co-operation between a food business and a specialist pest control company, dealing mostly with preventive measures.

intermediate host
the host in which the larval stages of endoparasites, such as tapeworms, develop.

intrinsic factors
inbuilt characteristics, such as nutrients, pH and a_w that influence the survival and multiplication of micro-organisms.

organoleptic
involving the use of the senses; the characteristics of food are often assessed by its appearance, smell and texture, while sound (eg. tapping bread) is sometimes used.

outbreak
a cluster, in time or place, of cases of illness caused by a particular organism.

pasteurisation
a method of heat treatment that destroys tuberculosis pathogens and reduces other pathogens to accepted safe levels for human health.

pest (food)
a creature that contaminates or destroys food intended for human consumption.

pest control
measures including the prevention of infestation to safeguard the fitness of food for human consumption.

preservation (food)
methods of treatment designed to delay the natural processes of decomposition and extend the period within which food is good to eat.

product recall
publicity and public information warning consumers about a product that is contaminated or may be contaminated, coupled with an offer to replace, or refund the cost of, the product.

product specification
a customer's detailed description of the content, design, composition and intended use of the product to be supplied.

ready-to-eat food
food that is not prepared or treated (such as by cooking) in a way that would kill any pathogens present immediately before the food is eaten.

risk
a measure, or scale, of the likelihood (or probability) that a hazard will occur.

sanitizer
the name in the UK for a chemical formulation that combines the properties of a detergent and a disinfectant.

sanitizing
another term for disinfection; American-English for disinfection.

shelf life
the period within which food is both safe for human consumption and at its best.

spoilage
the normal processes of deterioration, decay or 'going off'.

sterilisation
a process in which all living organisms are destroyed.

stock rotation
the practice of using a product with the shortest shelf life before using a similar one with a longer shelf life.

stored product pest
an insect associated with foods such as grain, flour, herbs, spices and nuts that are often stored for long periods.

target level
in HACCP, a specified value for a control measure that eliminates a hazard or minimises the risk from it at a critical control point.

temperature control
all aspects of food safety in which temperature is used as a measure to stop a hazard or reduce the risk from it.

tolerance
in HACCP, a specified variation from the target level which is acceptable for the safety of food.

ultra heat treatment (UHT)
a method of high temperature food treatment, usually applied to milk, designed to reduce spoilage organisms and extend the shelf life.

unfit food
food that is not safe or suitable, as defined by law, for human consumption.

use by
the date indicating the last day on which food is safe to eat.

CLEAN ENOUGH FOR FOOD

Most adults know something about cleaning and disinfection, however reluctant they may be to do their fair share of the household chores. As a manager with responsibility for food safety, you need to know more about cleaning methods and cleaning chemicals than you know already from your everyday experience. The problem is that you may be faced either with banal statements — such as 'mix with water and apply to surface' — or with mind-numbing detail that is almost incomprehensible to all but the specialist — for example 'this product contains sodium sesquicarbonate, polyphosphate and metasilicate which have more buffering power than products containing sodium carbonate and trisodium phosphate'.

This chapter aims to steer between the two extremes. It offers down-to-earth information to help you to comply with the law and enhance your company's business reputation and gives general information about cleaning methods and groups of chemicals to help you to choose the best forms of cleaning and disinfection for the type of food operation you manage. (Detailed material about cleaning chemicals is provided in the Reference section — see pages 356 to 357.)

THE BUSINESS CONTEXT

In Part 1 we said that the success of a food business is inextricably linked to the effectiveness of food safety measures. Thorough cleaning and, where appropriate, disinfection, play a central part in this success by:
- controlling microbiological, chemical and physical hazards — for example, by removing microbiological contaminants from surfaces and food environments, removing food scraps that could attract and nourish pests, disturbing areas where pests could hide and breed, and making it easier to see damage to the packaging of stored food
- preventing food-borne illness
- maintaining the operational effectiveness of utensils and machinery
- complying with food safety legislation.

Benefits
In turn, these measures are likely to help a food business to:
- maintain a pleasant working environment which may improve staff motivation and productivity
- reinforce food handlers' hygiene awareness and motivation
- create a better impression for customers
- reduce the amount of food that has to be thrown away
- minimise the cost of maintenance, repair and replacement of equipment, utensils and facilities.

In addition, clean and tidy food premises help to reduce workplace accidents caused by slipping or tripping.

WHAT DO WE REALLY MEAN BY CLEAN?

So far we have used the word *clean* in its everyday sense, but what does it really mean in the context of a food business? The word derives from an Old English word meaning pure or clear, but it is far easier to define by referring to its opposite — dirty. So most dictionaries state something like 'free from dirt, marks or soiling' or 'without dirt or filth' or just 'unsoiled'.

Clean for food

Most people recognise when something is physically clean because a surface is free from dirt, soiling or residue — there is nothing to be seen or touched.

Chemically clean means that all the residue and deposits from cleaning and disinfecting materials have been removed, usually by rinsing the item in water of drinking quality.

Microbiologically clean means that the number of micro-organisms on a work surface or equipment has been reduced to a level that current scientific knowledge deems acceptable for human health. This usually involves the use of disinfectants, which we discuss on pages 246 to 247 and 252 to 253.

It is, of course, one thing to check whether something is physically clean and quite another to confirm whether something is chemically or microbiologically clean. That is why it is suggested that you have equipment and surfaces checked scientifically from time to time — see pages 66 to 68. (There are, of course, legal limits and recommended maxima for chemicals such as mycotoxins, naturally occurring toxins and agricultural and veterinary residues.)

The process of cleaning

Cleaning (sometimes termed cleansing) is the *process* of making something clean. The process is necessary to control chemical, physical and microbiological contamination of food by keeping food premises, equipment and food-contact and hand-contact surfaces free from soiling, whether visible or not.

Energy for cleaning

There are many methods of cleaning but they all require energy in one form or another. The energy is generated by one or a combination of:
- movement (known as mechanical or kinetic energy) provided by:
  - personal physical effort (sometimes described as elbow grease), such as wiping, sweeping or scrubbing
  - the action of mechanical and electrical equipment, such as dishwashers or floor polishers

- water agitation (turbulence), as used in many clean-in-place (CIP) systems involving pipes
- temperature (thermal energy) — from hot water or steam
- chemicals (chemical energy) — in detergents, disinfectants and sanitizers.

COMBINING ENERGIES

The balance between these forms of energy depends upon factors such as the nature of the cleaning task being undertaken, the frequency with which the task is carried out, the equipment used and the time involved — not merely the time to complete the task but also, and more significantly, the time required for a chemical to work effectively or for hot water to be in contact with the item to be cleaned. These diagrams indicate very roughly the significance of the different forms of energy in a selection of cleaning processes.

Cleaning a work surface by hand

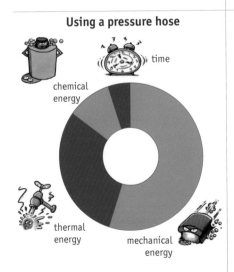

chemical energy

thermal energy

mechanical energy

time

Sweeping a floor with a broom

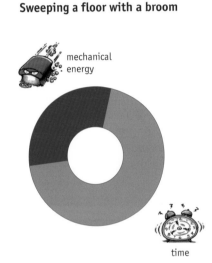

mechanical energy

time

Using a pressure hose

chemical energy

time

thermal energy

mechanical energy

Washing crockery in a dishwasher

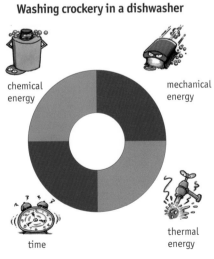

chemical energy

mechanical energy

time

thermal energy

WHAT SHOULD WE CLEAN, OR CLEAN AND DISINFECT?

Everything in food premises must be kept clean and the immediate area surrounding food premises must also be kept clean. It is as simple as that. However, as you well know, this is not the end of the story as there are many surfaces in food premises that could be microbiologically contaminated to a level that could cause food-borne illness or spoilage.

The use of *detergents* — chemicals that help to dissolve grease and remove dirt — combined with mechanical and thermal energy (as in washing dishes) removes dirt and may remove some microbes. Even so, many micro-organisms and their spores can survive this treatment, so a more lethal approach is required — disinfection.

Disinfection

In the British Standard 5283 *disinfection* is defined as 'the destruction of micro-organisms, but not usually bacterial spores; it may not kill all micro-organisms but reduces them to a level which is neither harmful to health nor the quality of perishable goods.' In other words, disinfection reduces microbiological contamination to an 'acceptable' level — one considered low enough to be safe for human health.

Surfaces and equipment that must be disinfected after cleaning include:
- food-contact surfaces — such as preparation or cutting boards, knives, work surfaces, mixing bowls, serving dishes and slicing machines
- hand-contact surfaces — such as taps, door handles (including those on refrigeration units), light switches, telephones, toilet seats and nail brushes
- cleaning materials and equipment — such as mops, cleaning cloths, scrapers and brushes — and waste disposal equipment — such as bins and their lids.

Types of disinfection
Disinfection can be carried out by:
- heat (as steam or hot water)
- chemicals
- a combination of thermal and chemical energy.

Ultraviolet radiation is used in some bakeries and at some water processing plants because it is particularly good at killing protozoa which can survive chlorination. The most common methods of disinfection in food premises use either heat (thermal energy) or chemicals (chemical energy).

Thermal disinfection
Hot water disinfection is usually limited to the use of a machine, such as a dishwasher, as the temperature is too high for comfortable skin contact. The temperature reached is around 88°C with a variable contact time of between one and 20 seconds.

Steam disinfection is usually used for areas of equipment that are inaccessible by hand. The process can corrode or otherwise damage materials and equipment and some specialists question whether it is effective for food safety and safe enough for staff to use without scalding themselves.

Chemical disinfection
Chemical disinfection is a second stage process: it must always follow cleaning and rinsing, otherwise the disinfectant may not work properly.

Thermal and chemical *disinfectants* need to be in contact with the surface for a specific time in order to work properly, and this *contact time* is specified by the manufacturer. Cutting short the contact time will stop disinfection from taking effect, but prolonging the contact time may also have undesirable effects. Some bacteria, for instance, can develop resistance to chemical disinfectants if they are not used in accordance with the manufacturer's instructions. For instance, it is unwise to leave cloths, mops and so on to soak in chemical disinfectants overnight.

Sanitizing and sanitizers
In some parts of the world it is more common to talk about *sanitizing* (also spelled sanitising) than disinfection. These two words mean the same thing but, just to make life a little more complicated, sanitizers are *not* the same as disinfectants! In the UK *sanitizers* combine the functions of a detergent and a disinfectant. They clean and disinfect in one go.

SANITIZERS
When we talk about sanitizers in the UK we mean a chemical formulation that combines the functions of a detergent and a chemical disinfectant.

A common confusion
Never confuse disinfection (or sanitizing) with *sterilisation*, which means the destruction of all pathogenic organisms. Sterilisation is a routine process for medical equipment, but is rarely achievable, or necessary, in normal food operations, although *commercial sterilisation* is used as a method of *preservation* (see pages 290 to 292.)

WHICH METHOD IS THE MOST APPROPRIATE?

Perhaps this question seems a little patronising at first. After all, you would not dream of asking staff to scrub an oven with a bottle brush or to try to disinfect a floor mop in a bratt pan with cooking oil.

Even so, from time to time it is worth reviewing how cleaning is undertaken in your workplace. By considering what is being cleaned, the type of soiling and the amount of soiling, you may be able to improve efficiency or reduce costs. Questions for you to answer include:
• what is the surface to be cleaned — for example, a wall, floor, work surface, toilet, piece of equipment?
• what kind of dirt must be cleaned — is it organic, such as animal fat, butter or blood; or inorganic, such as rust or limescale?

- how dirty is it — heavily or lightly soiled, or likely to be microbiologically contaminated?
- what is the condition of the dirt — for example, long-standing encrustation, fresh soiling, stained (soaked in) or burnt?
- how clean should the surface to be when cleaning is finished — physically, chemically or microbiologically clean, or all three?
- what equipment could be used — for example, a hand-held brush, electrical rotary mop, dishwasher, washing machine, jet wash?
- which chemicals would best achieve the level of desired cleanliness — for example, a detergent alone or a detergent followed by a disinfectant?
- how would the pH or hardness of the local mains water affect the efficiency of a chemical?
- how cost effective is the method chosen — for example, can the dilution be controlled, can a cheaper product do the same job, does a more expensive product use less personnel time?
- how can you monitor and test the effectiveness of the method chosen?

WATER HARDNESS
A characteristic of water caused by salts of calcium, magnesium and iron that causes soap to curdle and increases the consumption of soap or detergent and the deposition of limescale. The hardness is not necessarily related to a high pH.

Scale of the task

The size of the job should play a part in your decision-making. A small floor area, for instance, may be most effectively cleaned with a mop and bucket and the application of 'elbow grease' whereas a large floor area may be more effectively cleaned by using an electric machine that combines the functions of sweeping, vacuum cleaning and polishing.

Cleaning in place (CIP) is a method used in industrial-scale food premises for cleaning equipment and pipelines without having to dismantle them every day for manual or machine cleaning. The design of the equipment must ensure that the circulation of cleaning chemicals and rinsing water is continuous and is not disrupted by spurs or dead-ends in the pipeline. (Part or all of the system should be dismantled for inspection and manual cleaning from time to time.)

Cost-effective hygiene

While some items, such as cooking pots and trays, may be best washed by hand, a dishwasher probably offers a better standard of hygiene (see also page 249), coupled with savings in cost and time for cleaning crockery, glasses, utensils and cutlery.

The choice of cleaning equipment

Brushes

Commonly used for sweeping floors and scrubbing stubborn dirt, they should be kept clean and in good repair so that bristles are not shed onto food. Sweeping can raise dust and contaminate food, so the use of brushes should ideally be restricted to times and places where food is out of harm's way. Many specialists prefer the use of damp mops to clear up both food debris and spills during food preparation and production periods and in food stores.

Cloths

The use of cleaning cloths (particularly dishcloths, wiping cloths and drying-up cloths) should be limited as they often cause more problems that they resolve. Many studies have shown that cloths are the most heavily contaminated items in a food preparation area. Single-use paper may be preferable for cleaning a work surface and drying up. If re-usable cloths must be used, they should be replaced with fresh ones frequently during the work period and cleaned thoroughly before being soaked for the appropriate contact time in a frequently changed disinfectant solution.

Service cloths and oven cloths (or gloves) could also become hazardous if they are used for cleaning tasks or for drying hands.

Dishwashing machines

They have the advantage of disinfecting as well as cleaning, while freeing staff for other activities.

Floor mops and floor cloths

They should be cleaned and disinfected after use.

High pressure hoses

These are often used to clean the walls and floors in food processing plants. Some specialists advise against their regular use in food areas as they can spread isolated pockets of contamination throughout the food premises in air-borne droplets.

Sinks

The use of double sinks is often advocated, with one sink used for cleaning and disinfection and the other used for rinsing. It is also usually recommended to provide, where space permits, separate sinks for food preparation.

Steam hoses

These should generally be used only in special circumstances, such as deep cleaning, and by specially trained personnel as they can cause steam scalds. They are often used for cleaning the walls and floors of abattoirs and for reaching awkward corners of equipment or premises.

Vacuum cleaners

These include the domestic type and sit-on models and may include functions such as brushing, vacuuming and washing. They can usually clean large areas in one go, with less chance of causing dust, but may be difficult to use in restricted spaces.

Washing machines

Many premises, especially hotels and restaurants, have laundering equipment. Care should be taken to ensure that the equipment is positioned as far away from food areas as possible.

WHICH CHEMICALS ARE APPROPRIATE?

Cleaning products are available in many forms, including liquid, gel, foam, tablet, aerosol and powder. Before trying to answer the question of which is best for a particular task, we need to familiarise ourselves with a few technical terms applied to cleaning and disinfection materials.

There are five basic groups of chemicals used by manufacturers to formulate detergents and disinfectants. A product often contains chemicals from more than one group, designed to suit particular examples of cleaning circumstances. The groups are:

- surfactants
- sequestrants
- natural soaps
- solvents
- inorganic builders.

These groups are outlined on the following two pages, and you'll find more detailed information in the Reference section.

Surfactants

Surfactants reduce the surface tension of a liquid, so increasing the penetration of detergents. They are often referred to as wetting agents or, more technically, as synthetic surface-active materials.

WETTING AGENTS
A wetting agent (surfactant) is a substance which lowers the surface tension of the water or the cleaning solution, allowing it to have better contact with all the surfaces and to penetrate the soil.

There are many types of commercially available surfactant, almost all of which are petrochemical products. In the early stages of their development there were some environmental problems because sewage works could not easily treat the chemicals in the waste water, so foam formed on many rivers and waterways.

The problem has largely been overcome by formulating products that are more 'environmentally friendly' and biodegrade rapidly.

Types

They are usually classified according to their electrical charge when they are in solution, but we need not go into detail here!

Anionic surfactants

These are the most commonly used of the surfactants and can be found in most detergents including those in domestic use. They have very good wetting properties, are biodegradable and are non-toxic but they are not compatible with quaternary ammonium compounds (abbreviated to qats, quats or QUATS — see page 253) which are used as bactericidal agents.

Cationic surfactants

These are usually used for their bactericidal properties. They have some wetting properties but not as much as those of anionic surfactants. Their efficiency can be adversely affected by mineral salts and mineral-based soiling.

Amphoteric surfactants

These relatively costly chemicals are useful for removing grease — for instance, in ovens. However, they are unsuitable for use on food-contact surfaces.

Non-ionic surfactants

These are often mixed with the other surfactants because they are quite effective in removing oils and are not badly affected by hard water.

Sequestrants

These are chemicals that suppress or counteract the effect of other chemicals. They are used as ingredients in detergents simply as water-softening agents, so preventing the formation of scum or limescale.

Natural soaps

Most modern detergents are synthetic soap made from petrochemicals, but the original detergents — the so-called natural soaps — were manufactured by treating animal or vegetable fats with strong alkalis. With perfume added, these are still in use as toilet soaps and commercial laundry products. They do however form a scum in hard water.

Solvents

These are liquids, such as water and alcohol, used in products that remove oil and fat. Some also aid the rapid penetration of the detergent through layers of soil.

Inorganic builders

This group contains a range of chemicals.

Neutral fillers

These are added to make it easier to measure and handle the product, although cynics might say that they are included merely to bulk up the product and make it more profitable to the manufacturer. Examples of the substances used are water, magnesium sulphate, sodium sulphate, sodium chloride and borax.

Oxygen-release agents

Some laundry products include sodium perborate and hydrogen peroxide that release the available oxygen which acts as a mild bleach.

Caustic soda

This is highly alkaline and therefore not normally used in manual operations because of the risk of chemical skin burns or respiratory problems. It has good fat-removing properties and is often used in automatic milkbottle washing. It can be very corrosive.

Silicates

These highly alkaline materials, although less corrosive than caustic soda, have good wetting and emulsifying properties. They also help to suspend dirt particles in the liquid, so they can be rinsed away more easily.

EMULSIFYING

An emulsifier is a liquid that holds another substance, usually fat or oil, in suspension.

Phosphates

These can suspend and disperse soil (break lumps or areas of dirt into particles) and have water-softening characteristics.

Carbonates

The most common of these detergents is sodium carbonate (soda ash) which also has water-softening properties.

Chemical disinfectants

The number of chemical disinfectants available for use in the food industry is restricted because product must neither taint the food nor cause chemical food poisoning when used properly. Such is the concern over the effectiveness of, and possible harm from the use of, such chemicals that in many European countries chemical disinfectants must have official approval before they can be used in food premises. Until the mid 1990s chemicals used in the British dairy industry also had to be approved, but there is no longer a system of approval.

As with all chemicals, great care should be taken when using and storing disinfectants. Staff must be properly trained before they use them and supervisors must ensure that the manufacturers' instructions are followed to the letter.

There are many trade names for chemical disinfectants, so we outline just a few by their groups.

Chlorine

Chlorine is relatively cheap and is effective against most micro-organisms, provided that the manufacturers' instructions are followed. The chemical is available in many formulations and dilutions, but it is the amount of 'available', or 'free', chlorine that essentially determines how effective it will be. Chlorine-based compounds are probably the most commonly used chemical disinfectants.

Sodium hypochlorite is used most frequently: it works by oxidising the protein in the microbial cell structure.

Iodophors
Although more expensive than chlorine-based disinfectants, iodophors are very effective. They also have some detergent properties. As the name suggests, iodophors contain iodine: this is held in an alcohol solution which makes it particularly effective in the dairy and brewing industries where moulds and yeasts can be a problem. As with all chemicals the manufacturers' instructions need to be followed or they may become corrosive.

Quaternary ammonium compounds (qats, quats or QUATS)
While these disinfectants have the advantage of being odourless and non-corrosive, they are relatively expensive and, unless modified, are not very effective against Gram-negative bacteria.

Per-acetic acid
This is used widely in the dairy industry because of its effectiveness at low temperatures and on stainless steel and glass surfaces.

Alcohols
Ethanol and iso-propanol, two types of this group of chemical compound, are often the disinfecting agent in disinfectant wipes which are used where there is light soiling and for disinfecting hands and temperature probes.

ALKALINE ATTACK
We cannot attack bacteria by making food more alkaline because the flavour would suffer, but bleach and other powerful bactericidal disinfectants work by having a high pH level that destroys bacteria.

FACTORS IN CHEMICAL DISINFECTION

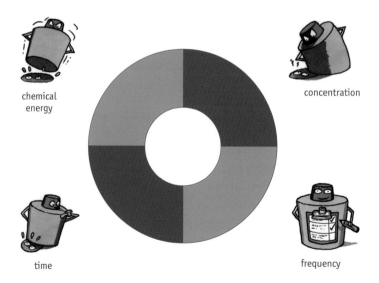

chemical energy

concentration

time

frequency

WHAT DOES EFFECTIVE CLEANING INVOLVE?

Whatever the type of cleaning task that needs to be carried out:
- all soil should be removed from the surface or item being cleaned
- the surface or item should be disinfected if disinfection is appropriate
- the contact time (for chemical and thermal disinfection) should be observed
- if chemicals are used in the cleaning process, all residue should be removed
- if the process involves wet cleaning, the surface or item should be dried or allowed to dry before it is used again.

Principles of cleaning

You could view the process of cleaning under the following general stages:
- task preparation
  - the process: selection of chemicals, materials and equipment, checking safety instructions, use of personal protective equipment (PPE) where appropriate
  - preparing the surrounding area: for example, by removing or covering food
  - preparing the surface to be cleaned, for example, by rinsing or sweeping to remove loose soiling
- cleaning – which may itself involve several stages (see the example of wet cleaning below)
- finishing
  - putting away clean items in the correct place so that they are free from hazards
  - storing chemicals safely and cleaning, repairing and maintaining cleaning equipment before storing it safely.

Wet cleaning and disinfection

Many cleaning tasks in food premises, such as washing large food storage containers in a sink by hand, may involve several steps within the cleaning stage.

1 Surface preparation — rinse to remove all loose and easily removed soil.
2 Washing — to remove, usually with the aid of a detergent, all the remaining soiling from the surface being cleaned.
3 First rinse — to remove all the detergent and loosened debris from the surface.
4 Disinfection — either with chemicals or hot water to reduce any remaining bacteria to an 'acceptable' level. (This stage is obviously applicable only when a reduction of micro-organisms is necessary, as with food-contact surfaces.)
5 Second rinse — to remove all trace of disinfectant.
6 Drying — to remove the residual water left from the second rinse. (Ideally allow the item to dry naturally. Otherwise, use a disposable cloth or a clean, dry fabric one.)

All the stages are not always necessary — for instance, to rinse items before washing them. When a sanitizer is used, several stages are combined because the chemical incorporates the function of both a detergent and a disinfectant.

WHEN SHOULD CLEANING BE CARRIED OUT?

The aim of cleaning is to remove contaminants and reduce the opportunities for microbial multiplication — in other words, to make items that come into contact with food as safe as possible for as long as possible. As ordinary cleaning processes rarely destroy all the pathogens that could cause a food-borne disease or accelerate spoilage, the aim of disinfection is to reduce pathogens to a low level that is considered safe for human health and helps to prolong product shelf life.

So cleaning needs to be carried out:
- whenever food appears to have been contaminated
- whenever there is a possibility that food has been contaminated
- whenever food-contact or hand-contact surfaces appear to have been contaminated
- whenever there is a possibility that food-contact or hand-contact surfaces have been contaminated
- as a matter of course to prevent microbial multiplication, chemical persistence or the build-up of dirt that could impair the way equipment or machinery operates.

In addition, disinfection needs to be carried out:
- whenever there is a possibility of microbial contamination
- whenever there have been ideal conditions, such as time and a danger zone temperature, for the multiplication of pathogens and spoilage organisms.

Before use
All utensils, equipment and facilities used for food must be clean and, where appropriate, disinfected before use. If a piece of equipment is used only occasionally, it may need to be cleaned after taking it out of storage and before use.

During use
Items and areas on which micro-organisms are likely to collect and multiply should be cleaned and disinfected throughout the work period. This is usually described as a *clean as you go* policy. It involves staff in clearing away and cleaning up as they work and immediately after completing a task.

If utensils and equipment are in constant use, they should be cleaned and disinfected frequently — for example, once every four hours, or at the end of every shift.

Where the same equipment, work surfaces and food areas must be used for preparing different types of food or for preparing raw as well as cooked or ready-to-eat foods (perhaps in very small premises), the equipment, utensil or surface must be cleaned and disinfected between different types of use.

After use

All food-contact surfaces must be cleaned and disinfected immediately after use and utensils and equipment should be stored in a clean area, protected from contamination, so that staff can have reasonable confidence that items are clean before they use them.

Hand-contact surfaces should be cleaned at least at the end of the working day or the work period, or more often depending on the level of use.

Structural features, such as walls and floors, and installed items, such as extractors, should be cleaned regularly according to the cleaning schedule (see pages 257 and 258).

Frequency

It is normally quite easy to decide how often cleaning should be carried out and to some extent the subject is covered by asking *when* cleaning should be undertaken. It would obviously be unacceptable to clean and disinfect a work surface only on the first Thursday of every month, but it would be unnecessary to wash the walls of a dry goods store once every hour of the working day.

The factors involved in the decision include microbiological, physical and chemical hazards — in other words, microbiological, physical and chemical contamination plus microbiological multiplication and survival.

Your *hazard analysis* (see 317 to 327) should help you to decide the frequency for any task and this should be shown in the cleaning schedule.

WHO SHOULD DO THE CLEANING?

The jobholder who carries out the cleaning really depends on the circumstances. For example, in a clean-as-you-go area it should probably be the person who made the mess who cleans it up, or someone in that immediate work team. However, the cleaning could be carried out by someone who is employed specifically as a cleaner or, in the case of scheduled deep cleaning, by an outside contractor, say every few months.

What is important is that the person who has been given the responsibility for a particular cleaning task should be properly trained for the job. They should also know:
• what they are responsible for cleaning
• how they should be cleaning
• which chemicals, if any, they should be using
• how often they should carry out the cleaning task
• what documentation they should be keeping
• why they should be cleaning and how it contributes to food safety.

HOW CAN YOU JUDGE THE EFFECTIVENESS OF CLEANING?

It is all well and good to establish criteria such as how often, with what and by whom, but how can you know how well cleaning is being carried out and whether it is making a positive contribution to food safety?

Daily supervision should indicate whether cleaning is done when it ought to be, whether the process is carried out in the prescribed way and whether something appears clean. The re-ordering rate for chemicals at least suggests that cleaning products are being used, while log books for detection equipment should provide evidence of levels of some types of contaminant. It may well be appropriate, however, to use rapid microbiological test methods to check the effectiveness of disinfection or to arrange for laboratory testing of samples from time to time, or both.

It is an excellent form of insurance is to make certain that staff involved in any cleaning activity, however minor, have been trained properly and are supervised so that they get it right first time, every time. It is also important that senior staff lead by example and help to motivate the staff to carry out what can be rather mundane tasks.

Cost

One of the factors in judging the effectiveness of cleaning is the cost of achieving an acceptable result. As we have seen, cleaning is basically the application of energy. All of these energies cost money, whether for the heating bills for water, for the purchase and maintenance of equipment and the purchase of chemicals, or for staff salaries.

Studies show that the labour cost of cleaning activities are up to 75 per cent of the total bill, so lowering this element of the cost by even five per cent would make a significant difference to your profit margins. It is for this reason that investment in equipment which cleans more quickly as well as more effectively than several human cleaners is often seen as a better option than using less detergent or cooler water. However, the effectiveness of good old-fashioned 'elbow grease' should never be underestimated.

When you review the cost of cleaning, make sure that any cost-cutting initiatives introduced still enable your staff to clean and disinfect surfaces, equipment and utensils thoroughly.

HOW SHOULD YOU MANAGE CLEANING?

Cleaning and disinfection are very important components of a safe food system so it is essential that they are carried out properly. *Cleaning schedules* are documents that help managers to plan what needs to be done on an hourly, daily, weekly, monthly, quarterly and annual basis and to help to ensure that all is actually carried out according to plan. Every food business should have a cleaning schedule. It could have a variety of designs but it is advisable to carry at least all the points suggested in the left-hand column of the chart below. Experiment with the layout, as it can make all the difference to how staff follow the schedule — grudgingly, willingly or perhaps enthusiastically.

CLEANING SCHEDULES

Point for inclusion	Examples and comments
What is to be cleaned	A mixing bowl.
How it is to be cleaned	Manually with a nylon brush.
Which chemicals should be used	A detergent followed by a disinfectant (and rinsing water).
What temperature the water should be	Optimum operating temperature for a particular chemical. For thermal disinfection, water needs to be above 82°C.
When it is to be cleaned	Disinfected *before* use and cleaned and disinfected *after* use.
How often it should be cleaned	Every time it is used, or weekly, monthly or quarterly depending on the item.
How long is required to complete the task	Between five and eight minutes. Ensure that sufficient time can be allocated.
Who must carry out the cleaning	Either the title of the jobholder or the name of the individual(s) responsible, or both. The name of the contracted specialist company.
The signature of the person who has carried out the cleaning	Personal guarantee that the cleaning has been carried out according to specification.
The signature of a supervisor to confirm that the standard of work has been checked	A safeguard giving a manager confidence that the work has been carried out to a required standard.

MAKING IT EASIER FOR OTHERS

- Emphasise that effective cleaning and disinfection help to prevent illness and create a favourable impression on customers and clients.
- Explain the hazards that can arise from inadequate cleaning.
- Outline the group and individual responsibilities for carrying out cleaning.
- Mention that it is a legal requirement to keep food premises clean.
- Train staff how to clean effectively and safely, including occupational safety measures such as the use of rubber gloves and aprons where appropriate.
- Emphasise the importance of checking how to use chemicals, including the dilution and method of application, before attempting to carry out a cleaning task with them.
- Create an appropriate procedure for keeping refrigerated and frozen food at a safe temperature while refrigerators and freezers are being cleaned.
- Make sure that senior staff, such as chefs, lead by good example.
- Insist that staff always wash their hands after completing a cleaning task.

PESTS UNDER CONTROL

FOOD PEST
An animal, insect
or bird which
contaminates or
destroys food.
Pests pose a
threat to stored
foodstuffs and to
the hygiene of
food-related
operations.

In some ways humans have made their own *pests*. The foods we grow, eat and store and the environments we create often provide valuable food sources and refuge for a wide range of insects, birds and small animals. In return they are, at best, inadvertently destructive or troublesome. At worst, they can be dangerously harmful, destroying crops and essential food supplies, contaminating food, causing food poisoning, spreading other diseases to humans and livestock, and creating occupational safety hazards by, for example, gnawing through electricity cables. Small wonder then that *pest control* is a prerequisite for food safety management.

Miniature invaders

When we mention pest control we are mainly talking about preventing *infestation* — the presence of food pests, usually in large numbers — in food premises. Indeed, something like 90 per cent of effective pest management is concerned with *active* prevention rather than *reactive* remedial measures (or in dealing directly with pests). As a consequence, pest management is inextricably linked to four other crucial aspects of food safety management:

- the design of the premises
- cleaning and disinfection
- the safe disposal of waste and rubbish
- hygiene practices.

When any of these goes wrong — if the building is badly designed or poorly cleaned, or if rubbish piles up or people are careless — then one of the first consequences is usually pest infestation. So, pest management also involves raising the staff's awareness of the hazards from pests, specific training in preventing infestation and effective supervision and monitoring of all methods.

A TIMELESS RELATIONSHIP

People, their health, food and pests have been closely linked ever since humans started to preserve and store food. Initially regarded as a nuisance to be tolerated, pests started to become a problem when stored foods were destroyed or rendered inedible, sometimes leading to human hunger or starvation. The direct fight against pests probably began in earnest when the pathogenic potential of pests began to be realised in the eighteenth and nineteenth centuries. Pest control then gradually developed into the *prevention* of infestation rather than trying to kill the pests — a crucial move from reactive to proactive types of food safety management, which is demonstrated today by *systematic* forms of food safety management including HACCP.

HARM FROM FOOD PESTS

Food pests create both microbiological and physical hazards — and food businesses have a legal responsibility to eliminate hazards to food or to reduce the risk from them to 'acceptably safe' levels. Clearly, pest infestation is a sign that a food business has not exercised *due diligence* in the management of food safety.

OUTSIDE THE LAW
The presence of pests in food premises is illegal.

The hazards from pests and the risk from those hazards depend largely upon the type of pest. Mice, for instance, can cause serious damage to stored foods and to food premises, but little economic damage is caused by houseflies. However, flies, which may have landed on rubbish tips and animal droppings, may be the *vectors* of serious diseases.

The main five plagues cited by the World Health Organization in 1999 — malaria, dengue fever, leishmaniasis, sleeping sickness and lymphatic filariasis — are all transmitted by insects or other vectors. Rats can carry a vast array of pathogenic bacteria that can become food-borne or water-borne and can cause potentially fatal conditions, such as leptospirosis (Weil's disease). Cockroaches are also laden with pathogenic micro-organisms, such as *Salmonella*.

Types of problem

Despite the variety of harm caused by pests, the problems can be divided into six main categories:

- direct damage to food
- consequent damage to food
- spoilage
- health hazards
- physical contamination of food
- physical damage.

You should also bear in mind that the inexpert use of pesticides can also cause chemical hazards.

HAZARDS
Pests create microbiological and physical hazards, while the inappropriate use of pesticides can cause chemical hazards.

Direct damage to food

Direct damage to food intended for people occurs in various ways. Rodents, for instance, consume all kinds of food. In contrast, *stored product pests* practice selective feeding, eating only a part of a food like a nut kernel but still making the whole batch of food *unfit* for human consumption. Another significant problem is caused by the larvae of some stored product pests which can destroy large quantities of food.

Consequent damage

Food can become unfit as a by-product of its infestation — for example, by becoming foul smelling or by losing its usual flavour or appearance.

Spoilage

Food starts to deteriorate as soon as it is harvested or slaughtered, and peeling, crushing or gnawing can accelerate the process. As soon as pests attack products like stored cereals their nutritional value also declines.

Health hazards

Insects, rodents and birds can cause food-borne illnesses, serve as vectors of cross-contamination and trigger skin ailments and allergies. The Indian meal moth, for example, can cause skin disease. Flour moths, grain weevils and cockroaches can provoke human respiratory problems.

Physical contamination of food

Every part of the body of every type of pest and every pest excretion and secretion has at some point been found in food products. Typical finds are:

- droppings
- eggs, larvae, insect exoskeletons, cocoons
- cobwebs from spiders, web-like residues from moths and beetles
- rodent hairs and bird feathers.

Physical damage

As well as causing damage costing thousands of pounds, pests can also create a wide range of health and safety problems. For example, rodents must gnaw to wear down their incisors which continue growing throughout their lives. Rats gnaw almost anything, including electricity cables, hoses, pipes and pipelines. This can lead to short-circuits, fires, floods or mechanical failures. Pests can also cause significant structural damage to food premises and to food packaging materials.

TYPICAL FOOD PESTS

As food safety manager you need to establish appropriate systems of pest management. To do so, you need an underpinning knowledge of the creatures that are most likely to be a threat to your business and of where and why they are likely to 'invade'. On the following pages, we summarise typical examples of food pests in the UK and Europe. Later in the chapter we look at proactive pest management.

Scientists often group pests according to their impact on humans. So, *storage* pests are a hazard to food in store, while *material* pests damage wood, textiles and so on. So-called *hygiene* pests may not be a direct danger to food, but their presence is objectionable, while *health* pests are injurious to human health as vectors and transmitters of disease. As some pests fall into more than one of these categories and as all pests are a hazard to food safety and hygiene, we have decided to consider pests under groups of animal.

OPEN INVITATION?

Food intended for people is often an attractive meal for pests. Buildings can become safe sleeping or nesting quarters, or shelter from cold, wind, rain and natural enemies.

RODENTS

Rodents are large group of gnawing mammals but only a few families, such as mice and rats, are classed as food pests. Rodents followed people into the towns and cities centuries ago and rodent populations do best by living near food premises, waste disposal sites and sewage works. Urbanisation and urban rubbish, among other things, have been blamed for an increase in rodent problems.

Signs of rodent infestation include droppings, gnaw marks, footprints and fur and tail marks. Rodents try to avoid crossing open spaces: where their fur touches walls or any other surface, such as pipes, sacks or containers, they tend to leave characteristic smear marks along well-established routes. Small numbers of rodents may be difficult to detect but you may find damaged food or food containers, destroyed packaging materials or other signs of feeding or nesting. It is important to encourage staff not to ignore damaged food containers or spilled goods as they may indicate rodent infestation.

Mice
Mice are vegetarian and prefer grain and cereals because of their high energy content. They can develop particular food preferences, for instance, for potato crisps. They usually live singly, but their immensely successful distribution is due to their reproductive ability — one female can give birth to about 45 young each year.

House mouse (*Mus musculus*)
Originally native in Mediterranean countries and the Asian steppes, the house mouse can now be found all over the world, usually near human settlements. Its favourite habitats are farm buildings, supermarkets and food manufacturing premises. As their preferred foraging range is no more than ten metres, mice try to live as close to their food source as possible. They can survive without drinking water, instead using the residual water in food.

Rats
Both the brown rat and the black rat are omnivorous, although they prefer cereals, meat, fish, nuts, eggs and fruit. The damage they cause is immense. Not only do they devour large quantities of food, but they can also destroy utensils and equipment by gnawing. They can cause serious physical contamination too, because each rat can produce about 200kg faeces and 55 litres of urine every year.

Their role as vectors is wide ranging and cannot be overestimated. They can transmit diseases including typhoid, cholera, tuberculosis, cryptosporidiosis, toxoplasmosis, listeriosis and other zoonoses and they are also associated with diseases such as tularaemia, leptospirosis and Hanta virus.

Since the Middle Ages they have had a significant role in distributing plague among urban and rural populations because the plague bacterium *Yersinia pestis* lives in

DISEASE SPREADERS
Rats can cause an alarming number of serious and life-threatening food-borne diseases including typhoid, cholera, tuberculosis, cryptosporidiosis and listeriosis.

the rat flea and is spread by rats. Rats are very good climbers and swimmers and access through waterways and unsecured sewage pipes poses no problem for them.

Black rat (*Rattus rattus*)
This is darker than the brown rat and its tail is longer than its body length. It made its way to Europe from India via Africa. Preferred habitats include grain stores, where it is warm and dry. The black rat does not depend on water sources as much as does the brown rat.

Brown rat/Norwegian rat (*Rattus norvegicus*)
During the Middle Ages the brown rat began its spread from its native eastern Asia and is now distributed all over the world. Brown rats are social animals and prefer to live in groups of several hundred. They live in and outside buildings and use urine marks to define their territory. In the urban environment they can be found in shops, storage areas, abattoirs and almost any food premises provided that there is access to a water source. They tend to be active at night and avoid people. If cornered, brown rats can be quite aggressive and may even attack humans.

INSECTS

Flies, cockroaches, ants and stored product pests come under this heading. Their small size, tough exoskeletons and large numbers make them difficult to eradicate and, as many are also highly mobile, they are often difficult to control.

Signs of infestation include seeing the insect itself and finding dead bodies, larvae, pupae, egg cases and, especially in the case of cockroach infestation, the exoskeletons left after casting. Storage moths and beetles leave web-like structures that are often mistaken for lumps of flour. Unusual smells may also indicate insect infestation. The adult form of most insects may be easy to detect, but as pests can enter your premises at earlier stages of their life cycles, it may be very difficult to identify the larval stage. They can be hidden inside some products and it is almost impossible to see the eggs.

Flies
Flies have always troubled humans, but it is only since the nineteenth century that people have appreciated that flies can carry and spread disease as a result of their habit of feeding on, and flying between, human food and human and animal faeces. The adult fly can feed only on *liquid* matter so the fly dissolves solids by regurgitating stomach acids onto the surface of the food then sucking up the resultant partially digested fluid. Flies are known to transmit typhoid, dysentery and microscopic parasites. Latest research suggests that they may also be vectors for *E. coli* 0157.

Housefly (*Musca domestica*)
This is probably the most familiar and certainly the most widely distributed of all insects. It has followed humans everywhere, adapting itself to breeding and

hibernating in various conditions. At a minimum temperature of 18°C the housefly can develop and multiply in any season of the year, with the female producing up to 600 eggs during its life. The development from egg to adult insect takes about three weeks in warm weather. In tropical latitudes, the housefly can be responsible for the spread of cholera.

Fruit fly (vinegar fly, genus *Drosophila*)

These very small flies are attracted to fermenting substances and they appear wherever fruit and vegetables are processed, for instance in the production of jams, jellies, juices, wines, beers, ciders and vinegar. The flies can cause considerable nuisance in kitchens and canteens by flying around in swarms. Infestation also accelerates fruit spoilage. They breed on overripe, decaying fruit and are a major problem in fruit and vegetable stores, canning factories and juice manufacturers. The female fly lays between 400 and 500 eggs during its life. The maggot larvae feed mainly on moulds and yeasts on the food material.

Whether fruit flies are also vectors of diseases is not known, although there is a strong suspicion that they are because they also settle on faeces.

Bluebottle (*Calliphora erythrocephala*)

With its characteristic iridescent blue body and loud buzzing, this fly is a member of a family that also includes greenbottles and flesh flies. They are sometimes collectively known as blow flies because of their habit of depositing ('blowing') their eggs on exposed meat, where they develop into maggots. Bluebottles are more likely than their close relatives to enter buildings in search of meat and they also frequent dustbins that contain meat and fish scraps. The female can produce up to 600 eggs in its lifetime.

Cockroaches

The two most common species in the UK are the German cockroach and the Oriental cockroach. They tend to infest premises where there is a constant ambient temperature and a reasonable level of humidity. Typical breeding areas are moist and dark and include beneath refrigerators, stoves or sinks, in and under cupboards and around plumbing. They are usually active only at night and seeing a cockroach during the day suggests an extremely serious level of infestation.

Cockroaches are omnivorous and are attracted to a wide range of foods, fouling what they do not consume and leaving a typical odour described as a 'roachy' smell: for those who recognise it, the smell is an unfailing indication of infestation.

They do not go through a complete metamorphosis from larva to adult (unlike a butterfly or beetle). A miniature cockroach, called a 'nymph', hatches from the egg differing only slightly from the adult form. As their hard exoskeleton (body covering) is very rigid and does not enlarge, cockroaches need to shed their exoskeleton in order to grow larger. The casts (the shed exoskeletons) indicate infestation and particles from them can cause respiratory allergic reactions (sometimes described as cockroach asthma). Cockroaches can also cause a number of food-borne diseases by carrying pathogenic bacteria from refuse or excrement to food. The bacteria may be carried on their feet and transferred to food or may be transmitted from the intestinal tract or regurgitated stomach contents.

German cockroach (*Blattella germanica*)
These are found in most parts of the world, usually indoors. Their life cycle depends very much on the ambient temperature: at 30°C it takes 50 to 60 days from egg to adult insect. The females are able to mate several times during their lifetime, every time producing an egg case containing 15 to 45 eggs. German cockroaches do not only attack foodstuffs but also packaging materials and textiles. This insect, which is only between 1cm and 1.5cm, is often carried into premises in cartons or other packaging materials.

Oriental cockroach (common cockroach, black 'beetle', *Blatta orientalis*)
This cockroach, measuring between 2cm and 2.7cm, is the more common in Britain. It deposits its egg cases in warm hidden places where they stay for about two months (unlike the German cockroach, which carries its egg case until a few hours before hatching). During their lives females can produce up to 18 egg capsules, each containing about 16 eggs, but the length of their life cycle depends on the suitability and abundance of food as well as on temperature and humidity: the Oriental cockroach does not need as much moisture as does the German cockroach.

Ants
Ants live in highly developed social organisations, taking distinct adult forms according to the tasks they perform in the colony. It makes little sense killing single worker ants by mechanical methods (such as squashing them): not only does the dying ant leave a chemical warning for others, but the infestation will persist as long as the queen ant remains unharmed at the centre of the colony. Ant nests are usually to be found outside buildings but the insects find their way inside through cracks and crevices in walls, doors and window sills. In kitchens and food premises ants are mainly a cause of annoyance, although food attacked by ants may become insipid and spoilage is accelerated. Most ant species are not known to transmit disease — the Pharaoh's ant (see below) is an exception.

Black garden ant (*Lasius niger*)
Black garden ants, which are about 4mm long, are found all over Britain. Worker ants enter buildings in search of food: when they find a rich source of sugar, they send out scent message to attract more ants. They form a line to transport the food into the nest where it feeds the queen and the workers tending the larvae. Old-fashioned remedies against ants rely on disrupting the scent communication by scattering aromatic plants such as lavender and marjoram along the ant trail.

Pharaoh's ant (*Monomorium pharaonis*)
Native to India, these ants were probably imported to Britain over a hundred years ago and have adapted to an indoor environment where there are high temperatures

and relatively high humidity. They owe their name to the first scientific description of the species, which was discovered during the examination of mummies of Egyptian rulers (or pharaohs).

At 2mm long, this ant is much smaller than the black garden ant. Its colonies take up only a tiny space in walls or floor crevices, behind broken tiles or cracks in furniture or wooden frames. One colony usually hosts several queens. These ants do not swarm like other ants but from time to time some queens leave the nest, followed by a stream of workers, to establish a new colony. Worker ants are attracted to meat, fat, cheese, sweets, bread and pastry but they also carry dead creatures such as cockroaches and decomposing mice into the nest. Eradication of an infestation is possible only by detecting and destroying the nest.

Pharaoh's ants can access almost any building and are frequently found in kitchens, canteens and bakeries, as well as in hospitals where they can contaminate dressings, catheters, intubation drains and other sterile items with bacteria picked up from wound liquids, faeces, sputum and hospital waste.

Stored product pests

Ever since humans started to grow crops and store them from one harvest to another, storage insects have been a constant companion — one of the principal stored product pests, the biscuit beetle, was found in the tomb of Tutankhamen who died in about 1352 BC. For a long time the infestation of grain, cocoa, tobacco and other goods must have been regarded as almost inevitable.

The presence of insects associated with stored products usually involves an immediate or potential risk of a substantial loss of food — most damage is caused by the larval form of the insect which needs the food as a carbohydrate (or starch) source for its development. As there are many stored product pests, we can mention only some of the principal representatives. As you will see, many pests are named after their preferred food — for example, *flour* moth and *grain* weevil — but this does not mean that you will never find them in another type of food.

Biscuit beetle (*Stegobium paniceum*)

This beetle, measuring between 2mm and 3.5mm long, causes considerable loss of products in dried goods stores. Although it feeds mainly on grain and flour, it can also be found in many other products such as dried noodles, rice, spices, chocolate, nuts, dried vegetables and even cork, leather and paper. The biscuit beetle is one of the very few pests that can live under extremely dry conditions and survives in a humidity of lower than eight per cent. In temperate climates, such as that of the UK, the biscuit beetle can produce about two generations a year.

Confused flour beetle (*Tribolium confusum*)

The common name of this beetle, which is found worldwide, comes from the Latin word confusum, which can be translated as *dark*, a description that helps to distinguish it from *Tribolium castaneum*, the chestnut-coloured flour beetle. In cooler climates it is restricted to warm stores of staples such as flour, but it also feeds on grain, pulses, pastry, chocolate, spices, dried fruits, nuts and animal feeds. Flour infested by this beetle produces a sour, evil-smelling odour, making it unfit for baking. The terminal segments of the beetle's abdomen contain glands that produce chemical substances which may have a carcinogenic effect on humans.

Grain weevil (*Sitophilus granarius*)
This is a familiar pest to anybody who stores grain and cereals in large quantities. It causes serious infestations of grain in undeveloped regions of Asia, Africa and South America where millet or kaffir corn is the staple diet of poor people. The larvae can grow in wheat, rye, barley, rice and corn as well as in sunflower seeds, millet, oats and chestnuts — one larva usually infests each grain. As the adult insect comes out from the grain, it leaves a distinct round hole.

Indian meal moth (*Plodia interpunctella*)
This insect occurs in warehouses, silos, mills and food-processing plants as well as in catering premises and homes. The insect got its common name from the United States where it was a pest of maize or Indian corn meal. It also infests dried vegetables, herbs, dried fruits, nuts, cocoa beans, chocolate, powdered milk, seeds and grain products. In warm climates it attacks a wider range of products including sultanas, raisins, currants, figs, dried apricots and lentils. The insect, or its larval form, is usually imported into the UK in such products.

Mealworm beetle (*Tenebrio molitor*)
This is better known for its larval form, the 'yellow mealworm', which can be bought as food for caged birds and lizards. It takes the larvae about 600 days to develop and its importance as a stored product pest in flour in domestic premises has diminished in recent decades with the decrease of home baking. However, the beetle is often still found in mills, flour stores and bakeries where it may transmit bacteria to food and can be an *intermediate host* for several tapeworm species. Infection occurs when whole or crushed mealworms are eaten.

Mediterranean flour moth (*Ephestia kuehniella*)
This moth is a serious nuisance in mills where, if it is present in large numbers, its web-like structures may clog conveyor spouts and other parts of the milling machinery. The larvae feed on flour, bran, flakes, grain and nuts and, in warm environments, may produce five generations a year.

Saw-toothed grain beetle (*Oryzaephilus surinamensis*)
The larvae of this insect are increasingly prevalent in warehouses, silos, mills and food processing plants. The larvae need high temperatures at around 30°C, so they are attracted to grain that has been stored before it has cooled properly after the drying process. At 3mm long, this insect can hide in crevices inaccessible to sprays and fumigants.

Birds

Food businesses often neglect to consider birds when they discuss pest management, even though pest controllers sometimes describe sparrows as 'flying mice' because of their potential for causing pathogenic contamination.

Wild birds, such as sparrows, starlings, seagulls, swallows and especially pigeons, are potential vectors of serious diseases. Feral pigeons, for instance, can spread toxoplasmosis and many other diseases. Birds can also be *carriers* of a number of parasites such as mites and lice. They can cause severe contamination through their excrement and large-scale infestation can produce offensive smells.

In urban environments birds have adapted to living around people and their waste. They feed on all kinds of rubbish including bread, fast-food leftovers, even mayonnaise and mustard. Birds roost in roof structures in and outside warehouses and other buildings and are hard to expel when they have found a suitable niche.

An additional problem is that birds, especially pigeons, often provoke human affection which makes their control a sensitive and sometimes unpopular measure.

Apart from seeing the bird itself, droppings, feathers and evidence of nest building are signs of infestation. Sparrows use every possible material when building their nests, including waste, pieces of packaging materials and old tissues. Birds undergo seasonal moulting when large numbers of feathers are shed. These are not only potential physical contaminants but can also carry pathogens and mites.

MANAGING THE HAZARDS

Effective pest management requires preventive, monitoring and control activities. Prevention includes measures such as appropriate design and construction of premises, the use of pest-proof containers and diligent cleaning. Regular inspections, monitoring and reviewing are required — for example, deliveries of food must be checked before storing, and food stores and baited traps must be inspected frequently. There must be immediate remedial action if necessary.

Integrated

It is common to tackle these activities in partnership with professional pest controllers. Partnership is the key here, as an arm's-length relationship may not produce the desired results. By developing a mutual understanding, both parties contribute time, expertise and action to keep pests out. Such an approach is usually described as *integrated pest management* (IPM). The essence of IPM is best explained as follows:
- co-operation between the food business and the pest control consultant
- staff training in environmental pest control
- preventive measures instead of chemical pest control once infestation is established
- prevention of re-infestation.

METHODS OF CONTROL

Pest control can be divided into three categories:
- environmental
- physical
- chemical.

Some methods of control should be used only by professional pest controllers, others can be carried out by the food company as a matter of course, while others still need the skill and diligence of *both* parties to be effective. Whichever is appropriate, the staff involved must be trained properly. As you will see, you should consider chemical controls to be a last resort.

Environmental control

Every food business should exercise environmental pest control measures, whether or not it engages external pest specialists. As you will see from the examples of measures given on the next page, environmental controls are really part and parcel of everyday food safety management. They involve denying pests the three things that make food premises attractive to them:
- access
- food
- shelter.

Access

To stop pests getting in to food premises, all possible points of entry must be sealed or restricted and controlled. So, for example, the brickwork around pipes should be sealed and kept in sound repair: remember that insects and even mice can get through tiny fissures and openings.

While it may be easier to deny birds and rodents access than it is to keep insects out of premises, screens on windows and strip curtains on external doors help considerably. Mechanical devices can help to keep food preparation areas insect-free, as many stored product pests enter the premises in sacks of dry goods, in the folds and crevices of packaging materials or clinging to wooden pallets or vehicles.

This is where effective staff training and constant staff vigilance provide a form of access barrier — trained staff can recognise the signs of infestation in typical deliveries of food to your premises and follow the procedures for rejecting unfit consignments. Regular daily inspections and vigilance, with prompt remedial action if required, help to stop your external defences being breached.

Food and shelter

Clean, tidy, well-maintained food premises, the essence of 'good housekeeping', are core defensive measures against pests and the damage and contamination they can cause. Regular cleaning routines disturb areas where pests might otherwise be harboured in dimly lit, out-of-the-way corners and installations (such as pipes and refrigerator coils), while removing food scraps minimises the risk of microbiological and physical contamination. If your premises are clean and tidy, staff are far more likely to spot the signs of any infestation that does occur despite all your best efforts. After all, pests are great opportunists.

Outside the premises
Remove vegetation from the immediate area around the premises: it could provide cover and habitat from which pests could migrate to the building. Do not cut corners on external maintenance and service, but do make sure to eliminate potential breeding grounds such as open or damaged gutters and drains.

Keep rubbish areas and storage containers scrupulously clean and tidy to eliminate harbourage and food debris. If rubbish builds up or bins overflow, check whether you need to arrange for additional bins or more frequent collections.

Emphasise to staff the importance of keeping bin bags inside the containers with the lids closed securely: some creatures, such as foxes and seagulls, can be persistent and ingenious at retrieving poorly protected refuse. Ensure that food is delivered at times when the premises are open so that food is not left outside.

Neglected maintenance and repairs can rapidly provide access to food premises and habitats for food pests.

Inside the premises
Establish appropriate cleaning schedules, paying special attention to any parts of the premises that tend to be neglected, such as the shafts of service lifts, areas under staircases and spaces behind shelves, piles of stock and equipment, or machinery that is not in regular use. Emphasise how important it is for staff to follow the *clean as you go* principle in order to remove food debris that could attract pests. Whenever possible, store food in rodent-proof containers with close-fitting lids. Where this is not practicable, ensure that paper and card packaging remains intact. Reusable food containers must be cleaned and disinfected before re-use.

Physical control

These methods accept that there are pests in the environment and are designed to catch them before they become a food hazard or to deter them from getting in to food premises. The methods available differ widely in their effectiveness — mechanical devices such as the mousetrap, for instance, prove effective only against individual mice and cannot deal with a large infestation.

Physical methods can usually be employed by trained food handlers as well as by professional pest controllers. However, it might be worth investing in professional advice before making a decision to use physical methods and before training staff how to deploy the devices, check them and dispose of trapped dead animals. Examples of devices include fly-swatters, insect-catchers that use sticky paper, electronic fly-killers, which use ultraviolet light, and preventive installations such as mesh screens on windows and other openings. For trapping larger animals, such as mammals and birds, there are traps, snares and nets available. Spikes on window ledges, the upper levels of buildings and on porches and architectural features can be used to deter birds, but nets can also be effective.

Ultraviolet (UV) fly-killers

UV fly-killers (also known as electrocutors and insect zappers) can be used in any kind of food business. It is especially important to position them properly and to maintain them carefully if they are to work safely and efficiently. If, for example, a fly-killer were installed right over a doorway, it might attract insects into the building. Alternatively, if one were positioned directly above areas where open food is prepared, dead flies could easily fall into the product. Even so, every fly-killing device needs a collecting tray that is large enough to catch even those parts of insects that would otherwise be quite widely distributed.

Models of fly-catcher with electrified grids can be replaced by ones that catch the insects on a sticky surface. In either case the fluorescent tubes need to be changed regularly (at least once every six months is recommended).

Chemical control

Chemical pest control should be adopted only as a corrective measure and your aim should always be to keep the premises permanently free of pests. The decision to use chemical methods of control should be made with considerable caution as any chemical substance in a food business creates a food hazard which needs to be monitored and supervised. Some substances may be directly harmful to human health and their application is best carried out only by professional specialists.

As we saw in Part 3, the word *pesticide* covers chemicals designed to kill pests. There are three main types, named after their intended target:
• rodenticides (to kill rodents)
• insecticides (to kill insects)
• acaricides (to kill mites).

Pesticides should not be confused with chemicals, such as pheromones and other attractants, which are *not* used to control an infestation but to monitor intrusion into an area.

Many pests have developed resistance to previously effective poisons. Rats and cockroaches, for example, show neophobic behaviour, learning to avoid particular bait formulations and 'teaching' the rest of the population to do so too.

Application of pesticides

There are many different methods of applying pesticides — as bait pellets, in spray or gel form or dispensed by fumigation (smoke or gas in a controlled area). None of these methods should be attempted by untrained staff and it is vital, even where contractors are employed, to alert *all* staff to the pest control measures and to warn them about the personal dangers and the possible contamination hazards involved if they touch, move or tamper in any way with bait stations or other form of pesticide.

If pesticides are applied as a surface film, aerosol or gas, you must ensure that the area is decontaminated thoroughly before any work with food resumes. If an existing infestation needs to be treated, product lines may need to be covered, open food removed and instructions given about disposing of potentially contaminated products.

Chemicals against pests

Until about one hundred years ago most pesticides were inorganic materials, such as sulphur, lead, copper, arsenic and mercury, or occasionally botanical compounds such as nicotine and pyrethrum. The development and extraordinary effectiveness of highly toxic DDT (dichlorodiphenyltrichloroethane) changed the nature of pest control and slowed down the development of other, less toxic substances.

Only when research proved that the gradual accumulation of pesticides created a possibility of global contamination did scientists start to look for less harmful solutions — and there is still a great deal of confusion about the toxicity of, and the necessity for, pesticides. Easy decontamination and biodegradability have become critical factors in the development of new pesticides.

Because pests adapt rapidly by their behaviour and their resistance to pesticides, it is necessary to make constant modifications to the formulations of pesticides to try and keep one step ahead.

KEEPING PERFORMANCE UNDER REVIEW

Pest management acknowledges that pest problems can vary enormously and may change over time. If infestation has occurred then access, food and shelter must have been provided and a first step before using chemicals should be to ask the following questions:
- why could it have happened?
- which pest prevention measures have been neglected?
- is it possible to get rid of the problem by removing sources of food, water and shelter?
- if not — how can infestation be prevented from happening again?

Taking professional advice

As the professional responsible for food safety in your business, you may have to listen to some constructive comments and criticism from the pest specialists. You could, for instance, be told that:
- you should improve general hygiene practices

- staff need better general hygiene training or specific training in pest prevention
- faulty or badly-designed processing equipment is harbouring pests
- transport vehicles used inside or outside your premises are moving pests into, or around, food areas
- the layout of your premises needs to be changed to improve workflow and reduce contamination
- your waste disposal system does not work as it should.

✱ MAKING IT EASIER FOR OTHERS

- Explain the potential food and health hazards from pests.
- Point out that the law requires the business to be free from pests.
- Emphasise the devastating impact that pests could have upon customer perception of the business and on trade.
- Explain that pests can literally eat into business profits, so damaging the company's profitability and viability.
- Encourage everyone to follow the company procedures for preventing infestation and reporting signs of infestation.
- Emphasise the message, 'Keep it tidy — keep it shut'. It works to prevent most kinds of contamination!

SAFE FOOD AT ITS BEST

It is difficult to draw a clear line between *temperature control* for the purposes of food *preservation* and temperature control for the purposes of *food safety* as the use of high and low temperatures are central to both. Generally speaking, preservation methods are industrial or large-scale processes aimed at extending the *shelf life* of food (and may include controls other than temperature), while temperature controls designed to keep food safe to eat are essential to almost every food business in almost every sector of the food industry.

PRACTICAL DIVISIONS

In this book we have gathered together the time and temperature methods that are primarily used for food safety into the chapter 'Controlling time and temperature' (see pages 277 to 284). Most of these controls are are likely to be necessary in any food establishment in any food sector. However, the *pasteurisation* of milk, which is usually an industrial process, appears in this chapter because it is mainly a food safety technique even though it does prolong shelf life a little.

Techniques mainly used to prevent *spoilage* and extend shelf life, including the *sterilisation* and *ultra heat treatment* (UHT) of milk, are covered in the chapter 'Maintaining quality over time' (see pages 285 to 298).

Of course, storage conditions are important to both food safety and shelf life and these are covered in the chapter 'Storing for safety and profit' (see pages 301 to 306), which also deals with labelling, date marks, deliveries, handling and stock rotation.

Safety and quality

Temperature control to ensure food safety is a cornerstone of the Hazard Analysis and Critical Control Point (HACCP) system (see pages 314 to 327). Preservation processes are also a part of the HACCP system to ensure that food remains safe as well as good to eat.

Different countries, industrial sectors and companies set slightly different rules for time and temperature control. The times and temperatures given below remind you of the danger zone temperatures and provide an at-a-glance reference to temperatures that are generally accepted to be good practice or are legal requirements where stated.

Oven cooking (a typical baking temperature)	180°C, time variable
Ice cream sterilisation	149°C for 2 seconds
UHT milk	132°C for 1 second
Canning	121°C, time variable
Milk sterilisation	100°C for 15 to 30 minutes
Normal boiling point of water	100°C
Minimum recommended core cooking temperature	Good practice is normally 72°C for 2 minutes for prime cooking
Minimum reheating temperature	Good practice is a core temperature of at least 70°C for 2 minutes, or an absolute minimum of 75°C if no time recommended; by law in Scotland, not less than 82°C
High-temperature short-time pasteurisation (HTST)	72.2°C for 15 seconds
Gelatine	71°C for 30 minutes (by law in Scotland)
Ice cream pasteurisation	Variable, eg. 71°C for 10 minutes
Egg pasteurisation	64.4°C for a minimum 2.5 minutes
Legal minimum hot holding temperature	63°C
Danger zone	5°C to 63°C
Human body temperature (average)	37°C
Legal maximum refrigeration/chill/cold holding temperature for specified foods	8°C (England, Wales and Northern Ireland)
Recommended maximum refrigeration/ chill/cold holding temperature	5°C
Normal freezing point of water	0°C
Typical freezer temperature	−18°C
Typical commercial freezing and frozen storage temperature	−26°C

CONTROLLING TIME AND TEMPERATURE

What is the main reason for food poisoning? Poor temperature control is the simple answer. Research over many years in several countries pins the blame on sloppy temperature practices. As we saw on page 74, such practices include inadequate cooling of hot food, unsuitable cold holding temperatures, preparing food long before it is to be served then leaving it at ambient temperatures, and inadequate hot holding or reheating.

None of the steps involved in keeping food at a safe temperature for a suitable time is difficult. So, while poor temperature control is the main cause of food poisoning, the main cause of poor temperature control can be firmly pinned on ineffective management. One of the most important elements of a food safety management system is time and temperature control. When properly managed, the risk of causing a food-borne illness is significantly reduced.

Type of control

You are no doubt familiar with the idea of temperature control, but you will see that in this book we take about *time and* temperature control because, for practical purposes, the two are usually inseparable. Forgetting the importance of time destroys the value of temperature control.

INSEPARABLE CONTROLS
Effective temperature control necessarily includes suitable time control.

Time and temperature control includes measures to:
- restrict the time that high risk foods are at a temperature that is likely to encourage the multiplication of pathogenic or spoilage micro-organisms
- destroy pathogens — for instance, by heating food
- restrict microbial activity — for instance, by holding food at a low temperature.

THE DANGER ZONE

A guiding principle of time and temperature control is to keep high risk foods out of the *danger zone* (5°C to 63°C) — the temperature range which is most suitable for pathogenic microbial multiplication.

In short, high risk foods should not be left at danger zone temperatures for long periods because many types of pathogen have time to multiply to levels that cause illness (see Part 3, especially the bacterial growth curve on pages 52 to 54).

Although you may understand this principle well, you may also know that in practice it is often impossible to prevent high risk foods from being in the danger zone at some stage — for example, during preparation.

In fact, it may be necessary for some foods to pass through the danger zone several times — for example, during thawing, cooking and cooling. This is where time becomes a crucial part of temperature management. It is essential to restrict the length of time that a food is at a danger zone temperature by, for instance, refrigerating a high risk food *immediately after* preparation and *until* it is needed. Temperatures outside the danger zone can be used to destroy pathogens or at least to restrict their multiplication.

Essential controls

The use of heat and cold conditions as food safety controls are discussed in detail later in this chapter. Before we look at the specifics, it is worth reminding ourselves of some useful rules of thumb:

- restrict the time that high risk foods are at a danger zone temperature
- cook food thoroughly, right through to the core or the thickest part of the food
- keep hot food really hot, at 63°C or hotter, if it is to be eaten hot
- keep cold food really cold, ideally at 5°C or cooler
- keep frozen food frozen, at −18°C or below
- thaw frozen food thoroughly before use, unless the manufacturer recommends cooking from frozen
- cool hot food as rapidly as possible if it is to be eaten cold or stored for later use
- avoid reheating food if at all possible; if not, reheat thoroughly right the way through the food.

MAINTAINING SAFE TEMPERATURES

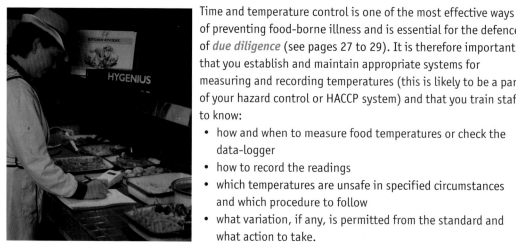

Time and temperature control is one of the most effective ways of preventing food-borne illness and is essential for the defence of *due diligence* (see pages 27 to 29). It is therefore important that you establish and maintain appropriate systems for measuring and recording temperatures (this is likely to be a part of your hazard control or HACCP system) and that you train staff to know:

- how and when to measure food temperatures or check the data-logger
- how to record the readings
- which temperatures are unsafe in specified circumstances and which procedure to follow
- what variation, if any, is permitted from the standard and what action to take.

The temperature of high risk food must be checked regularly and recorded. Staff must know exactly what to do if there is an unsatisfactory reading.

Types of temperature recording device

Some equipment, such as refrigeration and freezer units, indicates the temperature automatically and continuously: some produce a permanent record. Other devices measure the temperature of food or air. They include digital, infrared, probe and electronic thermometers. The devices must be calibrated regularly to ensure that the temperatures they indicate are accurate: this may have to be carried out by a specialist company. To prevent contamination and cross-contamination it is essential to train and monitor staff in cleaning and disinfecting recording devices thoroughly, particularly those with probes for inserting into food.

Reading temperatures

It is important to ensure that staff follow the manufacturer's instructions and use each device only within its approved temperature range. Whichever method is used, sufficient time must be allowed for the device to reach an accurate reading.

Meat and poultry are best checked towards the end of their cooking time by inserting a clean probe into the centre or thickest part of the flesh (for example, into the poultry breast or thigh). An ideal way to check the temperature of food under refrigeration is to insert a clean, disinfected probe into the centre of a tub of a commercial test medium (a gel made for the purpose) that has been kept in that particular refrigerator. Freezer temperatures, if not recorded automatically, can be taken by hanging the probe in the freezer unit, making sure that it does not touch the room or cabinet walls, or by placing it between packets of food or by resting it on top of food.

Ensuring an accuracy

When checking the temperature of solid food that is being cooked, reheated, cooled or thawed, it is important to check the *core temperature* — the temperature at the centre of the food or in the middle of the thickest part of the food. Liquid food should be stirred frequently before taking the reading to ensure that it is accurate for the temperature *throughout* the liquid.

WHEN TO TAKE TEMPERATURES

Temperatures should be checked as often as appropriate to the types of product and operation.

Examples

Deliveries of food	as soon as it arrives
Refrigerated units	daily and regularly; ideally within 15 minutes of the start of shift, then throughout the day
Freezer units	daily
Thawing food	towards predicted end of thawing period
Cooked and reheated food	towards predicted end of cooking or reheating period
Hot holding	frequently

Unsatisfactory readings

It is crucial to ensure that there are clear rules about target temperatures (or critical limits) and that they are written into the HACCP or hazard analysis plan (see pages 314 to 327).

Staff must know what to do if a temperature is incorrect. For example, the appropriate action regarding cooked food may be to continue cooking. However, if a refrigerated vending machine has two readings of 9°C or higher, the appropriate action may be for staff to report directly to you or to a supervisor so that checks can be made on the way the machine is operating and a decision reached on taking the machine out of service and possibly destroying the food it contained.

CORRECTIVE ACTION
Your company's rules for dealing with non-conforming temperature readings should be included in the HACCP plan and management policies.

Keeping records

Accurate temperature records help the business to monitor and maintain safe temperatures. They are also valuable evidence of due diligence in the event of an allegation of food-borne illness. The records should be kept where they are easily available to an inspector or auditor during a food hygiene inspection. It is suggested that the records be retained for several years in case they are needed to answer an allegation or defend legal action.

USE OF LOW TEMPERATURES

Refrigeration

Although refrigeration keeps food safe for only short periods, it is an invaluable temperature control that even the smallest food business can use. Refrigeration contributes to food safety because it affects one of the *intrinsic factors* for the survival and multiplication of micro-organisms. The ideal temperature for the multiplication of most pathogenic bacteria is between 5°C and 63°C (the danger zone), with the optimum temperature for most being around 37°C.

So, when food is kept above freezing point but below 10°C the multiplication rate of bacteria slows down dramatically and eventually, at a slightly different temperature for each species, stops altogether. Even so, many bacteria can still survive for quite long periods at low temperatures. Multiplication at below 5°C is restricted to some specialist organisms, such as the psychrotrophs *Yersinia enterocolitica*, *Listeria monocytogenes*, *Aeromonas hydrophila* and *Clostridium botulinum* Type E. Although the multiplication rate is slow, these organisms are still of significant concern. Parasites may also survive refrigeration temperatures.

The law and good practice

Legal requirements for chilled foods differ from country to country. In England, Wales and Northern Ireland, for instance, the storage temperature of foods which are not *ambient shelf stable* is set at 8°C. (There is a limited defence of some upward variation from the 8°C maximum under certain types of specified circumstance, and there limited specified tolerances.)

SAFETY MARGIN
Good practice is to keep refrigerated food at below 5°C.

The accepted *good practice*, however, is to hold chilled food at below 5°C: in reality, this is usually at 4°C to stop the formation at lower temperatures of ice crystals in salad vegetables, such as cucumbers.

Refrigeration and chiller units

The design of these cabinets should be suitable for the intended purpose and they should be constructed of easy-to-clean materials. Units should be placed away from heat sources and draughts and out of direct sunlight. Food must not be crammed into the unit in a way that prevents cold air from circulating so increasing the temperature of stored food to within the danger zone. Managers should ensure that there are sufficient refrigerators and chiller cabinets to cope with peaks in demand.

Cold holding (or chilling)

This term usually refers to the practice of keeping food cool for a relatively short time in a display cabinet or vending machine, commonly in retail or catering premises, sometimes for customer self-service. The food should legally be kept at below 8°C and ideally at below 5°C. This can be achieved in many ways and the most common is the circulation of cold air through the display. Ice is used for many displays, particularly for fish, shellfish and prepared salads: this gives the food a pleasing and appetising appearance as well as keeping it safe to eat.

Cooling

Inadequate cooling is a major cause of food-borne illness, so it is important to reduce the temperature of hot *high risk food* quickly so that it is at a danger zone temperature for the shortest period possible. The temperature control regulations (see pages 160 to 163) stipulate that such foods should be cooled as quickly as possible.

It is good practice to aim to reduce hot food to a refrigeration temperature within 90 minutes. This is best achieved by using a blast chiller. Other methods include cooling food in shallow trays, cutting large joints of meat or poultry into smaller portions, or using an ice bath — either where a cold container of the food is placed inside another of ice and cold water, or by putting the food in food bags before placing them in containers of ice and water.

Multi-use refrigerators should *not* be used for cooling hot food, as this may raise the temperature of the other foods stored there.

Cook-chill and cook-freeze

Many food businesses use a combination of cooking and chilling methods every day, but 'cook-chill' is the title given to a form of mass catering. It involves the preparation and cooking of a large number of meal portions which are packed, blast chilled and stored at below 3°C until they are required. They are then regenerated for service. The preparation, cooking, chilling and storing is often carried out at a central production unit before the food is distributed to satellite outlets, such as hospitals, for regeneration and serving.

Cook-freeze is a similar operation but, as the name implies, it involves freezing the cooked and portioned product instead of chilling it. There are specific guidelines for these processes.

Thawing

Some frozen products may be cooked from frozen following the manufacturer's instructions, but many must be thawed first. If food, such as joints of meat or whole poultry, is not thawed thoroughly before cooking, ice crystals may remain at the centre so that, although the surface of the food will cook, the temperature at the core may remain within the danger zone, providing ideal temperatures for microbial multiplication.

DEALING WITH LIQUIDS
Remove cooked meat joints and whole poultry from their juices before placing them in clean containers for the appropriate method of cooling. Use large shallow containers for cooling products in liquid as the large surface area accelerates the process.

COVER UP
Protect food from contamination during thawing.

Thawing should ideally be carried out either in a specially designed thawing cabinet or in a refrigerator set aside for the purpose. This keeps the food at a controlled temperature outside the danger zone during the period of thawing which can be several days if the product, such as a turkey, is large. It is unsafe to thaw food in a kitchen overnight, or worse still over several days, because the ambient temperature is most likely to be within the danger zone.

Frozen food should ideally reach refrigeration temperature right through to the core before it is cooked.

If your premises are so small that you have only one multi-purpose refrigerator, it is advisable *not* to buy large frozen items that require thawing before use. Where *small* items are thawed in a multi-purpose refrigerator, they should be placed on the lowest shelf to prevent juices from dripping and contaminating other products. Ensure that workflow is planned to take account of thawing times.

USE OF HIGH TEMPERATURES

Heating food is without question the best way to eliminate micro-organisms and it is a happy coincidence that the cooking of foods often makes them more palatable. One could argue that if everything were boiled and eaten immediately, the only food safety problems would arise from some of the toxins, notably *Staphylococcus aureus*, and the naturally occurring toxins. However, as boiling everything is not an viable option, we must consider alternative forms of heat treatment.

Cooking
Most forms of cooking or baking involve temperatures that are high enough to destroy pathogens (although spores and toxins may survive), provided that the food is cooked for long enough. The rule of thumb is 70°C or above for two minutes, so that the food is cooked thoroughly and evenly right the way through to the centre, or to the thickest part of the food or the bone. To do so, it is advisable to cook poultry stuffing separately and not in the chest cavity.

Reheating
Inadequate reheating can provide an ideal temperature for bacterial multiplication and is a common cause of food-borne illness (see page 74). If your business must reheat food, you must ensure that it is heated thoroughly and evenly. Ideally a core temperature of at least 70°C should be reached for at least two minutes, and in Scotland there is a legal requirement to reheat previously cooked food to a temperature of not less than 82°C.

Food should ideally be reheated immediately before consumption. However, if it must be kept hot before sale or service, it should be held at 63°C or hotter. The reheating of left-overs should be discouraged.

Hot holding

Hot holding is important for anything from a display cabinet for hot food in restaurants to a bain marie in a kitchen to a pizza delivery bag. Food should be held at above 63°C — in other words, outside the temperature danger zone. As with any time and temperature management, the temperature should be checked regularly to ensure that it has not fallen below 63°C.

Pasteurisation

This relatively mild form of heat treatment is applied to foods such as milk, eggs, fruit juice, ice cream, canned fruit, wine and canned ham. The time and temperature used varies according to the product and the exact method of pasteurisation that is chosen. Milk is usually heated to 72.2°C for 15 seconds — the method known as high temperature short time (HTST) pasteurisation.

This treatment was originally applied to milk to destroy tuberculosis pathogens, but it also reduces other pathogens in milk to accepted safe levels for human health.

Pasteurisation is not, however, a process of sterilisation (in which virtually all micro-organisms are destroyed), so a small number of organisms, especially spoilage types, survive the process and can survive in the milk even when it is correctly refrigerated. This is why pasteurised milk has a shelf life lasting days rather than weeks.

The main advantage of pasteurisation over other forms of heat treatment is that the flavour and composition of the food is relatively unchanged. Milk loses about 25 per cent of its vitamin content but the remaining amount is still so high that this does not significantly affect its nutritional value.

The pasteurised cheese debate

Some types of soft cheese are traditionally made with unpasteurised milk and there has been much debate about whether they are safe to eat. Those who favour compulsory pasteurisation maintain that pasteurised cheeses are safer and that food-borne infections such as *E. coli* 0157 and *Listeria monocytogenes* have such a low infective dose that heat treatment is the only way to reduce the risk of serious illness. Those opposed to compulsory pasteurisation argue that consumers should have the right to choose and that pasteurisation alters the flavour of cheese, increases costs and may even increase the risk to health because any bacteria that contaminate the product after pasteurisation will have no competition.

It is legal to sell unpasteurised milk products, but they must be labelled as such. Some companies also voluntarily label unpasteurised foods with a warning to people in the 'at risk group'.

The law requires hot food to be held at 63°C or above to help to control the growth of pathogenic micro-organisms or the formation of toxins. The temperature should be checked frequently.

STORING PASTEURISED FOODS Pasteurised products should usually be refrigerated as the process is designed for safety not for extending storage times.

⚙ MAKING IT EASIER FOR OTHERS

- Make sure that all food handlers understand the danger zone and essential controls, particularly:
  - keep hot food hot
  - keep cold food cold
  - keep frozen food frozen.
- Teach staff how to stack refrigerators to avoid cross-contamination and to allow cold air to circulate.
- Encourage staff to plan their workflow so that they open refrigerator doors as infrequently as possible and remove food from refrigeration just before it is needed.
- Ban staff from placing food above the load line in chest freezers or from storing unwrapped food in freezers.
- Ban the storage of food in ice-cream freezers (conservators) because the temperature will be too warm.
- Insist that everyone follows the house rules for approved methods of thawing frozen food and do not tolerate high risk food being thawed at ambient temperatures, for instance, overnight.
- Insist that everyone follows the house rules for cooling hot food.
- Remind staff to observe the standing time, or to stir the food, when items are heated in a microwave oven.
- Train staff how to check and record temperatures.
- Train staff to follow procedures for corrective action if temperatures are unsatisfactory.

MAINTAINING QUALITY OVER TIME

In our additive-conscious age, when the words natural, fresh and unprocessed have become familiar marketing slogans, food preservation and especially preservatives are sometimes viewed with mistrust. But storing food to prevent starvation is probably almost as old as the human species and can be seen as one of the first evolutionary adaptations distinguishing humans from other animals. Some rodents, such as squirrels, do store nuts and other foods but they are unable to treat them to make them last. Often they fail even to find their food stocks when they are needed. Only humans have found the secret of reliable food preservation and storage.

Keeping food palatable

The first methods of storage were determined by climate. People in cold parts of the world learned to use ice and cold larders while those in warmer regions developed methods of sun-drying. Even so, treating the food was only the first step and they also had to discover how to keep it in excellent condition.

One of the first big breakthroughs probably came with the discovery that liberal applications of salt can preserve foods such as meat and fish for long periods, regardless of climate. So important was this that salt became an early form of currency. (Our word 'salary' comes from the Latin for salt and gives us the expression 'to be worth your salt'.) We will probably never know whether it was the human liking for salty flavours that led to the discovery of its preserving properties, or its use as a preservative that gave us a taste for salt. (Some other animals, such as cows, seem to like salt, without having any knowledge of preservation methods.)

Later on, other methods such as smoking, pickling and curing were discovered. More recent technological developments have given us a wide range of methods, including heat treatment such as canning and sterilising; the addition of chemicals; and vacuum packing.

Preservation in the modern food industry

Our ancestors were probably more motivated by hunger than by food safety. After all, when starvation is the issue, even unpalatable food will be eaten. Today, however, when we talk about *food preservation* we are mostly concerned with preventing *spoilage* and extending *shelf life* — which is sometimes described as prolonging the 'eating quality' of the food.

Even so, preservation and safety are closely connected because most techniques for controlling spoilage are also methods for controlling pathogens. In law, too, there is no sharp distinction and legislation in most countries considers food to be *unfit* for human consumption if it has been spoiled. Of course in the food business, you need to consider both aspects when you are processing food for storage.

WHY FOOD SPOILS

Spoilage is simply any change in a food product that makes it unfit or unacceptable for its intended purpose: and that purpose is, of course, eating. All food eventually spoils but the process can be accelerated by bad practices such as careless handling and inappropriate transport or storage. The four main causes of spoilage are:
- micro-organisms
- enzymes
- oxidation
- contamination.

Spoilage by micro-organisms

Micro-organisms are present in all food unless it has been specially treated to eliminate them. The same principles that apply to controlling pathogenic micro-organisms (see pages 58 to 66 and 183 to 187) also apply to spoilage micro-organisms, so preventing them from:
- contaminating food
- multiplying if they are on food
- surviving.

Food is exposed to some micro-organisms even in the cleanest, most hygienic conditions and does not come to you in a sterile condition. So you must have in place effective methods for preventing microbial multiplication and survival.

As you know from Part 3, most techniques rely on one or more of the following approaches:
- removing nutrients
- reducing water activity (a_w)
- reducing or increasing temperature
- controlling and managing temperature and time
- creating an inhospitable hydrogen-ion concentration (pH)
- removing oxygen
- using microbial competitors.

As well as these methods, chemical preservatives may be used. These function in different ways, for example by disrupting the functioning of bacterial cells.

Spoilage by enzymes

CHEMICAL TRIGGER
A catalyst is a chemical that triggers off, or speeds up, a chemical reaction without itself being changed by the reaction.

Enzymes are chemicals produced by living organisms. They act as *catalysts* in essential biochemical reactions. Often designed for just one specific biochemical reaction, enzymes are usually large, complex protein molecules. We cannot live without enzymes as they sustain essential chemical reactions in our bodies. One estimate suggests that there may be as many as 3,000,000 enzymes in every human cell and there are others — such as those involved in digestion — which are found outside the cell walls.

Benefits
Enzymes are used extensively in food processing to speed up reactions within the food. Some of these uses are modern high-tech developments but others have been known since ancient times. Enzymes in yeast, for instance, have been used for thousands of years to help in the fermentation processes behind wine production, beer brewing and bread making.

Disadvantages
For all their usefulness, enzymes can also be destructive. Long after an animal or plant is dead, enzymes carry on precipitating chemical reactions which may produce unpalatable or even dangerous compounds — an example of the latter is a part of the process that leads to scombroid poisoning of fish. The longer you keep the food, the higher the concentration becomes of these substances — unless, of course, you do something to halt their action. Indirectly, enzymes can also be destructive by preparing the way for microbes, creating an environment that is favourable to their multiplication.

Controlling enzyme reactions
There are several ways of controlling enzyme reactions.

Temperature control
One of the most important and effective is by managing temperature. Most enzyme activity occurs between 20°C and 50°C, with 30°C to 35°C being optimal. Some enzymes are still active outside this range but they are much less effective.

Temperatures of 60°C to 70°C will destroy most enzymes. In fact the standard way of testing whether milk has been properly pasteurised is to check for the presence of the enzyme phosphatase. Correctly pasteurised milk should be heated to 72.2°C for 15 seconds. This destroys phosphatase, so any sign of this enzyme after the pasteurisation process indicates that the milk was not properly treated.

Low temperatures also control enzyme activity by preventing their production. In scombroid fish poisoning, for instance, the enzyme histidine decarboxylase is produced by bacterial action in the dead fish. Storing the fish at below 4°C controls bacterial activity and so controls enzyme production.

Hydrogen-ion control
Another way of controlling enzyme activity is by pH. Most enzymes function best in the pH range 4.5 to 8, so acidic foods and those processed in such a way that the pH is low, such as pickling, are less likely to spoil due to enzyme activity.

Rancidity of fats and oils
Rancidity in dairy products may be caused by hydrolysis (a chemical reaction), resulting in free fatty acids, or by the action of naturally occurring enzymes called lipases, producing odours and tastes which are usually described as 'off'.

Spoilage by oxidation

Oxidation typically happens in the presence of oxygen — for example, when you cut an apple in half and leave it exposed, the oxygen in the air causes a reaction that turns the cut surface brown. Processes of oxidation, known as redox or the oxidation-reduction potential (and often abbreviated to O/R or E_h) also have a significant impact upon micro-organisms. These are described more fully in the feature on pages 299 to 300. For now, the most important thing to know is that one way of preserving food from bacterial deterioration is by altering the amount of oxygen in the atmosphere around a food.

Spoilage by contamination

Contamination, as we have already seen, can be caused by almost anything and does not have to pose an actual risk to health but simply to be objectionable to consumers. Problems commonly occur as a result of bad handling, transport and storage that leads to microbiological, physical and chemical contamination.

REDUCING SPOILAGE

There are many ways of delaying spoilage. As you would expect, they include:
- altering the pH
- altering the a_w
- altering the E_h
- removing air or altering the air composition
- applying heat
- storing at low temperature
- chemical destruction or inhibition of microbial cells
- appropriate storage
- introducing competitive organisms.

These methods, which can be used alone or in combination, generally control the multiplication of pathogenic bacteria such as *Clostridium botulinum* but will not necessarily control moulds and yeasts. Although the preservation techniques listed above are varied, they fall into one of five basic categories of food preservation which are described on the following ten pages — low temperature, high temperature, dehydration, chemical or physical preservation.

LOW TEMPERATURE PRESERVATION

Reducing the temperature of food is a traditional method of preservation. As refrigeration (or chilling) is a short-term form of preservation only, it was discussed in the previous chapter — see pages 280 to 281.

Freezing

Freezing preserves the 'natural' freshness of foods over an extended period and for that reason has become extremely popular.

Keeping food at below 0°C, the normal freezing point of water, can eventually destroy some harmful organisms, particularly parasites. However, the main value of freezing as a method of preservation is that microbiological activity almost ceases due to the reduced a_w. Some moulds and yeasts can nonetheless still grow at very low temperatures.

Although some bacteria die when they are first frozen and some subsequently die during frozen storage, most become dormant. Even so, their spores and toxins can survive freezing.

Preparing food for freezing

All foods must be wrapped to minimise the loss of surface water and prevent irreversible damage from *freezer burn* (the formation of large ice crystals caused by the loss of surface water). In most cases this involves using plastic or foil wrappings, but some products, such as fish fillets, are sprayed to form a thin coat of ice before they are frozen in order to prevent dehydration. Products that are susceptible to oxidation, such as fatty foods, benefit from vacuum packing before they are frozen. Vegetables need to be blanched beforehand to destroy enzymes that might otherwise cause deterioration during storage.

A block of commercially frozen fish being prepared for bulk storage.

Freezing methods

There are several methods of commercial freezing and the one selected depends on the type of food to be frozen and the speed of the process. The longer the freezing process takes, the larger the ice crystals that are formed, and the greater likelihood of freezer burn.

Blast freezing

Food is passed on a conveyor belt through a tunnel of cold air. This is probably the most common method and is used for fish and meat products. The time taken to freeze the product depends on the type of food, its size and surface-to-mass ratio.

Plate freezing

Packaged foods such as blocks of frozen fish are inserted between two metal plates and cold air circulated around it.

Fluidised bed freezing

The food moves along a belt on an air cushion, allowing rapid freezing of individual items, often vegetables.

Cyrogenic freezing

Liquid nitrogen is sprayed onto a product, such as prawns, resulting in a quick freezing process.

HIGH TEMPERATURE PRESERVATION

As we mentioned in the previous chapter, heating foods is an effective way to destroy micro-organisms. In the following paragraphs we look at methods used primarily or exclusively to preserve foods.

Ultra heat treatment (UHT)

This method of heat treatment was developed to give milk a longer unrefrigerated shelf life without significantly affecting the flavour. The milk is heated to 132°C for one second, then aseptically packaged. Some people detect a small change in taste and smell but the use of *UHT* milk has increased dramatically over the years, especially in buffet-style and self-service catering, where it is often packaged in single portions. Ultra heat treated milk does not need to be refrigerated until after it has been opened.

Sterilisation

True *sterilisation* means the destruction of *all* micro-organisms. As this is both difficult to achieve and to verify in food, the phrase *commercial sterilisation* (sometimes known as *appertizing*) is usually used to describe the process when it is applied to food.

Commercial sterilisation

Commercial sterilisation involves heating the food to more than 100°C for anything from 15 to 30 minutes, usually by the application of steam and pressure.

Milk is sterilised in this way. The process modifies the flavour and texture of milk and impairs the nutritional value, including the vitamin content.

Ohmic heating and canning are typical forms of commercial sterilisation and are discussed below and on the following two pages. Pouches of food, such as sauces and soups, which have become popular in recent years, are also subject to similar treatment before being packaged aseptically.

Ohmic heating

This is a form of commercial sterilisation in which food is heated by passing an electrical current through it. The method is suitable only for small particulate, semi-liquid foods which can be pumped, such as chilli con carne or bolognese sauce. After heating, the food is aseptically packed. It can then be stored at an ambient temperature for several months.

Canning

The term canning refers to the process of putting food into metal, glass or plastic containers which are hermetically sealed and heat treated until the food is commercially sterile. The process is designed to kill the spores of *Clostridium botulinum* — hence the phrase *botulinum cook* — and to reduce to an acceptable level the heat-resistant spores of spoilage organisms. The time and temperature required are related to the pH of the food. Fruit and other products with a pH of less than 4.5 (acid foods) receive relatively less treatment than those with a pH greater than 4.5 (low-acid foods) which receive more robust heat treatment. The a_w of the food is also taken into account in determining the treatment.

The importance of destroying *C. botulinum* spores cannot be overstated as the botulinum toxin is the most dangerous substance to be dealt with. In practice it is assumed that all organisms present are spores and that they must be reduced to a level which no longer creates a human health hazard — in other words, so that the product is commercially sterile. This minimum sterilisation process is known as a 12D reduction: this is simply a mathematical way of expressing that however high the initial contamination may be, the end product is safe to eat.

F values

The time and temperature combination depends on the kind of food to be processed. The temperature is always 121°C, but the time varies as some foods have a higher possibility of being contaminated with spores than others, some products are denser than others, some products conduct heat more readily than others and so on.

The time is expressed as an equivalent F_0 value. The F is simply a mathematical symbol. When, for instance, a product requires heating for 3 minutes at 121°C to achieve sterility, it is simply stated as $F_0 = 3$. Other examples of values are canned salmon which has an F_0 of 7 and acid fruits, such as strawberries, which may be as low as $F_0 = 1$.

Stages of canning

Stage 1: Filling

After preliminary cleaning, sorting and processing, food is added to cans. Liquid is usually placed in the can first, to prevent air bubbles.

Stage 2: Exhausting

Steam is blown into the top of the open container above the contents, causing a vacuum and, to some extent, removing oxygen.

Stage 3: Sealing

The three seams (top, bottom and side) are hermetically sealed.

Stage 4: Processing

Cans are cooked to the time indicated by the F_0 value (above). Steam, hot water under pressure, or steam and air mixes may all be used as a heating medium.

Stage 5: Cooling

Cans are cooled in chlorinated water as quickly as possible. It is important that enough chlorine has been used during the water treatment to ensure that the cans do not become contaminated, but not so much that the chlorine corrodes the cans.

Stage 6: Labelling and storage
Cans must be dry before being labelled to prevent rusting.

Common problems with cans
Blown cans
Blown cans occur because of a build-up of gas — either hydrogen or carbon dioxide — as a result of microbial action. In the early stages a blown can is slightly swollen at one end and would flex under thumb-pressure. Reputable suppliers would withdraw such as can, known as a flipper, as it could quickly progress to a dangerous stage when the can becomes extended at each end so that it resembles a rugby ball (this is known as hard swell). At this stage, the can could explode if knocked or dropped.

Hydrogen swells
Dark stains inside a can are the result of acid foods acting on the internal surface where the lacquering has been damaged. Hydrogen sulphide forms in the can and reacts with the lining. The condition is not harmful but it does look unpleasant.

Damaged cans
Dents, corrosion, leaks and punctures can come about for any number of reasons — usually because of poor handling or storage. Damage of this kind can be dangerous to health as bacteria or moulds may enter the food through the punctured container and oxygen from the atmosphere may permit pathogenic or spoilage organisms to multiply to harmful levels.

CORNED BEEF TYPHOID OUTBREAK

When two cases of typhoid were first diagnosed in Aberdeen in May 1964 nobody predicted one of the largest food safety crises in the UK in the twentieth century, with 487 patients in hospital. The outbreak was eventually traced to just one catering-size can of Argentinian corned beef. The can had a flaw in its seam and the meat inside had become contaminated by untreated water used in the cooling stage of the canning process. When the corned beef was sliced in an Aberdeen shop, the slicing machine became contaminated and cross-contaminated other meats.

Television broadcasts played a new and significant part in the intense media coverage, for the first time providing a public health warning as well as widely airing public reaction. The lessons learned from the subsequent public enquiry changed attitudes and policies of public health professionals, politicians and others concerned with food safety. One of the main outcomes was the setting up in Scotland, and later in the rest of the UK, of methods of surveillance to give early public warning of outbreaks of food-borne illnesses and advice on the ways to avoid becoming ill.

PRESERVATION BY DEHYDRATION

Drying is one of the earliest food preservation methods employed by humans. It works by removing the moisture that bacteria need in order to be active. To be effective, the drying processes must reduce the moisture content or a_w to a point where the activities of both spoilage and pathogenic bacteria are inhibited.

Foods that have been subjected to a drying process fall into two categories: dried or desiccated foods, such as whole eggs, yolks or whites, and semi-dry foods such as biscuits, cakes and pastries. The former, known as low moisture (LM) foods, contain no more than 25 per cent moisture and have an a_w between 0.00 and 0.60. The latter are called intermediate moisture (IM) foods and have a water content of between 15 and 50 per cent and an a_w of between 0.61 and 0.85. The two types have different storage requirements and different shelf lives.

Methods of drying
There are several ways of drying food, some going back to ancient times and some involving advanced technology.

Sun drying
The simplest and oldest form of dehydrating food is sun drying, which is often used for fruits. Food is spread out under the sun and, provided the temperature remains high and the humidity is not too great, the process is usually successful. However, an extensive area is obviously required for large-scale production.

Spray drying
Foods such as milk are processed into a pasteurised slurry which is then sprayed into a hot air stream. Moisture is quickly lost due to the small droplet size and the food ends up as a powder.

Drum or roller drying
A food paste is spread on a roller or drum which is heated, causing water to evaporate. When enough water has been lost the dried 'cake' is simply scraped off the drum. A variation known as tunnel drying involves placing food on trays which are passed through a tunnel of hot air.

Freeze drying
The product is subjected to rapid freezing, which draws out water but creates smaller ice crystals than normal freezing and therefore does less physical damage. After freezing, the food is heated in a vacuum, causing the ice to turn to water vapour which is drawn off, leaving behind a dehydrated product such as instant coffee or vegetables used in instant soup mixes.

With this method of preservation, the reconstituted product tastes only minimally different to the original.

CHEMICAL PRESERVATION

The main use of chemical preservatives is against spoilage organisms but they do also have an effect on pathogens. In fact, it would be dangerous to use a chemical preservative that was effective only against spoilage organisms, as the pathogens would suddenly find themselves free to multiply without any competition. This does not happen in practice, because the chemicals used affect spoilage and pathogenic organisms in much the same way. Chemical preservatives can also be quite effective against spores, either by preventing their germination or by destroying bacteria as they germinate.

The chemical reactions involved in this form of preservation are quite complicated and in some cases not fully understood. For the purposes of food safety management, however, it is not necessary to understand the chemistry fully, but only to know which preservatives are used and what effect they have on food.

Salt

As discussed earlier, salt is an early method of food preservation which is often used to preserve meats and fish. It works by producing a drying effect. When food is salted a process known as plasmolysis takes place in which water is drawn out of the cells causing them to contract, stop growing and, in some cases, to die. In fact, in smoking processes (see page 298) it is usually the salt that causes the preserving effect rather than the smoking itself.

Sugar

As you will know if you have ever made jam, fruit can be preserved by the simple addition of sugar. Sugar preserves food in much the same way as salt: it reduces the a_w and so inhibits the growth of spoilage and pathogenic organisms. Much greater concentrations of sugar than salt are required to be effective, but most people have a sweet tooth and this method of preservation has found favour for centuries.

Sugar substitutes such as saccharine do not have the same preserving action as sugar itself, partly because they do not combine so readily with free moisture. Dietary products such as low-sugar jams can develop surface mould more quickly than traditional jams and need to be kept under refrigeration.

Benzoic acid

Together with some of its derivatives, benzoic acid was one of the first chemical preservatives to be given official approval. It works by disrupting the activity of cell membranes at a low pH, so making it useful in high-acid foods but completely ineffective at a neutral pH. The main use is therefore in foods such as cider, soft drinks, tomato ketchup and salad dressings.

Of course, a low pH inhibits the growth of bacteria in any case, but the main effectiveness of benzoic acid is in inhibiting yeast and mould. It does, however, also have an inhibitory effect against some bacteria at certain concentrations. The maximum permitted concentration is 0.1 per cent but, even at this level, benzoic acid can give a peppery or burning taste to fruit juices.

Sorbic acid

The action of sorbic acid is very similar to that of benzoic acid. It is widely used and is effective at a lower pH than benzoic acid. Sorbic acid is thought to inhibit the dehydrogenase enzyme system, which is involved in processing moisture in the microbial cell. It is particularly effective against mould and yeast growth although it also works reasonably well against aerobes such as *Salmonella* species and can prevent the outgrowth of vegetative cells from germinating spores. It is used mainly in foods such as bakery products, juices, salad dressings and cheese.

Proprionic acid

The main use of proprionic acid is to inhibit the growth of mould in bread, cakes and cheese, and rope (a soft, sticky texture) in bread dough, which are formed by *Bacillus subtilis*, the spores of which may survive baking. The acid acts in a similar manner to sorbic and benzoic acid and is also useful in low-acid foods.

Nitrites and nitrates

Sodium nitrite and sodium nitrate are used in curing meat because they stabilise the red meat colour, inhibit some spoilage and food poisoning organisms and enhance the meat's flavour. Their main use is against *Clostridium botulinum* although these chemicals are also effective against other organisms, particularly other *Clostridium* species. They are a useful preservative for fish but only for those in the low pH range.

The Perigo factor

For some time researchers were puzzled by the almost total absence of botulism toxin in cured, canned and vacuum-packed meat and fish products even when viable spores were present. Then in 1967 it was shown that if curing salts, such as sodium nitrite, were added *before* heat treatment — as in these forms of processing — the result was about ten times more effective against spore germination than when the chemical was added afterwards. This is known as the Perigo factor, or Perigo effect, after the surname of its discoverer.

Sulphur dioxide and sulphites

Sulphur compounds have been used as preservatives since at least the beginning of the nineteenth century. They are effective against bacteria although the exact mechanism is not known. The main use is in neutral or acid foods such as lemon juice, molasses, wine, fruit juice and meat products such as sausages and mince.

Antibiotics

Two antibiotics are used in food preservation. Nisin, which was first used in Swiss cheese to control *Clostridium butyricum*, is added to cheese to inhibit spoilage.

Natamycin is used as an antifungal agent, mainly for the control of surface mould and yeast, for instance on fruits and salami.

PHYSICAL PRESERVATION

Several very different processes fall into this category.

Altering the atmosphere

Techniques such as vacuum packing and modified atmosphere packaging (MAP) work by reducing the available oxygen.

Vacuum packing

In vacuum packing the product is placed in a plastic bag and the air is sucked out by a vacuum-packing machine, after which the bag is heat sealed. Not all the oxygen is removed from the package, but the little that remains is quickly used up by any aerobic organisms present, so increasing the levels of carbon dioxide and inhibiting aerobic growth. Even so, it is always advisable to keep vacuum-packed products under refrigeration.

The effectiveness of vacuum packing depends on the integrity of the plastic wrapping. Provided it is properly carried out, this method is relatively safe.

However, problems may still arise with *Yersinia enterocolitica* and *Staphylococcus aureus* bacteria for various reasons. *Clostridium botulinum* poses a potentially high risk in cooked vacuum-packed products because of the possible persistence of its spores. However, products contaminated with *C. botulinum* often undergo organoleptic changes that make them so unpalatable that it is unlikely that they would be eaten anyway.

Modified atmosphere packaging (MAP)

In MAP the air is flushed out of the packaging by a mixture of other gases, usually containing high levels of carbon dioxide and nitrogen. The reduction of oxygen affects micro-organisms in a similar way to that of vacuum packing and quite a long shelf life is achievable, especially when the food is then refrigerated.

Irradiation

Subjecting food to low levels of ionizing radiation is a reasonably effective way of destroying pathogens, bacterial spores, spoilage organisms, parasites and insects.

According to British law, irradiation is approved for use at specified doses for a limited range of products — herbs, spices and some medically prescribed special diets — and all irradiated food must be labelled as such. Although the process is strictly controlled and all the current scientific evidence suggests that there is no significant risk to human health, irradiation is still controversial and the subject of public concern. One of the perceived problems is that, as there are few apparent changes to irradiated foods, it is therefore difficult to detect whether food has been treated or not. Consumer resistance suggests that there is unlikely to be any substantial increase in the use of irradiated foods within the UK within the immediate future.

The process
Food irradiation involves bombarding food with a form of energy — ionising rays with strong penetration abilities, such as X-rays, gamma rays, microwaves and ultraviolet waves. In general, the shorter wavelengths of X-rays and gamma rays are the most powerful, with the lethal dose depending on the individual organism. Non-spore forming bacteria, yeasts and mould spores are killed at lower doses than spore forming bacteria. The highest irradiation values (which are measured in rads) are needed to inactivate viruses and enzymes. The nature and consistency of the food is also taken into account when calculating the rads required.

Possible advantages and disadvantages
The process can be employed to treat solid and packaged foods. Not only is this convenient, but it also helps to prevent the recontamination of the product.

There are some *organoleptic* effects which may be considered to modify the quality of the product — for example, colour changes and alterations in smell and taste. At high dosages some foodstuffs may undergo a change in structure. Some other concerns have also been raised, including:
- the possibility of decreased nutritional value — some vitamins may be affected but in general there is little cause for concern as radiation doses are low
- carcinogenic effects — none has been demonstrated to date
- residual radioactivity — doses are considered to be too low to pose a significant risk
- microbiological problems — it has been suggested that sub-lethal doses of radiation may allow micro-organisms to survive, possibly with genetic mutations, but no significant problems have ever been found
- altered flavour and smell — it is reported, for example, that doses at the higher end of the approved range may give chicken a 'wet dog' smell
- inappropriate use — fears have sometimes been expressed in the media that irradiation could be used to clean up microbiologically contaminated or spoiled foods before sale.

Smoking
This is a centuries-old method for treating food for storage, even though its value as a preservative is limited. It is thought that chemicals known as phenols, which are produced by the smoke, may have some preserving effect. If this is indeed true, then the effect can apply only at the surface.

Fish and ham have traditionally been smoked, but in recent years the process has been extended to a much wider range of products including many types of meat, sausages and cheese, although this is often done more for flavour than for preservation purposes. There are two types of smoking — hot smoking and cold smoking. The methods vary only in the time and temperature combinations.

The process

Smoking takes place in a kiln where food is suspended for a specified time over smouldering chips of oak or other hardwood. Modern kilns allow for careful monitoring and control of both time and temperature. Before smoking the food is often left for up to eight hours in dry salt or in a brine solution, sometimes with additional marinades. It is probably the salt rather than the smoking that has the main preserving effect: unless the food is of uniform thickness, the salt profile varies significantly and so does the preservative effect.

Hot smoking

The hot smoking process is essentially a form of cooking. The time and temperature combination is typically around 82°C for 30 minutes or 60°C for two to four hours. This form of treatment is used when smoking trout, kippers and some haddock and salmon.

Cold smoking

Cold smoking is carried out at much lower temperatures for a much longer time, typically 32°C to 38°C for 15 to 18 hours. The food is not actually cooked but merely cured and flavoured. Smoked salmon is prepared in this way.

MAKING IT EASY FOR OTHERS

- Train staff to understand and follow the rules for time and temperature control as they apply to methods of preservation undertaken on your premises.
- Ensure that suppliers' and manufacturers' instructions for storage and handling are observed.
- Emphasise the importance of observing *use by* and *best by* dates.
- Train food handlers to recognise the signs of spoilage.
- Make certain that staff understand that some 'preserved' products, such as pasteurised canned ham and vacuum-packed products, still need to be refrigerated.

finding the energy

The story behind some of the most important aspects of food technology makes it much clearer why manipulating the intrinsic factors of microbes works so well in many food safety and preservation techniques. One of these stories concerns the redox, or oxidation-reduction, reaction.

It is not essential to know about the redox reaction to pass a food safety course at managerial level. But a basic grasp of it, even if some of the explanatory terms we must use are unfamiliar, will help you to understand the importance of pH and why some organisms are aerobes, some anaerobes and some facultative anaerobes.

The redox potential indicates the ease with which a substrate or medium (in this case, the food) loses or gains electrons. A substrate that loses electrons is said to be oxidised while a substrate that gains electrons is said to be reduced. You may come across this expressed as E_h.

The E_h is strictly dependent on the pH. It can change due to the multiplication of certain bacteria on the food or because of technological influences during storage and preparation.

In turn, micro-organisms display varying degrees of sensitivity to the oxidation-reduction potential of the food they contaminate.

Like every living thing, the growth of micro-organisms requires energy. Microbes obtain the necessary energy by degrading, or using up, the nutrients present in the food.

One of the most relevant using-up processes — the scientific term is catabolism — is respiration. In this context, respiration does not mean breathing, as microbes do not breathe. It is an oxidation, or using up, process, of which familiar examples are the rusting of iron as it reacts with moist air or the browning of the cut surface of an apple.

In food the chemical process involves a hydrogen transfer from reduced substrates (such as sugars) to oxygen or other oxidised compounds.

All micro-organisms that are able to transfer hydrogen as H+ to molecular oxygen (O_2) are known as aerobes, and they can therefore live in the presence of air. If they can grow *only* in the presence of air, they are described as *obligate* aerobes.

The process of oxygen reduction leads to the formation of superoxide free radicals which are very toxic. Aerobic organisms contain a specific enzyme (superoxide dismutase or SOD), a catalyst in the reaction, which binds or destroys these radicals. Microbes that do not possess this enzyme are unable to grow in the presence of oxygen because oxygen is toxic to them. These are called anaerobes, a term derived from Greek words meaning without air.

Aerobic micro-organisms reduce the oxygen during respiration, so lowering the E_h value of the food. Anaerobic organisms have the same effect on the E_h, although the process involves substances other than oxygen. Aerobes will, however, multiply only where there are high E_h values. So, when the redox potential sinks below 0, the growth conditions are more favourable for anaerobes. In the middle E_h range, there is a transition stage where micro-aerophilic and facultative organisms can grow.

Food products usually have a low redox potential and it varies throughout the product. The surface of a product, for instance, may have a higher redox potential than deeper layers — the cosmos of a micro-organism is really very small!

Small pieces or particles of food are more exposed to oxygen than large ones because the ratio of their surface area to their body mass is higher. So, techniques like mincing, trimming, stirring, mixing and even squeezing food increases the food's exposure to oxygen. On the other hand, techniques like vacuum packing, the addition of reducing compounds (such as ascorbic acid) and heating processes have the effect of maintaining a low redox potential.

STORING FOOD FOR SAFETY AND PROFIT

Have you ever rummaged in a kitchen cupboard at home only to conclude that an essential ingredient for your meal is nowhere to be found? Exasperating, isn't it? But just imagine the trouble a food business would get itself into if it failed to keep sufficient supplies of the foods it needed.

WHY STORE FOOD?

No food business has the time to pop out to buy ingredients as needed, but convenience is only one aspect of the benefits of staying stocked up: even if your business buys all or many fresh ingredients on a daily basis, it still needs to store some staple products.

The budgetary benefits from bulk buying and storing food are self-explanatory, as cost-effectiveness is fundamental to every company.

Few companies can predict precisely what their orders will be day to day or week to week, so it is essential that they can fulfil their orders at the drop of a hat, even when there is an unexpectedly high demand. Storing food allows them to even out the peaks and troughs of demand and supply.

Similarly, storing foods enables companies to supply customers instantly with foods all year round, even when the produce is out of season. Rapid forms of transport allow the importation of foods, often in purpose-designed containers or packaging, from around the world every day.

There is another advantage to storing food, although it is not perhaps the first thing you would think of in an affluent country: that is, to help to avoid famine, an issue that is still of the greatest importance in many parts of the world.

Making storage work to best advantage

Perhaps we should remind ourselves that all these benefits assume that the food is stored in such a way that it retains its eating quality (its appearance, flavour, smell, texture and nutritional value) as well as remaining safe to eat.

As we mentioned in Part 1, contaminated and spoiled food must be thrown away, so increasing costs instead of controlling them.

THE PRINCIPLES OF STORAGE

The best way to store food depends upon three factors, which are the:
- amount of food to be stored
- type of food to be stored
- length of time in storage.

A question of quantity

It is obvious that there is a vast difference between storing breakfast cereals in an hotel or guest house and storing half a million tonnes of grain in a granary. Although the scale is vastly different, many of the other necessary conditions are similar. In the case of an hotel or guest house we are looking at a small dry goods store, whereas in the granary we would need lots of large grain silos.

Type casting

Let us use some typical ingredients of a traditional British breakfast to deal with the type of food to be stored. What is the difference in the storage requirements for breakfast cereal, grapefruit, sausage, bacon, egg, bread, milk, tea and coffee? The most significant difference is that some require refrigerated temperature control and some do not. How does the scale of storage count? In bulk storage the relative humidity may also need to be controlled.

Time on the shelf

Account has to be taken of how long something needs to be stored — is it hours, days, weeks, months or years? This determines, for example, whether the storage facility should be chilled, deep frozen, humidity controlled or just clean and tidy. *Shelf life* also introduces important issues of stock control that are covered later in the chapter.

ALL ROUND ESSENTIALS

The mention of 'just clean and tidy' in the previous paragraph has no doubt alerted you to some basic requirements for storage areas, no matter what their size, type or purpose. The following paragraphs outline these storage prerequisites.

Suitable for the purpose

This seems an obvious point to make, but you need to equip food premises with adequate storage space for the type of goods being stored and to ensure that any shelves, racking, pallets, packaging and containers conform to any relevant food legislation. There should be separate stores for non-food items such as cleaning equipment and chemicals, the latter ideally in a lockable facility. Provision should be made for the separate storage of different types of food, which may have varying requirements, such as those affecting temperature, gaseous atmosphere, stacking, accessibility and different stages of preparation — for example:

- canned and bottled food
- dairy products
- dry goods and cereals
- fish
- frozen food
- fruits
- liquids
- open food
- packaged food
- raw meat
- ready-to-eat food
- shellfish
- vegetables.

Whatever the size or type of food business, food must be kept in suitable storage in appropriate conditions.

Designed so that different foods can be stored separately

Raw foods and *high risk foods* that are cooked or *ready-to-eat* must be kept apart, ideally in separate storage areas. However, where space for storing raw or high risk foods is so restricted that there is room for only one refrigerator, then raw foods must be stored *below* cooked and ready-to-eat foods so they cannot cause contamination from dripping juices or blood.

Protected from contamination

Contamination comes in many forms, as we have already discussed. Apart from the possibility of falls, spills and transfer of contaminants, there are also issues of quality to consider. For instance, as we saw earlier in Part 4, some foods readily absorb odours from other foods, so becoming tainted. Care should therefore be taken to store separately anything which is liable either to pick up a taint or to give one.

Windproof and waterproof

The store, whether it be an outdoor silo, a small larder, a large walk-in cold store or a self-standing refrigerator, should be constructed in a way that excludes the draughts but is well ventilated to prevent condensation. It may seem incongruous to talk of a refrigerator housed in a kitchen as needing to be windproof and waterproof, but the same general principle does apply as it needs to be made of non-porous materials and sited out of draughts.

Protected from light

Some foods react with light, especially sunlight, and change colour. Storing any food in direct sunlight is likely to affect temperature control, which may compromise food safety and quality. Make sure that the lighting is correct and that shading, such as blinds, is provided where necessary.

Easy to clean

All surfaces, especially those that come into contact with food, should be designed and be of such materials that they are easy to clean.

Pest proofed

The main reasons for pest proofing storage areas are to:

- eliminate possible contamination of the food or the premises from rodents, birds or insects
- prevent economic loss due to damage caused by the voracious appetites of pests.

Free from pests

Even if storage areas are properly pest proofed, they should still be monitored for the presence of pests — because pests are great opportunists — and any infestation should be dealt with immediately.

CLEAN AND TIDY

Keeping storage areas clean and free from clutter helps to:

- reduce the possibility of contamination of the food
- minimise the possibility of harbouring pests by reducing potential shelter, nesting places and supplies of food
- show up damaged packaging or signs of pest infestation clearly
- maintain proper stock control.

Transport, delivery and loading areas

It is best to consider delivery vehicles and loading areas as an extension of food premises so they must also be designed, maintained and operated in ways that safeguard food from contamination, microbial multiplication or spoilage.

Storage areas, especially in larger businesses, are often linked directly to delivery and loading areas. The same dock and entrance are often used for both delivery and loading. However, there are circumstances — such as abattoirs — where the fresh meat should not be loaded in the same place where live animals may be brought in. In some food premises a double entry system is used where goods are unloaded through one door into an unpacking area and only then distributed through another door into the storage areas.

STOCK CONTROL

Whether the storage unit is a large warehouse or a small refrigerator, the importance of good stock control cannot be over-emphasised. It makes sense to do this — for safety, quality, customer care and, not least, economic reasons. Food spoilage is an ever-present concern in a food businesses and stock control is right at the heart of controlling loss by spoilage.

Product life cycle

Stock control really starts with your supplier checks and product specifications — see pages 307 to 308, even though some aspects of the care of stock are beyond your direct control.

Receiving

The controls you put in place for accepting or rejecting deliveries of food to your premises establish the best possible basic conditions for the food you then store.

Be certain to include the criteria for receiving food deliveries in staff training programmes — you may wish to designate individual members of staff who are authorised to accept or reject consignments of goods.

Storing and retrieving

Make sure that every member of staff who may be asked to store food knows what to do if he or she suspects that food safety may have been or will be compromised.

Emphasise the importance of placing the stock with the longest shelf life at the back of shelves, behind stock that is approaching its expiry date. With some kinds of storage facility, such as chest freezers, this may mean placing the food with the longest shelf life underneath food with a shorter shelf life. The whole point of this way of storing and retrieving food, known as *stock rotation*, is to help to ensure that a product with a short shelf life is used before one that can be stored safely for longer.

This is sometimes expressed as the FIFO system, which stands for *first in, first out*. While the phrase may make good sense to managers, it may need to be used with caution, if at all, with staff. They could interpret it to mean that they should use stored food according to the time it was delivered, regardless of the length of its shelf life.

In some food premises, such as supermarkets, the principles of stock rotation face the additional problem of customers who rummage through to find the item with the longest lasting date mark and therefore the longest safe storage period. Managers of such premises must always be aware that, no matter how carefully they have had the stock arranged, about two hours after opening for business, the stock may have become thoroughly mixed up.

Staff need to be trained how to store and retrieve food from storage areas: both food safety and occupational safety are at stake!

Shelf life and labelling

The shelf life of a food depends on its nature and type of preservation. The manufacturing and processing sector of the food industry carries out many tests to determine shelf life: obviously, the longer the shelf life can be extended, the more profitable it is likely to be.

Pathogens and spoilage organisms

Some foods, such as canned, bottled or dehydrated foods, have an extremely long safe storage period because most bacteria have been destroyed or the conditions are too harsh for remaining bacteria to multiply. Roughly the same conditions that allow for the multiplication of pathogens are ideal for the multiplication of spoilage organisms — just think back to the chapter on microbiology in Part 3. The foods that are likely to pose safety problems are generally the same ones that will readily support the multiplication of spoilage organisms.

Date marks

For this reason there are two legally recognised categories of *date mark* for food:

- *use by*
- *best before*.

Use by

This date mark, which usually gives a date only a few days after the date of purchase, states a day, month and year. It is a legal requirement for packaged high risk foods to have a *use by* date if they are not *ambient shelf stable* and therefore may become a health hazard. It is also an offence to sell them after the *use by* date has expired. As you can see, the *use by* date is largely concerned with food safety rather than quality.

Best before

This dates mark applies to foods other than those covered by a *use by* date and usually allows for a far longer storage period. The *best before* date is, as the name suggests, largely an issue of quality, although safety may also be involved. The manufacturer is in effect making a statement that the food will be at its best — of the quality they would wish consumers to enjoy — up until the date given.

Disposal of spoiled and damaged stock

SUSPECT FOOD

If in doubt, throw it out.

Any stock which appears to be spoiled or damaged must be examined thoroughly to ascertain its fitness for human consumption. If there is any doubt about its fitness it should be disposed of in such a way that it will not re-enter the food chain.

MAKING IT EASIER FOR OTHERS

- Train designated staff to take responsibility for receiving and checking deliveries of goods to your premises.
- Create clear procedures in your food safety policy for dealing with spoilt food or food in damaged packaging.
- Make sure that all staff know where and how to store different types of food.
- Emphasise the importance of storing high risk and highly perishable foods before others such as dry and canned goods.
- Explain how rough handling can accelerate spoilage and cause contamination.
- Emphasise and re-emphasise the importance of time and temperature control.
- Insist that all storage areas are kept clean and tidy.
- Encourage staff to report evidence of damage or signs of infestation.
- Make sure that stock is adequately rotated and that date marks are observed.

beyond your control?

Whatever the food business, there are two stages when food safety is usually out of your hands — before food reaches you and after it leaves you. So, what can you do to build in some measure of control to protect the consumer?

It is common for large food companies to make fairly rigorous checks on their suppliers. This might be done through site inspections, product specifications and audits. The food company may undertake the audit itself (customer audit) or it may contract an outside company or individual specialising in such work to do the audit (third party audit) on its behalf.

A food safety audit involves checking the supplier company and its operations against clearly defined criteria (the standards) that are required by the customer company. The criteria may be specific to the customer company, but more often they are agreed nationally and adopted by individual companies as their own standard.

Safeguards offered by an audit include information about whether a supplier is adhering to a product specification and whether its systems conform to the standard. It can also reveal whether the supplier is operating good management principles (GMP) and obeying the law. The information gleaned from an audit helps to protect both the customer company and the supplier by revealing non-conformation to the desired standards and giving the supplier the opportunity to take remedial action if necessary.

There are, however, some shortcomings to audits that you always need to bear in mind. For example, you may need to establish

307

whose standard a supplier conforms to where there is more than one customer, each with its own special requirements. There may be an industry-wide national standard to covers this situation to your company's complete satisfaction.

Many auditing or consultancy companies work to a national standard and are accredited as such, but it is also worth checking what their experience is and asking for a reference from one of their existing customers.

In the event of a court case, your established standards and your care in checking the auditors might help to support a due diligence defence. Every such defence is taken on its merits, but it is hard to imagine that a court would take much account of a company's claim of diligence if it had not taken account of the standard of the product delivered or of the people who are supposed to safeguard that standard.

As with many issues of food safety, there is always the consideration of cost. Is the cost of an audit justified in its contribution to food safety, especially for a small company? This is for you to decide, but you do need to make some kind of checks on what your suppliers send you.

Mainly because of the cost, small businesses often rely on suppliers' product specifications and documentary evidence. This is satisfactory provided the supplier can convince you that it does meet your standard. Take care to keep the product specification under review and occasionally get the product checked by a laboratory against the specification.

Small businesses often buy from wholesalers rather than direct from the manufacturer so they have to rely on the wholesalers' specifications. Ask each wholesaler to give you copies of its controls over its own suppliers, and incorporate the standard into your company's food safety policy and documentation.

Perhaps the trickiest question concerns how you control what customers do with the food once they have it. You cannot really control their actions, but you can build in some safeguards, or at least some warning, for your customers (the consumers or end-users) and your clients (companies that buy from you but do not themselves consume the product).

If you are a food manufacturer, say of liquid chocolate, supplying other manufacturers or caterers, it is fairly likely that the product information and advice you issue will be followed — and your clients are almost certain to have given you a product specification in the first place.

However, if your product — for instance, ready-to-eat meals — sells to the general public, how do you know that the consumer will store or reheat the product to the correct temperature?

All you can do is to provide clear and unambiguous labelling and to ensure that the stated shelf life takes into account as far as possible any problems with temperature abuse during storage.

Always assume that someone could do something silly with your product, and protect yourself as much as possible.

RISK MANAGEMENT

Until the mid 1970s the subject of risk was probably most closely associated with actuarial and insurance businesses. If the premiums for a life insurance policy were being assessed, it was easy for the lay person to see why a rock climbing instructor who went parachuting every weekend might be considered to be at a higher risk of injury or death than an office worker who went swimming once a week.

Since then, as you may know from some of your other responsibilities, it has become a legal requirement under health and safety at work legislation for companies with five or more employees to carry out a risk assessment of the occupational health hazards arising from the work being carried out.

In more recent years the consideration of risk has become increasingly important in the general process of all business management, covering aspects of risk as diverse as finance, occupational health, environmental impact, information technology and business continuity. You will find that the discussion of risk features more and more in the food industry in relation to food safety.

RISK IN THE FOOD INDUSTRY

How, then, does the subject of risk fit in with what we have already discussed about hazards in the food industry? In fact it is the other way around and hazards fit in to the much bigger topic of risk. But before we start to trip over terms, let's review and expand upon what we have mentioned so far.

Hazard and risk

From listening to general conversation or consulting a dictionary, you'll know that the three words hazard, risk and danger are pretty much interchangeable in everyday speech to describe the possibility that something unpleasant, unwelcome or harmful may happen. When it comes to managing public health, we do, however, need to be more specific in our use of words.

Early in the book we described a *hazard* as being any thing, condition or circumstance that could cause harm to the consumer. Later on we talked about *food hazards* as being anything microbiological, chemical or physical that might cause harm to the consumer. In comparison, we described *risk* as being a measure, or scale, of the likelihood (or probability) that a hazard will occur. (You may also come across the word *severity* in the context of risk analysis, where it is used to indicate the seriousness, gravity or magnitude of a hazard or its possible consequences.)

We spot hazards and estimate risks every day of our lives, without too much difficulty. For instance, we know that moving motor vehicles are a hazard. We evaluate the risk from crossing a road at a designated crossing point which has traffic lights, or from dashing across any section of a road when the traffic flow is light or vehicles seem to be travelling slowly. Even so, as the business use of the words hazard and risk can sometimes cause confusion, we hope that our lighthearted illustrations below will help you to make the distinction more easily. As you can see, the hazard always remains a hazard: what changes is the risk from the hazard.

High risk

The hazard

Medium risk

Low risk

No risk

WHAT DO WE NEED TO MANAGE?

As you are familiar with the discussion of managing *hazards*, you may still wonder why we also need to consider the management of *risk*? The answer is that hazard management is just one small part of risk management because:

- hazards to human health exist in all foods
- the risks from these hazards vary from food to food and from situation to situation
- some hazards cannot be eliminated, but we can influence the risk of their occurring — risks can be managed.

Benefits

Of course, customers expect that you will manage food so that it is safe to eat, whether they think of this as being risk management or not, and, for all the reasons mentioned in Part 1, it makes sound economic sense to do so. As you can infer from the existence of the defence of due diligence discussed in Part 1 and Part 3, the law quietly expects you to manage risks to food safety.

Effective risk management enables managers to set priorities which concentrate the company's food safety efforts at the points in the production process where they make the most significant difference.

MANAGING RISK
The management of risk enables managers to concentrate efforts at the points that make the greatest difference to the safety of food.

HOW DO WE NEED TO MANAGE RISK?

What forms of risk management are available to help us to manage food safety? Quality assurance schemes and microbiological and chemical testing may meet some of the criteria and the system of Hazard Analysis and Critical Control Point (HACCP) and various related systems of hazard analysis, which are discussed on pages 314 to 326, fulfil many requirements of a successful risk management system.

Prerequisites

Even so, there are certain *prerequisites* — things that must be in place first — if these systems are to work properly and bring real benefits. After all, there is no point in, for example, trying to produce safe food if the premises and equipment are not clean or, where relevant, disinfected.

The prerequisites include many of the issues we have already discussed, such as:

- the proper design and construction of the food premises
- thorough cleaning and disinfection procedures
- effective staff training and supervision (for instance, of personal hygiene)
- effective pest control
- waste management
- and, possibly, proper policies and procedures, which we discuss on pages 338 to 340.

Criteria for risk management

The general features to be expected from a risk management system are outlined on the following eight paragraphs. If you are new to the management of food safety, you may prefer to read the chapter on HACCP and hazard analysis first and return to these criteria later.

Proactive

Your system should be able to make you aware of a potential problem before it becomes a crisis of food safety or financial loss. There is little point in having such an advanced warning system if it alerts you to a problem when it is too late to do something about it or to salvage anything from the situation.

Timely

When the advance warning system works properly, it lets you know in good time that something has indeed gone wrong, whether by a system of warning bells, flashing lights or a message from staff, so that your crisis management plan (see page 328) can swing into action.

Measurable

Intrinsic factors, such as pH, and extrinsic factors, such as time and temperature (see pages 58 to 65), can be measured accurately and relatively cheaply, but your management of risk also needs to take into account factors such as appropriate timing, frequency and standards — for instance, when, how often and how well a food handler washes his or her hands.

Controllable

Your system needs to be based on factors that are genuinely controllable. It is relatively easy to train staff to check time and temperature and to satisfy those who are interested in auditing your records, but it would be unwise to base any decisions about food safety on trying to control how often a food handler rubs her nose with the back of her hand.

Understandable

When any new system is introduced it is essential for all the staff involved to know why the system is being put in; what benefits are expected to accrue from it; how much extra work, responsibility, inconvenience or time may be involved; what exactly they have to do; why they have to do it; when they have to do it; and what standards are expected of them.

Visible

Your risk management system should be clear to all. If *Salmonella* species are a hazard, for example, your system should openly acknowledge this and explain what staff should do to eliminate the hazard or minimise the risks from it. There is no point in denying that there is a potential problem or in trying to deal with it secretly. Only if all risks are looked at openly and honestly and with accountability can there be any hope of managing them effectively. Your staff, your customers and clients, and the enforcement authorities all need to be confident that every possible step is being taken to ensure that the food your company produces is safe to eat.

Cost-effective

For your peace of mind it might be reassuring to take a microbiological and chemical sample of product every five minutes, but the company would soon go bankrupt (or suffocate under the pile of data). The whole point about risk management is to prioritise and to concentrate the efforts at the critical points in the food production where it makes the most significant difference. You'll read more about such critical points on pages 318 to 320.

Rectifiable

To be cost-effective, safe, and legal you need to build in the opportunity to put things right before the product has been eaten (and caused illness), or has to be discarded or completely reprocessed.

FITTING THE BILL?

The systems of HACCP and hazard analysis are outlined on pages 314 to 326. At the time of writing, British law requires all food businesses to have a system of hazard analysis in place, while a few, such as some butchers, are required to have a full HACCP system in place.

HACCP AND HAZARD ANALYSIS

Hazard Analysis and Critical Control Point (*HACCP*) is a well-established system for managing risks in the food industry. It was initiated in the 1960s to give the burgeoning American space industry a system guaranteeing safe food for astronauts on space flights. By the 1990s the system was being adopted in many countries around the world, many of which have now incorporated it into legislation either in its complete form or as a simpler system of *hazard analysis*.

This chapter describes the HACCP system and how it can be established, then outlines the simpler hazard analysis system which is practised in many non-manufacturing food businesses in the European Union. In the process, we also look at some of the advantages and common pitfalls of these systems.

WHAT HACCP IS

Hazard Analysis and Critical Control Point is a formal, systematic and scientifically based approach to making decisions about the procedures affecting the safety of food. In broad terms, it involves identifying the *particular* hazards that could affect the safety of a food ingredient or product at any stage in a *particular* food business, then determining the most significant points (the 'critical control points') at which effective controls can be made. The system has been described as being the use of the simplest possible controls at the points where the controls matter most.

THE HACCP PRINCIPLES

The HACCP system consists of seven activities which are known as principles.

Principle 1
Carry out a hazard analysis.

Principle 2
Decide which points in the food production process are critical control points (CCPs).

Principle 3
Establish critical limits (tolerances or target levels).

Principle 4
Set up a system for monitoring the control of the CCP.

Principle 5
Establish corrective action to be taken when the monitoring system shows that a CCP is out of control.

Principle 6
Create procedures to verify that the HACCP system is working as planned.

Principle 7
Set up a documentation system to record all of the above.

IMPLEMENTING A HACCP SYSTEM

Putting the seven principles of a HACCP system into place is fairly straightforward, although it may be time-consuming at the outset.

Preliminary tasks

As with many other tasks, there are some essential preparatory steps. These are to:

- create a HACCP team
- describe the products or ingredients in turn
- identify the intended use and the consumers of the product in question
- construct a flow diagram which accurately shows all the process steps involved
- verify the flow diagram in the workplace.

You may also come across mention of 'the terms of reference' of a HACCP plan. This simply means that you need to decide the 'boundaries' of your plan. These could be the sorts of hazard your HACCP plan will cover — these would normally be microbiological and chemical as well as physical hazards — and whether the cut-off point is the sale of the product or its consumption.

Creating the team

The first part of the process is to assemble a team with sufficient expertise to formulate the HACCP plan. Where possible, the team should include representatives of all the company's job specialisms and levels of the staff hierarchy.

Other than in the smallest companies, it is typical to include food processing, technical, quality assurance, pest control and marketing staff, as well as external consultants and, most importantly, a representative of the management team who is sufficiently senior to make decisions and drive the project forward.

Some members of the team may be involved only for discussion of aspects of processes that are involved in their job description and others, such as cleaning and maintenance managers, might be co-opted from time to time, but there should always be a core membership.

It is, of course, impossible to have a large team in many small businesses. Even so, the principle of having more than one person applies, and consulting an external specialist is often advisable.

Training

While HACCP is not a difficult system to set up or operate, it is not something that can be undertaken at the drop of a hat.

Every member of the HACCP team should be aware of the principles of HACCP and and at least one member should have undertaken a specific training course on the subject. Ideally this person should have an advanced-level food safety qualification.

Describing the product

Before the HACCP team can carry out a hazard analysis (Principle 1), the team members need to describe each product used by the business. (If your company manufactures one product only, this activity will not be time-consuming. If your company produces or sells many product lines, you may be able to carry out a *generic* hazard analysis, which is discussed on page 323, but it is still important to understand all the principles involved in HACCP.) The description of the product needs to cover factors such as the ingredients, processing methods, packaging and storage requirements, shelf life and instructions for consumer use.

Identifying the intended use and the consumers of the product

It is important to establish both the intended use of each product and its most likely consumers, as the same type of product could be used, or abused, in various ways before consumption, or could be eaten by people in the 'at risk group'.

Let us take a seafood pizza as an example. Its intended uses could involve being made in a restaurant for immediate service and consumption on the premises, made in a factory and frozen for retail sale (after which the consumer could ignore the storage or preparation instructions), or made in a take-away and delivered hot to the consumer's home. The consumer could be of almost any age and could also include a hospital patient who is in the 'at risk group'.

Constructing a flow diagram

Before the HACCP team can carry out a hazard analysis on any product, the team members need to draw up a flow diagram showing *all* the steps in the process (process steps) for each product from the purchase of raw materials through all the stages of storage and preparation to the sale to the consumer. Although this activity could seem superfluous at first glance, it is an essential preliminary that enables you to carry out later parts of the HACCP process. It is very important to include all the process steps involved, even if they seem to be very minor activities. As an example, on the page opposite we show one company's flow diagram of how they make tea for themselves in the staff room. You may not agree with how they make the tea, but the point is to record all the process steps on the flow diagram.

Verifying the flow diagram in the workplace

The HACCP team needs to confirm the flow diagram on site, ideally by walking the route of the process steps and talking with the staff involved. No matter how well they have drawn up the flow diagram, they are almost bound to discover that something has been overlooked or that a process is actually carried out in a slightly different way to what was believed. It could simply be that the night shift legitimately does things in a slightly different way — they may need to store a product ready for cooking the next day, for example — and this needs to be taken into account. Whatever the reason, it is essential for the flow diagram to represent what *actually* happens. After all, the discrepancy between what should and what does happen may point you in the direction of a food safety hazard!

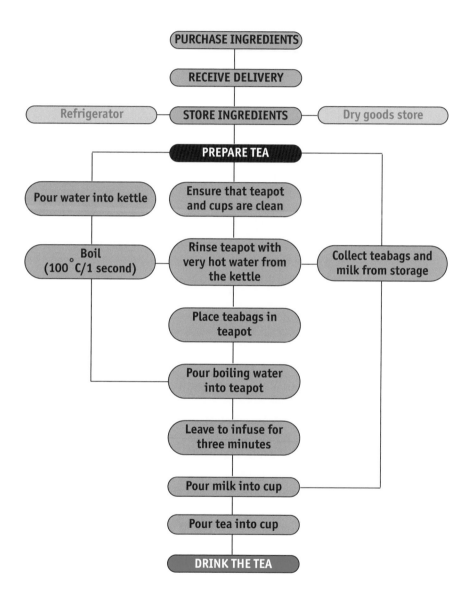

THE PRINCIPLES IN PRACTICE

HACCP involves identifying the food hazards, assessing the risks and establishing controls that stop the hazards, or reduce the risk from them to a minimum.

Principle 1 — Conduct a hazard analysis
In simple terms, a hazard analysis involves:
- describing all the hazards (microbiological, chemical and physical) that could occur at *each* process step for each product in turn
- describing all the measures that could control the hazards identified — these preventive measures may already be in operation.

Needless to say, there are many food hazards and the HACCP team will probably identify a large number, so it is essential to distinguish between those hazards which have a risk of occurring in the particular food business and those for which the risk is negligible. Assessing the risk from a hazard (how likely it is to occur) is one of the most difficult parts of designing a HACCP system. You may sometimes see this activity described as being the process of deciding which hazards are the 'significant' ones. Factors that could be included in the assessment are the:
- history of hazards in the company that have led to food-borne illness
- history of the hazard in connection with particular foods
- possibility that the hazard will occur even if there is no history of its occurrence.

Factors such as the severity of the consequences of a hazard and the number of people involved could also be considered, but not in cases where the risk is judged to be negligible.

Principle 2 — Identify critical control points
This principle involves determining the *critical control points* (*CCPs*) — the points at which the controls matter most. Such 'points' could be a location, practice, procedure or process — those at which a *loss of control* would lead to an unacceptable risk to health, but at which the *exercise of control* over one or more factors could prevent a hazard altogether, or minimise the risk that it will occur.

It is important to recognise this dual nature of critical control points. Some CCPs can *prevent* a hazard occurring altogether — for example, a botulinum cook will kill spores as well as pathogenic micro-organisms. (These are often referred to as CCP 1s.) Other CCPs, such as the refrigerated storage of high risk foods, can only minimise the risk that a hazard will occur. (These are known as CCP 2s.)

The correct identification of CCPs is at the heart of the HACCP system, but can be tricky at first. Codex Alimentarius, the international food safety organisation, has produced a decision tree to assist with this process, which is shown in Reference on page 359. If you are unaccustomed to using decision trees, you may find the simplified decision ladder (opposite) a little easier to use. By asking yourself the

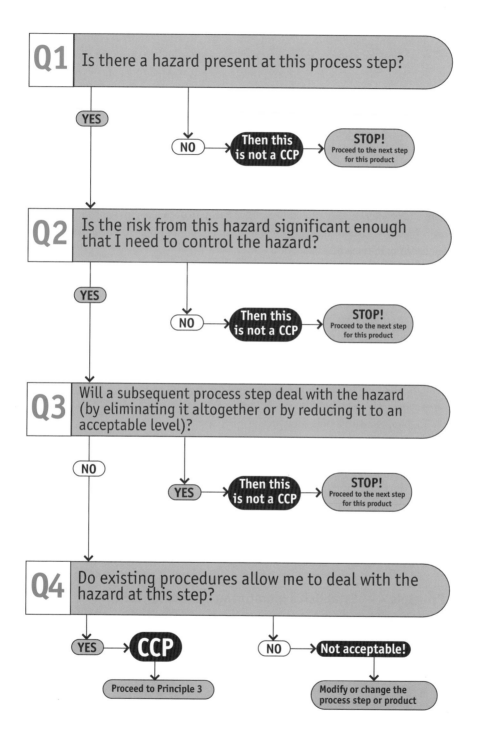

Q1 Is there a hazard present at this process step?

YES

NO → Then this is not a CCP → STOP! Proceed to the next step for this product

Q2 Is the risk from this hazard significant enough that I need to control the hazard?

YES

NO → Then this is not a CCP → STOP! Proceed to the next step for this product

Q3 Will a subsequent process step deal with the hazard (by eliminating it altogether or by reducing it to an acceptable level)?

NO

YES → Then this is not a CCP → STOP! Proceed to the next step for this product

Q4 Do existing procedures allow me to deal with the hazard at this step?

YES → **CCP** → Proceed to Principle 3

NO → Not acceptable! → Modify or change the process step or product questions in turn, you should be able to decide reasonably quickly what is or is not a critical control point. Question 3 is often the one that will make you certain whether or not a process step is a critical control point.

It is important to note that CCPs are concerned only with food safety and do not cover quality or matters of good practice. There is no limit to the number of CCPs you identify, but the fewer there are, the easier it is to keep them under control in practice.

Principle 3 — Establish critical limits

Critical limits are the 'borders' you establish between the safe and unsafe practices and processes affecting food and help you to ensure that each CCP is genuinely under control. Control criteria must be established at each critical control point to ensure the safety of the product. For example, the pasteurisation of milk requires a time and temperature combination of 72.2°C for 15 seconds. This control is a *target level* — a specified value for the control measure which has been shown to eliminate or minimise a hazard at a CCP.

As it is often impracticable for the target level to be achieved with one hundred per cent accuracy, there should also be a *tolerance* for each CCP — a specified variation from the target level which is acceptable in terms of food safety. For example, the time and temperature combination of 72.2°C for 15 seconds is the minimum target level for pasteurisation required by law, so there would be no point in permitting a downward tolerance. As a consequence, most pasteurising plants set themselves a slightly higher requirement than the legal target level — say, 73.2°C for 16 seconds, with a temperature tolerance of +/−1°C (in other words, +1°C or −1°C), coupled with a time tolerance of +/−1 second.

The HACCP plan should explain what staff should do if they discover that something is not meeting its target level or operating within its tolerance.

Apart from time and temperature, other common factors specified for target levels and tolerances are the pH, water activity, colour and texture. These target levels and tolerances should be written into the HACCP plan and form the basis on which the product's safety is founded.

Principle 4 — Establish a monitoring system for CCPs

This principle requires you to monitor (measure or observe) your control criteria — the critical limits you established under Principle 3. Effective monitoring of what happens each day enables you to take corrective action (Principle 5) where it is necessary.

As we have said many times in this book, there is no point in having a system set up if you do not keep a close eye on how it is working. Once all the CCPs have been established and targets and tolerances have been defined, the HACCP team must establish a system of monitoring. Among other things, the monitoring system should:

- give you, as manager, a picture of how well your controls are really working and whether there are any trends that indicate that remedial action is required
- detect any deviation from the target level or its tolerances
- reveal in good time any deviation, so that corrective action can be taken to regain control
- provide a written record of criteria such as time, temperature and pH, to help you to manage food safety and to provide evidence of due diligence if required.

In many cases recording and monitoring can be carried out continuously and automatically on-line, but a member of staff with a watch and a calibrated thermometer can be just as effective.

Members of staff must be specifically designated to be responsible for the monitoring and should be trained effectively so that they are in no doubt as to what is required of them and when.

Principle 5 — Establish corrective action

If the monitoring indicates that there has been a deviation from the target level at a particular critical control point, then corrective action must be taken, ideally without wasting the product. Your HACCP plan should specify:

- what the action is that should be taken
- who is responsible for taking the action.

Principle 6 — Establish verification procedures

Verification is the process of confirming periodically that your whole HACCP system is functioning effectively and just as planned. The word verify comes from the Latin for true, and your verification should ensure that the system is indeed running true to form. Verification is different to monitoring, which confirms whether particular, individual controls are working every day as they should.

Verification should be carried out at regular intervals as a matter of course to confirm that the whole system is still operating as it should. It should also take place whenever there is a change in the process — for example, when new ingredients or equipment are introduced — or when there is a system failure or new hazards are identified. Any such changes should be taken account of and the HACCP plan amended if necessary.

Some of the verification activities that companies undertake include:

- contracting an independent scientific study to confirm that the critical limits, tolerances and so on are justified
- taking measurements to confirm the accuracy of the monitoring
- collecting samples and sending them for microbiological analysis
- interviewing staff about the way they monitor critical control points.

Principle 7 — Establish a system of documentation

Keeping proper HACCP records is an essential part of the system, although the type of records is not specified. In practice, you need to ensure that two sets of records are kept — those associated with the setting up of the system and those associated with monitoring the system.

The former are an intrinsic part of the HACCP system and are best described as permanent records which are updates as necessary following verification. The latter are records of the system as it operates every day. These should be kept for a period of time which at least exceeds the shelf life of the product, plus a safety margin to allow for customer misuse of the product. (In some cases, there are legal minimum periods specified for retaining documents.)

EXAMPLES OF HOW HACCP WORKS

Let us take two examples to see how HACCP can help in the production of safe food.

Making tea — the CCPs

For the first example, consider the flow diagram for making tea, which is shown on page 317. Work your way through the decision ladder: identify a hazard, then ask yourself whether it is a significant one. Then consider what kind of control measure could be in place. If there is no later point in the operation where you can use a control measure, then you are at a critical control point. You will probably decide that there are three critical control points in this example — the receipt of goods, the boiling of the water and the storage of the milk in temperature-controlled conditions.

At the second process step — 'Receive delivery' — the hazards could include microbiological ones affecting the milk. The milk could have been transported at the wrong temperature, or it could have exceeded its *use by* date. The relevant control measures would be to check the temperature of the milk on delivery and the *use by* date of the consignment. In a later process step when the water is boiled, any microbes present in the water could survive the heating unless there is the control measure of heating the water to 100°C for at least one second. The refrigerator where the milk is stored is also a CCP, as the milk will not be temperature treated later in any way that would eliminate microbiological hazards before it is consumed.

Cooked chicken — the HACCP system

For this example we shall assume that we are preparing a cooked chicken product and consider just one CCP. The numbers in brackets refer to the relevant HACCP principle. One *hazard* (1) is the survival of micro-organisms such as *Salmonella* or *Campylobacter* species. The cooking stage is a critical control point (2). A control measure at this CCP is for the core temperature of the chicken to be raised to at least 75°C for at least two minutes. The *critical limits* (3) need to show how far below 75 °C is safe and how much less than two minutes is safe. The time and temperature need to be *monitored* (4) using, for instance, a probe thermometer and a clock. The reading should be recorded (7). If a reading is unsatisfactory, a *corrective measure* (5) is to increase the time or the heat input.

Vital information

The important thing is that any member of staff involved in monitoring the chicken should know:

- why a CCP is critical in ensuring the safety of the food
- what the time and temperature combination should be
- what the critical limit or tolerance is
- what needs to be done when something goes wrong
- what needs to be written down
- who needs to be told that there is a problem.

OTHER SYSTEMS OF HAZARD ANALYSIS

HACCP in its original, full form is applied to *one* product, such as baked beans, through all its production stages. (This is why you may hear HACCP described as *product-specific HACCP*.) Of course, this type of approach is impracticable in some businesses, such as bakeries or restaurants, which have a multitude of food or menu items to assess. So modified systems, known as *process-specific HACCP* or *generic HACCP*, have been developed which are more suitable for these types of food business. Such systems include Assured Safe Catering and 'hazard analysis'.

WHAT HAZARD ANALYSIS IS

As we have just described, hazard analysis is the first part of the HACCP system. It is *also* the name given to systems of control which are based on HACCP but do not include all of its principles. In hazard analysis systems the hazards associated with process steps are considered in a more general way. So, although foods do not all go through exactly the same processes, the general steps are the same and it is reasonable to assume that there are typical hazards associated with particular process steps. The process steps may include:

- purchasing
- receipt of ingredients and products
- storage before preparation
- preparation
- heat treatment
- cooling
- storage before service or sale
- hot or cold holding
- reheating
- service or sale.

Regulations covering general food hygiene (see Part 3) require the proprietor of a food business to identify any step in the activities of the food business that is critical to ensuring the safety of food. In addition, the proprietor must ensure that 'adequate safety procedures are identified, implemented, maintained and reviewed' in the workplace. The regulations list five principles for carrying out the legal requirements.

Analyse the food hazards in the food business.

Identify the points where food hazards may occur.

Decide which of the points identified are critical to ensuring food safety — the regulations call them critical points.

Identify and implement effective control and monitoring procedures at the critical points.

Review the food hazards, critical points and the control and monitoring procedures periodically and whenever the business's operations change.

An example

Let us suppose that one of the process steps was to store a food under refrigeration. One generic hazard is the multiplication of pathogenic and spoilage organisms if the refrigerator is too warm and the food is stored there for some time. The hazard would be relevant for any food or product that needs to be refrigerated, so control measures for time and temperature would deal with all such products.

BENEFITS AND PROBLEMS

HACCP and hazard analysis have had a mixed reception from the British food industry and food safety enforcers, so it is worth taking a moment to review some of the generally discussed pros and cons.

Benefits

The traditional (pre-HACCP) method of checking the safety of food is end-product testing. This involves sending samples of a finished food item to a laboratory for, for instance, microbiological tests (see pages 66 to 68.) This is a slow and expensive process which deals only with selected hazards, is sometimes inaccurate and means 'wasting' the food samples. Sometimes the process is perceived as being the responsibility of quality assurance specialists rather than as being an everyday matter of food safety practice involving all.

In contrast, HACCP and other systems of hazard analysis are generally viewed as being:
- proactive and rapid, because problems are dealt with as they occur rather than later when it may be too late
- inexpensive, because laboratory controls are minimised

- cost-effective, because there is less wastage due to inadequate processing
- all-embracing, because all significant hazards are considered, not just selected ones
- relevant to all personnel, not just quality assurance staff.

A difficult reputation for setting up the system

HACCP (and sometimes hazard analysis) has sometimes been criticised for being 'difficult' so we mention some of these objections here.

It has to be acknowledged that some of the material produced on the subject is complicated and some people may have gained the false impression that they were obliged to buy bulky and costly ready-made packages in order to carry out the systems. Like any specialist subject and system, there are some special terms associated with HACCP and hazard analysis and these may have been off-putting to some people when they first tried to get to grips with the subject.

It is true that two procedures may seem tricky at first (and might benefit from some specialist advice). These are the risk assessment ('significant' hazards) aspect of hazard analysis (Principle 1) and the setting of critical limits (Principle 3).

The rest can be carried out easily, and we assure you that the HACCP and hazard analysis systems are simple to operate by anyone with a knowledge of their particular food business and that the principles of the systems can be applied in any type of food business. Indeed, if food managers have insufficient knowledge of their own food businesses to implement a simple hazard analysis plan, it is hard to understand how they could possibly run any aspect of that business!

Problems with implementation

HACCP and hazard analysis are good, well-proven systems for ensuring safe food. However, the systems are not a cure-all and there have been some difficulties in their implementation. Of course, it could be argued that the only thing in a food business which is worse than no HACCP or hazard analysis system in place is a system that exists but does not work, so lulling everyone into a false sense of security. Some of the issues that regularly crop up are outlined below.

Prerequisites

There is no point in even trying to introduce a HACCP or hazard analysis system unless the prerequisites mentioned on page 311 are in place. These systems will not function in a food business where the staff have no idea about hygiene, nothing is cleaned or disinfected and which is overrun with mice or cockroaches.

Communication

Good communication lies at the heart of the success of any system. It needs to involve everyone concerned with food production and sale or service in the individual food business, everyone in the food chain from producer to retailer, the consumer, the media, the legislator and the enforcer. Some of the links in the necessary chain of communication may have broken in the past so, for instance, everyone's priorities were not always the same, there were misunderstandings about individual expectations of each other or of where responsibilities lay. The result may at times have been that some of the people best placed to benefit from HACCP or hazard analysis were themselves responsible for many of the problems encountered.

SMEs and non-manufacturing businesses

The majority of food businesses in Europe (some estimates put it as high as 95 per cent) fall into the categories of small- or medium-size enterprises (SMEs) or non-manufacturing food businesses. This can create a few challenges when establishing and maintaining a HACCP or hazard analysis system — challenges such as creating a HACCP team in a one-person or very small business, finding the necessary expertise in-house for setting the critical limits or maintaining food safety standards during busy periods. However, flexibility and pragmatism, as well as some sound advice from outside specialists, can go a long way, as they usually do in SMEs.

Documentation

The EU General Hygiene Directive 93/43 asks for adherence to some of the principles of HACCP but not for documentation. This has caused more argument across Europe than anything else to do with this directive.

Some member countries apply the directive to the letter, others insist on a full HACCP system (in other words, with documentation), while others seem to take a mid-way position. Many SMEs point out that they are in the business of producing food, not mountains of documents, especially as so many of them are one-person businesses. In contrast, the enforcers tend to argue that it is impossible to control food premises properly unless the company keeps accurate records.

A pragmatic approach

We cannot enter this lengthy debate here, so we offer just two simple suggestions for your consideration — food businesses should:

- keep such documents as they consider necessary to provide themselves with a defence of due diligence should they need it
- not expect environmental health officers to rely solely on documents, but should expect EHOs to make thorough inspections to find out for themselves whether or not a food business is operating safely.

Whatever else you do, make sure you do not merely create an unbreakable paper chain, rather than providing a safe food chain.

Verification (or review)

There is a tendency to assume that once a system of HACCP or hazard analysis has been created, it can look after itself. This ignores the fact that the HACCP system requires verification (and the hazard analysis system requires a review). In neglecting to undertake these processes, a legal requirement is overlooked.

Training

We have said similar things earlier in this book, but it is worth emphasising that all the time, effort and money spent on establishing and implementing systems will be wasted if the employees in a food business are not properly trained. In most cases the job training need only be at a basic level, with the simplest of introductions to the fact that the company has a hazard analysis or HACCP system. Refresher training should happen on a regular basis.

Even the best of HACCP or hazard analysis systems will not work if the food handlers ignore, or are ignorant about, the need to wash their hands, let alone the more complicated aspects of food hygiene.

THE WAY FORWARD?

The continuing high level of statistics for food-borne illnesses worldwide, even when there are occasional improvements in a part of the picture, provide ample evidence that traditional methods of food control were not always totally effective. Can HACCP or hazard analysis change this? Only time will tell, but for the food manager these systems should at the very least ensure fewer sleepless nights about food safety.

 MAKING IT EASIER FOR OTHERS

- Ensure that all food staff have a basic awareness of the importance of the hazard analysis or HACCP system operating in your workplace.
- Make sure that at least one member of your HACCP or hazard analysis team has been trained to at least an advanced level in food safety.
- Bring in experts if necessary to complement the skills of the in-house members of your HACCP or hazard analysis team.
- Establish clear procedures for dealing with critical limits and tolerances.
- Train all the relevant staff in monitoring, recording and remedial action procedures.
- Encourage staff to report hazards to their manager or supervisor.

TURNING A CRISIS TO ADVANTAGE

Imagine the scene: you turn up at work one morning to find your way barred by television crews and newspaper reporters. They ask you about a food poisoning outbreak. People are in hospital. Some are critically ill. A child is dead. Your business may be responsible. Would you like to comment?

Most people would regard this as a crisis. Even when a company thinks it has done everything possible that a responsible organisation can do, mistakes and the unforeseen can occur, leaving the business in the glare of hostile publicity. In the period before the cause of an outbreak of food-borne illness has been discovered the spotlight may well fall on the innocent and the guilty alike.

So how do you prepare for the day when it could fall on you?

PREPARATION, PREPARATION, PREPARATION

Planning is your best insurance policy. Most companies do not have any kind of crisis plan, so, when things go wrong, they really do go horribly wrong, often ending up by ruining the business.

But how can you possibly plan for and manage a crisis? After all, a crisis is by definition a period of severe difficulty.

The ancient origins of the word (from Greek, Latin and Middle English) hold the clues, because a crisis can also be translated as a time of decision or as a *turning point*. Assuming that your company already does everything possible to justify a defence of due diligence under food safety legislation, a crisis management plan can make difficult, urgent decisions easier to make and may even eventually enable you to turn a potential business disaster into a positive business benefit!

Getting ready

The time to start your planning is now, not when the press is baying at your door. At that point you will need to put all your energy and clear thinking into dealing with the immediate situation. Prepare a three-stage plan of actions to be taken:
- in advance, as a matter of course
- during a crisis
- after a crisis.

This chapter outlines issues you should consider and actions you could take to plan for and manage an event we all hope will never happen — after all, the whole point of this book is to help you to prevent such situations. We deal only with crises affecting food safety so, although the advice holds good for many other kinds of crisis, you may wish to put it into the bigger picture of managing the business.

PLANNING AHEAD

Perhaps your company already has a crisis management plan. If so, is it up to date, comprehensive and well practised? Does everyone know about it and understand their part? Will it work if key people are on holiday or ill or just out of the office? Does it include a strategy for dealing with the media? Is there a press spokesperson? Do managers know what to say and how to say it? Do they know what *not* to say? Do they realise that their actions could make or break the company?

If you do not already have a plan, or the plan needs an overhaul, a good way to start is by thinking about what could go wrong. Unless you have a realistic view of what might happen, you will not be able to plan for it. Ask yourself questions such as:

- what are the things that could go wrong — what is the very worst that could happen and what are the most likely to happen?
- how would the public be affected?
- what would the fallout be for the company — a minor inconvenience or bankruptcy; refunding the cost of a tin of beans, or paying out millions in damages; a minor dent in your reputation or the death of the business?
- what would you tell your customers — how could you keep their confidence and their custom?

Once you have a general idea of the kind of crises that could happen in your business you can start planning for specific situations.

Consider different scenarios

Your initial information about a problem could come from many sources and your planned response will probably need to be shaped by the source of the information and the perceived seriousness of the problem. Typical sources include:

- suppliers
- trade organisations
- customers
- consumer organisations
- environmental health officers
- government departments
- the police
- blackmailers
- media
- contacts in the food industry.

There are numerous possible responses. For example, your strategy for dealing with a blackmailer, no matter how serious the threat, may be to give no publicity at all. In contrast, your response to the possibility of the physical contamination of a product may be to issue a *product recall* which could involve the maximum publicity in a bid to inform as many customers as possible.

Establish a crisis team

As well as considering a range of response strategies you need to designate the members of the team that will go into action at the first sign of a problem, co-ordinating the company's responses and deciding what to say to the staff, press and public. The team may vary depending on the type of crisis but there should usually be a core group. In a larger company the team would probably include all the following people:

- senior manager or director able to take major decisions
- marketing or sales manager
- legal expert
- food safety expert
- quality assurance manager
- production manager
- press spokesperson
- external food safety or management consultant.

Owner-managers and managers of small businesses may need to draw upon the help of nominated outsiders in a crisis, as one or two people are unlikely to cope with doing everything when the chips are down.

Appoint a spokesperson

Someone in the crisis team needs to be designated as the spokesperson who deals with the press. Having one person in this role improves the chance of putting across a single, consistent message and minimises the possibility of confusion among journalists and customers. It does not matter whether the spokesperson is the managing director, the food safety manager, the sales director or a member of the canteen staff. What is most important is that the person should be capable, unflappable, believable, concerned and well briefed. Look for someone with a trustworthy manner — someone from whom you would be confident to buy a second-hand car.

Draw up a communications policy

Communication lies at the heart of all business relationships, as it does of most human relationships. It can lose customers or gain them, it can give you a good press or a bad press and it can turn a crisis into a disaster or into an opportunity. Consider two managers faced with a crisis. One tells the press, "We have never had a problem before so I don't see how this can be our fault." The other says, "We have been working very hard to find out exactly what has caused this problem. We will keep you informed as soon as we know anything. In the mean time, we have taken the following precautionary steps..." Customers are much more likely to forgive the second company than the first.

Try to involve your spokesperson and the other members of the crisis team in drawing up the communications policy. Don't forget to keep your staff, suppliers and customers in the picture as you scurry to deal with reporters. Staff may become anxious or even unco-operative in the absence of hard facts. Remember that many people show some of their best characteristics in a crisis, if they are given the chance to do so. After a bomb destroyed a large part of the Docklands area of London in 1996, customers rallied round with help that enabled one company to get itself back on its feet.

There are no hard and fast rules for your communications policy, but it is worth considering the following suggestions.

Put customers and the public first

Treat customers and the public with respect. Don't interrupt or be dismissive, but acknowledge their point of view, even if they are rude or misinformed. Show that you take their concerns seriously and appreciate their right to information.

Be honest and direct

Leave it to experts to find out the facts. Don't deny or accept responsibility until the evidence is in, but explain what you are doing to resolve the crisis. Never is it more true that little lies become big lies than when dealing with a crisis. All communications must be truthful and above reproach. Any attempt to hide or misrepresent the facts will probably come out eventually — not only will you have more explaining to do, but your credibility will be in tatters.

Be prepared, practical and positive

Focus on the constructive measures you have taken to improve the situation. Decide in advance what you are going to say. Don't be tempted to make up ad hoc answers.

IF A CRISIS OCCURS

Management during a crisis is different: normal roles and rules may be suspended temporarily in the interests of dealing with the emergency. In this situation you need to think quickly, clearly and with a view of the big picture.

Teamwork is even more important than before and managers must put the interests of public health first, followed by the long-term interests of the company — ahead of financial targets, deadlines, personal concerns or egos. There may need to be even greater flexibility than normal if production or service is to continue because even greater attention will need to be paid to food safety and product quality.

Going into action

As soon as you are aware of a crisis, bring your crisis management plan into action. Make sure that members of the crisis team meet immediately.

Among the questions they should ask themselves are:
- what has happened?
- who is already affected?
- who else could be affected?
- why has it happened — can this be ascertained immediately with any certainty?
- what can the company do to correct the situation immediately?
- is additional specialist advice required from outside the company?
- should production or service be halted?
- should a product recall be instigated?
- who will liaise with any investigating officials such as environmental health officers and other specialists (see page 333)
- what should be done to ensure that no one destroys, interferes with or disturbs potential evidence, such as suspect food?
- when is it appropriate to issue a press statement?
- what can be done to maintain good customer relationships?

Devising a plan

The team must place actions in order of priority in a staged plan. They must consider how to prevent the problem recurring as well as solving the immediate problem — and that must, of course, take precedence. Some things will need to be done immediately, others later in the day, others the following day, and still others weeks or months later, or once the crisis is over.

THE ROLE OF INVESTIGATING AUTHORITIES

Let us backtrack for a moment. Why might an environmental health officer (EHO) approach your business other than for a routine inspection or at your request for advice? The legal duties of EHOs include safeguarding food so that it is fit for human consumption. This involves general monitoring of the food chain and food operations. It also includes investigating consumer complaints about food and allegations of food-borne illness. These activities not only protect consumers and public health, but they also help to exonerate innocent food businesses if they are accused of blame!

Your business might also become involved in an investigation if there is an outbreak of food-borne illness. While a *case* is just one incidence of illness, an *outbreak* is a cluster, in time or place, of cases of illness caused by a particular organism. The public health authorities, such as the Public Health Laboratory Service, are always alert to the possibility of outbreaks and warn the medical and environmental health authorities when they suspect from their data that an outbreak is occurring. If the outbreak is a significant one, an outbreak investigation team is then set up to co-ordinate all actions that need to be taken to deal with the problem.

Outbreak investigation team
The size and composition of an investigating team varies but the core members are:
- a consultant in public health medicine
- an environmental health officer, or several
- a consultant microbiologist
- secretarial support staff.

Depending on the circumstances, the team may also include some or all of the following specialists:
- a consultant in infectious diseases
- press officers
- an infection control nurse
- a veterinarian
- a general practitioner (GP)
- a public analyst
- a toxicologist
- a virologist
- representatives of government departments and agencies.

The investigation
All investigations follow a similar pattern, involving interviewing patients and establishing what they have eaten over the period prior to the onset of symptoms. The team tries to find a common feature, either a food or product that all the victims have eaten, or a restaurant or shop that has supplied them. If any suspect food is still available in the home, restaurant or shop, it is taken away for analysis.

Other actions that the investigating team might undertake include:
- taking clinical and environmental samples
- inspecting suspected premises
- identifying the need for medical care facilities

- agreeing measures to control the outbreak and prevent further spread, for example by means of exclusion of personnel, withdrawal of foods thought to be hazardous or the closure of premises
- determining the issuing of advice to the public and professionals and the setting up of a helpline
- issuing press releases and dealing with the press
- liaising with government departments and agencies
- producing a report that includes any lessons learned from the outbreak.

Why your business?

Outbreak investigations are undertaken to safeguard public health, not to make the lives of food managers difficult. So while you must always do everything possible to *prevent* food-borne illness, you also need to be *prepared* for the authorities to knock on your door and to tell you that they 'think' there may be a problem with one of your products. Whatever you do, do not be tempted to try to send them packing just because they said 'think'. You are legally obliged to co-operate, but from a business viewpoint, if there is even the remotest possibility that you may have a problem, then it is in your interest to reveal it so that it can be dealt with.

Best interests

Keep in mind your responsibilities for safeguarding public health and business wealth by:

- bringing your crisis management plan into action
- carrying out your own internal investigation with external help if necessary
- co-operating fully with the authorities
- not destroying, disturbing or interfering with evidence.

Benefiting from the investigation?

How does an investigation end up exonerating or pointing the finger of blame at a particular product or business? In fact the results of investigations are often inconclusive.

The origin of the problem is sometimes revealed promptly because samples reveal that all the patients were affected by the same organism which matches exactly those found in samples of the suspect food. Things rarely happen quite so neatly and, however diligent the investigators may be, they often have to rely on educated guesswork and epidemiological evidence (findings about the spread of the illness) to determine the likely cause.

Sometimes it is impossible to make even an informed guess as to the cause. Usually, however, a tentative conclusion is formed. Even if there is only the slightest hint that your company could be responsible in some way, do bear in mind that the investigators would be foolhardy to draw a provisional conclusion without having satisfied themselves that they have sufficient evidence to justify it.

Whatever the outcome, try to use the lessons learned or suggested to review your HACCP system or hazard analysis system and overall standards of food safety.

WHEN THE CRISIS IS RESOLVED

Some crises are never truly resolved and some organisations never recover, typically those that failed to draw up, or implement, a crisis management plan. Assuming that you have a plan and have put it into action, you stand a good chance of pulling through. But this is not the end of the story as there are still some vital things to be done.

Thank anyone who has been involved in helping to put things back on a normal footing, whether staff, suppliers, consultants or customers. After all, appreciation can go a long way. If appropriate, thank customers for their patience.

Work with specialists, such as environmental health officers, to make certain that lessons have been learned and measures are in place to prevent anything similar happening in the future. Take the time to evaluate and revise your crisis management plan. What was good about it? What did not work so well and could be improved? What came up that was not covered by the plan?

From crisis to opportunity?

It may seem like a disaster at the time, but, if you handle it well, a crisis can end up strengthening your business rather than destroying it. After all, you should now have enhanced food safety mechanisms in place, a workforce united by having pulled through difficult circumstances and customers who respect you for the professionalism, integrity and honesty with which you handled the situation.

MAKING IT EASIER FOR OTHERS

- Reinforce the message that food safety affects everyone.
- Create a simple procedure for dealing with customer complaints about food and allegations that your company caused illness.
- Consider a system whereby staff refer customer complaints and allegations direct to their supervisor or manager, rather than attempting to deal with it themselves. This may be especially worthwhile if you employ a lot of young employees or have a high staff turnover.
- Prepare a crisis management plan.
- Make certain that everyone knows what to do if the worst happens.
- Work as a team with a single external voice.
- Emphasise the importance of co-operation with investigating authorities.

🎖 MANAGEMENT MATTERS

Cleaning and pest control services are sometimes outside the direct control of food managers. Even so, you must ensure that your company has in place and maintains proper procedures for cleaning and disinfection, the disposal of rubbish and waste and pest control.

Inadequate cleaning procedures can cause, or fail to control, a large number of hazards including:

- microbiological contamination — for example, when food debris is not removed from food contact surfaces promptly and thoroughly
- microbiological multiplication — for example, when food-contact or hand-contact surfaces are not cleaned and disinfected promptly
- cross-contamination — for example, when the same cleaning equipment, such as a cleaning cloth, is used in areas designated for the storage or preparation of raw foods as well as in areas set aside for preparing cooked or ready-to-eat foods
- physical contamination — for example, from debris from brushes and mops, or from grease or burnt food and other food debris that could contaminate the next batch of food that is prepared, or from packaging materials that are not disposed of properly and promptly
- chemical contamination — for example, from the purchase of cleaning chemicals that are not food-safe, the use of inappropriate dilutions of chemicals, the unsuitable storage of cleaning chemicals close to food or the storage of chemicals in food containers
- pest infestation — because particles of food and undisturbed areas attract pests.

Ignoring pest management could have a dire impact upon your company's legal record, budget and profits and could lead to serious illness or injury, so:

- establish clear procedures that are easy for staff to follow
- ensure that all food staff clean as they go
- emphasise the importance of keeping all parts of the premises clean at all times
- store food off the floor in pest-resistant packaging or containers and make sure that staff replace lids securely
- teach staff how to check and rotate stock
- encourage staff to report any sign of infestation.

Effective pest management may require cultural and educational changes in your business and better teamwork that involves everyone from the cleaning staff to the senior managers. Hazards from inadequate pest control include:

- bacterial contamination — carried or excreted by pests
- cross-contamination — particularly from flying insects that move from food to food or from sources of contamination, such as rubbish tips, to food premises
- chemical contamination — from the careless use or residual traces of pesticides
- physical contamination — from their bodies, droppings and nest materials.

Temperature control throughout the food chain is an important key to producing safe food and all food-contact staff should be given the opportunity to learn how microbial survival and multiplication affect the safety of food. All aspects of temperature control are important, of course, but you may wish to take the hint from the statistics about the causes of food poisoning (see page 74) and particularly reinforce the message about safe cooling, holding temperatures (both cold and hot) and reheating, if you permit reheating at all.

Managers have a crucial role to play, not only in emphasising 'safe' temperatures and setting a good example in their own everyday work, but also in ensuring that:
- workflow takes full account of temperature control and not just contamination hazards
- there are procedures for every aspect of temperature control that are clear to all and easy for every member of staff to follow.

As with so many other aspects of food safety, this may involve management teamwork. In a large organisation this could involve chefs and warehouse, distribution and sales managers, for example.

Systems of HACCP and hazard analysis can help you to make procedures clear to all and to improve your control, but, like any system, HACCP and its modified forms are only as good as the daily monitoring of control points and regular reviewing of the effectiveness of the system.

Ever since the principles of HACCP became compulsory for all kinds of food businesses, the system has experienced an evolution of its own. Some companies use it wisely as an umbrella concept, while others have adopted an over-cautious and usually unworkable approach, making every tiny process step a critical control point. A lot of the frustration of recent years comes from the misunderstanding that HACCP should cover *all* controls — including personal hygiene, cleaning and disinfection, maintenance schedules, pest control, waste disposal and so on. However, HACCP works much better if a company concentrates on such prerequisites before advancing towards HACCP.

Systems should work for you, not make you and your colleagues into slaves of the system. Used wisely, your food safety systems should enhance your company's operational efficiency and the safety and, possibly, the quality of the food you produce.

INTEGRATED MANAGEMENT

Hats, rats, buildings, temperature, training, personal hygiene, personal habits, extrinsic factors, intrinsic factors, critical control points, critical limits, tolerances and teamwork — just a few of the topics we have discussed so far. We cannot pretend that food safety is anything but a vast subject, so how can you make your knowledge work well for your company, for consumer safety and for profit?

Suggestions about ways to manage the details of food safety have been provided throughout the book, but you may feel it would be advantageous to pull all these points together into a workable, comprehensive, easy-to-understand and easy-to-operate system.

The idea of implementing overall control systems is not new. Some accreditation and industry bodies have developed hygiene accreditation systems which take different types of food safety management systems, including farm-to-fork approaches and HACCP, and provide an all-embracing concept. Many companies have developed individual guidelines for good practice (such as good manufacturing practice —GMP), often in preparation for, or as the first step towards, official certification of quality management. But what can *you* do to integrate all aspects of food safety?

PULLING EVERYTHING TOGETHER

A Swiss scientist, Friedrich Untermann, suggests that we think about food safety management as being rather like a house. You do not start building a house with the roof, of course, but with the foundations. Only then do you work upwards. You might want to think of the foundations and basement as being the design, construction and equipping of the premises. On the floors above are fundamental requirements such as personal hygiene, cleaning and disinfection, pest and waste control, temperature and humidity controls and the separation of clean and dirty processes. At roof level you have the food safety control measures appropriate to your particular company.

Beyond the basement

All of your control measures need to be within the framework of your organisation's overall business aims and stated policies. Many companies publish a food safety policy, which states the company's intention to meet it legal obligations to provide safe products and its responsibilities towards its customers. It may also include an organisational flow chart indicating where management responsibility lies. Detailed statements about policies and the ways in which staff should implement them are usually integrated in operational, standards or staff manuals or software. They usually include topics such as personal hygiene, temperature control, storage and transport control, physical contamination, disposal of unfit stock, dealing with visitors, reporting illness, product recalls and allegations of food poisoning. A few examples of issues often covered by policies are given on the following two pages.

Personal hygiene

Product safety and product hygiene depend on the behaviour, attitude and action of staff and there is no chance of implementing an effective food safety system if the people who run it are not aware of the basic personal hygiene rules. All food handlers must be trained thoroughly and supervised diligently and other staff, such as finance managers, administrative staff, maintenance staff and sub-contractors must also be made aware of the impact that they could have upon the safety of food. Policies usually include the company's rules about the access and movement of personnel, eating and drinking on the premises, jewellery and personal adornment, protective clothing and personal cleanliness.

Visitor policies

As well as dealing with the actions of staff, a company also has to deal with visitors such as external maintenance engineers, cleaning staff, pest controllers, customers and suppliers. As they could all pose a threat to food safety, you should formulate rules for areas other than public access areas. These might cover such issues as how to authorise admission to the premises, insisting that visitors wear suitable protective clothing (supplied by the company) and observe all in-house hygiene rules, and whether visitors should be accompanied at all times. You should also consider displaying the company hygiene rules in reception areas and at entrances to production areas. You may wish to make part of the procedure for admission to the site a requirement for visitors to read the rules.

Regular training, encouragement and supervision help staff to gain confidence and competence in their individual contribution towards food safety.

Glass and blade registers

Sharp objects are on top of the list of physical contaminants. A written policy can state the company's attitude towards preventive measures and describe appropriate controls. In high risk areas all sources of glass should be either eliminated or protected. If you cannot achieve this immediately, establish a schedule for replacing breakable objects. Use the list of such items to help you to check the state of these objects, to record breakages and describe corrective actions.

A blade register describes the cutting tools authorised by the company. Any other unauthorised tools, such as knives with break-off blades, should be banned from the premises.

Incident reports

A food safety incident (or food hygiene incident) is anything visible or easily detectable that might endanger the safety of the consumer — for example, glass splinters in a food room, traces of physical or chemical contamination, accumulating waste, unauthorised items or utensils in food areas. To introduce a reporting system you need to establish a list of types of event that could compromise product safety — your hazard analysis will already contain most of this information — and state the procedures for dealing with it. Not only will an incident reporting procedure allow records to be kept of the incident itself, but it will also provide a permanent note of the resulting corrective action. This information can then be fed back into the review of hazards and assist you generally in gauging the company's potential weak points for food safety.

Product recalls

A public *product recall* is probably the nightmare of every food business, but procedures for such an eventuality should be in place, as we discussed in 'Turning a crisis to advantage' on pages 328 to 335. Your policies should cover the recall procedures to be followed, taking into account the likely length of time it will take for the recall notices to come to the attention of suppliers and your market. You should have a system in place that enables you to trace all your materials and ingredients from source right through to the finished product.

Consumer allegations about illness

A customer complaint of food poisoning could, if it were badly handled, easily turn into a public relations disaster, whether or not the allegation was justified. Make sure that you formulate and make clear to staff the procedure to be followed. You may decide that staff should immediately refer the customer to a supervisor or manager, or you may create a form to be filled in by the member of staff and the customer. Whichever procedure you choose, make certain that staff are aware of the importance of remaining polite and attentive, without admitting liability.

Keep records of complaints, whether they are eventually justified, disproven or malicious. Use them to review food safety (and customer relationship) procedures and to record any appropriate corrective action.

MANAGING FOOD SAFETY

Systems work only if they are used properly, monitored and reviewed — and that requires confident and competent staff who know what they should be doing and understand why they should be doing it. It also requires up-to-date, motivated supervisors and managers who lead by good example. The investment in training, motivation and systems is in time, energy, commitment and money, but prevention is always less costly than the cure.

A manager like you with the responsibility for food safety has a big and continuous task, but food safety is indeed achievable, provided that you manage it diligently.

REFERENCE

MEASUREMENTS AND SYMBOLS

Abbreviations

Mass and volume

kg	kilogram (1,000 kg = 1 metric ton)
g	gram
µg	microgram (one millionth of a gram)
l	litre
ml	millilitre
cu	cubic (cubic metres are, for example, also expressed as m^3)

Linear measurement and area

km	kilometre
m	metre
cm	centimetre
mm	millimetre
µm	micrometre or micron (one millionth of a metre, also expressed as 10^{-6}m)
nm	nanometre (one billionth of a metre, also expressed as 10^{-9}m)
sq	square (square metres are, for example, also expressed as m^2)

Chemical symbols

CO_2	carbon dioxide
H	hydrogen
H_2O	water
N	nitrogen
NH_3	ammonia
NO_3^-	nitrate
NO_2^-	nitrite
O	oxygen
O_2	free (or molecular) oxygen
O_3	ozone

Others

a_w	available water; moisture
C	the Celsius temperature scale (often referred to as centigrade)
E_h	oxidation-reduction (or redox) potential
pH	scale of acid and alkali

Examples of numbers expressed to the power of ten

10^3	1 thousand	1,000
10^6	1 million	1,000,000
6×10^6	6 million	6,000,000
25×10^6	25 million	25,000,000
50×10^6	50 million	50,000,000
25×10^9	25 billion	25,000,000,000
16×10^{10}	160 billion	160,000,000,000

PATHOGENIC MICRO-ORGANISMS

These tables provide an at-a-glance reference to the most common causes of food-borne diseases. Under the heading 'Type of illness' we have given the classification used in this book, followed, where appropriate, by a note of other classifications you may encounter in other publications written in English. The onset and duration periods are typical average ranges for the organism and are based on the findings of a Department of Health working group.

BACTERIA

Bacillus cereus

Type of illness	Bacterial food poisoning — *Bacillus cereus* poisoning. (Alternatively, classed as a bacterial intoxication, or as a toxin-mediated infection.)
Cause of illness	One of two kinds of toxin: 1) released in the food before it is consumed (emetic syndrome), and acts on the upper gastro-intestinal tract 2) released in the body (diarrhoeal syndrome) in the intestinal tract.
Illness	1) *Emetic syndrome* Onset time: 1-5 hours. Symptoms: mainly vomiting, abdominal pains, sometimes diarrhoea. Duration: 6-24 hours. 2) *Diarrhoeal syndrome* Onset time: 8-16 hours. Symptoms: watery diarrhoea, abdominal pains, sometimes vomiting. Duration: 12-24 hours.
Carrier status	None.
Source	Soil, dust and vegetation. Very common in the natural world.
Food commonly involved	Cereals, grains, rice and rice-based products, corn, cornstarch and products containing cornstarch, soya beans and soya products, meat, fish, milk, vegetables, pasta and tofu.
Control measures	Preventing cross-contamination. Controlling time and temperature during preparation and holding, such as cooking, cooling and hot-holding. Storing in temperature-controlled conditions (usually under refrigeration). Avoiding reheating food.

Brucella

Rod-shaped, aerobic, Gram-negative, zoonotic.

Type of illness	Bacterial food-borne infection — brucellosis, Malta fever (*B. melitensis*) or Bang's disease (*B. abortus*).
Cause of illness	Enteric fever, invasion of the bloodstream. The infection can occur as droplet infection (inhaling Brucella-infected dust), contact infection or food-borne infection.
Illness	Onset time: 5-30 days (*B. melitensis*). Symptoms: fever, headache, general weakness, depression, generalised muscle aches. Duration: can turn into a persistent chronic stage for years.
Carrier status	Yes.
Source	Intestines of sheep, goats and cattle; also found in deer, caribou and dogs. Occurs worldwide but especially in Mediterranean countries, Central and South America and Central Asia.
Food commonly involved	Milk, dairy products and meat products.
Control measures	Controlling time and temperature control, especially during pasteurisation or sterilisation of milk and milk products. Observing high standards of hygiene in slaughterhouses. Excluding infected employees from handling food.

Campylobacter jejuni

Microaerophilic, Gram-negative, spiral-shaped rod, toxin-producing, zoonotic (can infect humans and animals).

Type of illness	Bacterial food-borne infection — campylobacter-enteritis.
Cause of illness	Acute infectious bacterial diarrhoea and gastro-enteritis caused by the invasive abilities of the organism. Only a few cells are required to cause infection (low infective dose). The common route is cross-contamination. Human-to-human transmission is of minor significance.
Illness	Onset time: 2-5 days, sometimes longer. Symptoms: watery and bloody diarrhoea, fever, headache, abdominal pain and nausea. Potential complications: meningitis, septicaemia, Reiter's syndrome, Guillain-Barré syndrome, Miller-Fisher syndrome. Duration: 2-7 days, but relapses are common and the patient can be infectious for 10 days or more.
Carrier status	Yes.
Source	Wild birds (such as seagulls, crows and feral pigeons), poultry, sheep, cattle, pigs, sewage and untreated water supplies.
Food commonly involved	Raw meat and offal, poultry, raw milk and untreated water sources.
Control measures	Strictly controlling time and temperature during the pasteurisation or sterilisation of milk and milk products. Preventing cross-contamination, particularly by effective cleaning and disinfecting and by separating utensils and equipment used for preparing raw and cooked foods. Observing high standards of personal hygiene. Using only potable sources of water.

Clostridium botulinum

Anaerobic, Gram-positive, rod-shaped, spore-forming, neurotoxin-producing. The spores are highly heat resistant.

Type of illness	Bacterial food poisoning — botulism. (Alternatively classed as a bacterial intoxication.)
Cause of illness	Consumption of an exotoxin — a highly toxic neurotoxin — produced on the food. Infant botulism is caused by the consumption by babies and young children of botulinum spores which then germinate in the intestine.
Illness	Onset time: 12-36 hours. Symptoms: double vision, difficulty in speaking and swallowing, headache, nausea, fatigue, constipation, vomiting, dizziness, muscle paralysis and damage to the nervous system. Mortality rate: 30%-65%. Duration: 1-10 days, although longer is common. Death is likely to occur within eight days of the onset of symptoms unless an anti-toxin is given.
Carrier status	None.
Source	Soil and water.
Food commonly involved	Meat, fish and vegetables; inadequately processed low-acid foods; home-canned products; vacuum-packed meats and other vacuum-packed foods; continuous stockpots; baked/jacket potatoes that have not been subject to effective temperature control. Infant botulism is often caused by spore-contaminated honey.
Control measures	Strict control of time and temperature (botulinum cook), especially in canning, bottling and vacuum packing.

Clostridium perfringens

Anaerobic, Gram-positive, rod-shaped, spore-forming, toxin-producing.

Type of illness	Bacterial food poisoning. (Alternatively, classed as an intoxication or as a toxin-mediated infection.)
Cause of illness	An enterotoxin. (Spores are formed in food as it cooks. When the food is cooled too slowly, the spores germinate and multiply. After the food is eaten, the organism sporulates in the intestine, releasing an endotoxin.)
Illness	Onset time: 8-18 hours. Symptoms: diarrhoea and abdominal pain; fever and vomiting are rare. Can be fatal for elderly and immuno-compromised people. Duration: 12-24 hours.
Carrier status	No.
Source	Human and animal intestinal tract, soil, dust, spices.
Food commonly involved	Cooked meat and poultry, gravy, sauces, spices, various foods that have been cooled too slowly.
Control measures	Strict control of time and temperature, especially in cooking, cooling and reheating. Avoiding reheating more than once, if at all. Preventing cross-contamination (eg. raw vegetables and cooked foods). Cleaning and disinfecting food preparation areas and utensils thoroughly and regularly.

Escherichia coli

Rod-shaped, aerobic and facultative anaerobic, Gram-negative, toxin-producer. This bacterium is naturally present in the human intestine and only some types are pathogenic.

Type of illness	Bacterial food poisoning. The illnesses are known by various popular names such as traveller's diarrhoea. (Alternatively, classed as an intoxication.)
Cause of illness	One of several enterotoxins invading intestinal cells and destroying the intestinal lining.
Illness	Onset time: 12-72 hours is usually quoted, but varies between hours and several days depending on the organism and the health of the person. Symptoms: can include acute abdominal pain, fever, water or bloody diarrhoea, kidney damage and failure. The illness can be life threatening, especially to those in the 'at risk' group. Duration: 1-14 days.
Carrier status	Yes.
Source	Humans and animals, especially cattle; the natural environment including water; sewage.
Food commonly involved	Beef, especially minced beef (as in beefburgers), and meat products (including gravy); raw milk; milk products; fish; drinking water; some unpasteurised fruit juice products, such as cider.
Control measures	Cooking thoroughly and observing strict time and temperature control — for example, the internal temperature of beefburgers. Preventing cross-contamination. Observing strict personal hygiene. Using potable water. Ensuring the safe disposal of sewage.

E. coli 0157

Type of illness	Bacterial food-borne infection. (Alternatively, classed as an intoxication or a toxin-mediated infection.)
Cause of illness	Shiga-like toxins — verotoxin, verocytotoxin. The toxin causes damage to the intestinal epithelial cells. Blood vessels are damaged and bleeding occurs. The infective dose is very low and can be as few as 10 cells.
Illness	Onset time: varies between hours and several days depending on the number of bacteria ingested and the health of the person; 48 hours is typical. Symptoms: fever, vomiting abdominal pain and diarrhoea. Potential complications: a second stage — haemolytic uremic syndrome (HUS) — can follow, which is characterised by kidney failure and loss of red blood cells. Can be life threatening. Duration: variable; typically 1-8 days.
Carrier status	None.
Source	Intestinal tract of cattle and sheep; birds.
Food commonly involved	Beef (particularly minced beef) and meat products, raw or underpasteurised milk and drinking water.
Control measures	Controlling time and temperature. Cooking food thoroughly. Avoiding cross-contamination. Observing strict personal hygiene, especially with regard to hands.

Listeria monocytogenes

Facultative anaerobic, rod-shaped, Gram-positive, psychrotropic, halophilic.

Type of illness	Bacterial food-borne infection — listeriosis.
Cause of illness	Bacteria invade body tissue and bloodstream creating changes in the composition of the red blood cells. Non-pregnant, healthy individuals are usually resistant to infection, but may be life threatening to unborn babies, pregnant women, the elderly and individuals with weakened immune systems
Illness	Onset time: 1-70 days, typically up to 21 days. Symptoms: fever, septicaemia, meningitis, nausea. Potential complications: abortion, premature birth, still-birth. Duration: depends on symptoms.
Carrier status	Yes.
Source	Soil, water, sewage, human and animal carriers.
Food commonly involved	Raw milk and raw-milk products such as soft cheeses, ready-to-eat foods such as prepared salads, coleslaw, cook-chill products, sausages, pâté and raw vegetables, salad vegetables and seafood.
Control measures	Observing thorough hygiene practices in abattoirs and dairies. Strictly controlling time and temperature during the pasteurisation or sterilisation of milk and milk products. Washing (and treating, where appropriate) vegetables and salad ingredients. Preventing cross-contamination. Observing high standards of personal hygiene. Using only potable water supplies. Labelling or avoiding serving raw milk and or raw-milk products to susceptible individuals, particularly pregnant women and nursing mothers as the bacterium can affect unborn children or breast-fed infants. Observing *use by* dates of refrigerated foods with the greatest care.

Mycobacterium tuberculosis and *Mycobacterium bovis*

Rod-shaped, Gram-positive, zoonotic, aerobic rods with exceptional resistance to drying processes and chemical disinfectants.

Type of illness	Bacterial food-borne infection — tuberculosis.
Cause of illness	Enteric fever; invasion of the bloodstream. The infection can occur as droplet infection, contact infection or food-borne infection. Direct infection of the lung by inhalation only needs very few cells.
Illness	Onset time: 4-12 weeks. Symptoms: pulmonary or extra-pulmonary tuberculosis. The initial infection usually goes unnoticed. Duration: can turn into a persistent chronic stage.
Carrier status	Yes.
Source	Human carriers, cattle, some wild animals such as badgers, opossum and deer.
Food commonly involved	Raw milk and dairy products.
Control measures	Strictly controlling the time and temperature during pasteurisation and sterilisation of milk and milk products. Not using raw milk or raw-milk products. Excluding infected employees from handling food. Preventing cross-contamination. Observing high standards of personal hygiene.

Salmonella species

Large group of rod-shaped, facultative anaerobic, Gram-negative bacteria.

Salmonella Enteritidis and *Salmonella* Typhimurium

Type of illness	Bacterial food poisoning — salmonellosis. (Alternatively, classed as an infection.)
Cause of illness	Invasion of the body by large numbers of bacteria (typically, 100,000 per gram of food) which have already multiplied on the food.
Illness	Onset time: 6-96 hours, typically 12-48. Symptoms: diarrhoea, vomiting, fever, abdominal pain. Can be life threatening, particularly for people in the 'at risk' group. Duration: typically 1-7 days, but can last up to three weeks.
Carrier status	Yes.
Source	Human and animal intestinal tracts and faeces. The infection route is via raw foods of animal origin, such as meat, poultry, eggs and egg products and milk, or via faeces and fertilisers — for instance, on vegetables. Insects, birds, vermin and domestic pets are also sources.
Food commonly involved	Meat and meat products, poultry, eggs and egg products such as mayonnaise, raw milk, dairy products, fish and seafood, some beansprouts such as alfalfa.
Control measures	Observing high standards of personal hygiene. Controlling time and temperature, especially in cooking, cooling and reheating. Preventing cross-contamination: strict separation of raw and cooked foods. Cleaning and disinfecting thoroughly. Ensuring effective pest management.

Salmonella species continued over the page

Salmonella Typhi and *Salmonella* Paratyphi

Type of illness	Bacterial food-borne infections — *S.* Typhi: enteric fever, typhoid/typhoid fever (not to be confused with typhus, which is an infectious disease caused by Rickettsiae); *S.* Paratyphi — enteric fever, paratyphoid.
Cause of illness	Enteric fever: invasion of the bloodstream at a very small infective dose.
Illness	Onset time: 3-56 days; typically 12-20 days. Symptoms: fever, spleen enlargement (*S.* Typhi), severe diarrhoea. *S.* Typhi is fatal in 2%-10% of cases. Duration: up to 40 days; typically 10-14 days. Paratyphoid is less severe than typhoid and its occurrence is more sporadic.
Carrier status	Yes.
Source	Human carriers (*S.* Typhi); human and animal intestines (*S.* Paratyphi).
Food commonly involved	Milk, dairy products, drinking water, meat and seafood.
Control measures	Using only potable water supplies. Ensuring the safe disposal of human faeces. Observing strict personal hygiene and kitchen hygiene. Controlling time and temperature thoroughly, especially during cooking and pasteurising. Using shellfish only from approved sources. Excluding infected persons from handling food. Ensuring effective pest management.

Shigella dysenteriae
Rod-shaped, facultative anaerobic, Gram-negative, acid tolerant.

Type of illness	Bacterial food-borne infection — shigellosis (bacillary dysentery).
Cause of illness	A powerful toxin (Shiga toxin) which inhibits protein synthesis in the invaded cells. The minimum infective dose is very low.
Illness	Onset time: 1-3 days. Symptoms: watery, sometimes bloody diarrhoea, stools with blood and mucous, fever, abdominal pain, severe dehydration and sometimes vomiting. Duration: normally up to 2 weeks; depending on symptoms and treatment, the patient can excrete the organism for several months even after the symptoms have stopped.
Carrier status	Yes.
Source	Human carriers.
Food commonly involved	Milk, eggs and egg products, water, flour, vegetables, fruits, salad vegetables, shellfish, salads and dairy products.
Control measures	Using only potable water. Controlling the disposal of waste water and sewage. Observing high standards of personal hygiene and kitchen hygiene. Controlling time and temperature. Excluding infected persons from handling food. Ensuring effective pest management.

Staphylococcus aureus

Round (coccal), facultative anaerobic, Gram-positive, halophilic. Some are toxin-producers.

Type of illness	Bacterial food poisoning — staphylococcal gastro-enteritis. (Alternatively, classed as a bacterial intoxication.)
Cause of illness	Exotoxin poisoning when large numbers of the bacteria are toxin-producers. Illness is usually caused by consuming the toxin, not the living organism.
Illness	Onset time: 2-6 hours. Symptoms: acute vomiting, diarrhoea, nausea, abdominal pain and sometimes collapse. Body temperature may drop. Duration: 12-48 hours.
Carrier status	Yes.
Source	Human body — nose, throat, skin, hands and hair, and in boils, pimples, sties, septic lesions, burns and wounds — and animals.
Food commonly involved	Ham, poultry, egg products, dairy products, potato salads, raw goat's and cow's milk, cream and cheese, and almost any other product of animal origin or product touched by hand.
Control measures	Observing high standards of personal hygiene especially with regard to handwashing. Excluding people with skin infections, colds and so on from working with food. Controlling time and temperature, especially when cooking, cooling and reheating.

Vibrio parahaemolyticus

Comma-shaped, facultative anaerobic, Gram-positive, halophilic.

Type of illness	Food poisoning. (Alternatively, classed as an infection.)
Cause of illness	Invasion of the body by large numbers of bacteria (about 10,000 per gram of food) which have multiplied in food.
Illness	Onset time: 4-96 hours; typically 12-24 hours. Symptoms: vomiting, diarrhoea, abdominal pain, fever and dehydration. Can be life threatening to people in the 'at risk group'. Duration: up to 7 days.
Carrier status	Yes.
Source	Marine shellfish and fish, especially from warm waters. (Some species of *Vibrio* are naturally present in some marine creatures.) Also food from sewage-contaminated marine waters.
Food commonly involved	Fish and shellfish including clams, oysters, lobsters, crabs and prawns.
Control measures	Buying seafood only from approved sources, and checking legal requirements and quality standards for supplies. Controlling time and temperature rules. Avoiding serving raw or lightly cooked seafood, especially to those in the 'at risk group'.

Yersinia enterocolitica

Rod-shaped, facultative anaerobic, Gram-negative, psychrotrophic.

Type of illness	Bacterial food poisoning — yersiniosis. (Alternatively, classed as an infection.)
Cause of illness	Invasion of the intestinal tissue by the living organism.
Illness	Onset time: 1-14 days; typically 3-7 days. Symptoms: diarrhoea, fever, headache and abdominal pain. Potential complications: reactive arthritis, mesenteric lymphadenitis, terminal ileitis and pseudo appendicitis. Duration: up to 40 days.
Carrier status	Yes.
Source	The natural environment, including soil and water, and animals.
Food commonly involved	Milk and milk products, egg products, raw meat (especially raw pork), vegetables, poultry and vacuum-packed products.
Control measures	Controlling time and temperature, especially with chilled products. Observing high standards of personal hygiene. Using only potable water.

Hepatitis A

Type of illness	Viral infection — hepatitis.
Cause of illness	Viral infection. Transmission usually occurs via the faecal-oral route. People can harbour the virus for six weeks before showing symptoms and are infectious for about one week before symptoms appear.
Illness	Onset time: 15-50 days. Symptoms: fever, nausea, vomiting, abdominal pain, liver disease, jaundice. Duration: 1 week-several months.
Carrier status	Yes.
Source	Human intestinal tract. Faeces, urine and blood may be infected.
Food commonly involved	Water, raw shellfish, raw vegetables and any food prepared by bare hands. Ready-to-eat foods, such as salads and bakery products, are often implicated.
Control measures	Ensuring the highest standards of personal hygiene, especially with regard to handwashing. Controlling time and temperature, especially when cooking. Avoiding cross-contamination.

Norovirus (previously known as Norwalk and Norwalk-like viruses)

Type of illness	Viral infection — Norwalk gastro-enteritis/Norovirus gastro-enteritis.
Cause of illness	Viral infection, often associated with traveller's diarrhoea and transmitted by the faecal-oral route.
Illness	Onset time: 1-2 days. Symptoms: fever, nausea, projectile vomiting, diarrhoea, abdominal pain. Headache and fever are possible. Duration: 1-3 days.
Carrier status	Possible.
Source	Human intestinal tract. Sewage-contaminated water.
Food commonly involved	Raw shellfish, raw vegetables, salads, fruit, water.
Control measures	Observing the time and temperature rules, especially for cooking. Avoiding cross-contamination. Observing high standards of personal hygiene, especially with regard to handwashing. Buying seafood only from approved sources. Taking special care when storing live mussels and cockles. Avoiding serving raw or lightly cooked seafood, especially to individuals in the 'at risk group'.

Rotavirus

Type of illness	Viral infection — rotavirus gastro-enteritis.
Cause of illness	Viral infection. Once the virus has invaded the host cell, it is transported to the lysosomes (organs within the cell containing vital enzymes).
Illness	Onset time: 1-3 days. Symptoms: fever, nausea, vomiting and watery diarrhoea, often leading to dehydration. Duration: 4-8 days.
Carrier status	Probable.
Source	Human intestines and sewage-contaminated water.
Food commonly involved	Raw seafood, untreated water, raw vegetables and salad ingredients.
Control measures	Observing high standards of personal hygiene, especially with regard to handwashing. Avoiding touching food by hand. Controlling time and temperature.

Type of parasite	Organism	Definitive host	Intermediate host	Food involved	Prevention
Protozoa	*Cryptosporidium parvum*	Humans, many mammals, reptiles and birds	None	Water and vegetables and fruit that have been washed with contaminated water	Observing high standards of personal hygiene. Using only potable water. Disposing of sewage safely. Cooking food thoroughly. Freezing below -20°C.
	Giardia lamblia	Humans, rats, beavers and muskrats	None		
Tapeworms	*Taenia saginata*	Humans	Cattle	Beef	Controlling time and temperature when cooking and freezing. Avoiding cross-contamination and contact with animals. Inspecting meat. Controlling water pollution and other forms of environmental pollution.
	Taenia solium	Humans	Pigs and humans	Pork	
	Diphyllobothrium latum	Humans	Crustaceans and fish	Fish	
	Echinococcus granulosus	Dogs	Humans	Food contaminated by dog faeces	
Flukes	*Fasciola hepatica*	Humans and cattle	Water snails	Watercress	Avoiding eating wild watercress and other water plants from non-approved sources.
Roundworms	*Trichina spiralis*	Humans, pigs and rats	None	Pork and horsemeat	Avoiding eating raw or undercooked meat. Cooking meat thoroughly. Pickling or freezing meat. Inspecting meat.

Mycotoxin	Aflatoxin	Patulin	Ochratoxin	Ergot alcaloids
Producing organism	*Aspergillus flavus, A. parasiticus*	*A. clavatus, A. giganteus, A. terreus*	*A. ochraceus, Penicillium viridicatum*	*Claviceps purpurea*
Foods commonly involved	Nuts, cereals, dried fruits	Fruit, fruit juices, bread	Cereals, corn, nuts, dried beans, cocoa, coffee, soya beans	Rye, other cereals
Effect on humans	Carcinogenic, hepatotoxic Acute symptoms: hepatitis	Carcinogenic Causes chromosomal changes in animal and plant cells	Carcinogenic, hepatotoxic, nephrotoxic	Neurotoxic Can cause gangrene
Common preventive measures	At source: fungus-free seeds, rapid drying processes, storage under controlled dry conditions. Also storage and transport under controlled anaerobic conditions; frozen storage ($-18\,^\circ$C). Preservation criteria: $a_w < 0.8$ / pH < 3 or > 6.5			

CHEMICALS

Pest control chemicals

Formulation	Examples
Baits	Most rodenticides, ant baits
Dusts (finely ground mineral or pesticide combined with a dry carrier)	Boric acid, diatomaceous earth, pyrethrum, silica aerogel, sulphur
Fumigants (poison gas)	CO_2
Granules (pesticides and carrier combined with a binding agent)	Many insecticides
Sprays: • aerosols • emulsifiable concentrates • flowables • micro-encapsulated materials • slurry • water-soluble concentrates • wettable powders	Pyrethrins Many pesticides Sulphur, copper compounds Many pesticides Bordeaux mixture (hydrated lime and copper sulphate) Insecticidal soaps *Bacillus thuringiensis*

Category	Examples
Attractants	Compounds, including pheromones (sexual hormones), that attract pests to traps or poisons
Repellents	Compounds that repel the target pest
Desiccants	Compounds that kill by adhering to insect cuticle, drying out the insect (eg. diatomaceous earth, silica aerogel)
Insect growth regulators (juvenile hormones)	Compounds mimicking insect hormones that regulate insect development
Poisons: • contact poisons • stomach poisons • fumigants • pass-throughs	Materials that penetrate the skin or outer membranes and disrupt the physiology of the organism (eg. insecticidal soaps, pyrethrins) Materials that attack the pest after it has ingested the poison (eg. boric acid) Respiratory poisons that kill by suffocation (eg. CO_2 against storage pests) Poisons that pass through an animal's digestive system and kill insects that attempt to inhabit the dung
Sterilants	Compounds, such as methyl bromide (which is used for fumigation), which kill many life forms.

Detergents and chemical disinfectants

FUNCTIONS AND LIMITATIONS OF CLEANING CHEMICALS

Category of aqueous cleaner	Approx. concentrations for use (%)	Examples of chemicals used	Functions	Limitations
Clean water	100	(Water usually contains dissolved air and minerals in small amounts.)	Solvent and carrier for soils and chemical cleaners.	Hard water leaves deposit on surfaces. Residual moisture may allow microbial growth on washed surfaces. Promotes rusting of iron.
Strong alkalis	1-5	Sodium hydroxide Sodium orthosilicate Sodium sesquisilicate	Detergents for removing fat and protein. Precipitate water hardness. Produce alkaline pH.	Highly corrosive. Difficult to remove by rinsing. Irritating to skin and mucous membranes.
Mild alkalis	1-10	Sodium carbonate Sodium sesquicarbonate Trisodium phosphate Sodium tetraborate	Detergents. Buffers at pH 8.4 or above. Water softeners.	Mildly corrosive. High concentrations are irritating to skin.
Inorganic acids	0.5	Hydrochloric Sulphuric Nitric Phosphoric Sulphamic	Produce pH 2.5 or below. Remove precipitates from surfaces.	Very corrosive to metals but can be partially inhibited by amines. Irritating to skin and mucous membranes.
Organic acids	0.1-2	Acetic Hydroxyacetic Lactic	Remove inorganic precipitates and other acid-soluble substances from surfaces.	Moderately corrosive but can be removed by various organic nitrogen compounds.
	0.1-2	Gluconic Citric Tartaric Levulinic Saccharic	Remove inorganic precipitates and other acid-soluble substances from surfaces.	Moderately corrosive but can be removed by various organic nitrogen compounds.
Anionic wetting agents	0.15 or less	Soaps Sulphated alcohols Sulphated hydrocarbons Aryl-alkyl polyether sulphates Sulphonated amides Alykl-aryl sulphonates	Wet surfaces. Penetrate crevices and woven fabrics. Emulsify oils, fats, waxes and pigments. Compatible with acid and alkaline cleaners and may be synergistic. Effective general detergents.	Some foam excessively. May be incompatible with cationic wetting agents.
Non-ionic wetting agents	0.15 or less	Polyethonoxyethers Ethylene oxide-fatty acid condensates Amine-fatty acid condensates	Excellent detergents for oil. Used in mixtures of wetting agents to control foam.	May be sensitive to acids.

Category of aqueous cleaner	Approx. concentrations for use (%)	Examples of chemicals used	Functions	Limitations
Cationic wetting agents	0.15 or less	Quaternary ammonium compounds	Some wetting effect. Antibacterial action.	Not compatible with anionic wetting agents. Inactivated by many minerals and some soils.
Sequestering agents	Variable depending on water hardness	Tetrasodium pyrophosphate Sodium tripolyphosphate Sodium hexameta-phosphate Sodium tetraphosphate Sodium acid pyrophosphate Ethlyenediamine tetra-acetic acid (sodium salt) Sodium gluconate with or without 3% sodium hydroxide	Form soluble complexes with metal ions such as calcium, magnesium and iron to prevent film formation on equipment and utensils. See also strong and mild alkalis opposite. Phosphates are inactivated by protracted exposure to heat.	Phosphates are unstable in acid solutions.
Abrasives	Variable	Volcanic ash Seismotite Pumice Feldspar Silica flour Steel wool Chore balls made of metal or plastic	Combined with scrubbing action they remove dirt from surfaces. Can be used with detergents for difficult cleaning jobs.	Scratch surfaces. Particles may become embedded in equipment and later appear in food. Skin damage possible if protective gloves not worn.
Chlorinated compounds	1	Dichlorocyanuric acid Trichlorocyanuric acid Dichlorohydantoin	Used with alkaline cleaners to increase peptizing of proteins and minimise milk deposits.	Not germicidal because of high pH. Concentrations vary depending on the alkaline cleaner and conditions of use.
Amphoterics	1-2	Mixtures of a cationic amine salt or a quaternary ammonium compound with an anionic carboxy compound, a sulphate ester or a sulphonic acid	Loosen and soften charred food residues on ovens or other metal and ceramic surfaces.	Not suitable for use on food contact surfaces.
Enzymes	0.3-1	Proteolytic enzymes produced in cultures of aerobic spore-forming bacteria	Digest proteins and other complex organic soils.	Inactivated by heat. Some people become hypersensitive to products containing enzymes. Some have contained *Salmonella*.

SICKNESS — EXCLUSION FROM WORK

The table summarises the Department of Health guidelines for dealing with food handlers who have been diagnosed with a food-borne illness (middle column) and symptom-free food handlers who have been in contact with someone suffering from a food-borne illness (right-hand column).

Organism/illness	Criteria for allowing a food handler to return to work when free from symptoms and after	Criteria for dealing with a symptom-free food handler who has been in contact with sufferer
Aeromonas species	48 hours after they have passed a normal stool, but strict hygiene measures must be followed	No criteria
Bacillus species	as above	No criteria
Campylobacter species	as above	No criteria
Clostridium botulinum	No criteria	Treatment of those at risk
Clostridium perfringens	as *Aeromonas* species	No criteria
Cryptosporidium species	as *Aeromonas* species	No criteria
Entamoeba histolytica	3 negative stools	Microbiological screening
E. coli (excluding VTEC)	as *Aeromonas* species	No criteria
E. coli (VTEC)	2 negative specimens	Microbiological screening
Giardia lamblia	No criteria	Microbiological screening
Hepatitis A	7 days after onset of jaundice or other symptoms	No criteria
Salmonella species (except *S.* Typhi and *S.* Paratyphi)	as *Aeromonas* species	No criteria
Salmonella Typhi and *S.* Paratyphi	6 consecutive negative stool specimens have been passed at 2 weekly intervals starting 2 weeks after the completion of antibiotic therapy	3 consecutive negative stools have been passed at weekly intervals starting 3 weeks after the last contact with the case
Shigella species	When normal stools are being passed	None
Staphylococcus aureus	After any septic lesions have healed	None
Taenia solium	After treatment	Until treated
Vibrio parahaemolyticus	as *Aeromonas* species	None
Viral gastro-enteritis	as *Aeromonas* species	None
Yersinia species	as *Aeromonas* species	None

HACCP DECISION TREE

This decision tree is a traditional version based on the Codex Alimentarius decision tree for determining critical control points in the Hazard Analysis and Critical Control Point system.

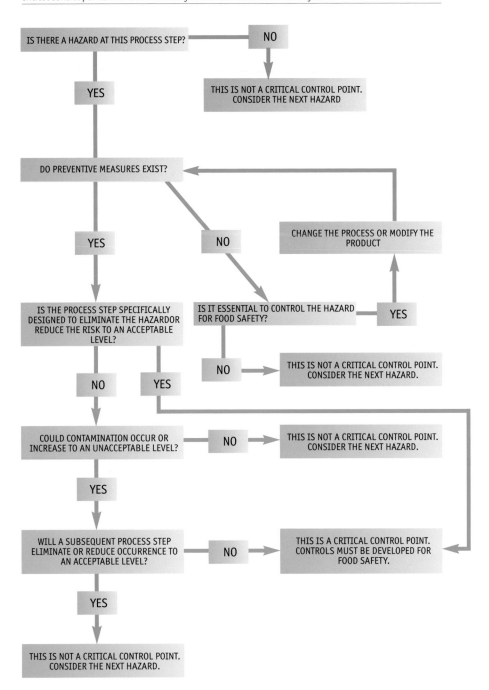

GLOSSARY

acaricide — a PESTICIDE designed to kill mites.

acceptable daily intake (ADI) — the amount of a chemical, determined on the basis of all the known facts, that can be consumed every day for an individual's lifetime without causing harm.

acid — a chemical compound that releases hydrogen ions (H+) when dissolved in water. A solution with a pH of less than 7 is acidic.

acute disease — an illness in which the symptoms develop rapidly following infection.

acute poisoning — the short-term adverse effect of eating food containing a high level of a toxic substance.

additives — substances, such as preservatives, colourings and flavourings, which are deliberately added to food to improve its taste, appearance or shelf life.

adulterant — a substance or item that adversely alters the nature of a food.

aerobic — description of organisms, such as bacteria, that require 20 per cent oxygen in the atmosphere to be able to multiply.

aflatoxin — a mycotoxin, produced mainly by moulds of the genera *Aspergillus* and *Penicillium*.

alga (pl: algae) — simple plants, many single-celled, including the seaweeds.

alkali — a chemical compound that releases hydroxide ions (OH-) when dissolved in water. A solution with a pH of more than 7 is alkaline. Such chemicals are highly corrosive, but are frequently used as DISINFECTANTS in low concentrations.

alkaloid — one of a group of chemical substances which are produced by some plants (such as members of the nightshade family) and fungi, and which have a specific effect on the animals that consume them. Alkaloids include nicotine, cocaine, morphine and atropine.

allergy/allergic reaction — an identifiable immunological response to food, toxins or other substances. The symptoms vary considerably and may include rash, vomiting, breathlessness, diarrhoea or migraine.

ambient shelf stable — a description of foods that can safely be stored at ordinary room temperatures for a specified period.

ambient temperature — the environmental temperature, often used to describe 'normal' room temperature.

anaerobic — description of organisms, such as bacteria, that require the absence of oxygen to be able to multiply. Obligate anaerobes are poisoned by oxygen.

anatomy — the study of the form and structure of an organism.

antibiotic — a substance, such as penicillin, that is produced by micro-organisms and destroys or inhibits the growth of bacteria.

antibody — a blood protein which counteracts the growth and harmful action of ANTIGENS (foreign bodies or substances) such as bacteria or pollen grains.

antigen — a substance, such as a bacterial toxin, that triggers the formation of an ANTIBODY.

antiserum — blood serum containing ANTIBODIES which act against specific ANTIGENS.

antitoxin — an ANTIBODY produced in response to a bacterial toxin.

appertizing — another term for commercial STERILISATION, named after the Swiss-French chef Nicholas Appert. See COMMERCIALLY STERILE.

aseptic — free from contamination by MICRO-ORGANISMS. Often used to describe a method of packaging.

atmosphere — the gases surrounding Earth: the air we breathe.

at risk group — people at greatest risk from food-borne disease, including pregnant women and unborn children, breast-fed infants, the very young, the elderly and people who are ill or convalescing or who have weakened immunity to disease.

atropine — a poisonous alkaloid produced by members of the nightshade family.

audit — a systematic examination of processes and standards to determine whether activities and results comply with a company's documented procedures and standards and whether they are suitable to achieve the stated objectives. Often conducted by an independent consultant.

authorised officer — someone legally authorised to act in matters relating to food safety. In England, Wales and Scotland the authority is conferred by the Food Safety Act 1990.

autotroph — an organism that can synthesise organic compounds from inorganic sources. PHOTOSYNTHESIS, where sunlight is used to convert carbon dioxide and water into organic compounds, is an example of autotrophism. See also HETEROTROPH.

a_w — water activity: the moisture available to an organism. It is defined as $a_w = P/P_0$ where 'P' represents the vapour pressure of the food and 'P_0' represents the vapour pressure of water at the same ambient temperature. The a_w of pure water is 1, so food has an a_w value below 1.0.

bacteria (s: bacterium) — ubiquitous single-celled micro-organisms of various shapes, most of which are harmless, or even beneficial, to humans but which also include a small number of PATHOGENS.

bacterial growth curve — the changes in size in a bacterial colony (the population development) as recorded on a graph.

bacterial monitoring — continuous observation or checking of bacterial contamination.

bacterial spore — a dormant form of some bacteria that enables survival under adverse conditions. (See also ENDOSPORE and SPORE.)

bacterial toxin — a poisonous substance produced by pathogenic bacteria.

bactericide — a substance that kills bacteria.

bacteriology — the study of bacteria.

bacteriophage — a virus that is parasitic within bacteria.

base/basic — another term for ALKALI/alkaline.

best before — a date marked on food that indicates the period within which the food is at its best.

binary fission — an asexual form of reproduction, typical of bacteria, in which a 'mother' cell splits into two identical 'daughter' cells.

biocide — a poisonous substance that harms or kills living organisms.

biodegradable — a substance that will naturally decay over time without producing noxious substances.

botulinum cook — a method of high temperature food preservation designed to kill the spores of the pathogenic bacterium *Clostridium botulinum* and to reduce the spores of spoilage organisms to a level accepted as being safe for human health .

budding — an asexual form of reproduction, typical of yeast, in which several 'daughter' cells sprout from one 'mother' cell.

canning — a preservation method in which food is hermetically sealed in metal, glass or plastic containers and heat treated until it is commercially sterile.

carcinogen — a substance with the ability to trigger cancer.

carrier — a person who shows no symptoms of an infectious disease, but who carries it and may transmit it to others.

carry-over effect — the consequences of toxic substances being carried from one food in the food chain to another until they accumulate in the body fat tissue or organs of animals used for human food. The chemicals can be secreted in human breast milk.

case — a single incidence of illness.

catalyst — a chemical that initiates or accelerates a chemical reaction without changing itself in the process.

cell — the functioning unit of most organisms.

cell division — an asexual method of reproduction whereby a cell divides into two, each half containing identical genetic information. (see also BINARY FISSION.)

cell membrane — the layer between the cell wall and the inner cellular space in bacterial, fungal and plant cells which controls interactions of the cell with its surrounding medium.

cell mortality — death rate of cells.

cell wall — a strong and rigid structure surrounding bacterial, plant and fungal, but *not* animal cells. The cell wall is largely permeable.

chemical contaminants — so-called non-biological chemicals which are accumulated in food as a consequence of environmental pollution. They include heavy metals, radio nuclides and industrial hazards, such as dioxins, other polychlorinated compounds and polyaromatic hydrocarbons.

chemical energy — a form of energy involved in cleaning. (Also the energy stored within an atom or molecule which can be released by a chemical reaction.)

chemical hazard — any chemical which is potentially harmful to the consumer.

chemically clean — the removal of all residue and deposits from cleaning and disinfecting chemicals, usually by rinsing with potable water.

chemical preservation — any process, such as the addition of salt and sugar to food during processing, which is designed to extend the shelf life of food by eliminating or restricting the multiplication of spoilage organisms.

chemical residues — substances which are deliberately or accidentally added to, or brought into contact with, a food during its growth. Residues tend to be veterinary products, feed additives, pesticides and herbicides.

chemistry — a science dealing with the composition of substances and their combinations and changes under various conditions.

chronic disease — an illness in which the symptoms last for a relatively long time and may take some time to develop following infection.

chronic poisoning — the consumption over a long period of food containing a low level of a toxic substance.

ciguatera — the most common type of fish poisoning induced by species of toxic algae.

cilia — hair-like structures on bacteria which usually move.

clean — free from dirt, marks or soiling.

clean as you go — the recognised good practice of cleaning up throughout food preparation and immediately after completing the task.

cleaning — the process of making something clean; usually a combination of the application of MECHANICAL, CHEMICAL and THERMAL ENERGY.

cleaning schedule — a management plan for effective cleaning and, where appropriate, disinfection, detailing what, how and when something is to be cleaned.

clean in place (CIP)— a method of cleaning without first dismantling equipment. Common in breweries and diaries for cleaning pipes that carry food.

cocci — spherical bacterial cells.

code of practice — advisory or guidance notes without formal legal status, the observance of which may help a due diligence defence. Statutory codes of practice are issued to EHOS about enforcing legislation.

Codex Alimentarius Commission — food standards and advice organisation: a subsidiary of the World Health Organization and the Food and Agriculture Organization of the United Nations.

commensal — a description of a form of SYMBIOSIS. A close, harmonious, biological relationship between one organism (the commensal), such as a benign bacterium and another, such as a human, in which the commensal benefits without harming the other organism.

commercial freezing — the rapid freezing and storage of foods at temperatures below −18°C; typically at −22°C or colder.

commercially sterile — a method of high temperature preservation, also known as APPERTIZING, in which STERILISATION is assumed but cannot be measured accurately. The process is designed to kill pathogenic micro-organisms. 'Sterilised' milk, for example, is treatedin this way.

contact time — the period when a disinfectant must remain on, or must surround, a surface in order to achieve disinfection.

contaminant — any unwanted material, object or substance in food.

contamination — any unwanted matter in food. The presence in food, or the process of transferring to food, any unwanted material, object or substance.

controlled atmosphere packaging (CAP) — the precise adjustment of the composition of the air surrounding packaged food to prolong its shelf life.

core temperature — the temperature measured at the centre or in the thickest part or food, or at the bone.

critical control point (CCP) — in HACCP, the point at which the exercise of control over one or more factors could eliminate a hazard or minimise the risk from it. The point where control matters most.

critical limit — in HACCP, the border between what is safe and unsafe. A value at a CCP outside of which the product would be unsafe.

cross-contamination — the transfer of a contaminant from one contaminated product, such as raw meat, to another previously uncontaminated product, such as a ready-to-eat food.

cryptosporidiosis — a form of food-borne illness provoked by the parasite *Cryptosporidium parvum*.

cytoplasm — a complex semi-liquid suspension of enzymes, metabolic and end products inside the living cell.

danger zone — an expression describing the preferred temperature range of pathogenic food-borne bacteria. Temperatures from 5°C to 63°C at which most food-borne pathogens multiply easily. The temperature range to be avoided for high risk foods.

date mark — a date or code indicating the period within which food should be consumed. Legally recognised date marks include *use by* and *best before* dates.

DDT (dichlorodiphenyltrichloroethane) — an organochloric compound used as a pesticide in the 1940s and 1950s which accumulates in the food chain.

death (or decline) phase — the final stage of a BACTERIAL GROWTH CURVE.

definitive (or primary) host — the host on or in which a parasite carries out its sexual stage. The terminal host of a parasite.

dehydration — the process of removing water/moisture from a product. The medical condition resulting from the loss of body fluid.

denature — a structural change in protein or nucleic acid caused by heat, chemicals or high or low pH.

depuration — cleansing or purification of shellfish.

detergent — a formulation of chemicals designed to facilitate the removal of food and grease particles from dishes, equipment, utensils, surfaces and so on.

diarrhoeal syndrome — symptoms involving excessive and frequent loosening of the bowel.

diarrhoeic shellfish poisoning (DSP) — ('diarrhetic' in American English) poisoning from shellfish that have become temporarily poisonous following the seasonal ingestion of toxic plankton.

dinoflagellatae — small protozoa (algae).

dioxin — an extremely toxic substance formed, for example, by burning plastics.

direct contamination — the route of contamination direct from the source of contamination to food. This is the case when, for example, a contaminated food touches, drips or falls onto an uncontaminated one.

disinfectant — a chemical formulation or the application of heat (as steam or hot water) to achieve disinfection.

disinfection — the reduction of PATHOGENIC MICRO-ORGANISMS to a level accepted as being safe for human health according to current scientific understanding. Disinfection does not usually destroy bacterial spores. British Standard BS 5283 states that disinfection may not kill all micro-organisms but reduces them to a level which is neither harmful to health nor the quality of perishable goods.

DNA (deoxyribonucleic acid) — the genetic material inside every cell of an organism.

dormant — literally 'asleep'; used to distinguish inactive forms or stages in the life cycle of an organism, such as bacterial ENDOSPORES.

dosing — the dilution of cleaning chemicals to the correct concentration for safe and effective use.

due diligence — a defence under Section 21 of the Food Safety Act 1990 that every practicable measure was taken to avoid committing an offence under the Act.

dysentery — infection of the lower bowel causing pain, fever and diarrhoea.

ectoparasite — a parasite thriving on a host's body surface.

E$_h$ — see OXIDATION-REDUCTION POTENTIAL.

EHEC — enterohaemorrhagic *E. coli*. See VTEC.

EIEC — enteroinvasive *E. coli*, which multiplies in the surface cells of the intestine and particularly , affects the very young and the very old. A toxin is *not* formed.

electrolyte — a liquid capable of conducting electricity due to the presence of positive or negative ions.

ELISA test — an immunological test method.

emergency prohibition notice/order — legal notification issued under Section 12 of the Food Safety Act 1990 for closing a food business because of a suspected imminent risk to health. An Emergency Prohibition Notice is issued by an authorised officer and an Emergency Prohibition Order confirming the Notice is issued by a court.

emetic syndrome — acute vomiting, sometimes accompanied by abdominal pain and occasionally by diarrhoea, typically caused by *Bacillus cereus*.

emulsify — the mixing of two liquids where one exists as a colloid (small particles) dispersed within the other.

endoparasite — a parasite living within its host; in the tissues, organs or circulatory systems.

endospore — the full name for an asexual SPORE that develops inside the cell of some bacterial genera when the bacterium is under threat; a dormant form, or stage, of some types of bacteria that enables the organism to survive unfavourable conditions.

endotoxin — a TOXIN present inside a bacterial cell which is released when the cell disintegrates.

enterotoxin — a TOXIN affecting the intestine.

enzyme — a type of protein that can trigger chemical reactions in an organism without itself undergoing any change.

EPEC — enteropathogenic *E. coli*. The serotype responsible for many cases of childhood diarrhoea.

epidemic — the existence and spread of an infectious disease to a large number of people within a certain area.

ergot — a mycotoxin from the fungus *Claviceps purpurea* that affects grain, particularly rye.

ergotism — also called St Anthony's fire. An illness caused by the ingestion of ergot. Symptoms include hallucinations and gangrene.

ETEC — enterotoxigenic *E. coli*. The serotype responsible for 'traveller's diarrhoea'.

exotoxin — a toxin released from the cell of a living bacterium into its surroundings.

exposure — in public health, a state of having no protection from contact with something harmful.

extrinsic contamination — contamination from sources other than the raw food itself.

extrinsic factors — external factors (such as temperature and atmosphere) that influence the growth and survival of micro-organisms.

facultative — a description indicating that a micro-organism can live in a variety of conditions: either in the presence, or in the absence, of an environmental factor. For example a facultative anaerobe is a bacterium that can survive with or without oxygen.

faecal coliform — an organism, such as *E. coli*, the presence of which indicates faecal contamination.

farm to fork — a popular expression describing all the many possible stages from the moment of harvesting (fruit, grain and vegetable crops), slaughter (animals) or catching (fish) of food until it is eaten by the consumer. The phrase is commonly used to highlight the long chain of food safety controls that are necessary to ensure public health. The phrase 'plough to plate' is used in the same way.

fascioliasis — an illness provoked by the liver fluke *Fasciola hepatica*.

flagellum (pl: flagellae) — slender thread-like structure enabling bacteria to 'swim' in liquids.

flatworms — worms with a flat body lacking blood vessels. Many parasites are flatworms.

flora (microbial)/microflora — the assemblage of microbial species normally found in a particular habitat, such as the intestine.

food — products used for human consumption, including drink; articles and substances of little or no nutritional value, such as chewing gum; and articles and substances used as ingredients in the preparation of food. What counts as 'food' is defined by law in each country and may vary slightly. In the UK the word 'food' does *not* include live animals; fodder or feeding stuff for animals; controlled drugs within the meaning of the Misuse of Drugs Act 1971; or any other exceptions which may be made by Ministers.

food-borne disease/illness — a general description of any illness from contaminated food. In this book the phrase covers *any* type of illness that is caused, or is probably caused, by the consumption of contaminated food, water or other drink.

food-borne infection — an infection caused by PATHOGENS that are carried by food but are not dependent upon it.

food-contact surface — any surface that comes into contact with food.

food flow — the stages (such as growing, harvesting or slaughtering, transport, storage, preparation,display and sale) that a particular food follows from farm to fork.

food handler — any person in a food business who, by his or her action, inaction, management, decision or advice can directly influence the safety of any food that is handled by that business at any stage.

food hazard — anything microbiological, chemical or physical that might cause harm to the consumer.

food hygiene — all the processes involved in keeping food safe to eat.

food poisoning — any illness, caused by, or thought to be caused by, pathogens or toxins in food. The term is sometimes also used as a simple general term for all kinds of illness related to food.

food safety — the protection of human health by preventing edible substances (defined by law) from becoming hazardous and by minimising the risks from those hazards. Also used to indicate the absence of harm to people from food.

food safety policy/food hygiene policy — a document that makes clear a company's intentions towards, and objectives for, food safety standards.

food spoilage — see SPOILAGE.

freezer burn — the accidental dehydration of food caused by large ice crystals formed when the freezing process is too slow or food thaws slightly and is refrozen. a form of food spoilage.

fungal spore — the reproductive stage of fungi.

fungicide — a PESTICIDE designed to kill fungi.

fungus (pl: fungi) — a group of micro-organisms (including moulds and yeasts) and macro-organisms (mushrooms and toadstools) with rigid cell walls.

gastro-enteritis — inflammation of the mucous membrane of the gut.

gene — the smallest unit of heredity; a segment of DNA; a distinct sequence of nucleotides forming part of a chromosome.

generic HACCP — a modified system of HACCP, also known as process-specific HACCP, that is applied in food businesses such as restaurants and bakeries, where it would impracticable to apply the system to each product. 'HAZARD ANALYSIS' IS one such modified system.

genetic material — genetic 'information'; the sum of all hereditary material.

genus (pl: genera) — a classification category, ranking above species, of organisms sharing many characteristics.

germination — the growth of endospores into vegetative bacteria. (Also applied to the initial stages of plant seed growth.)

giardiasis — an illness caused by the parasitic PROTOZOAN *Giardia lamblia*.

Gram reaction — a test that distinguishes important basic characteristics of bacteria.

growth curve — see BACTERIAL GROWTH CURVE.

growth optimum — the peak of a GROWTH CURVE.

HACCP — an abbreviation, usually pronounced 'hassup', for Hazard Analysis and Critical Control Point, which is a system for identifying, assessing and controlling hazards and risks associated with food and drink. The ICMSF definition of HACCP is 'a systematic approach to the identification and assessment of the microbiological hazards and risks associated with food and the definition of means for their control.'

haemagglutinin — a substance which causes the clumping together of red blood cells.

haemoglobin — an oxygen-carrying protein in mammal blood.

haemolysis — breakdown of red blood cells. It can have several causes e.g. action of micro-organisms, poisons or as the result of an allergic reaction.

haemorrhage — loss of blood.

halophile — a salt-loving or salt-tolerant MICRO-ORGANISM.

hand-contact surface — any surface touched by hand. The surface may subsequently be touched by food, or micro-organisms on the surface may be transferred to food.

hazard — a source of danger: any thing, condition or circumstance that could cause harm to the consumer. See also FOOD HAZARD.

hazard analysis — the systematic identification of food hazards and the estimation of their severity and the degree of risk from them. The term is applied the first principle of HACCP and to a generic form of HACCP.

Hazard Analysis and Critical Control Point — see HACCP.

heavy metal — a metal with a high relative atomic mass such as copper, lead and zinc. Such metals are a cause of environmental pollution.

herbicide — a PESTICIDE designed to kill unwanted plants or weeds.

hermaphrodite — an organism that possesses both male and female reproductive organs.

heterotroph — an organism that derives its nutrients from organic substances. See also AUTOTROPH.

high risk food — a food, typically high in protein and moisture, that is at high risk of CONTAMINATION by spoilage bacteria or pathogens and requires strict time and temperature control to remain safe to eat. High risk foods are sometimes referred to as 'high care foods' or 'potentially hazardous foods'.

host — an organism providing nourishment and shelter, on or within its body, for a parasite.

HTST — high temperature short time. A form of PASTEURISATION.

hurdle concept/technology — the controlled manipulation of factors essential to microbial survival and multiplication to increase the shelf life of food.

immune system — the combined action of the body's various means of fighting infection.

immunocompromised — impairment of the immune system.

immunological — pertaining to immunity.

improvement notice — a notice served by an authorised officer under Section 10 the Food Safety Act 1990 requiring improvements to be made in a food premises.

incubation period — the length of time between infection by an organism and the first appearance of symptoms of a disease; also known as 'onset'.

indicator organisms — ones that suggest faecal contamination and inadequate cleaning and disinfection.

indirect contamination — contamination introduced by a VEHICLE OF CONTAMINATION.

infection — the presence and multiplication of a pathogen in the body, producing disease. The process of infecting or stage of being infected.

infective dose — the number of micro-organisms required to cause symptoms of a disease.

infestation — the presence, usually in large numbers, of a food pest.

ingest — feed. The taking in of food and drink by an organism and their subsequent digestion.

inherent — existing within something; inbuilt.

inorganic — not composed of organic (carbon-based) matter; mineral.

insecticide — a PESTICIDE designed to kill insects.

integrated pest management (IPM) — a style of pest management based on co-operation between a food business client and a specialist pest control company (PCP), dealing mostly with preventive measures.

intermediate (or secondary) host — the host in which the larval stages of endoparasites, such as tapeworms, develop.

intoxication — the state or process of poisoning by a chemical substance or the products of bacteriological action.

intrinsic contamination — contamination associated with the food itself.

intrinsic factors — inbuilt or inherent characteristics such as nutrients, pH and a_w that influence the survival, growth and multiplication of micro-organisms.

irradiation — the use of gamma radiation to destroy pathogenic and spoilage organisms in food.

kinetic energy — see MECHANICAL ENERGY.

lag phase — the first stage of bacterial growth in which an organism adapts to its surroundings and does not reproduce.

leaching — the washing out of the soluble constituents of a solid by passing a solvent, such as water, through it. Heavy metals sometimes contaminate the food chain when they leach from landfill sites (rubbish tips), as a result of rain or underground water..

learning spiral — a sequence of experiencing, sharing, adjusting, applying and communicating knowledge.

log (or logarithmic) phase — the stage of rapid bacterial multiplication.

log scale — a scale of measurement in which an interval of one unit represents a tenfold multiplication of the quantity measured. Bacterial growth is often measured on a logarithmic scale.

macro-molecule — a molecule containing a very large number of atoms.

malicious tampering — the intentional contamination of a product.

mechanical energy — a form of energy, also known as KINETIC ENERGY, involved in the process of cleaning. Energy possessed by a body by virtue of its motion.

mesophile — an organism preferring temperatures between 10°C and 55°C.

metabolism — the sum total of the chemical changes carried out in the cells of a living organism.

metabolite — a substance required for METABOLISM or which is formed in metabolism.

microaerophile — an organism that does not require much oxygen.

microbe — see MICRO-ORGANISM.

microbial competition — microbial activity in which one type of micro-organism gains superiority over another.

microbiologically clean — a surface or equipment on which the number of micro-organisms has been reduced to a level accepted as being safe for human health.

microbiology — the science of the study of microbes.

micro-organism — any organism that is so small that it can be observed only through a microscope.

miracidium — free-swimming larval stage of a parasitic fluke.

mobile — moveable. (Compare with MOTILE.)

modified atmosphere packaging (MAP) — the preservation of food by controlling the chemical composition of the air in hermetically sealed packaging.

moisture — in general discussion about food and food safety, the word refers to the water activity (see a_w) of food. Also used to describe dampness, condensed water/water vapour.

monitoring — in HACCP, the measurement or observation at a critical control point (CCP) of the criteria which allow corrective actions to be taken.

morphology — the science of the structure and shape of organisms.

mortality rate — death rate.

motile — capable of independent, or self-propelled, movement. Usually used to describe cells, but *not* animals or equipment.

moulds — strictly aerobic filamentous FUNGI which can spoil food and cause food poisoning by poisonous metabolites (MYCOTOXINS).

multiplication — microbial reproduction, for instance by BINARY FISSION (bacteria) or BUDDING (yeast).

mutagenic — causing genetic alteration.

mycotoxicosis — an illness caused by the toxins produced by some fungi.

mycotoxin — a toxic substance produced by some fungi. Mycotoxins can cause serious acute and/or chronic diseases.

myristicine — compound present in the oil of nutmeg.

natural toxins — poisonous substances which are inherent in the product.

'nature or substance or quality' — a legal requirement to sell food that is constituted as the consumer expects.

nephrotoxic — damaging or poisonous to the kidneys.

neurotoxin — a poison which acts on the nervous system.

neutral — a pH of 7.0.

nitrate — a naturally occurring chemical used in agriculture and as a food additive which may cause food poisoning.

nitrite — a chemical used as a food additive which may cause food poisoning.

nitrogen — colourless, odourless, gas element (represented by the letter N) which makes up 78% by volume of the Earth's atmosphere. It is an essential component of proteins and nucleic acids.

nitrogen cycle — major environmental element cycle. Nitrates in the soil are taken up by plants and passed to animals through the food chain. Denitrifying bacteria return some nitrogen to the atmosphere.

nitrosamine — a chemical compound that can cause food poisoning.

nucleus — a structure within some types of cell (not bacterial cells) that contains DNA.

obligate — describes a microbe that is obliged to live in particular conditions to survive — for instance, an obligate aerobe must have oxygen, while an obligate anaerobe must live in oxygen-free conditions.

ochratoxin — mycotoxin produced by the genus *Aspergillus*.

onset/onset period — see INCUBATION

oocyst — cyst containing a reproductive cell formed by a parasitic organism.

organic chemistry — the chemistry of compounds of carbon, whether natural or synthetic.

organism — individual life form capable of maintenance, growth and reproduction.

organoleptic — involving the use of the senses; the characteristics of food are often assessed by its appearance, smell and texture and even sound, for instance the tapping of bread.

outbreak — two or more linked cases of the same infection or food-borne illness; a cluster, in time or place, of cases of illness caused by a particular organism; a situation where the observed number of cases unaccountably exceeds the expected number.

oxalic acid — poisonous acid with a sour taste, present in rhubarb leaves.

oxidation — the process of oxidising, that is, reaction with oxygen or a chemical reaction involving the loss of electrons. Oxidation can spoil food. The turning brown of cut apple is the result of oxidation.

oxidation-reduction potential (E_h) — the value used to describe the ease with which a medium loses or gains electrons. It sums up the effects of both oxidising and reducing factors in food and is influenced by bacterial growth.

paralytic shellfish poisoning — food poisoning caused by shellfish which have become temporarily poisonous following the seasonal ingestion of toxic plankton.

parasites — plants or animals that derive shelter and sustenance in or on other organisms, thriving on their body substance or metabolites.

pasteurisation — a method of heat treatment of liquids, such as milk and beer, that destroys tuberculosis PATHOGENS and reduces other pathogens to accepted safe levels for human health.

pathogen — an organism which can cause disease.

patulin — a mycotoxin produced by moulds of the genera *Aspergillus* and *Penicillium*.

Perigo factor — a not fully understood phenomenon which occurs when nitrite is added before food is heated and produces an effect which is ten times more inhibitory than when the nitrite is added *after* the heating.

peripheral nervous system — the nervous system outside the brain and the spinal cord.

permeability — the degree to which a surface or membrane will admit the passage of substances. Permeability depends on the structure or texture of the membrane as well as on the nature of the diffusing matter.

personal protective equipment (PPE) — any clothing, equipment or device designed to protect food from contamination or the wearer from injury. In food businesses such items include rubber gloves, overalls, hats, hairnets and aprons.

person in charge — the person given the authority by the employer to take charge of food premises at any given time.

pest — an unwanted animal, including insects and birds, which contaminates or destroys food, or whose presence in food premises is undesirable.

pesticide — a collective term for several groups of chemical substances designed to kill animal pests and noxious plants and protect crops and stored products. They include insecticides (insect control), rodenticides (rodent control), acaricides (mite control), herbicides (for plant protection) and fungicides (for controlling unwanted fungi, such as mould.

pH scale — a logarithmic scale used to express acidity or alkalinity. 7.0 represents neutral. A reading below 7 is acid, above 7 is alkaline. It can be defined as $-\log_{10}c$ where c is equal to the hydrogen ion concentration in moles per litre.

phagetyping — a method of identifying bacteria by using host-specific viruses which only attack certain bacteria strains.

photosynthesis — a process by which green plants use sunlight to synthesise nutrients from carbon dioxide and water.

phylum — a high-level category of taxonomic classification of organisms. Organisms are classified into the following hierarchy: phylum, class, order, family, genus, species.

physical contaminants — foreign bodies in food which can provoke both harm and/or disgust depending on their nature.

physically clean — the state achieved when all visible or tangible evidence of dirt or residue or foreign material has been removed by cleaning from a surface or piece of equipment.

physiology — science dealing with the normal functions of organisms.

plasma membrane — see CELL MEMBRANE.

plasmid — a structure in a cell composed of DNA which can reproduce independently. Plasmids often control instructions for cell activities.

poison — any substance which either kills or causes damage when introduced into a living organism.

polyaromatic hydrocarbons — derivatives of phenol; often highly carcinogenic.

polymerase chain reaction (PCR) test — a genetic test method depending on the activity of the individual replication enzyme taking place in the sample due to the DNA amplification.

potable — safe to drink. Generally used to describe water treated for use as drinking water.

predisposition — the tendency to suffer from a particular condition.

preservation (food) — methods of treatment designed to delay the natural processes of decomposition and to extend the period within which the food is at its best for consumption.

prion — the abbreviation for proteinaceous infectious particle; an abnormal (or rogue) form of mammal protein found, for example, in the brain. Prions are one of the prime suspects implicated in brain-wasting diseases of animals and humans, such as scrapie in sheep, bovine spongiform encephalopathy (BSE) in cattle (commonly known as mad cow disease) and variant Creutzfeldt-Jakob Disease (vCJD) in humans. The suspected role of prions in these illnesses is, however, still controversial. Prions are not viruses, although their impact has sometimes associated with them in the past, sometimes as virions.

product recall — the process of retrieving a product that is contaminated or may be contaminated, usually involving publicity and public information. This is usually coupled with an offer to replace, or refund the cost of, the product.

product specification — a customer's detailed description of the content, design, composition and intended use of the product to be supplied.

product-specific HACCP — the full, original form of HACCP, which is designed to be applied to one product through all its process stages.

protozoan (pl: protozoa) — single-celled animal with a more complex internal structure than a bacterium. Some protozoa, such as *Entamoeba histolytica*, are pathogenic.

PSP — see PARALYTIC SHELLFISH POISONING.

psychrophile — an organism preferring temperatures between −5°C and 20°C.

psychrotroph — an organism preferring temperatures between 0°C and35°C.

qats/QUATS — quaternary ammonium compounds: a non-corrosive disinfectant.

quality assurance — ensuring the repeatability of a defined quality in a product.

ready-to-eat — food produced for immediate consumption, without further treatment (except, in some cases, for heating). A food that is either eaten raw, or is not prepared or treated (such as by cooking) immediately before it is eaten in a way that would kill any pathogens present.

re-emergent pathogens — a term created by the World Health Organisation to describe the reappearance of pathogenic bacteria which were thought to have been eliminated.

residue — small amounts of a substance that remain after the main part has gone.

ribosome — tiny particle within a cell consisting of RNA and associated proteins.

risk — a measure, or scale, of the likelihood (or probability) that a hazard will occur.

risk analysis — a process involving risk assessment, risk communication and risk management.

RNA —ribonucleic acid; a nucleic acid present in all living cells which acts as a messenger for the control of the synthesis of proteins.

rodenticide — a pesticide designed to kill rodents.

sanitizer/sanitiser — term used in the UK for a chemical formulation combining the properties of a detergent *and* a disinfectant. In America the term is often used for any kind of chemical disinfectant. Compare with DETERGENT and DISINFECTANT.

sanitizing/sanitization — another term for chemical disinfection used particularly in America. The American Food Code (model for food safety legislation) defines sanitization as the application of cumulative heat or chemicals on cleaned food contact surfaces to create a 99.999 per cent reduction in pathogens of public health importance.

scombroid poisoning — an illness from a toxin that can be formed in oily fish, such as mackerel and tuna.

selectively permeable — a membrane allowing only a selection of substances to pass through it.

serotyping — an immunological method for identifying bacteria by means of specific antigen/antibody reactions.

severity — in HACCP, the magnitude or seriousness of the possible consequences of a hazard.

shelf life — the period within which food is both safe for human consumption and at its best.

smoking (food process) — a method of introducing a smoked flavour to food products which may, in some cases, have a preservative effect.

solanine — a poisonous compound present in nightshade, green potatoes and related plants.

solutes — the the substance dissolved in a solvent to form a solution.

source of contamination — point of origin of a contaminant.

spoilage — deterioration of food; the normal processes of deterioration, decay or 'going off'.

spore (bacterial) — contraction of 'endospore'; the dormant, survival forms of *Clostridium* and *Bacillus* bacteria which are resistant to heat, acid, salt and most other adverse conditions. When conditions become favourable, the spores germinate and release vegetative bacterial cells. Unlike fungal spores, bacterial endospores do not multiply.

spore (fungal) — a reproductive cell of a fungus.

sporocyst — a parasitic fluke in the initial stage of infection.

sporozoite — a motile spore-like stage in the life cycle of some parasitic protozoa.

sporulation — spore production.

stationary phase — a stage of the bacterial growth curve at which the bacterial population has reached its maximum.

sterile — a condition in which all living organisms have been destroyed.

sterilisation — the destruction of all living organisms.

stock rotation — the practice of using a product with the shortest shelf life before using a similar one with a longer shelf life.

stored product pest — an insect, sometimes known as a storage insect, associated with foods such as grain, flour, herbs, spices and nuts that are often stored for long periods.

substrate — a substance on, or from which, an organism lives, grows, multiplies or obtains its nourishment. Also a substance on which an enzyme acts.

supplier's certificate — a supplier's guarantee of the wholesomeness of a product based on criteria set by the purchasing company.

surfactant — a substance which increases the wetting or penetrating action of a detergent.

swabbing technique — a bacterial monitoring technique involving the measurement of the uptake of micro-organisms from a surface and incubation in a standard or selective medium.

symbiosis — the close association between two species, particularly where there is benefit to both species. See also COMMENSAL.

target level — in HACCP, a specified value for a control measure that eliminates or minimises the risk from a hazard at a critical control point (CCP).

taxonomy — the naming, description and classification of organisms.

temperature — a measure, or scale, of the degree of hotness or coldness of a substance.

temperature control — all aspects of food safety in which temperature is used as a measure to stop a hazard or reduce the risk from it. The most basic rules of temperature control regarding high risk foods are to keep hot food hot and to keep cold food cold. See also DANGER ZONE.

thermal energy — one of three forms of energy involved in the process of cleaning. Thermal energy is usually provided by hot water or by steam.

thermophile — a heat-loving micro-organism that thrives at between 40°C and 80°C.

tolerance — in HACCP, a specified variation from the target level which is deemed to be acceptable for food safety.

toxic — a description of *any* poisonous substance.

toxin — a poisonous substance produced by some bacteria and fungi; usually a complex enzyme (a type of protein) which is fatal to other proteins. Organisms producing toxins are toxigenic.

trophozoite — the growing stage in the life cycle of some protozoan parasites.

tuberculosis — a chronic bacterial disease, which may be food-borne, air-borne or by contact, caused either by the bacteria *Mycobacterium tuberculosis* or *M. bovis*.

typhoid/typhoid fever — the illness caused by the bacterium *Salmonella* Typhi. The disease is also known as enteric fever.

typhus — an illness, sometimes known as 'spotted fever' and not to be confused with typhoid/typhoid fever, which is caused by rickettsiae, a group of parasitic organisms.

ultra heat treatment (UHT) — a method of high temperature food treatment, usually applied to milk, designed to reduce spoilage organisms and extend the shelf life.

unfit (food) — food that is not safe or suitable, as defined by law, for human consumption. All food which is sold must meet food safety requirements. That is it must not be unfit for human consumption, must not have been rendered injurious to health and must not be contaminated to an extent that it would not be reasonable to expect it to be eaten. Additionally, it is an offence to treat food so as to render it injurious to health.

unicellular — having only one cell.

use by — the date indicating the last day on which food is safe to eat.

vacuum-packing — a type of food packaging where the air has been removed to create a vacuum which prevents the multiplication of aerobic organisms.

vector — animals, including insects and birds serving as vehicles of contamination.

vegetative cell — living, reproducing cell.

vehicle of contamination— any substance, object or living being which carries contamination from one point to another. The route taken is known as indirect contamination.

verification — in HACCP, is the checking or reviewing of the entire HACCP system to ensure that it is operating according to plan.

virion — a virus-like particle, sometimes discussed in connection with prions.

virology — the scientific study of viruses.

virulence — the degree or severity of harm that a pathogenic organism can cause.

virus — an extremely small infective organism, ranging from $1/10$ to $1/100$ the size of one bacterium, that can multiply only within living cells. A virus particle consists of only a single strand of nucleic acid surrounded by a protein coat which acts as a protective shell and enables the virus to link itself to the surface of a host cell.

VTEC — verocytotoxin-producing *E. coli*. The term verocytotoxin refers to the type of cells it affects in laboratory work. It is an extremely virulent serotype of the bacterium, which is also referred to as the serotype 0157:H7 and as EHEC (enterohaemorrhagic *E. coli*).

water activity — see a_w.

winter vomiting disease — viral infection caused by Rotavirus that usually affects children of primary school age.

workflow — the logical route organised through food premises for food, food handlers, equipment and rubbish at each stage from the delivery of raw food to the dispatch, sale or service of finished products.

xerophile — an organism that likes dry conditions and can survive low a_w values.

yeast — a microscopic unicellular fungus which can contaminate food and cause spoilage.

zoonosis (pl: zoonoses) — a disease of animals that can also infect humans.

TAKING IT FURTHER

British Institute of Cleaning Services
3 Moulton Court
Anglia Way
Moulton Park
Northampton NN3 6JA
T: 01604 678710
U: www.bics.org.uk

professional, educational and awarding body

Centers for Disease Control
www.cdc.gov

American centre for disease surveillance

Chartered Institute of Environmental Health
Chadwick Court
15 Hatfields
London SE1 8DJ
T: 020 7827 5800
F: 020 7827 5865
E: customersupport@chgl.com
U: www.cieh.org

*professional, educational and awarding body
for food safety and other environmental health
matters*

Codex Alimentarius Commission
www.codexalimentarius.net

*a food safety and standards organisation: a
subsidiary of the World Health Organization
(WHO) and the Food and Agriculture
Organization (FAO)*

**Department of the Environment, Food and
Rural Affairs (DEFRA)**
www.defra.gov.uk

*the UK government department
concerned with food and related matters*

Department of Health (DoH)
www.doh.gov.uk

the UK government health department

European Law
www.europa.eu.int/eur-lex

site summarising European law

Eurosurveillance
www.eurosurveillance.org/eurosurv/index.htm

European disease surveillance organisation

European Union
europa.eu.int

Food Standards Agency
www.foodstandards.gov.uk

*the UK's food safety and standards
organisation*

The Food Safety Authority of Ireland
www.fsai.ie

*The Republic of Ireland's (Eire) food safety and
standards organisation*

Hansard
www.parliament.the-stationery-office.co.uk/pa/cm/cmhansrd.htm

the official record of Parliament (UK)

Her Majesty's Stationery Office
www.hmso.gov.uk

*source of copies of UK legislation and
government departmental reports*

**Local Authorities Co-Ordination Body on Food
and Trading Standards** (LACOTS)
www.lacots.com

*organisation co-ordination and giving advice
to enforcement bodies*

National Registry of Food Safety
Professionals
1200 East Hillcrest Street
Suite 303
Orlando, Florida 32803
T: (407) 228 6405
F: (407) 894 7748
U: www.nrfsp.com

professional, educational and awarding body
in the USA; sister organisation of the CIEH

Public Health Laboratory Service
www.phls.co.uk

British disease surveillance organisation

The Royal Environmental Health Institute
of Scotland
3 Manor Place
Edinburgh EH3 7DH
T: 0131 225 6999
F: 0131 225 3993
U: www.rehis.org

professional, educational and awarding body for food
safety and other environmental health matters

The Royal Institute of Public Health
28 Portland Place
London W1B 1DE
T: 020 7580 2731
F: 020 7580 6157
E: info@riph.org.uk
U: www@riph.org.uk

professional, educational and awarding body for food
safety and other public health matters

The Royal Society for the Promotion
of Health
38A St George's Drive
London SW1V 4BH
T: 020 7630 0121
E: rshealth@rshealth.org.uk
U: www.rsph.org

professional, educational and awarding body for food
safety and other public health matters

Scottish Centre for Infection and
Environmental Health
www.show.scot.nhs.uk/scieh

disease surveillance organisation for Scotland

The Society of Food Hygiene Technology
PO Box 37
Lymington
Hampshire SO41 9WL
www.sofht.co.uk/training/auth_trainer.htm

British professional, educational and awarding body

SQF Institute
Rue de Grand-Chêne 6/4
1003 Lausanne
Switzerland

International organisation managing safe food and quality
management systems

United States Department of Agriculture (USDA)
www.usda.gov

World Health Organization
www.who.int/home-page

the United Nations' public health body, based in
Switzerland

Institute of Food Science and Technology
www.ifst.org

British professional organisation for the food industry

BIBLIOGRAPHY

Entires are listed alphabetically by author's surname

Lisa M Ackerley, 'Food Hygiene and Food Poisoning: A Study of Public Perceptions', PhD thesis, University of Birmingham, 1991

M R Adams and M O Moss, *Food Microbiology*, The Royal Society of Chemistry, Cambridge, 1995

A Dictionary of Biology, Oxford University Press, Oxford, 2000

Advisory Committee on the Microbiological Safety of Food, *Interim Report on Campylobacter,* HMSO, London, 1993

Michael Agnes (ed), *Webster's New World College Dictionary,* IDG Books Worldwide Inc, Foster City, California, 2001

Patricia Barnes-Svarney, *The New York Public Library Science Desk Reference,* Macmillan, New York, 1995

BBC News Online, *BSE and CJD Crisis Chronology*, 2001

Lutz Bertling, *Erlaubt-Verboten in Gastronomie und Gemeinschaftsverpflegung,* Deutscher Fachverlag, Frankfurt a. Main, 1996

R C Bowman and E D Emmett, *A Dictionary of Food Hygiene*, Chadwick House Group Ltd, 1998

Frank L Bryan, *Hazard Analysis Critical Control Point Evaluations*, World Health Organization, Geneva, 1992

Codex Alimentarius, *Hazard Analysis and Critical Control Point (HACCP) System and Guidelines for Its Application,* 1997

Concise Science Dictionary, Oxford University Press, Oxford, 1996

Department of Health, *FSA Review of BSE Controls*, CJD Policy Unit, May 2000

Department of Health, *Management of outbreaks of food borne illness,* Department of Health, UK, 1994

Robert H Dreisach, *Handbook of Poisoning*, Lange Medical Publications, Los Altos, California, 1980

Dagmar Engel, *Hygiene – Eigenkontrolle in Bäckerei/Konditorei/Café,* Gildebuchverlag, Alfeld/Leine, 1998

Dagmar Engel, *HACCP in Training – Food Safety Principles Made Easy*, Chandos Publishing (Oxford) Ltd, Oxford, 2000

Dagmar Engel, *Teaching HACCP – Theory and Practice from the Trainer's Point of View*, Food Control, Elsevier Applied Science Publishers Ltd, No 2-3, 1998

Environmental Health News, Chadwick House Group Ltd, various editions 1999-2001

Food Standards Agency, FSA attitudes survey: research and press releases, 05 February, 2001

Tina Garrity, 'European food safety – food law regulations drafted', *Trainers' Exchange*, Volume 11 Issue 1, Chadwick House Group Ltd, Spring 2001

Faith Goodfellow, Faith Murray and Sabeha Ouki, 'Water-related chemical incidents: a national survey', *Health and Hygiene*, Volume 21 Number 2, The Royal Institute of Public Health and Hygiene, April 2000

Walter Heeschen, *Handbuch Lebensmittelhygiene*, Behr's Verlag, Hamburg, 1996

Herts Advertiser, St Albans, 2000 and 2001

Norman E Hickin, *Household Insect Pests,* Associated Business Programmes Ltd, London, 1974

Director Publications, *Director* (magazine of the Institute of Directors), London, 2000-2001

Kushik Jaga and Harsha Duvvi, 'Risk reduction for DDT toxicity and carcinogenesis through dietary modification', *The Journal of The Royal Society for the Promotion of Health*, Volume 121 Number 2, June 2001

Michael Jacob, *Safe Food Handling*, World Health Organization, Geneva, 1989

James M Jay, *Modern Food Microbiology*, Chapman and Hall, New York, 1996

James M Jay, *Modern Food Microbiology*, Aspen Publishers Inc, Gaithersburg, Maryland, 2000

Allan Jones, Rob Reed and Jonathan Weyers, *Practical Skills in Biology*, Longman, Harlow, 2000

Lothar Leistner, 'User Guide to Food Design', *Food Preservation by Combined Processes*, European Commission, Brussels, 1994

Donald MacDonald and Dagmar Engel, *A Guide To HACCP – Hazard Analysis For Small Businesses,* Highfield Publications, Sprotborough, 1996

Michael T Madigan, John M Martinko and Jack Parker, *Brock Biology of Microorganisms*, Prentice Hall International Inc, 2000

Tom Makin, *Microbial Contamination of Potable Water and Mechanisms of Control* in conference papers of The European Union and Food Control Conference for the Estonian Industry, ABLI International Ltd, 1996

Norman Marriott, *Principles of Food Sanitation*, Van Nostrand Reinhold Company, Inc, New York, 1989

Adrian Meyer, 'Commensal Rodent Control' in *Proceedings of the 3rd International Conference on Urban Pests*, Executive Committee of the International Conference on Urban Pests, Prague, 1999

Klara Miller, *Toxicological Aspects of Food*, Elsevier Applied Science Publishers Ltd, London, 1987

R T Mitchell, *Practical Microbiological Risk Analysis*, Chandos Publishing (Oxford) Ltd, Oxford, 2000

Sara Mortimore and Carol Wallace, *HACCP — A Practical Approach,* Chapman & Hall, London, 1994

J W Munro, *Pests of Stored Products*, Hutchinson & Co Ltd, London, 1966

Claire Nash, *Food Safe to Eat*, VisàVis Publications, St Albans, 2002

Claire Nash, *The Food Safety Training Pack*, Chadwick House Group Ltd, London, 2000

Claire Nash, *The Hygiene Challenge*, VisàVis Publications, St Albans, 1997

National Advisory Committee on Microbiological Criteria for Foods, *Hazard Analysis and Critical Control Point Principles and Application Guidelines*, US Food and Drug Administration, 1997

Richard North, *Some Observations on Food Hygiene Inspections*, Chadwick House Group Ltd, 1999

Notifications of Infectious Diseases, Public Health Laboratory Service, 2001

NSF International Conference and Exhibition, *Food Safety in Travel and Tourism*, conference papers, Barcelona, 2000

William Olkowski, Sheila Daar and Helga Olkowski, *Common Sense Pest Control*, The Taunton Press Inc, Newtown, 1991

John Postgate, *Microbes and Man*, Cambridge University Press, Cambridge, 2000

Stanley B Prusiner, 'The Prion Diseases', *Scientific American*, Issue 0896

Hans Riemann, *Food-borne Infections and Intoxications,* Academic Press, New York 1969

Hans-Jürgen Sinell, *Einführung in die Lebensmittelhygiene,* Verlag Paul Parey, Berlin/Hamburg, 1985

Sinner — see page 378

David A Shapton and Norah F Shapton, *Principles and Practices for the Safe Processing of Foods*, Butterworth-Heinemann Ltd, Oxford, 1991

Richard A Sprenger, *Hygiene for Management,* Highfield Publications, Sprotborough, 1995 and 1999 editions

Heinrich Steinbrink, *Gesundheitsschädlinge*, Gustav Fischer Verlag, Stuttgart, 1989

Sue Stevenson and Claire Nash, *Food Safety Management*, Chadwick House Group Ltd, 2000

TFIS, *Hazard Analysis and Critical Control Point* (HACCP Verification Manual), Technical Food Information Spectrum Inc, 1997

The Hutchinson Science Desk Reference, Helicon Publishing Ltd, Oxford, 1999

The Inquiry into BSE and Variant CJD in the United Kingdom, HMSO, October 2000

The Macquarie Concise Dictionary, The Macquarie Library Pty Ltd, New South Wales, 1998

The New Oxford Dictionary of English, Oxford University Press, Oxford, 1998

The Oxford Dictionary for Writers and Editors, Oxford University Press, Oxford, 2000

The Penguin Dictionary of Science, Penguin 1986

The Royal Society of Health, *Hygiene and Product Safety Management Systems for Food and Beverage Processing Companies* (Accreditation Scheme), The Royal Society for the Promotion of Health, London, 1997

The Scottish Office, *The Investigation and Control of Outbreaks of Foodborne Disease in Scotland*, Department of Health, 1996

Clarence Wilbur Taber, (Clayton L Thomas (ed)), *Taber's Cyclopedic Medical Dictionary*, F A Davis Company, Philadelphia, 1993

Jill Trickett, *The Prevention of Food Poisoning*, Stanley Thornes Ltd, Cheltenham, 1996

J A Troller, *Sanitation in Food Processing*, Academic Press, New York, 1983

Report of the Committee on the Microbiological Safety of Food Parts I and II, HMSO 1990, 1991

Friedrich Untermann and Ulrich Dura, 'Das HACCP-Konzept: Theorie und Praxis', *Fleischwirtschaft*, 76 (7), 1996

Christopher Wills, *Plagues — Their Origins, History and Future*, Flamingo, London, 1996.

Workshop on Foodborne Viral Infections, HMSO 1994

ACKNOWLEDGEMENTS

Many people and organisations have contributed directly or indirectly to the preparation of this book and we would particularly like to thank: Les Barker, Director, Environmental Solutions Partnership Ltd, London; David Barnes, C P Consultants, Devon; John Barrow, Managing Director, HACCP International Ltd, England; Derrick Blunden, Marketing Manager, International Food Hygiene, Positive Action Publications, England; Martin Cole, International Commission on Microbiological Specifications for Foods, Australia; Alex Douglas, Higher Executive Officer, Scottish Executive, Edinburgh; Focus Public Relations, London; Tina Garrity, Research Officer, Chartered Institute of Environmental Health; Tony Girdwood, Stobhill Hospital, Glasgow; Ann Goodwin, Assistant Secretary, Chartered Institute of Environmental Health; John Hall, Thompsons Solicitors, London; Roy Hayter, chef/co-proprietor, Lloyds Hotel, Llanidloes; Herts Advertiser, St Albans; Ben Inns, Bedfordshire; Johnson Wax Professional, UK; Ned Kingcott, Chief Environmental Health Officer, Food Standards Agency, London; Maria Laybourn, Safeway Stores plc; Mary Locking, Epidemiologist, Scottish Centre for Infection and Environmental Health, Glasgow; Audrey Lynch, Senior Press Officer, Communicable Disease Surveillance Centre, Northern Ireland; McDonald's Restaurants Ltd, UK; Morris McAllister, Director, Food Standards Agency, Northern Ireland; Dick Madely, formerly Professor, Department of Virology, Newcastle University; Tom Makin, Consultant Bacteriologist, Royal Liverpool University Hospital; Carole Milligan, Director, Environmental Solutions Partnership Ltd, London; Jenny Millward, Food Safety Team Manager, Birmingham Metropolitan District Council; Bob Mitchell, Head, Environmental Surveillance Unit, Public Health Laboratory Services, Colindale; Martin Müller, Germany; Richard North, consultant, Brussels and UK; Bill Reilly, Deputy Director, Scottish Centre for Infection and Environmental Health, Glasgow; Safeway Stores plc; the staff of The Science Photo Library, London; Julie Snelling, Senior Technical Enforcement Officer, Slough Borough Council; Mike Sweeney, Chief Executive, British Institute of Cleaning Services; Dee Waite, Technical and Development Manager, Chadwick House Group Ltd; Alette Weaver, Head of Diet and Nutrition Surveys Branch, Food Standards Agency, London.

In addition to the bibliography on pages 372 to 373, we are delighted to acknowledge the following as specific sources of information or comment (page numbers in bold):

13 The comment about the return of the customer was made by Robert Tyler, President of the British Meat Trades Federation, at a conference at the University of Reading, 20 January 1998. **14** FSA attitudes survey: from research and press releases issued by the Food Standards Agency, 05 February, 2001. **19** Self-diagnosis of food poisoning based on research and press releases issued by the Food Standards Agency, 05 February, 2001. **20** Graphs based on data published by the Health Protection Agency (for England and Wales), the Scottish Centre for Infection and Environmental Health and the Communicable Disease Surveillance Centre, Northern Ireland. **21-22** For other estimates of the cost of food poisoning, see also page 140 of *Food Microbiology*, M R Adams and M O Moss, Royal Society of Chemistry, 1999. **24** Information about re-emergent pathogens has also been based upon 'The Importance of HACCP for the public and the economy', Yasmin Motarjemi, lecture at the International Food Safety HACCP Conference, Noordwijk an Zee, February 1997. **27** Due diligence: Food Safety Act 1990, Section 21. **33** *Environmental Management at Work*, GEMS Environmental Management Services (Editors: Claire Nash and Caroline Smith); Chadwick House Group Ltd, 1999. **63** The table showing the effect on bacteria at different temperatures over time is based upon reasearch published in *Practical Hygiene in the Foodservice Profession*, SwissAir Catering Services. **70** For a more detailed discussion about the revised nomenclature of Salmonella species, see also James M Jay, *Modern Food Microbiology*, Aspen Publishers Inc, Gaithersburg, Maryland, 2000. **79** The description of *Clostridium perfringens* (*C. welchii*): 'Clostridium welchii food poisoning', Hobbs B et al, *Journal of Hygiene*, 51 75-101, 1953. **83** For a more detailed discussion about cholera and to see a copy of the illustration mentioned, see Christopher Wills, *Plagues — Their Origins, History and Future*, Flamingo, London, 1996. **120** Toffee pecan pie packaging reproduced by permission of Marks and Spencer plc, 2001. **153** Cutting reproduced by permission of The Herts Advertiser, St Albans, 2001. **154** and **156** Cuttings reproduced by permission of *Environmental Health News*, 2000 and 2001. **227** A Message from the Bored: originator unknown. Reprinted by permission of John Frater, The Royal Environmental Health Institute of Scotland.

232 L M Ackerley, 'Food Hygiene and Food Poisoning: A Study of Public Perceptions', PhD thesis, University of Birmingham, 1991. **245** and **253** Our illustrations are based very loosely on the 'Sinner diagrams' (Reinigungskreis nach Sinner), the models created by the former chemist at the Fa. Henkel company in Düsseldorf. Although these diagrams are widely used in continental Europe, we regret that, at the time of publication, we have been unable to establish Sinner's first name or the date of publication of this influential model. The website of the University of Bielefeld includes information in German featuring the diagrams — see http://dc2.uni-bielefeld.de/dc2/wsu-haush/kap_01.htm/ **309** For a definition of severity, see also Frank L Bryan, *Hazard Analysis Critical Control Point Evaluations*, World Health Organization, Geneva, 1992. **314** R T Mitchell said in *Practical Microbiological Risk Analysis*, Chandos Publishing (Oxford) Ltd, Oxford, 2000, 'HACCP is the use of the simplest possible controls where it matters most'. The table at the bottom of this page is based upon *Hazard Analysis and Critical Control Point (HACCP) System and Guidelines for Its Application*, Codex Alimentarius Commission, 1997 and on *Hazard Analysis and Critical Control Point Principles and Application Guidelines*, US Food and Drug Administration, as adopted by the National Advisory Committee on Microbiological Criteria for Foods, 1997. **318** Part of our definition draws on that of Frank L Bryan, *Hazard Analysis Critical Control Point Evaluations*, World Health Organization, Geneva, 1992, 'A CCP is an operation (practice, procedure, location or process) at which control can be exercised over one or more factors to eliminate, prevent or minimize a hazard.' **319** This decision ladder is adapted from original training materials developed by Dagmar Engel and Donald MacDonald in 1998. For a more conventional HACCP decision tree based on the Codex Alimentarius model, see page 359. **338** Friedrich Untermann's model is generally known as 'the Untermann house'. See Friedrich Untermann and Ulrich Dura, 'Das HACCP-Konzept: Theorie und Praxis', *Fleischwirtschaft*, 76 (7), 1996. **355** The table is adapted from William Olkowski, Sheila Daar and Helga Olkowski, *Common Sense Pest Control*, The Taunton Press Inc, Newtown, 1991. **356-357** Adapted from 'Functions and Limitations of Cleaning Chemicals', with permission of the International Commission on Microbiological Specifications for Foods. **359** The decision tree shown here is based on 'Example of Decison Tree to Identify CCPs' on the Codex Alimentarius website www.codexalimentarius.net/ and the website of the National Advisory Committee on Microbiological Criteria for Foods http://vm.cfsan.fda.gov/~comm/nacmcfp.html/defs

We have endeavoured to include all sources, but will be glad to include additional information if appropriate.

INDEX

hurdle technology/concept 65, 169, 366
hydrogen-ion concentration — see pH
hyphae 109

I

ice cream 18, 283
immune system 51, 119, 366
immunocompromised 366
immunological 366
immunological test 51
impedance method 67
improvement notice 150, 155-156, 158, 366
inappropriate practices 118
incident report 339
incubation period — see ONSET
indicator organisms 366
indirect contamination 169, 171, 179, 199, 366
industrial pollution 138-140
industry guides 163
infant botulism 78
infants 19, 55, 91, 93, 123, 137
infection 39, 71, 72, 366
infectious diseases 234-235
infectious intestinal disease (IID) 19
infective dose 39, 73, 96, 102, 169, 178, 367
infestation 242, 260, 367
ingest 367
inherent 39, 117, 169, 187, 367
Indian meal moth 267
inorganic 367
inorganic builders 251-252
insecticides 135, 272, 367
insects 264-268
inspections (food safety) — see ENVIRONMENTAL
   HEALTH OFFICER
integrated management 338-340
integrated pest management (IPM) 136, 242,
   269, 367
intermediate/secondary host 367 — see also
   HOST
internal audit — see AUDIT
International Commission on Microbiological
   Specifications for Food (ICMSF) 41
intestinal peristaltic 57
intestinal system 56
intoxication 39, 71, 72, 367
intrinsic contamination 39, 145-146, 169, 189-
   191, 199, 367
intrinsic factors 39, 58-61, 65-66, 312, 367
introduced chemicals 117
investigation (of an outbreak) 332-335
irradiation 65-66, 296-297, 367
itai-itai disease 139

J

jam 59
jewellery 235

K

kinetic energy — see MECHANICAL ENERGY
Koch, Robert 24
Krebs, Sir John 14

L

labelling 15, 120, 155, 158, 296, 308
Lactobacilli 46, 63
Lactobacillus reuteri 64
lag phase 40, 53, 54, 367
Lanarkshire *E. coli* outbreak 88
landscaping 205
larval forms 100, 103, 104, 107, 268
Lasius niger 266
leaching 141, 367
lead 138-139
lead poisoning 138-139
learning spiral 367
legal issues — see LEGISLATION
legislation 4-6, 27-31, 97, 142, 150-164, 201,
   204, 209, 210, 211-212, 214, 218, 225, 243,
   261, 283, 296, 308, 309, 324
   – British 152-164
   – butchers 163
   – compliance 155, 203
   – decisions 152
   – defence 156
   – directives 151, 218, 326
   – England 151, 152, 153-164
   – European 151-152
   – Food Safety Act 1990 4, 6, 152, 153-159,
   163-164
   – labelling 155, 158, 296
   – 'nature or substance or quality' 150, 154,
   158, 368
   – Northern Ireland 151, 152-153, 159, 150-161
   – notices 155-156
   – obstruction 155
   – orders 156
   – power of entry 155
   – premises 201
   – primary 152
   – regulations 151
   – Scottish 151, 152, 153-162, 162-163
   – secondary 152
   – seizure 156
   – UK 151-153, 163
   – Wales 151, 152, 153-162, 159, 160, 163
Leptospira interrogans 178
leptospirosis 178

N

National Advisory Committee on Microbiological Criteria for Foods, USA 41
naturally occurring chemicals 123-128
natural soaps 251
'nature or substance or quality' — see LEGISLATION
nematode — see ROUNDWORM
nephrotoxic 131, 368
nervous system 56, 57
neurotoxin 40, 56, 57, 77, 126, 368
neutral (pH) 40, 60, 368
nitrate 40, 136-137, 295, 368
nitrite 40, 136-137, 295, 368
nitrogen 136, 368
nitrogen cycle 136, 368
nitrosamines 40, 136-137, 368
non-food items 148, 192-193
Norovirus 95, 97, 177, 178, 351
Northern Ireland 19, 20
Norwalk and Norwalk-like viruses — see NOROVIRUS
Norwegian rat 264
nose 233
notices (legal) — see LEGISLATION
notified cases (of food poisoning) 20
nucleic acid (viral) 95-96
nucleus 50, 368
numbers expressed to the power of ten 341
nutmeg 125
nutrient content 58-59

O

objectionable matter 145
obligate (definition of) 40, 368
obligate aerobe 40, 63-64, 300, 368
obligate anaerobe 40, 64, 368
obstruction 155, 159
ochratoxin 131-132, 354, 368
ohmic heating 290
onset 39, 40, 73, 368
oocyst 101, G
orders (legal) — see LEGISLATION
organic chemistry 368
organism 40, 45, 368
organoleptic (effects) 242, 296, 297, 368
Oriental cockroach 265-266
Oryzaephilus surinamensis 268
outbreak 12, 18, 78, 88-89, 92, 333, 368
oxalic acid 125, 368
oxidation 288, 289, 369
oxidation-reduction potential (Eh) 299-300, 368
oxygen 63-64
oxygen-free 64
ozone 64

P

packaging 9, 26, 147, 191-192
paralytic shellfish poisoning 19, 128, 369
parasites 18, 42, 99-107, 179, 289, 353, 369
 − characteristics 100
 − flatworms 103-106
 − illness 101-107
 − life cycle 100-107
 − protozoa 101-103
 − roundworms 106-107, 353
paratyphoid 92
pasteurisation 242, 275, 283, 287, 320, 369
pathogen/pathogenic 24, 25, 40, 42, 46, 62, 63, 277-278, 283, 285, 305, 369
 − definition of 40
pathogenic organisms 342-354
patulin 131, 354, 369
PCR test 68, 369
peanuts 130, 131
penalties 159
penicillin 114, 123
Penicillium notatum 115
Penicillium genus 131
Pennington Report 88
Pennington, Professor Hugh 163
perfume 236
Perigo factor 295, 369
peripheral nervous system 126, 369
permeability 369
personal hygiene 28, 148, 193, 210-212, 230-237, 339
 − monitoring 231
 − policy 230-231
 − training 219, 230, 231
personal protective equipment (PPE) 212, 234, 235-236, 369
person in charge 3, 7, 369
pesticides 135-138, 272-273, 355, 369
pesticide residue 16
pests 181, 185, 191, 242, 260-274, 369
 − control of 242, 260, 270-273, 355
 − definition of 242, 260, 369
 − infestation 242, 260
 − management of 269, 273
 − problems 261-262
 − proofing 209, 304
 − types of 262-269
pH 40, 54, 57, 58, 60−61, 287, 291, 294, 299
pH scale 57, 60, 61, 369
phagetyping 40, 51, 68, 369
Pharoah's ant 266−267
pharyngeal fascioliasis 106
phenol 137
PHLS (Public Health Laboratory Service) 21, 235, 333
PHLS Northern Ireland 21
photosynthesis 47, G
phylum 369

trophozoite 102, G
tuberculosis 85, 90-91, 283, G
turkey X disease 130
typhoid/typhoid fever 91-93, 292, 372
Typhoid Mary 92, 234
typhus 372
Typhus abdominalis 91-93

U

ultra heat treatment (UHT) 242, 275, 290, 372
ultraviolet fly-killers 272
undercooking 19
unfit (food) 3, 5, 150, 154-155, 156, 242, 285,
  372
  – definition of 3, 5, 372
uni-cellular 372
United Kingdom 2, 14, 16, 18, 19, 74
United States of America (USA) 6, 18, 22, 41, 74,
  77
Untermann, Friedrich 338
US Centers for Disease Control and Prevention
  (CDC) 74
use by 242, 306, 372
utensils 207
utilities 210-211

V

vaccine 96
vacuum packing 289, 296, 300, 372
vector 169, 171, 372
vegetables 172-173, 176, 289
vegetative cell 56, 372
vehicles of contamination 40, 73, 169, 170-171,
  179-181, 372
vending machines 209
ventilation 212, 213-214
verification (HACCP) 321, 326-327, 372, 372
verocytotoxin 88
vertical directives 151
viability (of a spore) 55
vibrio 48
Vibrio cholerae 24, 83, 177
Vibrio foetus 87
Vibrio parahaemolyticus 60, 63, 71, 83-84, 175,
  177, 349
Vicia faba 125
vinegar fly — see FRUIT FLY
virion 372
virology 45, 372
virulence 372
virus 40, 42, 45, 95-98, 351-352, 372
  – characteristics 95-96
  – definition of 40, 372
  – food-borne illness 96-98
  – multiplication 95

viscera 127
visitor policy 340
vomiting 57
VTEC (verocytotoxin) 372 — see also E. COLI O157

W

Wales 4, 6, 19, 20, 21
walls 204, 207
warehousing 9
wash-hand basins 211
washing up 211
waste 205, 206
waste reduction 32-33
water 59, 73, 174, 177-178, 210
water activity (a$_w$) 38, 40, 54, 58, 59-60, 293,
  372
water hardness 248
waterproof dressings 236
Weil's disease — see LEPTOSPIROSIS
wetting agent 250
windows 209-210
winter 19
winter vomiting disease 19, 97, 372
wood 147, 193
working environment 212-214
work surfaces 207
workflow 199, 203, 204, 206-207, 372
World Health Organization (WHO) 18, 24, 65,
  138, 141, 261

X

xerophile 40, 60, 372

Y

yeast 45, 108-110, 287, 288, 289, 294, 295, 296,
  297, 372
  – definition of 372
Yersin, Alexandre 84
Yersinia enterocolitica 24, 71, 84, 175, 296, 350
Yersinia pestis 84, 263-265
yew 124

Z

Zahorsky 97
zinc 141
zoonosis 86, 372